Modal Logic for Philosophers

Designed for use by philosophy students, this book provides an accessible yet technically sound treatment of modal logic and its philosophical applications. Every effort has been made to simplify the presentation by using diagrams in place of more complex mathematical apparatus. These and other innovations provide philosophers with easy access to a rich variety of topics in modal logic, including a full coverage of quantified modal logic, nonrigid designators, definite descriptions, and the *de re–de dicto* distinction. Discussion of philosophical issues concerning the development of modal logic is woven into the text.

The book uses natural deduction systems and includes a diagram technique that extends the method of truth trees to modal logic. This feature provides a foundation for a novel method for showing completeness, one that is easy to extend to systems that include quantifiers.

James W. Garson is professor of philosophy at the University of Houston. He has held grants from the National Endowment for the Humanities, the National Science Foundation, and the Apple Education Foundation. He is also the author of numerous articles in logic, semantics, linguistics, the philosophy of cognitive science, and computerized education.

W0010529

Modal Logic for Philosophers

JAMES W. GARSON
University of Houston

CAMBRIDGE UNIVERSITY PRESS
Cambridge, New York, Melbourne, Madrid, Cape Town,
Singapore, São Paulo, Delhi, Mexico City

Cambridge University Press
32 Avenue of the Americas, New York, NY 10013-2473, USA

www.cambridge.org
Information on this title: www.cambridge.org/9780521682299

First published 2006
Reprinted 2008, 2012

A catalog record for this publication is available from the British Library.
Garson, JamesW., 1943–
Modal logic for philosophers / JamesW. Garson.
p. cm.
Includes bibliographical references (p.) and index.
ISBN-13: 978-0-521-86367-4 (hardback)
ISBN-10: 0-521-86367-8 (hardback)
ISBN-13: 978-0-521-68229-9 (pbk.)
ISBN-10: 0-521-68229-0 (pbk.)
1. Modality (Logic) – Textbooks. I. Title.
BC199.M6G38   2006
160 – dc22   2006001152

ISBN 978-0-521-86367-4 Hardback
ISBN 978-0-521-68229-9 Paperback

for Nuel Belnap, who is responsible for anything he likes about this book

Contents

Preface

The main purpose of this book is to help bridge a gap in the landscape of modal logic. A great deal is known about modal systems based on propositional logic. However, these logics do not have the expressive resources to handle the structure of most philosophical argumentation. If modal logics are to be useful to philosophy, it is crucial that they include quantifiers and identity. The problem is that quantified modal logic is not as well developed, and it is difficult for the student of philosophy who may lack mathematical training to develop mastery of what is known. Philosophical worries about whether quantification is coherent or advisable in certain modal settings partly explains this lack of attention. If one takes such objections seriously, they exert pressure on the logician to either eliminate modality altogether or eliminate the allegedly undesirable forms of quantification.

Even if one lays those philosophical worries aside, serious technical problems must still be faced. There is a rich menu of choices for formulating the semantics of quantified modal languages, and the completeness problem for some of these systems is difficult or unresolved. The philosophy of this book is that this variety is to be explored rather than shunned. We hope to demonstrate that modal logic with quantifiers can be simplified so that it is manageable, even teachable. Some of the simplifications depend on the foundations – in the way the systems for propositional modal logic are developed. Some ideas that were designed to make life easier when quantifiers are introduced are also genuinely helpful even for those who will study only the propositional systems. So this book can serve a dual purpose. It is, I hope, a simple and accessible introduction to propositional modal logic for students who have had a first course in formal logic (preferably one that covers natural deduction rules and truth trees). I hope, however, that students who had planned to use this book to learn only propositional modal logic will be inspired to move on to study quantification as well.

A principle that guided the creation of this book is the conviction that visualization is one of the most powerful tools for organizing one's thoughts. So the book depends heavily on diagrams of various kinds. One of the central innovations is to combine the method of Haus diagrams (to represent Kripke's accessibility relation) with the truth tree method. This provides an easy and revealing method for checking validity in a wide variety of modal logics. My students have found the diagrams both easy to learn and fun to use. I urge readers of this book to take advantage of them.

The tree diagrams are also the centerpiece for a novel technique for proving completeness – one that is more concrete and easier to learn than the method of maximally consistent sets, and one that is extremely easy to extend to the quantifiers. On the other hand, the standard method of maximally consistent sets has its own advantages. It applies to more systems, and many will consider it an indispensable part of anyone's education in modal logic. So this book covers both methods, and it is organized so that one may easily choose to study one, the other, or both.

Three different ways of providing semantics for the quantifiers are introduced in this book: the substitution interpretation, the intensional interpretation, and the objectual interpretation. Though some have faulted the substitution interpretation on philosophical grounds, its simplicity prompts its use as a centerpiece for technical results. Those who would like a quick and painless entry to the completeness problem may read the sections on the substitution interpretation alone. The intensional interpretation, where one quantifies over individual concepts, is included because it is the most general approach for dealing with the quantifiers. Furthermore, its strong kinships with the substitution interpretation provide a relatively easy transition to its formal results. The objectual interpretation is treated here as a special case of the intensional interpretation. This helps provide new insights into how best to formalize systems for the objectual interpretation.

The student should treat this book more as a collection of things to do than as something to read. Exercises in this book are found embedded throughout the text rather than at the end of each chapter, as is the more common practice. This signals the importance of doing exercises as soon as possible after the relevant material has been introduced. Think of the text between the exercises as a preparation for activities that are the foundation for true understanding. Answers to exercises marked with a star (*) are found at the end of the book. Many of the exercises also include hints. The best way to master this material is to struggle through the exercises on your own as far as humanly possible. Turn to the hints or answers only when you are desperate.

Many people should be acknowledged for their contributions to this book. First of all, I would like to thank my wife, Connie Garson, who has unfailingly and lovingly supported all of my odd enthusiasms. Second, I would like to thank my students, who have struggled though the many drafts of this book over the years. I have learned a great deal more from them than any of them has learned from me. Unfortunately, I have lost track of the names of many who helped me make numerous important improvements, so I apologize to them. But I do remember by name the contributions of Brandy Burfield, Carl Feierabend, Curtis Haaga, James Hulgan, Alistair Isaac, JoBeth Jordon, Raymond Kim, Kris Rhodes, Jay Schroeder, Steve Todd, Andy Tristan, Mako Voelkel, and especially Julian Zinn. Third, I am grateful to Johnathan Raymon, who helped me with the diagrams. Finally, I would like to thank Cambridge University Press for taking an interest in this project and for the excellent comments of the anonymous readers, some of whom headed off embarrassing errors.

Introduction: What Is Modal Logic?

Strictly speaking, modal logic studies reasoning that involves the use of the expressions 'necessarily' and 'possibly'. The main idea is to introduce the symbols □ (necessarily) and ◇ (possibly) to a system of logic so that it is able to distinguish three different *modes* of assertion: □A (A is necessary), A (A is true), and ◇A (A is possible). Introducing these symbols (or operators) would seem to be essential if logic is to be applied to judging the accuracy of philosophical reasoning, for the concepts of necessity and possibility are ubiquitous in philosophical discourse.

However, at the very dawn of the invention of modal logics, it was recognized that necessity and possibility have kinships with many other philosophically important expressions. So the term 'modal logic' is also used more broadly to cover a whole family of logics with similar rules and a rich variety of different operators. To distinguish the narrow sense, some people use the term 'alethic logic' for logics of necessity and possibility. A list describing some of the better known of these logics follows.

System	Symbols	Expression Symbolized
Modal logic	□	It is necessary that
(or Alethic logic)	◇	It is possible that
Tense logic	G	It will always be the case that
	F	It will be the case that
	H	It has always been the case that
	P	It was the case that
Deontic logic	O	It is obligatory that
	P	It is permitted that
	F	It is forbidden that

1

Locative logic	Tx	It is the case at x that
Doxastic logic	Bx	x believes that
Epistemic logic	Kx	x knows that

This book will provide you with an introduction to all these logics, and it will help sketch out the relationships between the different systems. The variety found here might be somewhat bewildering, especially for the student who expects uniformity in logic. Even within the above subdivisions of modal logic, there may be many different systems. I hope to convince you that this variety is a source of strength and flexibility and makes for an interesting world well worth exploring.

1

The System K: A Foundation for Modal Logic

1.1. The Language of Propositional Modal Logic

We will begin our study of modal logic with a basic system called K in honor of the famous logician Saul *K*ripke. K serves as the foundation for a whole family of systems. Each member of the family results from strengthening K in some way. Each of these logics uses its own symbols for the expressions it governs. For example, modal (or alethic) logics use $\Box$ for necessity, tense logics use **H** for what has always been, and deontic logics use **O** for obligation. The rules of K characterize each of these symbols and many more. Instead of rewriting K rules for each of the distinct symbols of modal logic, it is better to present K using a generic operator. Since modal logics are the oldest and best known of those in the modal family, we will adopt $\Box$ for this purpose. So $\Box$ need not mean necessarily in what follows. It stands proxy for many different operators, with different meanings. In case the reading does not matter, you may simply call $\Box$A 'box A'.

First we need to explain what a *language for propositional modal logic* is. The symbols of the language are $\bot$, $\rightarrow$, $\Box$; the propositional variables: p, q, r, p', and so forth; and parentheses. The symbol $\bot$ represents a contradiction, $\rightarrow$ represents 'if . . then', and $\Box$ is the modal operator. A *sentence of propositional modal logic* is defined as follows:

$\bot$ and any propositional variable is a sentence.
If A is a sentence, then $\Box$A is a sentence.
If A is a sentence and B is a sentence, then $(A \rightarrow B)$ is a sentence.
No other symbol string is a sentence.

In this book, we will use letters 'A', 'B', 'C' for sentences. So A may be a propositional variable, p, or something more complex like (p→q), or ((p→⊥)→q). To avoid eyestrain, we usually drop the outermost set of parentheses. So we abbreviate (p→q) to p→q. (As an aside for those who are concerned about use-mention issues, here are the conventions of this book. We treat '⊥', '→', '□', and so forth as *used* to refer to symbols with similar shapes. It is also understood that '□A', for example, refers to the result of concatenating □ with the sentence A.)

The reader may be puzzled about why our language does not contain negation: ~ and the other familiar logical connectives: &, ∨, and ↔. Although these symbols are not in our language, they may be introduced as abbreviations by the following definitions:

(Def~)   ~A $=_{df}$ A→⊥
(Def&)   A&B $=_{df}$ ~(A→ ~B)
(Def∨)   A∨B $=_{df}$ ~A→B
(Def↔)   A↔B $=_{df}$ (A→B)&(B→A)

Sentences that contain symbols introduced by these definitions are understood as shorthand for sentences written entirely with → and ⊥. So for example, ~p abbreviates p→⊥, and we may replace one of these with the other whenever we like. The same is true of complex sentences. For example, ~p&q is understood to be the abbreviation for (p→⊥)&q, which by (Def&) amounts to ~((p→⊥)→~q). Replacing the two occurrences of ~ in this sentence, we may express the result in the language of K as follows: ((p→⊥)→(q→⊥))→⊥. Of course, using such primitive notation is very cumbersome, so we will want to take advantage of the abbreviations as much as possible. Still, it simplifies much of what goes on in this book to assume that when the chips are down, all sentences are written with only the symbols ⊥, →, and □.

EXERCISE 1.1   Convert the following sentences into the primitive notation of K.

a) ~~p
b) ~p&~q
c) p∨(q&r)
d) ~(p∨q)
e) ~(p↔q)

Our use of ⊥ and the definition for negation (Def~) may be unfamiliar to you. However, it is not difficult to see why (Def~) works. Since ⊥ indicates a contradiction, ⊥ is always false. By the truth table for material implication, A→⊥ is true (T) iff either A is false (F) or ⊥ is T. But, as we said, ⊥ cannot be T. Therefore A→⊥ is T iff A is F. So the truth table for A→⊥ corresponds exactly to the truth table for negation.

The notion of an argument is fundamental to logic. In this book, an *argument* H / C is composed of a list of sentences H, which are called the *hypotheses*, and a sentence C called the *conclusion*. In the next section, we will introduce rules of proof for arguments. When argument H / C is provable (in some system), we write 'H ⊢ C'. Since there are many different systems in this book, and it may not be clear which system we have in mind, we subscript the name of the system S (thus: H ⊢$_S$ C) to make matters clear. According to these conventions, p, ~q→~p / q is the argument with hypotheses p and ~q→~p and conclusion q. The expression 'p, ~q→~p ⊢$_K$ q' indicates that the argument p, ~q→~p / q has a proof in the system K.

1.2. Natural Deduction Rules for Propositional Logic: PL

Let us begin the description of K by introducing a system of rules called PL (for *p*ropositional *l*ogic). We will use natural deduction rules in this book because they are especially convenient both for presenting and finding proofs. In general, natural deduction systems are distinguished by the fact that they allow the introduction of (provisional) assumptions or hypotheses, along with some mechanism (such as vertical lines or dependency lists) for keeping track of which steps of the proof depend on which hypotheses. Natural deduction systems typically include the rule Conditional Proof (also known as Conditional Introduction) and Indirect Proof (also known as Reductio Ad Adsurdum or Negation Introduction). We assume the reader is already familiar with some natural deduction system for propositional logic. In this book, we will use vertical lines to keep track of subproofs. The notation:

$$
\begin{array}{|l}
\_\, A \\
\ \ \vdots \\
B
\end{array}
$$

indicates that B has been proven from the hypothesis A. The dots indicate intervening steps, each of which follows from previous steps by one of the following five rules. The abbreviations for rule names to be used in proofs are given in parentheses.

The System PL

Hypothesis

|_ A   A new hypothesis A may be added to a proof
                   at any time, as long as A begins a new subproof.

Modus Ponens

A   This is the familiar rule Modus Ponens.
A→B   It is understood that A, A→B, and B must
------   all lie in *exactly the same subproof.*
B   (MP)

Conditional Proof

|_ A   When a proof of B is derived from the hypothesis A,
| :   it follows that A→B, where A→B lies outside
| B   hypothesis A.

A→B   (CP)

Double Negation

~~ A   The rule allows the removal of double
--------   negations. As with (MP), ~~A and A
A   (DN)   must lie in the same subproof.

Reiteration

A   Sentence A may be copied into a new subproof.
:   (In this case, into the subproof headed by B.)
|_ B
| :

| A   (Reit)

These five rules comprise a system for propositional logic called PL. The rules say that if you have proven what appears above the dotted line, then you may write down what appears below the dotted line. Note that in applying (MP) and (DN), *all sentences involved must lie in the same subproof*. Here is a sample proof of the argument p→q, ~q / ~p, to illustrate how we present proofs in this book.

$$
\begin{array}{ll}
p \to q & \\
\sim q & \\
q \to \bot & (\text{Def}\sim) \\
\quad p & \\
\quad p \to q & (\text{Reit}) \\
\quad q & (\text{MP}) \\
\quad q \to \bot & (\text{Reit}) \\
\quad \bot & (\text{MP}) \\
p \to \bot & (\text{CP}) \\
\sim p & (\text{Def}\sim)
\end{array}
$$

The proof begins by placing the premises of the argument (namely p→q and ~q) at the head of the outermost subproof. Then the conclusion (~p) is derived from these using the five rules of PL. Since there are no rules concerning the negation sign, it is necessary to use (Def~) to convert all occurrences of ~ into → and ⊥ as we have done in the third and last steps. We do not bother writing the name (Hyp) where we used the hypothesis rule. That the (Hyp) rule is being used is already clear from the presence of the subproof bracket (the horizontal "diving board" at the head of a subproof).

Most books use line numbers in the justification of steps of a proof. Since we only have four rules, the use of line numbers is really not necessary. For example, when (CP) is used, the steps at issue must be the beginning and end of the preceding subproof; when (DN) is used to produce A, it is easy to locate the sentence ~~A to which it was applied; when (MP) is used to produce B, it is easy enough to find the steps A and A→B to which (MP) was applied. On occasion, we will number steps to highlight some parts of a proof under discussion, but step numbers will not be part of the official notation of proofs, and they are not required in the solutions to proof exercises.

Proofs in PL generally require many uses of Reiteration (Reit). That is because (MP) cannot be applied to A and A→B unless both of these sentences lie in the same subproof. This constant use of (Reit) is annoying, especially in longer proofs, so we will adopt a convention to leave out the (Reit) steps where it is clear that an official proof could be constructed by adding them back in. According to this more relaxed policy, the proof just given may be abbreviated as follows:

$$
\begin{array}{ll}
p{\to}q & \\
{\sim}q & \\
q{\to}\bot & (\text{Def}{\sim}) \\
\quad p & \\
\quad q & (\text{MP}) \\
\quad \bot & (\text{MP}) \\
p{\to}\bot & (\text{CP}) \\
{\sim}p & (\text{Def}{\sim})
\end{array}
$$

We will say that an argument H / C is provable in PL (in symbols: H $\vdash_{PL}$ C) exactly when it is possible to fill in a subproof headed by members of H to obtain C.

$$
\begin{array}{l}
\text{H} \\
\vdots \\
\text{C}
\end{array}
$$

It is possible to prove some sentences outside of any subproof. These sentences are called *theorems*. Here, for example, is a proof that p$\to$(q$\to$p) is a theorem.

$$
\begin{array}{ll}
\quad p & \\
\quad\quad q & \\
\quad\quad p & (\text{Reit}) \\
\quad q{\to}p & (\text{CP}) \\
p{\to}(q{\to}p) & (\text{CP})
\end{array}
$$

EXERCISE 1.2 Prove the following in PL.

a) p$\to$q / (q$\to$$\bot$)$\to$(p$\to$$\bot$)
b) p$\to$q, p$\to$(q$\to$$\bot$) / p$\to$$\bot$
c) Show (p$\to$q)$\to$($\sim$q$\to$$\sim$p) is a theorem of PL.

1.3. Derivable Rules of PL

PL is a complete system for propositional logic. Every valid argument written in the language of propositional logic has a proof in PL. However, proofs involving the abbreviations ~, &, v, and ↔ may be very complicated. The task of proof finding is immensely simplified by introducing derivable rules to govern the behavior of the defined connectives. (A rule is derivable in a system iff it can be proven in the system.) It is easy to show that the rule Indirect Proof (IP) is derivable in PL. Once this is established, we may use (IP) in the future, with the understanding that it abbreviates a sequence of steps using the original rules of PL.

Proof of Derivability:

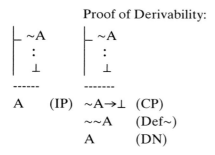

The (IP) rule has been stated at the left, and to the right we have indicated how the same result can be obtained using only the original rules of PL. Instead of using (IP) to obtain A, (CP) is used to obtain ~A→⊥. This by (Def~) is really ~~A, from which we obtain A by (DN). So whenever we use (IP), the same result can be obtained by the use of these three steps instead. It follows that adding (IP) to PL cannot change what is provable.

We may also show derivable a rule (⊥In) that says that ⊥ follows from a contradictory pair of sentences A, ~A.

Proof of Derivability:

```
A            A
~A           ~A
-----        -----
⊥    (⊥In)   A→⊥   (Def~)
             ⊥     (MP)
```

Once (IP) and (⊥In) are available, two more variations on the rule of Indirect Proof may be shown derivable.

Proof of Derivability:

```
 _ ~A            _ ~A
|   :           |   :
|   B           |   B
|   :           |   :
|  ~B           |  ~B
-------         ---------
A      (~Out)   |  ⊥       (⊥In)
                   A        (IP)
```

EXERCISE 1.3 Show that the following variant of Indirect Proof is also derivable. (Feel free to appeal to (⊥In) and (IP), since they were previously shown derivable.)

```
 _ A
|  :
|  B
|  :
| ~B
-------
~A      (~In)
```

With (~Out) available it is easy to show the derivability of a variant of Double Negation.

Proof of Derivability:

```
A            A
----         ----
~~A          | _ ~~~A
             |   ~A      (DN)
             |    A      (Reit)
                ~~A      (~Out)
```

Now it is easy to prove the rule of Contradiction (Contra), which says that from a contradiction anything follows:

Proof of Derivability:

```
⊥                    ⊥
----                ----
A    (Contra)       | ─ ~A
                    |  ⊥    (Reit)
                    A      (IP)
```

It is possible to show that the standard natural deduction rules for the propositional connectives &, v, and ↔ are also derivable.

```
A              A&B          A&B
B              -----        -----
-----          A (&Out)     B (&Out)
A&B (&In)
```

```
A              B            AVB
-----          -----        | ─ A
AVB  (vIn)     AVB  (vIn)   | :
                            | C

                            | ─ B
                            | :
                            | C
                            -----
                            C  (vOut)
```

```
A→B                     A↔B                  A↔B
B→A                     ---------            --------
--------                A→B  (↔Out)          B→A  (↔Out)
A↔B  (↔In)
```

(It is understood that all steps in these derivable rules must lie in the same subproof.) The hardest demonstrations of derivability concern (&Out)

and (vOut). Here are derivations for (vOut) and (one half of) (&Out) to serve as models for proofs of this kind. You will show derivability of the other rules in the next exercise.

(vOut)

AvB

> │ A
> │ ⋮
> │ C

> │ B
> │ ⋮
> │ C

A→C   (CP) (first subproof)
B→C   (CP) (second subproof)
~A→B   (Defv) (first line)

> │ ~C
> │ > │ A
> │ │ C   (MP)
> │ │ ~C   (Reit)
> │ ~A   (~In)
> │ B   (MP)
> │ C   (MP)
> │ ⊥   (⊥In)

C   (IP)

(&Out)

A&B

~(A→~B) (Def&)

> │ ~B
> │ > │ A
> │ │ ~B   (Reit)
> │ A→~B   (CP)
> │ ~(A→~B)   (Reit)

B   (~Out)

EXERCISE 1.4 Show that (&In), the other half of (&Out), (vIn), (↔In), and (↔Out) are all derivable. You may use rules already shown to be derivable ((~Out) and (~In) are particularly useful), and you may abbreviate proofs by omitting (Reit) steps wherever you like. (Hint for (&Out). Study the proof above. If you still have a problem, see the discussion of a similar proof below.)

The following familiar derivable rules: Modus Tollens (MT), Contraposition (CN), De Morgan's Law (DM), and (→F) may also come in handy during proof construction. (Again it is assumed that all sentences displayed in these rules appear in the same subproof.) Showing they are derivable in PL provides excellent practice with the system PL.

A→B   A→B
~B   --------
--------   ~B→~A   (CN)
~A   (MT)

~(AvB)   ~(A&B)
------------   -----------
~A&~B (DM)   ~Av~B (DM)

~(A→B)   ~(A→B)
-----------   -----------
A (→F)   ~B (→F)

To illustrate the strategies in showing these are derivable rules, the proof for (→F) will be worked out in detail here. (It is similar to the proof for (&Out).) We are asked to start with ~(A→B) and obtain a proof of A. The only strategy that has any hope at all is to use (~Out) to obtain A. To do that, assume ~A and try to derive a contradiction.

1. ~(A→B)
   ----
2. | ~A
   | ????
   A   (~Out)

The problem is to figure out what contradiction to try to prove to complete the subproof headed by ~A. There is a simple principle to help guide the solution. When choosing a contradiction, watch for sentences containing ~ that have already become available. Both ~A and ~(A→B) qualify, but there is a good reason not to attempt a proof of the contradiction A and ~A. The reason is that doing so would put us in the position of trying to find a proof of A all over again, which is what we were trying to do in the first place. In general, it is best to choose a sentence different from the hypothesis for a (~In) or (~Out). So the best choice of a contradiction will be ~(A→B) and its opposite A→B.

1. ~(A→B)
    ----
2. | ~A
    | ????
    | A→B
    | ~(A→B)   1 (Reit)
    A   (~Out)

The remaining problem is to provide a proof of A→B. Since (CP) is the best strategy for building a sentence of this shape, the subproof necessary for (CP) is constructed.

1. ~(A→B)
    ----
2. | ~A
    | | A
    | | ????
    | | B
    | A→B   (CP)
    | ~(A→B)   1 (Reit)
    A   (~Out)

At this point the proof looks near hopeless. However, that is simply a sign that (~Out) is needed again, this time to prove B. So a new subproof headed by ~B is constructed with the hope that a contradiction can be proven there. Luckily, both A and ~A are available, which solves the problem.

1. ~(A→B)
    ----
2. | ~A
3. | | A
4. | | | ~B
5. | | | A   3 (Reit)
6. | | | ~A   2 (Reit)
7. | | B   5 6 (~Out)
8. | A→B   7 (CP)
9. | ~(A→B)   1 (Reit)
10. | A   8 9 (~Out)

EXERCISE 1.5 Show that (MT), (CN), (DM), and the second version of (→F) are derivable rules of PL.

In the rest of this book we will make use of these derivable rules without further comment. Remember, however, that our official system PL for propositional logic contains only the symbols → and ⊥, and the rules (Hyp), (MP), (CP), (Reit), and (DN). Given the present collection of derivable rules, constructing proofs in PL is a fairly straightforward matter.

Proofs involving ∨ tend to be difficult. However, they are often significantly easier if (∨Out) can be used in the appropriate way. Let us illustrate by proving p∨q / q∨p. We make p∨q a hypothesis and hope to derive q∨p.

| p∨q
  :
| q∨p

At this point many students will attempt to prove either p or q, and obtain the last step by (∨In). This is a poor strategy. As a matter of fact, it is impossible to prove either p or q from the available hypothesis p∨q. When faced with a goal of the form A∨B, it is a bad idea to assume the goal comes from (∨In), unless it is obvious how to prove A or B. Often when the goal has the shape A∨B, one of the available lines is also a disjunction. When this happens, it is always a good strategy to assume that the goal comes from (vOut). In our example, we have pvq, so we will use this step to get our goal qvp using (vOut).

⌐ pvq
  ⋮
  qvp   (vOut)

If qvp follows from pvq by (vOut), we will need to complete two sub-proofs, one headed by p and ending with qvp and the other headed by q and ending with qvp.

⌐ pvq
   ⌐ p
     ⋮
     qvp

   ⌐ q
     ⋮
     qvp
  qvp   (vOut)

Now all we need to do is complete each subproof, and the goal qvp will be proven by (vOut). This is easily done using (vIn).

⌐ pvq
   ⌐ p
     qvp   (vIn)

   ⌐ q
     qvp   (vIn)
  qvp   (vOut)

In order to save paper, and to see the structure of the (vOut) process more clearly, I suggest that you put the two subproofs that are introduced by the (vOut) rule side by side:

⌐ pvq
   ⌐ p   ⌐ q
     qvp   (vIn)   qvp   (vIn)
  qvp   (vOut)

This way of notating proofs will play an important role in showing parallels between proofs and the truth tree method in Section 7.1.

EXERCISE 1.6   Prove the following using the (∨Out) strategy just described. Place the paired subproofs introduced by (∨Out) side by side to save space.

a) p∨q, p→r, q→s / r∨s
b) p∨(q&r) / (p∨q)&(p∨r)
c) ~p∨~q / ~(p&q)
d) p∨(q∨r) / (p∨q)∨r

1.4. Natural Deduction Rules for System K

Natural deduction rules for the operator □ can be given that are economical and easy to use. The basic idea behind these rules is to introduce a new kind of subproof, called a boxed subproof. A *boxed subproof* is a subproof headed by □ instead of a sentence:

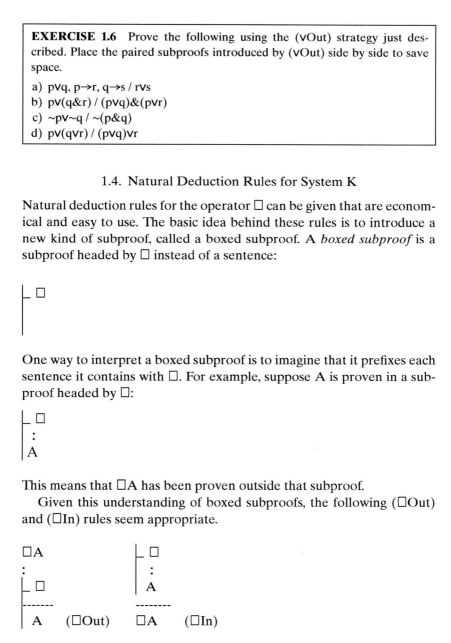

One way to interpret a boxed subproof is to imagine that it prefixes each sentence it contains with □. For example, suppose A is proven in a subproof headed by □:

This means that □A has been proven outside that subproof.

Given this understanding of boxed subproofs, the following (□Out) and (□In) rules seem appropriate.

The ($\Box$Out) rule says that when we have proven $\Box$A, we may put A in a boxed subproof (which indicates that A prefixed by a $\Box$ is proven). The ($\Box$In) rule says that once we have proven A in a boxed subproof, (indicating that A prefixed by $\Box$ is proven), it follows that $\Box$A is proven outside that subproof. ($\Box$Out) and ($\Box$In) together with natural deduction rules for PL comprise the system K.

System K = PL + ($\Box$Out)+ ($\Box$In).

There is an important difference between boxed and ordinary subproofs when it comes to the use of (Reit). (Reit) allows us to copy a sentence into the next deepest subproof, provided the subproof is headed by a *sentence* B.

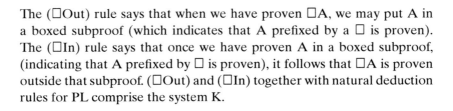

```
A
| B
|
| :
|-----
|  A   (Reit)
```

But the (Reit) rule does *not* allow A to be copied into a boxed subproof:

```
A
| □
|
| :
|-----
|  A   (INCORRECT USE OF (REIT))
```

This is incorrect because it amounts to reasoning from A to $\Box$A, which is clearly fallacious. (If A is so, it doesn't follow that A is necessary, obligatory, etc.) So be very careful when using (Reit) *not* to copy a sentence into a boxed subproof.

Strategies for finding proofs in K are simple to state and easy to use. In order to prove a sentence of the form $\Box$A, simply construct a boxed subproof and attempt to prove A inside it. When the proof of A in that boxed subproof is complete, $\Box$A will follow by ($\Box$In). In order to use a sentence of the form $\Box$A, remove the box using ($\Box$Out) by putting A in a boxed subproof. The following proof of □p&□q ⊢ □(p&q) illustrates these strategies.

1.	□p&□q		
2.	□p	(&Out)	[1]
3.	□q	(&Out)	[2]
4.	□		[4]
5.	p	(□Out)	[6]
6.	q	(□Out)	[7]
7.	p&q	(&In)	[5]
8.	□(p&q)	(□In)	[3]

The numbers to the right in square brackets are discovery numbers. They indicate the order in which steps were written during the process of proof construction. Most novices attempt to construct proofs by applying rules in succession from the top of the proof to the bottom. However, the best strategy often involves working backwards from a goal. In our sample, (&Out) was applied to line 1 to obtain the conjuncts: □p and □q. It is always a good idea to apply (&Out) to available lines in this way.

1.	□p&□q		
2.	□p	(&Out)	[1]
3.	□q	(&Out)	[2]

Having done that, however, the best strategy for constructing this proof is to consider the conclusion: □(p&q). This sentence has the form □A. Therefore, it is a good bet that it can be produced from A (and a boxed subproof) by (□In). For this reason a boxed subproof is begun on line 4 and the goal for that subproof (p&q) is entered on line 7.

1.	□p&□q		
2.	□p	(&Out)	[1]
3.	□q	(&Out)	[2]
4.	□		[4]
5.			
6.			
7.	p&q		[5]
8.	□(p&q)	(□In)	[3]

The proof is then completed by applying (□Out) to lines 2 and 3, from which 7 is obtained by (&In).

EXERCISE 1.7 Prove the following in K (derivable rules are allowed):

a) □p / □(pvq)
b) □(p→q) / □p→□q
c) □(p&q) / □p&□q
d) □(pvq), □(p→r), □(q→r) / □r
e) □pv□q / □(pvq) (Hint: Set up (vOut) first.)

1.5. A Derivable Rule for ◇

In most modal logics, there is a strong operator (□) and a corresponding weak one (◇). The weak operator can be defined using the strong operator and negation as follows:

(Def◇)   ◇A $=_{df}$ ~□~A

(◇A may be read 'diamond A.') Notice the similarities between (Def◇) and the quantifier principle ∀xA ↔ ~∃x~A. (We use ∀ for the universal and ∃ for the existential quantifier.) There are important parallels to be drawn between the universal quantifier ∀ and □, on the one hand, and the existential quantifier ∃ and ◇ on the other. In K and the systems based on it, □ and ◇ behave very much like ∀ and ∃, especially in their interactions with the connectives →, &, and v. For example, □ distributes through & both ways, that is, □(A&B) entails □A&□B and □A&□B entails □(A&B). However, □ distributes through v in only one direction, □Av□B entails □(AvB), but *not* vice versa. This is exactly the pattern of distribution exhibited by ∀. Similarly, ◇ distributes through v both ways, and through & in only one, which mimics the distribution behavior of ∃. Furthermore, the following theorems of K:

$$□(A → B) → (□A → □B)$$

and

$$□(A → B) → (◇A → ◇B)$$

parallel important theorems of quantificational logic:

$$\forall x(Ax \rightarrow Bx) \rightarrow (\forall xAx \rightarrow \forall xBx)$$

and

$$\forall x(Ax \rightarrow Bx) \rightarrow (\exists xAx \rightarrow \exists xBx).$$

To illustrate how proofs involving $\Diamond$ are carried out, we will explain how to show $\Box(p\rightarrow q) \rightarrow (\Diamond p\rightarrow\Diamond q)$ is a theorem. The strategies used in this proof may not be obvious, so it is a good idea to explain them in detail. The conclusion is the conditional, $\Box(p\rightarrow q) \rightarrow (\Diamond p\rightarrow\Diamond q)$, so the last line will be obtained by (CP), and we need to construct a proof from $\Box(p\rightarrow q)$ to $\Diamond p\rightarrow\Diamond q$. Since the latter is also a conditional, it will be obtained by (CP) as well, so we need to fill in a subproof from $\Diamond p$ to $\Diamond q$. At this stage, the proof attempt looks like this:

```
1. | _ □(p→q)                        [1]
2. |   | _ ◇p                        [3]
   |   |   ???
   |   |   ◇q
   |   ◇p→◇q                   (CP)   [4]
   | □(p→q)→(◇p→◇q)            (CP)   [2]
```

Since we are left with $\Diamond q$ as a goal and we lack any derivable rules for $\Diamond$, the only hope is to convert $\Diamond q$ (and the hypothesis $\Diamond p$) into $\Box$ using (Def$\Diamond$).

```
1. | _ □(p→q)                        [2]
2. |   | _ ◇p                        [4]
3. |   |   ~□~p          (Def◇)       [6]
   |   |   ???
   |   |   ~□~q                       [7]
   |   |   ◇q            (Def◇)       [5]
   |   ◇p→◇q            (CP)         [3]
   | □(p→q)→(◇p→◇q)     (CP)         [1]
```

At this point there seems little hope of obtaining ~□~q. In situations like this, it is a good idea to obtain your goal with (~Out) or (~In). In our case we will try (~In). So we need to start a new subproof headed by □~q and try to derive a contradiction within it.

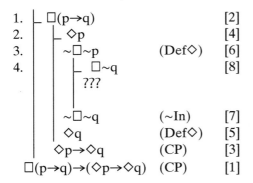

1. | □(p→q)   [2]
2. | ◇p   [4]
3. | ~□~p   (Def◇)   [6]
4. | □~q   [8]
   | ???
   |
   | ~□~q   (~In)   [7]
   | ◇q   (Def◇)   [5]
   | ◇p→◇q   (CP)   [3]
   | □(p→q)→(◇p→◇q) (CP)   [1]

The most crucial stage in finding the proof is to find a contradiction to finish the (~In) subproof. A good strategy in locating a likely contradiction is to inventory steps of the proof already available that contain ~. Step 3 (namely, ~□~p) qualifies, and this suggests that a good plan would be to prove □~p and reiterate ~□~p to complete the subproof.

1. | □(p→q)   [2]
2. | ◇p   [4]
3. | ~□~p   (Def◇)   [6]
4. | □~q   [8]
   | ???
   | □~p   [10]
   | ~□~p   (Reit)   [9]
   | ~□~q   (~In)   [7]
   | ◇q   (Def◇)   [5]
   | ◇p→◇q   (CP)   [3]
   | □(p→q)→(◇p→◇q) (CP)   [1]

At this point our goal is □~p. Since it begins with a box, (□In) seems the likely method for obtaining it, and we create a boxed subproof and enter ~p at the bottom of it as a new goal.

```
1.  ┌─ □(p→q)                          [2]
2.  │  ┌─ ◇p                           [4]
3.  │  │  ~□~p             (Def◇)       [6]
4.  │  │  ┌─ □~q                        [8]
    │  │  │ ┌─ □                        [11]
    │  │  │ │  ???
    │  │  │ │  ~p                       [12]
    │  │  │ □~p            (□In)        [10]
    │  │  │ ~□~p           (Reit)       [9]
    │  │  ~□~q             (~In)        [7]
    │  │  ◇q               (Def◇)       [5]
    │  ◇p→◇q               (CP)         [3]
    □(p→q)→(◇p→◇q)         (CP)         [1]
```

But now it is possible to use (□Out) (and (Reit)) to place p→q and ~q into the boxed subproof, where the goal ~p can be obtained by (MT), Modus Tollens. So the proof is complete.

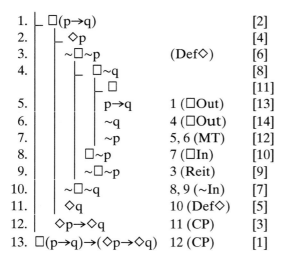

```
1.  ┌─ □(p→q)                                    [2]
2.  │  ┌─ ◇p                                      [4]
3.  │  │  ~□~p                    (Def◇)           [6]
4.  │  │  ┌─ □~q                                   [8]
    │  │  │ ┌─ □                                   [11]
5.  │  │  │ │  p→q              1 (□Out)           [13]
6.  │  │  │ │  ~q               4 (□Out)           [14]
7.  │  │  │ │  ~p               5, 6 (MT)          [12]
8.  │  │  │ □~p                 7 (□In)            [10]
9.  │  │  │ ~□~p                3 (Reit)           [9]
10. │  │  ~□~q                  8, 9 (~In)         [7]
11. │  │  ◇q                    10 (Def◇)          [5]
12. │  ◇p→◇q                    11 (CP)            [3]
13. □(p→q)→(◇p→◇q)              12 (CP)            [1]
```

EXERCISE 1.8 Show that the following sentences are theorems of K by proving them outside any subproofs:

a) □(p&q) ↔ (□p&□q)
b) (□p∨□q) → □(p∨q)
c) (◇p∨◇q) ↔ ◇(p∨q)
d) ◇(p&q) → (◇p&◇q)

As you can see from Exercises 1.8c–d, proofs in K can be rather complex when ◇ is involved. We have no rules governing ◇, and so the only strategy available for working with a sentence of the form ◇A is to translate it into ~□~A by (Def◇). This introduces many negation signs, which complicates the proof. To help overcome the problem, let us introduce a derivable rule called (◇Out).

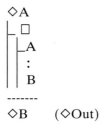

◇B   (◇Out)

EXERCISE 1.9   Show that (◇Out) is a derivable rule of the natural deduction formulation for **K**. (Hint: From the two subproofs use (CP) and then (□In) to obtain □(A→B). Now use the strategy used to prove □(p→q)→(◇p→◇q) above.)

To illustrate the use of this rule, we present a proof of problem d) of Exercise 1.8: ◇(p&q) → (◇p&◇q). Since this is a conditional, a subproof headed by ◇(p&q) is constructed in hopes of proving ◇p&◇q. This latter sentence may be obtained by (&In) provided we can find proofs of ◇p and ◇q. So the proof attempt looks like this so far:

```
┌  ◇(p&q)
│  ???
│  ◇p
│  ???
│  ◇q
│  ◇p&◇q              (&In)
◇(p&q) → (◇p&◇q)   (CP)
```

The (◇Out) rule comes in handy whenever a sentence of the shape ◇A is available, and you are hoping to prove another sentence of the same shape. Here we hope to prove ◇p, and ◇(p&q) is available. To set up the (◇Out), subproofs headed by □ and p&q must be constructed, within which p must be proven. But this is a simple matter using (&Out).

```
1. │  ◇(p&q)
2. │ │ □
3. │ │ │ p&q
4. │ │ │ p                       3      (&Out)
5. │  ◇p                        1, 4   (◇Out)
   │  ???
   │  ◇q
   │  ◇p&◇q                            (&In)
   │ ◇(p&q) → (◇p&◇q)                 (CP)
```

Using the same strategy to obtain ◇q completes the proof.

```
 1. │  ◇(p&q)
 2. │ │ □
 3. │ │ │ p&q
 4. │ │ │ p                      3      (&Out)
 5. │  ◇p                       1, 4    (◇Out)
 6. │ │ □
 7. │ │ │ p&q
 8. │ │ │ q                      7      (&Out)
 9. │  ◇q                       1, 8    (◇Out)
10. │  ◇p&◇q                    5, 9    (&In)
11. ◇(p&q) → (◇p&◇q)           10      (CP)
```

Since we will often use (◇Out), and the double subproof in this rule is cumbersome, we will abbreviate the rule as follows:

```
◇A
│ □, A
│  ⋮
│  B
------
◇B          (◇Out)
```

Here the subproof with □, A at its head is shorthand for the double subproof.

```
│ □, A                    │ │ □
│  ⋮     abbreviates:     │ │ │ A
│  B                      │ │ │ ⋮
                          │ │ │ B
```

We will call this kind of abbreviated subproof a *world-subproof.* This abbreviation is a special case of the idea that we will adopt for arguments, namely, that a sequence of subproofs can be abbreviated by listing the hypotheses in a single subproof. For example, instead of writing

$$
\begin{array}{l}
\vdash\ \text{A} \\
\quad \vdash\ \text{B} \\
\qquad \vdash\ \text{C}
\end{array}
$$

we may write:

$$\vdash\ \text{A, B, C}$$

instead.

Given the world-subproof abbreviation, it should be clear that ($\Box$Out) can be applied to a boxed sentence $\Box$A to place A into a world-subproof directly below where $\Box$A appears. Using world-subproofs, we may rewrite the last proof in a more compact format.

$$
\begin{array}{ll}
\vdash\ \Diamond(p\&q) & \\
\quad \vdash\ \Box,\ p\&q & \\
\qquad p & (\&\text{Out}) \\
\quad \Diamond p & (\Diamond\text{Out}) \\
\quad \vdash\ \Box,\ p\&q & \\
\qquad q & (\&\text{Out}) \\
\quad \Diamond q & (\Diamond\text{Out}) \\
\quad \Diamond p\&\Diamond q & (\&\text{In}) \\
\Diamond(p\&q) \rightarrow (\Diamond p\&\Diamond q) & (\text{CP})
\end{array}
$$

EXERCISE 1.10

a) Redo Exercise 1.8c using ($\Diamond$Out) with world-subproofs.

b) Show that the following useful rules are derivable in K:

$$
\begin{array}{cc}
\sim\Box\text{A} & \sim\Diamond\text{A} \\
\text{-------} & \text{-------} \\
\Diamond\sim\text{A} \quad (\sim\Box) & \Box\sim\text{A} \quad (\sim\Diamond)
\end{array}
$$

c) Using the rules ($\sim\Box$) and ($\sim\Diamond$) and other derivable rules if you like, prove $\Box\sim\Box p\ /\ \Box\Diamond\sim p$ and $\Diamond\sim\Diamond p\ /\ \Diamond\Box\sim p$.

1.6. Horizontal Notation for Natural Deduction Rules

Natural deduction rules and proofs are easy to use, but presenting them is sometimes cumbersome since it requires the display of vertical subproofs. Let us develop a more convenient notation. When sentence A is proven under the following hypotheses:

```
⌊ B
 ⌊ □
  ⌊ C
   ⌊ D
    ⌊ □
     ⋮
     A
```

we may first abbreviate it as follows:

```
⌊ B, □, C, D, □
 ⋮
 A
```

This can in turn be expressed in what we will call horizontal notation as follows:

   B, □, C, D, □ ⊢ A

Notice that B, □, C, D, □ is a list of the hypotheses (in order) under which A lies, so we can think of B, □, C, D, □ / A as a kind of argument. Of course □ is not strictly speaking a hypothesis, since hypotheses are *sentences*, but we will treat □ as an honorary hypothesis nevertheless, to simplify our discussion. When we write 'B, □, C, D, □ ⊢ A', we mean that there is a proof of A under the hypotheses B, □, C, D, □, in that order. We will use the letter 'L' to indicate such lists of the hypotheses, and we will write 'L ⊢ A' to indicate that A is provable given the list L. Notice that L is a list; *the order of the hypotheses matters*. Given this new notation, the rules of K may be reformulated in horizontal notation. To illustrate, consider Conditional Proof.

```
⌊ A
 ⋮
 B
-----------
A→B  (CP)
```

This rule may be applied in any subproof, so let L be a list of all the hypotheses under which A→B lies in the use of this rule. Then the conclusion of this rule may be expressed in horizontal notation as L ⊢ A→B. To indicate the portion of the rule above the dotted line we consider each sentence that is not a hypothesis. In this case, the only such sentence is B. Now B lies under the hypothesis A, and all hypotheses L under which A→B lies. So the horizontal notation for this line is L, A ⊢ B. Putting the two results together, the horizontal notation for the rule (CP) is the following:

L, A ⊢ B

L ⊢ A → B

In similar fashion, all the rules of K can be written in horizontal notation. A complete list follows for future reference.

Horizontal Formulation of the Rules of K

Hypothesis   L, A ⊢ A   (Hyp)

Reiteration   L ⊢ A

          L, B ⊢ A   (Reit)
(Note that B in the conclusion is the head of the subproof into which A is moved.)

Modus Ponens   L ⊢ A
              L ⊢ A→B

              L ⊢ B   (MP)

Conditional Proof   L, A ⊢ B

              L ⊢ A→B   (CP)

Double Negation   L ⊢ ~~A

              L ⊢ A   (DN)

□In   L, □ ⊢ A

              L ⊢ □A   (□In)

□Out   L ⊢ □A

                        L, □ ⊢ A   (□Out)

EXERCISE 1.11   Express (&Out), (IP), and (◇Out) in horizontal notation.

Instead of presenting proofs in subproof notation, we could also write them out in horizontal notation instead. For each line A of the proof, one constructs the list L of all hypotheses under which A lies, and then writes L ⊢ A. In the case of a hypothesis line A, the sentence A is understood to lie under **itself** as a hypothesis, so the horizontal notation for a hypothesis always has the form L, A ⊢ A. When several sentences head a subproof, like this:

| p
| q
|_ r

it is understood that this abbreviates three separate subproofs, one for each sentence. Therefore, the horizontal notation for these steps is given below:

|_ p   p ⊢ p
| |_ q   p, q ⊢ q
| | |_ r   p, q, r ⊢ r

For example, here is a proof written in subproof form on the left with the horizontal version to the right.

| □p&□q   □p&□q ⊢ □p&□q   (Hyp)
| □p   (&Out)   □p&□q ⊢ □p   (&Out)
| □q   (&Out)   □p&□q ⊢ □q   (&Out)
| |_ □
| | p   (□Out)   □p&□q, □ ⊢ p   (□Out)
| | q   (□Out)   □p&□q, □ ⊢ q   (□Out)
| | p&q   (&In)   □p&□q, □ ⊢ p&q   (&In)
| □(p&q)   (□In)   □p&□q ⊢ □(p&q)   (□In)

EXERCISE 1.12   Convert solutions to Exercises 1.7c–d into horizontal notation.

When proofs are viewed in horizontal notation, it becomes apparent that the rules of K apply to *arguments* L / C. In all proofs, the (Hyp) rule first introduces arguments of the form L, A ⊢ A (where L is empty in the first step), and then rules are applied to these arguments over and over again to create new provable arguments out of old ones. You are probably more familiar with the idea that rules of logic apply to sentences, not arguments. However, the use of subproof notation involves us in this more general way of looking at how rules work.

1.7. Necessitation and Distribution

There are many alternative ways to formulate the system K. Using boxed subproofs is quite convenient, but this method was not invented when the first systems for modal logic were constructed. In the remainder of this chapter, two systems will be presented that are *equivalent* to K, which means that they agree with K exactly on which arguments are provable. The traditional way to formulate a system with the effect of K is to add to propositional logic a rule called Necessitation (Nec) and an axiom called Distribution (Dist). We will call this system TK, for the *t*raditional formulation of K.

System TK = PL + (Nec) + (Dist).

$$\vdash A$$
$$\text{-------}$$
$$\vdash \Box A \quad \text{(Nec)} \qquad\qquad \vdash \Box(A{\to}B){\to}(\Box A{\to}\Box B) \quad \text{(Dist)}$$

The rule of Necessitation may appear to be incorrect. It is wrong, for example, to conclude that grass is *necessarily* green ($\Box A$) given that grass is green (A). This objection, however, misinterprets the content of the rule. The notation '⊢ A' above the dotted line indicates that sentence A is a *theorem*, that is, it has been proven *without the use of any hypotheses*. The rule does not claim that $\Box A$ follows from A, but rather that $\Box A$ follows when A is a *theorem*. This is quite reasonable. There is little reason to object to the view that the theorems of logic are necessary.

The derivation of a sentence within a subproof does not show it to be a theorem. So Necessitation does not apply within a subproof. For example, it is incorrectly used in the following "proof":

1. | p
2. | □p   1 (Nec) INCORRECT USE! (Line 1 is in a subproof.)
3. p→□p (CP)

We surely do not want to prove the sentence p→□p, which says that if something is so, it is so necessarily. The next proof illustrates a correct use of (Nec) to generate an acceptable theorem.

1. | p
2. | pvq   (vIn)
3. p→(pvq)   (CP)
4. □(p→(pvq)) 3 (Nec)   CORRECT USE (Line 3 is not in
                                            a subproof.)

It is easy enough to show that (Nec) and (Dist) are already available in K. To show that whatever is provable using (Nec) can be derived in K, assume that ⊢ A, that is, there is a proof of A outside of all hypotheses:

⋮
A

For example, suppose A is the theorem p→(pvq), which is provable as follows:

| p
| pvq   (vIn)
p→(pvq) (CP)

The steps of this proof may all be copied inside a boxed subproof, and (□In) applied at the last step.

| □
| ⋮
| A
□A (□In)

The result is a proof of □A outside all hypotheses, and so we obtain ⊢ □A. In the case of our example, it would look like this:

```
┌ □
│ ┌ p
│ │ pvq          (vIn)
│ │ p→(pvq)      (CP)
│ □(p→(pvq))     (□In)
```

To show that (Dist) is also derivable, we simply prove it under no hypotheses as follows:

```
┌ □(A→B)
│ ┌ □A
│ │ ┌ □
│ │ │ A                  (□Out)
│ │ │ A→B                (□Out)
│ │ │ B                  (MP)
│ │ □B                   (□In)
│ □A→□B                  (CP)
□(A→B)→(□A→□B)           (CP)
```

1.8. General Necessitation

K can also be formulated by adding to PL a single rule called General Necessitation (GN). Let H be a list of *sentences*, and let □H be the list that results from prefixing □ to each sentence in H. So for example, if H is the list p, q, r, then □H is □p, □q, □r.

H ⊢ A

□H ⊢ □A   (GN)

The premise of General Necessitation (GN) indicates that A has a proof from H. The rule says that once such an argument is proven, then there is also a proof of the result of prefixing □ to the hypotheses and the conclusion.

General Necessitation can be used to simplify proofs that would otherwise be fairly lengthy. For example, we proved □p, □q ⊢ □(p&q) above in eight steps (Section 1.4). Using (GN), we can give a much shorter proof, using horizontal notation. Simply begin with p, q ⊢ p&q (which is provable by (Hyp) and (&In)), and apply (GN) to obtain the result.

p, q ⊢ p	(Hyp)
p, q ⊢ q	(Hyp)
p, q ⊢ p&q	(&In)
□p, □q ⊢ □(p&q)	(GN)

EXERCISE 1.13   Produce "instant" proofs of the following arguments using (GN).

a) □p ⊢ □(pvq)
b) □p, □(p→q) ⊢ □q
c) □(pvq), □(p→r), □(q→r) ⊢ □r
d) □~p, □(pvq) ⊢ □q
e) □(p→q), □~q ⊢ □~p

Now let us prove that (GN) is derivable in PL + (Nec) + (Dist). Since we showed that (Nec) and (Dist) are derivable in K, it will follow that (GN) is derivable in K. First we show that the following rule (□MP) is derivable in any propositional logic that contains Distribution.

H ⊢ □(A→B)

H, □A ⊢ □B   (□MP)

The proof is as follows:

H ⊢ □(A→B)	Given
H, □A ⊢ □(A→B)	(Reit)
⊢ □(A→B)→(□A→□B)	(Dist)
H, □A ⊢ □(A→B)→(□A→□B)	(Reit) (many times)
H, □A ⊢ □A→□B	(MP)
H, □A ⊢ □A	(Hyp)
H, □A ⊢ □B	(MP)

To show that (GN) is derivable, we must show that if H ⊢ A, then □H ⊢ □A for any list of sentences H. This can be shown by cases depending on the length of H. It should be clear that (GN) holds when H is empty, because in that case, (GN) is just (Nec). Now suppose that H contains exactly one sentence B. Then the proof proceeds as follows:

$$
\begin{array}{ll}
B \vdash A & \text{Given} \\
\vdash B \rightarrow A & \text{(CP)} \\
\vdash \Box(B \rightarrow A) & \text{(Nec)} \\
\Box B \vdash \Box A & \text{(}\Box\text{MP)}
\end{array}
$$

In case H contains two members B_1 and B_2, the proof is as follows:

$$
\begin{array}{ll}
B_1, B_2 \vdash A & \text{Given} \\
\vdash B_1 \rightarrow (B_2 \rightarrow A) & \text{(CP) (two times)} \\
\vdash \Box(B_1 \rightarrow (B_2 \rightarrow A)) & \text{(Nec)} \\
\Box B_1, \Box B_2 \vdash \Box A & \text{(}\Box\text{MP) (two times)}
\end{array}
$$

EXERCISE 1.14   Now carry out the same reasoning in case H contains three members B_1, B_2, and B_3.

(GN) can be shown in general when H is an arbitrary list $B_1, \ldots, B_i$ using the same pattern of reasoning.

$$
\begin{array}{ll}
B_1, \ldots, B_i \vdash A & \text{Given} \\
\vdash B_1 \rightarrow \ldots (B_i \rightarrow A) & \text{(CP) (i times)} \\
\vdash \Box(B_1 \rightarrow \ldots (B_i \rightarrow A)) & \text{(Nec)} \\
\Box B_1, \ldots, \Box B_i \vdash \Box A & \text{(}\Box\text{MP) (i times)}
\end{array}
$$

This completes the proof that (GN) is derivable in K. It follows that anything provable in PL + (GN) has a proof in K. In Section 9.4 it will be shown that whatever is provable in K is provable in PL + (GN). So PL + (GN) and K are simply two different ways to formulate the same notion of provability.

1.9. Summary of the Rules of K

Rules of PL

Hypothesis

⌞ A (Hyp)

Reiteration

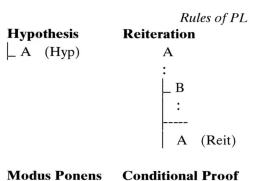

A

⋮

⌞ B

⋮

A   (Reit)

Modus Ponens

A

A→B

B   (MP)

Conditional Proof

⌞ A

⋮

B

A→B   (CP)

Double Negation

~~A

A   (DN)

Derivable Rules of PL

⌞ ~A

⋮

⊥

A   (IP)

A

~A

⊥ (⊥In)

A

~~A   (~~In)

⌞ ~A

⋮

B

⋮

~B

A   (~Out)

⌞ A

⋮

B

⋮

~B

~A   (~In)

A

B

A&B (&In)

A&B

A (&Out)

A&B

B (&Out)

```
A                    B                    AvB
-----                -----                 ⌐ A   ⌐B
AvB  (vIn)    AvB (vIn)           │   :   │  :
                                          │   C   │  C
                                          ------
                                          C   (vOut)
```

```
A→B                           A↔B                    A↔B
B→A                           -----                  -----
-----                         A→B   (↔Out)    B→A  (↔Out)
A↔B  (↔In)
```

```
A→B                           A→B
~B                            --------
-----                         ~B→~A   (CN)
~A   (MT)
```

```
~(AvB)                        ~(A&B)
-------                       --------
~A&~B   (DM)                  ~Av~B   (DM)
```

```
~(A→B)                        ~(A→B)
--------                      --------
A   (→F)                      ~B   (→F)
```

$$K=PL+(\Box Out)+(\Box In)$$

```
□A              ⌐ □
:               │  :
 ⌐ □            │  A
------          --------
│  A  (□Out)    □A   (□In)
```

Derivable Rules of K

◇A
⌊ □, A
⁞
│ B

◇B   (◇Out)

~□A   ~◇A
-----   -----
◇~A   (~□)   □~A   (~◇)

General Necessitation

H ⊢ A

□H ⊢ □A   (GN)

The Traditional Formulation of K: tK=PL+(Nec)+(Dist).

Necessitation

⊢ A

⊢ □A   (Nec)

Distribution

⊢ □(A→B)→(□A→□B)   (Dist)

2

Extensions of K

2.1. Modal or Alethic Logic

A whole series of interesting logics can be built by adding axioms to the basic system K. Logics for necessity and possibility were the first systems to be developed in the modal family. These modal (or alethic) logics are distinguished from the others in the modal family by the presence of the axiom (M). (M stands for 'modal'.)

(M) $\Box A \rightarrow A$

(M) claims that whatever is necessary is the case. Notice that (M) would be incorrect for the other operators we have discussed. For example, (M) is clearly incorrect when $\Box$ is read 'John believes', or 'it was the case that', (although it would be acceptable for 'John knows that'). The basic modal logic M is constructed by adding the axiom (M) to K. (Some authors call this system T.) Notice that this book uses upper case letters, for example: 'M' for systems of logic, and uses the same letter in parentheses: '(M)' for their characteristic axioms. Adding an axiom to K means that instances of the axiom may be placed within any subproof, including boxed sub-proofs. For example, here is a simple proof of the argument $\Box\Box p / p$ in the system M.

1.	$\Box\Box p$	
2.	$\Box\Box p \rightarrow \Box p$	(M)
3.	$\Box p$	1, 2 (MP)
4.	$\Box p \rightarrow p$	(M)
5.	p	3, 4 (MP)

Line 2: □□p→□p counts as an instance of (M) because it has the shape
□A→A. (Just let A be □p.) Proof strategies in M often require using
complex instances of (M) in this way.

Any interesting use of an axiom like (M) pretty much requires the use
of (MP) in the next step. This can make proofs cumbersome. To make
proofs in M shorter, it is useful to introduce the following derivable rule,
which we will also call (M).

The Rule (M)

   □A

   A   (M)

With this rule in hand, the proof of □□p / p is simplified.

1. ⌊□□p
2. │ □p   1 (M)
3. │ p   2 (M)

In the future, whenever axioms with the form A→B, are introduced, it
will be understood that a corresponding derived rule of the form A / B
with the same name is available.

EXERCISE 2.1

a) Prove A→◇A in M. (Hint: Use the following instance of (M): □~A→~A.)
b) Prove □A→◇A in M.
c) Prove (M): □A→A in K plus A→◇A.

The rule (M) allows one to drop a □ from a formula whenever it is the
main connective. You might think of this as an elimination rule for □.
Exercise 2.1c shows that the system M may be formulated equivalently
using A→◇A in place of (M), or by adopting a ◇ introduction rule that
allows one to prefix any proven formula with a ◇. This corresponds to
the intuition that A must be possible if it is true.

Many logicians believe that M is too weak, and that further principles
must be added to govern the *iteration*, or repetition, of modal operators.
Here are three well-known iteration axioms with their names.

(4)   □A→□□A

(B)   A→□◇A

(5)   ◇A→□◇A

> **EXERCISE 2.2**   Write an essay giving your reasons for either accepting or
> rejecting each of (4), (B), and (5).

To illustrate the use of these axioms (and their corresponding rules), here
are some sample proofs that appeal to them. Here is a proof of $\Box p / \Box\Box\Box p$
that uses (4).

1. $\quad \Box p$
2. $\quad \Box p \to \Box\Box p$ $\qquad$ (4)
3. $\quad \Box\Box p$ $\qquad\qquad$ 1, 2 (MP)
4. $\quad \Box\Box p \to \Box\Box\Box p$ $\quad$ (4)
5. $\quad \Box\Box\Box p$ $\qquad\qquad$ 3, 4 (MP)

Using the derived rule (4), the proof can be shortened.

1. $\quad \Box p$
2. $\quad \Box\Box p$ $\qquad$ 1 (4)
3. $\quad \Box\Box\Box p$ $\quad$ 2 (4)

Next we illustrate a somewhat more complex proof that uses (B) to prove
the argument $p / \Box\Diamond\Diamond p$.

1. $\quad p$
2. $\quad \Diamond p$ $\qquad$ Solution to Exercise 2.1a
3. $\quad \Box\Diamond\Diamond p$ $\quad$ 2 (B)

Note we have taken advantage of the solution to Exercise 2.1a to save
many steps in this proof. Feel free to do likewise in coming exercises.
Finally, here is a proof that uses (5) to prove $\Diamond p / \Box\Box\Diamond p$.

1. $\quad \Diamond p$
2. $\quad \Box\Diamond p$ $\qquad$ 1 (5)
3. $\quad\quad \Diamond p$ $\qquad$ 2 ($\Box$Out)
4. $\quad\quad \Box\Diamond p$ $\quad$ 3 (5)
5. $\quad \Box\Box\Diamond p$ $\quad$ 4 ($\Box$In)

You can see that strategies for proof finding can require more creativity
when the axioms (4), (B), and (5) are available.

Although names of the modal logics are not completely standard,
the system M plus (4) is commonly called S4. M plus (B) is called B
(for Brouwer's system) and M plus (5) is called S5. The following chart

reviews the systems we have discussed so far.

System M = K + (M): $\Box A \rightarrow A$.
System S4 = M + (4): $\Box A \rightarrow \Box \Box A$.
System B = M + (B): $A \rightarrow \Box \Diamond A$.
System S5 = M + (5): $\Diamond A \rightarrow \Box \Diamond A$.

It would be more consistent to name systems after the axioms they contain. Under this proposal, S4 would be named M4 (the system M plus (4)), and S5 would be M5. This is, in fact, the common practice for naming systems that are less well known. However, the systems S4 and S5 were named by their inventor C. I. Lewis, before systems like K and M were proposed, and so the names 'S4' and 'S5' have been preserved for historical reasons.

EXERCISE 2.3 Prove in the systems indicated. You may appeal to any results established previously in this book or proven by you during the completion of these exercises. Try to do them without looking at the hints.

a) $\Box\Box A \leftrightarrow \Box A$ in S4. (Hint: Use a special case of (M) for one direction.)
b) $\Box\Box{\sim}A / \Box{\sim}{\sim}\Box{\sim}A$ in K.
c) $\Diamond\Diamond A \leftrightarrow \Diamond A$ in S4. (Hint: Use the solution to Exercise 2.1a for one direction, and use 2.3b for the other.)
d) $\Box\Diamond\Diamond A \leftrightarrow \Box\Diamond A$ in S4. (Hint: Use (GN) with the solution for 2.3c.)
e) $\Box\Diamond A \leftrightarrow \Diamond A$ in S5. (Hint: Use a special case of (M) for one direction.)
f) (B) in S5. (Hint: Use the solution to Exercise 2.1a.)
g) $\Box{\sim}\Box{\sim}{\sim}A / \Box{\sim}\Box A$ in K.
h) $\Diamond\Box A \rightarrow A$ in B. (Hint: Use this version of B: ${\sim}A \rightarrow \Box\Diamond{\sim}A$, and the previous exercise.)
i) $\Diamond\Box A \leftrightarrow \Box A$ in S5. (Hint: In one direction, use Exercise 2.1a. In the other, use (${\sim}\Box$) (see Exercise 1.10b), this instance of (5): $\Diamond{\sim}A \rightarrow \Box\Diamond{\sim}A$, and the solution to g.)

The scheme that names a system by listing the names of its axioms is awkward in another respect. There are many equivalent ways to define provability in S5. All of the following collections of axioms are equivalent to S5 = M+(5).

M+(B)+(5)
M+(4)+(5)
M+(4)+(B)+(5)
M+(4)+(B)

By saying S5 is equivalent to a collection of rules, we mean that the arguments provable in S5 are exactly the ones provable with the rules in that collection. For example, consider M+(B)+(5). This is equivalent to S5, because we showed in Exercise 2.3f that (B) is provable in S5. Therefore (B) adds nothing new to the powers of S5. Whenever we have a proof of an argument using (B), we can replace the use of (B) with its derivation in S5.

EXERCISE 2.4

a) Prove (4) in S5. (Hint: First prove □A→□◇□A (a special case of (B)) and then prove □◇□A→□□A using the solution to Exercise 2.3i.)

b) Using the previous result, explain why S5 is equivalent to M+(4)+(5), and M+(4)+(B)+(5).

c) Prove S5 is equivalent to M+(4)+(B) by proving (5) in M+(4)+(B). (Hint: Begin with this special case of (B): ◇A→□◇◇A. Then use (4) to obtain □◇◇A→□◇A.)

It is more natural to identify a formal system by what it proves rather than by how it is formulated. We want to indicate, for example, that M+(5) and M+(4)+(B) are really the same system, despite the difference in their axioms. If we name systems by their axioms, we will have many different names ('M5', 'MB5', 'M45', . . and so on) for the same system. For a system like S5, which has many equivalent formulations, it is just as well that there is a single name, even if it is somewhat arbitrary.

Exercise 2.3 was designed to familiarize you with some of the main features of S4 and S5. In S4, a string of two boxes (□□) is equivalent to one box (□). As a result, any string of boxes is equivalent to a single box, and the same is true of strings of diamonds.

EXERCISE 2.5   Prove □□□A↔□A, ◇◇◇A↔◇A, and □□□□A↔□A in S4, using the strategies employed in Exercises 2.3a and 2.3c.

The system S5 has stronger principles for simplifying strings of modal operators. In S4 a string of modal operators of the same kind can be replaced for the operator, but in S5 strings containing both boxes and diamonds are equivalent to the last operator in the string. This means that one never needs to iterate (repeat) modal operators in S5 since the additional operators are superfluous.

EXERCISE 2.6   Prove ◇□◇A↔◇A and □◇□A↔□A in S5.

The following chart reviews the iteration principles for S4 and S5.

S4:   □□ .. □ = □   ◇◇ .. ◇ = ◇
S5:   00 .. □ = □   00 .. ◇ = ◇, where 0 is □ or ◇

The axiom (B): A→□◇A raises an important point about the inter-pretation of modal formulas. (B) says that if A is the case, then A is nec-essarily possible. One might argue that (B) should always be adopted in modal logic, for surely if A is the case, then it is necessary that A is possible. However, there is a problem with this claim that can be exposed by noting that ◇□A→A is provable from (B). (See Exer-cise 2.3.h.) So ◇□A→A should be acceptable if (B) is. However, ◇□A→A says that if A is possibly necessary, then A is the case, and this is far from obvious.

What has gone wrong? The answer is that we have not been careful enough in dealing with an ambiguity in the English rendition of A→□◇A. We often use the expression 'if A then necessarily B' to express that the conditional 'if A then B' is necessary. This interpretation of the English corresponds to □(A→B). On other occasions we mean that if A, then B is necessary: A→□B. In English, 'necessarily' is an adverb, and since adverbs are usually placed near verbs, we have no natural way to indicate whether the modal operator applies to the whole conditional, or to its consequent. This unfortunate feature creates ambiguities of scope, that is, ambiguities that result when it is not clear which portion of a sentence is governed by an operator.

For these reasons, there is a tendency to confuse (B): A→□◇A with □(A→◇A). But □(A→◇A) is not the same as (B), for □(A→◇A) is a theorem of M, and (B) is not. So one must take special care that our positive reaction to □(A→◇A) does not infect our evaluation of (B). One simple way to protect ourselves is to consider the sentence: ◇□A→A, where ambiguities of scope do not arise.

EXERCISE 2.7   Prove □(A→◇A) in M.

One could engage in endless argument over the correctness or incor-rectness of (4), (B), (5) and the other iteration principles that have been suggested for modal logic. Failure to resolve such controversy leads some people to be very suspicious of modal logic. "How can modal logic be logic at all," they say, "if we can't decide what the axioms should be?" My answer is to challenge the idea that we must decide on the axioms in order for modal logic to be coherent. Necessity is a many-sided notion, and so we should not expect it to correspond to a single logic. There are several viable modal systems, each one appropriate for a different way in which we understand and use the word 'necessarily'. This idea will be explored in more detail when we provide semantics for modal logics in Chapter 3.

2.2. Duals

The idea of the dual of a sentence is a useful notion in modal logic. The following pairs of symbols are defined to be *mates* of each other.

& ∨
□ ◇
∀ ∃

We have not introduced quantifiers ∀ and ∃ in our logics yet, but we will later, and so they are included now for future reference. Let A* be the sentence that results from replacing each symbol in A on the above list with its mate. Now we may define the *dual* for sentences that have the shapes A→B and A↔B, provided →, ↔, and ~ do not appear in A or B. The dual of A→B is B*→A* and the dual of A↔B is A*↔B*. Notice that sentences that do not have the shapes A→B or A↔B do not have duals. The best way to understand what duals are is to construct a few. The dual of (B): A→□◇A is (□◇A)*→(A)*, that is ◇□A→A. The dual of □(A&B)→(◇A∨◇B) is (◇A∨◇B)*→□(A&B)*. But (◇A∨◇B)* is □A&□B and □(A&B)* is ◇(A∨B), and so we obtain (□A&□B)→◇(A∨B), which is, therefore, its own dual.

EXERCISE 2.8 Find the duals of the following sentences.

a) □A→□□A
b) (□A&□B)↔□(A&B)
c) ◇A→□◇A
d) □(A∨B)→(□A∨□B)
e) ∀x□Ax↔□∀xAx
f) □(□A→A) (trick question)
g) □A→◇A
h) A→□◇A

The reason duals are interesting is that adding an axiom to K is equivalent to adding its dual as an axiom. Since sentences with the shape

A→□◇A are provable in B, it follows that all sentences of the (dual) shape ◇□A→A are provable in B as well. In fact, we could have used ◇□A→A instead of A→□◇A to define the system B. Being able to recognize duals can be very helpful in working out proof strategies and for appreciating the relationships between the various modal logics.

EXERCISE 2.9   Using duals, produce alternatives to the axioms (M), (4), and (5).

EXERCISE 2.10   To help verify that an axiom is equivalent to its dual, reconstruct proofs of the following facts:

a) The dual of (M) is derivable in K plus (M). (Exercise 2.1a)
b) The dual of (4) is derivable in K plus (4). (Exercise 2.3c)
c) The dual of (B) is derivable in K plus (B). (Exercise 2.3h)
d) The dual of (5) is derivable in K plus (5). (Exercise 2.3i)

2.3. Deontic Logic

A number of modal logics can be built from the basic system K that are not appropriate for necessity and possibility. They lack the characteristic axiom of M: □A→A. Deontic logics, the logics of obligation, are an important example. Deontic logics introduce the primitive symbol **O** for 'it is obligatory that', from which symbols for 'it is permitted that' and 'it is forbidden that' are defined as follows:

(DefP)   **PA** =$_{df}$ ~**O**~A
(DefF)   **FA** =$_{df}$ **O**~A

The symbol '**O**' in deontic logic plays exactly the same role as □ did in the system K. A basic system D of deontic logic can be constructed by adding the characteristic deontic axiom (D) to the rules of K, with **O** playing the role of □.

System D = (OOut) + (OIn) + (D).

```
 OOut              OIn
 OA                |_O
 :                 :
|_O                 A
|------            |--------
|  A   (OOut)      OA   (OIn)
```

(D)   **OA→PA**

Although the principles of K seem reasonable for deontic logic, one feature has bothered some people. The rule of Necessitation is derivable in K, so **O**A follows when A is a theorem. For example, since p→p is provable in PL, **O**(p→p) will follow. However, it is odd to say that p→p is obligatory (though just as odd, I would think, to deny that p→p is obligatory). Questions about whether A is obligatory or not do not arise when A is a theorem, because the language of obligation and permission applies to sentences whose truth values depend on our actions. No matter what we do, p→p will remain true, so there is no point in commanding or even permitting it.

Even though our feelings about K are, for this reason, neutral, K does lead to reasonable results where we do have strong intuitions. For example, the theorems about K concerning the distribution of operators over the connectives all seem reasonable enough. We will be able to prove that **O**(A&B) is equivalent to **O**A&**O**B, that **O**(A∨B) is entailed by **O**A∨**O**B but not vice-versa, that **P**(A∨B) is equivalent to **P**A∨**P**B, that **O**(A→B) entails **P**A→**P**B, and so forth. These are widely held to be exactly the sort of logical properties that **O** and **P** should have. Later, when we learn about modal semantics, we will find further support for the view that deontic logics can be built on the principles for K.

2.4. The Good Samaritan Paradox

There is a second problem with using K for deontic logic that has been widely discussed (Aqvist, 1967). The objection concerns a special case of the deontic version of General Necessitation (GN):

A ⊢ B

OA ⊢ OB

Now imagine that a Good Samaritan finds a wounded traveler by the side of the road. Assume that our moral system is one where the Good Samaritan is obliged to help the traveler. Consider the following instance of (GN):

1. The Good Samaritan binds the traveler's wound ⊢ the traveler is wounded.
2. The Good Samaritan ought to bind the traveler's wound ⊢ the traveler ought to be wounded.

Argument (1) appears to be logically valid, for you can't fix a person's wounds if the person is not wounded. However, the second argument (2) appears to be invalid. It is true that the Good Samaritan should help the traveler, but it is false that the traveler ought to be wounded. So it appears we must reject (GN) since it leads us from a valid to an invalid argument.

Let us resolve the paradox by symbolizing (1) in deontic logic. Although a full analysis requires predicate letters and quantifiers, it is still possible to present the gist of the solution to the problem using propositional logic. (For a more sophisticated treatment, see Exercise 18.18 in Chapter 18.) The central issue concerns how we are to translate sentence (3).

(3) The Good Samaritan binds the traveler's wound.

Sentence (3) really involves two different ideas: that the traveler is wounded, and that the Good Samaritan binds the wound. So let us use the following vocabulary:

W = The traveler is wounded.
B = The Good Samaritan binds the wound.

Now arguments (1) and (2) may be represented as an instance of (GN) as follows.

W&B ⊢ W

O(W&B) ⊢ **OW**

However, this does not count as a reason to reject (GN), for if it were, the argument **O**(W&B) ⊢ **OW** would need to have a true premise and a false conclusion. However, the premise is false. It is wrong to say that it ought to be the case that both the traveler is wounded and the Good Samaritan binds the wounds, because this entails that the traveler ought to be wounded, which is false.

One might object that the claim that the Good Samaritan ought to bind the traveler's wound, appears to be true, not false. There is, in fact, a way to represent this where it is true, namely W&**OB**. This says that the traveler is wounded and the Good Samaritan ought to bind the wound. In this version, W does not lie in the scope of the modal operator, so it does not claim that the traveler ought to be wounded. But if this is how the claim is to be translated, then (1) and (2) no longer qualify as an instance of (GN), for in (GN) the **O** must include the whole sentence W&B.

W&B ⊢ W

W&**OB** ⊢ **OW**   not an instance of (GN)!

So the Good Samaritan paradox may be resolved by insisting that we pay close attention to the scope of the deontic operator **O**, something that is difficult to do when we present arguments in English. Sentence (3) is ambiguous. If we read it as **O**(W&B), we have an instance of (GN), but the second argument's premise is false, not true. If we read (3) as W&**O**B, the premise of that argument is true, but the argument does not have the right form to serve as a case of (GN). Either way it is possible to explain why the reasoning is unsound without rejecting (GN).

2.5. Conflicts of Obligation and the Axiom (D)

We have already remarked that we do not want to adopt the analogue of (M), **O**A→A, in deontic logic. The reason is that if everything that ought to be is the case, then there is no point to setting up a system of obligations and permissions to regulate conduct. However, the basic deontic system D contains the weaker axiom (D), which is the analogue of □A→◇A, a theorem of M.

(D)   **O**A→**P**A

Axiom (D) guarantees the consistency of the system of obligations by insisting that when A is obligatory, it is permissible. A system that commands us to bring about A, but doesn't permit us to do so, puts us in an inescapable bind.

Some people have argued that D rules out conflicts of obligations. They claim we can be confronted with situations where we ought to do both A and ~A. For example, I ought to protect my children from harm, and I ought not to harbor a criminal, but if my child breaks the law and I am in a position to hide him so that he escapes punishment, then it seems I ought to turn him in because he is a criminal (**O**A), and I ought not to turn him in to protect him from harm (**O**~A). However, it is easy to prove ~(**O**A&**O**~A) in D, because (D) amounts to **O**A→~**O**~A, which entails ~(**O**A&**O**~A) by principles of propositional logic. So it appears that **O**A&**O**~A, which expresses the conflict of obligations, is denied by D.

I grant that conflicts of obligation are possible, but disagree with the conclusion that this requires the rejection of D. Conflicts of obligation arise not because a single system of obligations demands both A and ~A, but because conflicting *systems* of obligation pull us in different directions. According to the law, there is no question that I am obligated to turn in my son, but according to a more primitive obligation to my children, I should hide him. Very often, there are higher systems of obligation that are designed specifically to resolve such conflicts. If **O** is used to express obligation in a higher moral system that says that the law comes first in this situation, then it is simply false that I should refrain from turning him in, and it is no longer true that both **OA** and **O~A**.

Sometimes we have no explicit system that allows us to resolve conflicts between different types of obligation. Even so, we still do not have a situation where any one system commands both A and ~A. In our example, we have two systems, and so we ought to introduce two symbols: (say) **O**$_l$ for legal, and **O**$_f$ for familial obligation. Then **O**$_l$A is true but **O**$_l$~A is false, and **O**$_f$~A is true while **O**$_f$A is false when A is read 'I turn in my child'. The axiom (D) is then perfectly acceptable for both deontic operators **O**$_l$ and **O**$_f$, and so the conflict of obligations does not show that (D) is wrong.

2.6. Iteration of Obligation

Questions about the iteration of operators, which we discussed for modal logics, arise again in deontic logic. In some systems of obligation, we interpret **O** so that **OOA** just amounts to **OA**. 'It ought to be that it ought to be' is just taken to be a sort of stuttering; the extra 'oughts' just don't add anything. If this is our view of matters, we should add an axiom to D to ensure the equivalence of **OOA** and **OA**.

(OO)   **OA** ↔ **OOA**

If we view **(OO)** as composed of a pair of conditionals, we find that it 'includes' the deontic analogue **OA**→**OOA** of the modal axiom (4), □A→□□A. In system M, the converse □□A→□A is derivable, so it guarantees the equivalence of □□A and □A. But in deontic logic, we don't have (M), and so we need the equivalence in **(OO)**. Once we have taken the point of view that adopts **(OO)**, there seems to be no reason not to accept the policy of iteration embodied in S5 and simply ignore any extra deontic operators. So we would add an equivalence to guarantee the equivalence of **OPA** and **PA**.

(OP)   **PA** ↔ **OPA**

There is another way to interpret **O** so that we want to reject both **(OO)** and **(OP)**. On this view, 'it ought to be that it ought to be that A' commands adoption of some obligation that we may not already have. This is probably a good way to look at the obligations that come from the legal system, where we generally have legal methods for changing the laws and, hence, our obligations. Most systems that allow us to change our obligations do so only with limits, and these limits determine the obligations that are imposed on us concerning what we can obligate people to do. Under this reading, **OO**A says that according to the system, we have an obligation to obligate people to bring about A, that is, that no permissible changes in our obligations would release us from our duty to bring about A. Similarly, **OP**A says that we have an obligation in the system to permit A, that is, that we are not allowed to change the obligations so that people aren't permitted to do A. For example, according to a constitutional system, one might be allowed to make all sorts of laws, but not any that conflict with the fundamental principles of the constitution itself. So a system of law might obligate its citizens to permit freedom of speech (**OP**s), but this would be quite different from saying that the system permits freedom of speech (**P**s).

If this is how we understand **O** and **P**, it is clear that we cannot accept (**OO**) or (**OP**). If A is obligatory, it doesn't follow that it has to be that way, that is, that it is obligatory that A be obligatory. Also, if A is permitted, it doesn't follow that it *has* to be permitted. On this interpretation of obligation it is best to use the deontic logic D and drop (**OO**) and (**OP**).

There is one further axiom that we may want to add in deontic logics regardless of which interpretation we like. It is (OM).

(OM) $O(OA \rightarrow A)$

This says that it ought to be the case that if A ought to be the case, then it is the case. Of course, if A ought to be, it doesn't follow that A is the case. We already pointed out that $OA \rightarrow A$ is not a logical truth. But even so, it *ought* to be true, and this is what (OM) asserts. In almost any system of obligation then, we will want to supplement D with (OM).

EXERCISE 2.11   Show that sentences of the following form can be proven in D plus (OO): $OA \rightarrow OPA$.

2.7. Tense Logic

Tense Logics (Burgess, 1984; Prior, 1967) have provoked much less philosophical controversy than have deontic or even modal logics. This is probably because the semantics for tense logics can be given in a very natural way, one that is hard to challenge. Still there is no one system for tense that everyone agrees on. There are many tense logics, each one corresponding to a different set of assumptions made about the structure of time. There is general agreement, however, that these logics can all be based on the principles of K. A lot is known about how assumptions about the structure of time correspond to the various systems, a topic to be covered in Chapter 5.

In tense logic, we have two pairs of operators, one pair for the future, and the other pair for the past. The operators **G** and **F** abbreviate the expressions 'it always will be that' and 'it will be that', whereas **H** and **P** abbreviate 'it always was that' and 'it was that'. **G** and **H** are the strong operators and behave like □, whereas **F** and **P** are weak and behave like ◇. As we would expect, the operators in each pair are interdefinable.

(DefF)   FA =$_{df}$ ~G~A   (DefP)   PA =$_{df}$ ~H~A

So we can construct tense logic using only **G** and **H**. Of course we could start with **F** and **P** instead. This has some merit because **F** and **P** are the standard tense operators in English. However, that would complicate the rules for tense logics, and we would lose the parallels with the other logics in the modal family. A minimal system of tense logic called Kt results from adopting the principles of K for both **G** and **H**, plus two axioms to govern the iteration of **G** and **H**.

System Kt = PL + (**GOut**) + (**GIn**) + (**HOut**) + (**HIn**) + (**GP**) + (**HF**)

```
 GA           |_G            HA           |_H
 :            |  :           :            |  :
|_G           |  A          |_H           |  A
|------       |--------     |------       |--------
|  A  (GOut)   GA  (GIn)    |  A  (HOut)   HA   (HIn)
```

(GP)   A→GPA   (HF)   A→HFA

The axiom (HF) may appear to be incorrect, for it says that if A, then it always was the case that it will be that A. This may seem to have deterministic overtones. When we develop semantics for tense logic in Section 5.2, we will show that this worry results from a simple confusion and that (HF) is perfectly acceptable. At the same time, we will explain which axioms are correctly associated with deterministic assumptions about the nature of time.

Note that the characteristic axiom of modal logic, (M): □A→A, is not acceptable for either **H** or **G** since A does not follow from 'it always was the case that A', nor from 'it always will be the case that A'. However, it is acceptable in a closely related system where **G** is read 'it is and always will be', and **H** is read 'it is and always was'.

EXERCISE 2.12   Show that sentences of the following forms can be proven in Kt:

a) **PGA→A**
b) **FHA→A**

EXERCISE 2.13   Define what a dual is for tense logics.

2.8. Locative Logic

Now let us discuss a logic that can be interpreted as a logic of time, space, or of *locat*ions in general. Systems of this kind have been called topological logics (Rescher and Urquart, 1971, Ch. 2), but to avoid confusion with the very different subject of topology, the term 'locative logic' is chosen here. In locative logic, operators Ta, Tb, Tc, and so forth are added to the notation of PL. The sentence TnA is read 'It is the case at (or as of) n that A', where the term n may abbreviate such expressions as 'now', 'forty years ago', 'noon on July 26, 1943', 'the Eiffel Tower', 'latitude 40 degrees, longitude 30 degrees', 'John's point of view', and so forth.

In this sort of logic, we want Tn~A and ~TnA to be equivalent. If not A holds at n (Tn~A), then it is not the case that A holds at n (~TnA). Similarly if it is not the case that A holds at n (~TnA), then ~A must hold at n (Tn~A). A basic system T of locative logic results from adopting the principles of K along with Tn~A ↔ ~TnA. (It is understood that in the principles of K the □ is replaced with Tn throughout.)

System T = K + (T~).
(T~)   Tn~A ↔ ~TnA

Because of the presence of (T~) in T, we cannot distinguish a strong and a weak operator. The deontic axiom (D): □A→◇A is equivalent to □~A→~□A by (Def◇) and contraposition; the converse ◇A→□A amounts to ~□A→□~A, and so (T~) is the locative analogue of □A↔◇A, which ensures that the strong and weak operators are equivalent. It will come as no surprise, then, that the T operator behaves like □ as well as ◇ by distributing across &, ∨, and → both ways.

EXERCISE 2.14 Show that sentences of the following shapes are provable in T:

a) Tn(A∨B) ↔ (TnA∨TnB)
b) Tn(A&B) ↔ (TnA&TnB)
c) Tn(A→B) ↔ (TnA→TnB)

A system stronger than T can be constructed by adding an axiom that is an analogue of (4).

(TT)   TnA→TmTnA

Since there is no distinction between strong and weak operators in T, we might think of this as the analogue of (5) as well. This axiom is appropriate when the term n picks out a fixed "position". For example, if A is the case at noon, July 26, 1943, then this is itself the case at any other time. However, the axiom is not acceptable when n abbreviates an expression like '5 hours ago', which does not pick out any one time, but refers to different times depending on the time at which it is evaluated. If A is true 5 hours ago, it doesn't follow that this is so at noon, July 26, 1943.

Because of the presence of (T~), the addition of (TT) to T entails TmTnA→TnA. So the resulting system can demonstrate the equivalence of TmTnA and TnA, which means that any string of T-operators is equivalent to the right-most one, exactly as was the case in S5.

EXERCISE 2.15 Show that TmTnA ↔ TnA is provable in T plus (TT).

2.9. Logics of Belief

We may introduce operators Ba, Bb, Bc, and so forth so that Bn is read 'n believes that'. We might think of Bn as a locative operator where the term n refers to a person's "position" on what is or isn't so. But there are basic differences between a logic of belief and locative logic. First of all, we clearly do not want ~BnA ↔ Bn~A. A person who doesn't believe A does not necessarily believe ~A; he may have no beliefs one way or the other. So we will have to reject the axiom that yields the belief analogue of ◇A→□A, and we need to distinguish strong from weak operators in this logic.

Some people have argued that the analogue of (D) is also unacceptable for belief. On this view it is possible for a person to hold contradictory beliefs so that both BnA and Bn~A are true. If this is so, BnA→~Bn~A would have a true antecedent and a false conclusion.

There are also some difficulties with adopting the rules of K in belief logic, for these rules would sanction the inference from any theorem A to BnA. As a result, the principles of K ensure that every theorem of logic is believed. But that view is controversial to say the least. Let us imagine a very complicated theorem of logic, say one that would fill a whole book if it were written down. It would be unlikely that a person could understand it, much less believe it. So it seems wrong to adopt a rule that ensures that all theorems are believed. One might argue in reply that all theorems of logic count as the same belief, so that any person who is committed to any simple tautology (say pv~p) is thereby committed to any other theorem. However, this reply takes a fairly nonstandard attitude toward what count as identical beliefs. So it would appear that constructing a logic of belief is a difficult project. It seems that virtually all of the principles we have discussed for modal logics are controversial on some grounds or other. For this reason we may feel at a loss. Part of the problem is that acceptability of the axioms we are considering depends on one's theory of what beliefs are and how to tell the difference between them. This is a difficult problem in the philosophy of mind. Until it is solved, we cannot commit ourselves to any particular logic.

However, there is another way of looking at belief logic. Instead of describing belief *behavior*, a logic of belief might be a *normative* theory, recording what people ought to believe (whether they actually do so or not). On the normative reading, BnA says that n ought to believe A. Now the project of building a belief logic looks more promising. Clearly we will want to rule out contradictory beliefs, by accepting (D): BnA→~Bn~A. Furthermore, the objection to the principles of K no longer worries us. There may be a theorem of logic that is too long for me to believe, but I ought at least to believe it. So it looks as though a normative belief logic should be at least as strong as D.

EXERCISE 2.16   Write an essay giving reasons for or against accepting (M), (4), and (5) in a normative belief logic.

2.10. Provability Logic

(This section is for students with some knowledge of the foundations of mathematics.)

Modal logic has been useful in clarifying our understanding of central results concerning provability in the foundations of mathematics (Boolos, 1993). Provability logics are systems where the propositional variables p, q, r, and so forth range over formulas of some system S for mathematics, for example Peano's system PA for arithmetic. Godel showed that arithmetic has strong expressive powers. Using code numbers for arithmetic sentences, he was able to demonstrate a correspondence between sentences of mathematics and facts about which sentences are and are not provable in PA. For example, he showed that there is a sentence C that is true just in case no contradiction is provable in PA and there is a sentence G (the famous Godel sentence) that is true just in case it itself is not provable in PA.

In provability logics, □p is interpreted as a formula (of arithmetic) that expresses that what p denotes is provable in a given system S for arithmetic. Using this notation, sentences of provability logic express facts about provability. Since ⊥ indicates a contradiction, ~□⊥ says that S is consistent, and □A→A says that S is *sound* in the sense that when it proves A, A is indeed true. Furthermore, the box may be applied to any sentence. So, for example, when S is PA, □~□⊥ makes the dubious claim that PA is able to prove its own consistency, and ~□⊥ → ~□~□⊥ asserts (what Godel proved in his second incompleteness theorem) that if PA is consistent then PA is unable to prove its own consistency.

Although provability logics form a family of related systems, the system GL is by far the best known. It results from adding the following axiom to K:

(GL) □(□A→A)→□A

The axiom (4): □A→□□A is provable in GL, so GL is actually a strengthening of K4. However, axioms such as (M): □A→A, and even the weaker (D): □A→◇A, are not available (nor desirable) in GL. In provability logic, provability is not to be treated as a brand of necessity. The reason is that when p is provable in a given system S for mathematics, it does not follow that p is true since S may not be consistent. Furthermore, if p is provable in S (□p), it need not follow that ~p lacks a proof (~□~p = ◇p). S might be inconsistent and so prove both p and ~p.

Axiom (GL) captures the content of Loeb's Theorem, an important result in the foundations of arithmetic. □A→A says that S is sound for A, that is, that if A were proven, A would be true. Such a claim might not be secure since if S goes awry, A might be provable and false. Axiom (GL) claims that if S manages to prove the sentence that claims soundness for a given sentence A, then A is already provable in PA. Loeb's Theorem reports a kind of modesty on the part of the system PA (Boolos, 1993, p. 55). PA never insists (proves) that a proof of A entails A's truth, unless it already has a proof of A to back up that claim.

It has been shown that system GL is adequate for provability in the following sense. Let a sentence of GL be *always provable* exactly when the sentence of arithmetic it denotes is provable no matter how its variables are assigned values to sentences of PA. Then the provable sentences of GL are exactly the sentences that are always provable. This adequacy result has been extremely useful since general questions concerning provability in PA can be transformed into easier questions about what can be demonstrated in GL. For example, it is a straightforward matter to prove $\sim\Box\bot \to \sim\Box\sim\Box\bot$ in GL, and this allows us to demonstrate immediately the content of Godel's second incompleteness theorem, namely, that if PA is consistent, then PA cannot prove its consistency.

EXERCISE 2.17   Prove $\sim\Box\bot \to \sim\Box\sim\Box\bot$ in GL.
(Hint: Begin with the following instance of GL: $\Box(\Box\bot\to\bot)\to\Box\bot$. Use (Def~) and principles of K to demonstrate $\Box\sim\Box\bot \to \Box(\Box\bot\to\bot)$. Put these two results together to obtain $\Box\sim\Box\bot\to\Box\bot$, and then apply Contraposition to the result.)

3

Basic Concepts of Intensional Semantics

3.1. Worlds and Intensions

A pervasive feature of natural languages is that sentences depend for their truth value on the context or situation in which they are evaluated. For example, sentences like 'It is raining' and 'I am glad' cannot be assigned truth values unless the time, place of utterance, and the identity of the speaker is known. The same sentence may be true in one situation and false in another. In modal language, where we consider how things might have been, sentences may be evaluated in different possible worlds.

In the standard *extensional semantics*, truth values are assigned directly to sentences, as if the context had no role to play in their determination. This conflicts with what we know about ordinary language. There are two ways to solve the problem. The first is to translate the content of a sentence uttered in a given context into a corresponding sentence whose truth value does not depend on the context. For example, 'It is raining' might be converted into, for example, 'It is raining in Houston at 12:00 EST on Dec. 9, 1997 . .'. The dots here indicate that the attempt to eliminate all context sensitivity may be a never-ending story. For instance, we forgot to say that we are using the Gregorian Calendar, or that the sentence is to be evaluated in the real world.

There is a more satisfactory alternative. Instead of trying to repair ordinary language by translating each of its context-dependent sentences into a complex one that makes the context of its evaluation explicit, the account of truth assignment is adjusted to reflect the fact that the truth value depends on the context. The central idea of *intensional semantics* is to include contexts in our description of the truth conditions of sentences in this way.

To do this, let us introduce a set **W**, which contains the relevant contexts of evaluation. Since logics for necessity and possibility are the paradigm modal logics, **W** will be called the set of (possible) *w*orlds. But in the same way that $\Box$ is a generic operator, **W** should be understood as a generic set including whatever contexts are relevant for the understanding of $\Box$ at issue. No attempt is made in intensional semantics to fix the "true nature" of **W**, and there is no need to do so. When one wishes to apply modal logic to the analysis of a particular expression of language, then more details about what the members of **W** are like will be apparent. If $\Box$ is a temporal operator, for example, **W** will contain times; if $\Box$ means necessarily, **W** will contain possible worlds, and so on. The semantics given here lays out only the broadest features concerning how truth values are calculated, allowing it to be used for many different applications.

Some students worry that this failure to define **W** in more detail is a defect. However, a similar complaint could be lodged against the semantics for quantificational logic. There a domain **D** of quantification is introduced, but no attempt is made to say exactly what **D** contains. This is only proper, for it is not the province of logic to decide ontological questions about what really exists, or what the quantifier "really" means. The same point can even be made for propositional semantics. The truth values T (true) and F (false) are, as far as semantics goes, merely two separate objects. There is no attempt to explain what a truth value really is, nor is one needed.

In intensional semantics, an *intensional model* (for a language) is defined as a pair <**W**, **a**> where **W** is understood as a (nonempty) set of contexts (called worlds), and **a** is an assignment function for the language. In extensional semantics, the assignment function **a** would assign truth values to sentences directly. So if g abbreviates 'grass is green' and s abbreviates 'snow is green', then assignment **a** might give truth values as follows: $\mathbf{a}(g)=T$ and $\mathbf{a}(s)=F$. However, in intensional semantics, the truth value of sentence A depends on the world **w** at which A is evaluated. For this reason, an *assignment* in intensional semantics assigns to A a different truth value for each of the possible worlds **w** in **W**. The truth value of A on assignment **a** *at world w* is notated $\mathbf{a_w}(A)$. So, for example, if **r** is the real world, then $\mathbf{a_r}(g)=T$, and $\mathbf{a_r}(s)=F$, but in the case of an unreal world **u**, where grass is white and snow is green, we would have $\mathbf{a_u}(g)=F$, and $\mathbf{a_u}(s)=T$. We will call $\mathbf{a_w}(A)$ the *extension* of A (on **a** at **w**).

3.2. Truth Conditions and Diagrams for → and ⊥

The main task of semantics is to give the *truth conditions* for the logical symbols ⊥, →, and □. This means that a definition must be provided that explains how the truth values of complex sentences depend on the values of their parts. In propositional logic the truth conditions for the connectives are ordinarily given by the familiar truth tables. Instead diagrams will be used in this book to present and calculate truth conditions.

To represent that A is true at world **w** ($\mathbf{a_w}(A)=T$), we will draw a region, labeled by **w**, which contains A.

$$\boxed{A}^{\mathbf{w}} \qquad \mathbf{a_w}(A)=T$$

To show A is false at **w** ($\mathbf{a_w}(A)=F$), we could place A outside the region.

$$A \; \bigcirc^{\mathbf{w}} \qquad \mathbf{a_w}(A)=F$$

An assignment should not be allowed to give sentences truth values in an arbitrary way. For example, if $\mathbf{a_w}(p)=T$ and $\mathbf{a_w}(q)=F$, we do not want $\mathbf{a_w}(p{\rightarrow}q)$ to be T. To complete our definition of what an assignment **a** is, we must lay down conditions on how **a** assigns values to ⊥ and to sentences containing →. First, we will insist that **a** respects the idea that ⊥ stands for a contradictory sentence by stipulating that **a** always assigns ⊥ the value F in all the possible worlds.

(⊥) $\mathbf{a_w}(\bot)=F$.

In this and all future statements about **a**, it is assumed that **w** is any member of **W**. Second, we stipulate that **a** assigns values to sentences of the form A→B according to the truth table for the material conditional. The table can be summarized in the following condition:

(→) $\mathbf{a_w}(A{\rightarrow}B)=T$ iff $\mathbf{a_w}(A)=F$ or $\mathbf{a_w}(B)=T$.

The conditions (⊥) and (→) together fix the truth conditions for all the other connectives. For example, the truth clause of ~ must be (~).

(~) $\mathbf{a_w}(\sim A)=T$ iff $\mathbf{a_w}(A)=F$.

This can be shown as follows:

$$\mathbf{a_w}(\sim A)=T \quad \text{iff} \quad \mathbf{a_w}(A\to\perp)=T \qquad (\text{Def}\sim)$$
$$\text{iff} \quad \mathbf{a_w}(A)=F \text{ or } \mathbf{a_w}(\perp)=T \quad (\to)$$
$$\text{iff} \quad \mathbf{a_w}(A)=F \qquad \text{because } (\perp) \text{ rules}$$

out the possibility
that $\mathbf{a_w}(\perp)=T$.

The semantical condition ($\sim$) ensures that $\sim$A is true in a world exactly when A is false in the world. This means that the following two diagrams are equivalent:

It is inconvenient to have sentences "dangling" outside worlds in our diagrams, so when we want to show that $\mathbf{a_w}(A)$ is F, we will put $\sim$A inside the world **w** instead.

The condition ($\sim$) ensures the following:

($\sim$F)   If $\mathbf{a_w}(\sim A)=F$, then $\mathbf{a_w}(A)=T$.

We can represent this fact in a diagram as follows:

This diagram represents a rule for adding sentences to worlds. Above the line, we have shown $\sim$A is F in **w** by putting $\sim\sim$A there; below the line, we show what follows, namely, that A is T in **w**.

We will also want to diagram the condition ($\to$), which gives the truth behavior of $\to$.

($\to$) $\mathbf{a_w}(A\to B)=T$ iff $\mathbf{a_w}(A)=F$ or $\mathbf{a_w}(B)=T$.

To do so, two diagrams are needed, one for when A→B is true and one for when A→B is false. First, consider what ($\to$) tells us when $\mathbf{a_w}(A\to B)=F$. In that case $\mathbf{a_w}(A\to B)\neq T$, and by ($\to$) it follows that it is not the case that $a_w(A)=F$ or $a_w(B)=T$. But this amounts to saying that $a_w(A)=T$ and $a_w(B)=F$.

Summarizing, we have the following fact:

$(\rightarrow F)$ If $a_w(A\rightarrow B)=F$, then $a_w(A)=T$ and $a_w(B)=F$.

$(\rightarrow F)$ can be expressed in the following diagram:

$$
\boxed{\begin{array}{c} \underline{\sim(A\rightarrow B)} \\ A \\ \sim B \end{array}}^{\,w} \quad
\begin{array}{l} \text{If} \quad a_w(A\rightarrow B)=F, \\ \text{then} \quad a_w(A)=T \\ \text{and} \quad a_w(B)=F. \end{array}
$$

The diagram says that if we find $\sim(A\rightarrow B)$ in world **w**, we may also add both A and $\sim$B to **w**. This amounts to saying that if $A\rightarrow B$ is F in **w**, then A is T in **w** and B is F in **w**.

In case $A\rightarrow B$ is true, condition $(\rightarrow)$ tells us the following:

$(\rightarrow T)$ If $a_w(A\rightarrow B)=T$, then $a_w(A)=F$ or $a_w(B)=T$.

Here is the diagram for the condition $(\rightarrow T)$.

$$
\boxed{\begin{array}{c} \underline{A\rightarrow B} \\ \diagup\diagdown \\ \sim A \qquad B \end{array}}^{\,w} \quad
\begin{array}{l} \text{If} \quad a_w(A\rightarrow B)=T, \\ \text{then} \quad a_w(A)=F \text{ or } a_w(B)=T. \end{array}
$$

Above the line, we have indicated that $A\rightarrow B$ is T in **w**. Below the line we have constructed two branches, indicating that *either* A is F *or* B is T in **w**. If you know the tree method for checking for validity in propositional logic, this use of branches to indicate alternatives will be familiar.

EXERCISE 3.1   Create diagrams that express the following facts:

a) If $a_w(A)=T$ and $a_w(A\rightarrow B)=T$, then $a_w(B)=T$.

b) If $a_w(A\rightarrow B)=T$ and $a_w(B)=F$, then $a_w(A)=F$.

c) $a_w(A\&B)=T$ iff $a_w(A)=T$ and $a_w(B)=T$. (Use two diagrams, one indicating what happens when $a_w(A\&B)=T$, and the other when $a_w(A\&B)=F$.)

3.3. Derived Truth Conditions and Diagrams for PL

The propositional logic connectives &, $\vee$, and $\leftrightarrow$ are defined in terms of $\rightarrow$ and $\sim$ (actually $\sim$ is defined in turn using $\perp$). Given (Def&), (Def$\vee$),

(Def↔), and the truth conditions (→) and (~), it is possible to calculate the truth clauses for &, ∨, and ↔. Diagrams are an especially perspicuous way to present this sort of reasoning. For example, the truth clause for & is (&):

(&) $a_w(A\&B)=T$ iff $a_w(A)=T$ and $a_w(B)=T$.

This can be presented in two diagrams as follows:

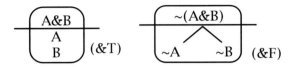

These diagrams can be shown derivable as follows:

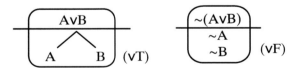

Similar methods may be used to show the derivability of (∨), the truth condition for ∨, which can be expressed in the following diagrams for ∨:

(∨) $a_w(A\lor B)=T$ iff $a_w(A)=T$ or $a_w(B)=T$.

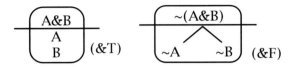

EXERCISE 3.2   Show that the above diagram rules follow from the rules for ~ and →.

So far, diagrams for ↔ have not been given. It may be just as easy for you to work out truth conditions for ↔ by converting A↔B into (A→B)&(B→A) and using the rules for → and &. However, if you are interested in derived rules for ↔, the following pair will do. They indicate the basic facts about the ↔ truth table. When A↔B is T, the values of A and B match, so either A and B are both T or A and B are both F. When A↔B is F, the values for A and B fail to match, which means that either A is T and B is F or A is F and B is T.

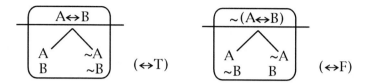

These diagrams together correspond to the following derived truth clause for ↔:

(↔) $a_w(A↔B)=T$ iff $a_w(A)=T$ iff $a_w(B)=T$.

3.4. Truth Conditions for □

So far, nothing has been said about truth conditions for the modal operator □. A simple way of defining them is to stipulate that □A is true iff A is true in every possible world. We will call this the *global interpretation* of □. Although the global interpretation is appropriate for some uses of 'it is necessary that', it is too restrictive for a generic modal operator. Imagine, for example, that □ symbolizes the future tense operator 'it will always be the case that'. On this interpretation, □A does not say that A is true at all worlds (times), it claims that A is true at times *in the future*. It is enough for □A to be true at **w** if A is true at all times *later than* **w**. Similarly, in deontic logic, where □ is read 'it is obligatory that', the truth of □A does not demand the truth of A in *every* possible world, but only in worlds where people do what they ought. Even in modal logic, we may wish to restrict the range of possible worlds that are relevant in determining whether □A is true. For example, I might say that it is necessary for me to turn my paper in on time, even though I know full well that there is a possible world where I turn it in late. In ordinary speech, the necessity of A does not demand truth of A in *all* possible worlds, but only in a certain class of worlds that I have in mind (for example, worlds where I avoid penalties for late papers). To provide a generic treatment of □, we must say that □A is true in **w** iff A is true in all worlds that are related to **w** in the right way. So for each operator □, we introduce a corresponding (binary) relation **R** on the set of possible worlds **W**, traditionally called the *accessibility relation* (or the *Kripke relation* in honor of Saul Kripke, who first proposed it). The accessibility relation **R** holds between worlds **w** and **v** iff **v** is a world where A must be true if □A is true at **w**. Exactly what **R** is will depend on our reading of □. In a future tense logic, for example, **R** is the relation **earlier than** on the set of times **W**. In Chapter 5, we will say more about how **R** is understood.

Since the accessibility relation **R** is needed to give the truth conditions for □, we need to add it to our intensional models. So let a *K-model* (for a language) be a triple <**W**, **R**, **a**>, where **W** is not empty, and **R** is a binary relation on **W**. The initial part of the K-model <**W**, **R**> is called the *frame* of the model. The assignment function **a** in a K-model obeys the truth clauses (→) and (⊥), together with the following condition for □:

(□) $a_w(□A)=T$ iff   for each **v** such that wRv, $a_v(A)=T$.

This condition is equivalent to a pair of conditions, one for when □A is true and one for when □A is false.

(□T)   If $a_w(□A)=T$, then for each **v** such that wRv, $a_v(A)=T$.
(□F)   If $a_w(□A)=F$, then for some **v** such that wRv, $a_v(A)=F$.

To see why (□F) follows from (□), note that if $a_w(□A)=F$, then $a_w(□A)≠T$, so it follows by (□) that it is not the case that for each **v** such that wRv, $a_v(A)=T$. But that means that there must be some world **v** such that wRv where $a_v(A)=F$.

Chapter 5 will explain how details concerning the semantical behavior of the various modal operators may be reflected in this treatment of □ by introducing special conditions on **R**. For example, to obtain the global interpretation, simply stipulate that wRv for all worlds **w** and **v**. Then (□) has the effect of saying that $a_w(□A)=T$ iff $a_v(A)=T$ in all possible worlds **v**.

Condition (□) is the first clause that involves the worlds in a fundamental way. The clause for ~ has the property that the extension of ~A at **w** depends on the extension of A at the same world, and similarly for →. But we cannot determine the extension of □A at **w** on the basis of the extension of A at **w**. For □A to be T at **w**, A must be T at all accessible worlds. This means that the extension of A at a world does not determine the extension of □A at that world; instead we must know the whole *intension* of A, that is, we need to know the truth values A takes in other worlds. This is the defining feature of the intensional operator □. It is not truth functional because the extension (truth value) of A (in **w**) does not determine the extension of □A (in **w**). However, this failure does not rule out a semantical analysis of □ because we can still specify the truth value of □A in terms of the *intension* of A, that is, the pattern of truth values that A has across all the possible worlds.

The truth condition for □ may be represented in diagrams, provided that we have a way to represent the accessibility relation **R**. We will represent **wRv** by drawing an arrow from world **w** to world **v**.

This arrow represents a pathway that makes **v** accessible from **w**.

Condition (□) may then be represented by two diagrams, one for when □A is true (□T), and the other for when □A is false (□F). Here is the diagram for (□T):

(□T)   If $a_w(\Box A)=T$, then for each **v** such that **wRv**, $a_v(A)=T$.

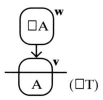

Above the line, we see a world **w** where □A is T, and another world **v** that is accessible from **w**; below the line we record what follows from this, namely, that A is T in **v**.

For (□F) we have the following diagram:

(□F)   If $a_w(\Box A)=F$, then for some **v** such that **wRv**, $a_v(A)=F$.

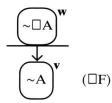

Here we see that □A is F at **w**. From this it follows that there is another world **v** accessible from **w**, at which A is F.

Notice the difference in the position of the horizontal line in the last two diagrams. *This is crucially important.* In the case of (□T), the parts above the line must already be in place before the conclusion may be drawn. The line cuts through situation **v**, indicating that the existence of **v** and the arrow from **w** to **v** must be already available before A may be placed in **v**. In the case of (□F), only world **w** is above the line, which shows that once we know □A is F, we know there must be some accessible world where A is F. This means that (□T) and (□F) behave very differently. In order to apply (□T), we must have □A in world **w** *and an arrow to another world* **v** before the rule can be applied.

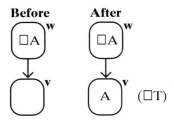

On the other hand, (□F) is quite different. To apply this rule, all we need is ~□A in world **w**. We do not need to have the arrow pointing to another world. Instead, the rule requires the introduction of a new arrow and a new world where ~A is placed.

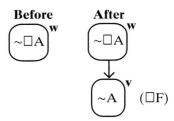

3.5. Truth Conditions for ◇

(Def◇), the definition of ◇ in terms of □, along with the truth conditions (□) and (~), entails that the truth clause for ◇ must be the following:

(◇) $a_w(◇A)=T$ iff for some **v**, **wRv** and $a_v(A)=T$.

We will give the proof in one direction using diagrams and leave the other direction as an exercise. We want to show (◇T), which corresponds to the following diagram:

($\Diamond$T)   If $a_w(\Diamond A)=T$ then for some **v**, **wRv** and $a_v(A)=T$.

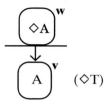

The proof can be presented using diagram rules for ($\Box$) and ($\sim$) as follows:

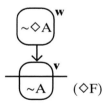

EXERCISE 3.3

a) For the following diagram rule for ($\Diamond$F), draw diagrams for **Before** and **After** the rule is applied.

($\Diamond$F)   If $a_w(\Diamond A)=F$ and **wRv**, then $a_v(A)=F$.

b) Show that ($\Diamond$F) follows from ($\Box$), ($\sim$), and (Def$\Diamond$) using diagrams.

3.6. Satisfiability, Counterexamples, and Validity

The purpose of providing semantics for a language is to give a careful definition of what it means for an argument to be valid. We are now ready to give this definition for a generic intensional operator $\Box$. Remember that a K-model for a language was a triple $<\mathbf{W}, \mathbf{R}, \mathbf{a}>$, consisting of a nonempty set of worlds $\mathbf{W}$, a (binary) relation $\mathbf{R}$, and an assignment function $\mathbf{a}$ that assigns to each sentence of the language at every world $\mathbf{w}$ in $\mathbf{W}$ a truth value (either T or F) according to the truth conditions $(\bot)$, $(\rightarrow)$, and $(\Box)$.

The definition of validity is developed by first defining the terms 'satisfied', 'satisfiable', and 'counterexample'.

A list of sentences H *is satisfied at w* on assignment $\mathbf{a}$
iff $\mathbf{a_w}(B)=T$ for every member B of H.

We write '$\mathbf{a_w}(H)=T$' to indicate that H is *satisfied* at $\mathbf{w}$ on $\mathbf{a}$.

A list of sentences H is *K-satisfiable*
iff there is a K-model $<\mathbf{W}, \mathbf{R}, \mathbf{a}>$ for a language containing sentences of H and a world $\mathbf{w}$ in $\mathbf{W}$ where $\mathbf{a_w}(H)=T$ (i.e. where H is satisfied at $\mathbf{w}$).

When a list of sentences H is K-satisfiable, it is logically possible for the sentences to be true together. Some logic books call satisfiable sets logically consistent (or consistent for short).

An argument H / C has a *K-counterexample*
iff the list H, ~C is K-satisfiable.

So the argument H / C has a K-counterexample exactly when it is possible to find a model and a world where the hypotheses are all true and the conclusion is false.

An argument H / C is *K-valid*
iff H / C has no K-counterexample.

We will also say that a *sentence* A *is K-valid* iff the argument /A is K-valid, that is, when the argument with no hypotheses and A as its conclusion is K-valid.

It will be useful to introduce a few abbreviations. To indicate that the argument H / C is K-valid, we will write: 'H $\vDash_K$ C'. Since an argument has a K-counterexample exactly when it is *not* K-valid, 'H $\nvDash_K$ C' indicates that H / C has a K-counterexample. Finally, '$\vDash_K$ A' says that the sentence A is K-valid.

This definition of validity may seem to be unnecessarily long-winded, especially since there is a more direct way to do the job. The basic intuition is that a valid argument has the feature that if all its hypotheses are T, then so is its conclusion. In the case of modal logic, an alternative (and more direct) definition would go like this:

H ⊨$_K$ C iff
for all K-models <**W**, **R**, **a**> and all **w** in **W**,
if **a$_w$**(H)=T, then **a$_w$**(C)=T.

However, we have chosen the long-winded definition to set the stage for later developments and to establish the relationship between validity and other important logical concepts such as that of a counterexample and a satisfiable set. It is worth pausing a moment to check that the long-winded definition and the alternative definition say the same thing. This can be done by showing that the alternative definition is equivalent to the long-winded one. Here is how. Note that H ⊨$_K$ C holds iff H / C has no K-counterexample. But to say that H / C has no K-counterexample is to say that H, ~C is not K-satisfiable, which means in turn that you cannot find a K-model <**W**, **R**, **a**> with a **w** in **W** where **a$_w$**(H)=T and **a$_w$**(C)=F. But that just means that for all K-models <**W**, **R**, **a**> and all **w** in **W**, if **a$_w$**(H)=T, then **a$_w$**(C)=T. This is the alternative definition.

EXERCISE 3.4

a) Show that ⊨$_K$ A iff for all models <**W**, **R**, **a**> and all **w** in **W**, **a$_w$**(A)=T. (Hint: Unpack the definition for ⊨$_K$ A.)
b) Show that H ⊨$_K$ A iff for all models <**W**, **R**, **a**> and all **w** in **W**, if **a$_w$**(H)=T, then **a$_w$**(A)=T.
c) Create a diagram that shows that H ⊭$_K$ C, that is, that the argument H / C has a K-counterexample.

3.7. The Concepts of Soundness and Completeness

The main reason for developing semantics for a logical system is to provide a standard for correctness – a way to distinguish the valid arguments from the invalid ones. The semantics for a logic gives a formal account of which arguments are the valid ones. However, there is no guarantee that a system of rules that we happen to chose is correct. There may be provable arguments of the system that are not valid, and there may be valid arguments that are not provable. One of the primary concerns of this book will be to show that the rules for the various modal logics are adequate. When the rules are *adequate*, the arguments that are provable are exactly the valid ones. Showing adequacy of a system of logic S involves two steps. First we must show *soundness* of S.

(Soundness)   If an argument is provable in S, then it is valid.

Showing soundness is relatively easy. The hard part is showing *completeness*.

(Completeness)   If an argument is valid, then it is provable in S.

The material in the next chapters is designed to provide tools for showing completeness of modal logics.

3.8. A Note on Intensions

We have referred to $a_w(A)$ (the truth value of A at world w assigned by a) as the *extension* of A (on w). On the other hand $a(A)$, the *intension* of A (on assignment a), is a function that describes the whole pattern of truth values assigned to A (by a) at the different possible worlds. Here is an example to make the idea of an intension more concrete. Consider, for example, the following abbreviations:

g='Grass is green'   s='Snow is green'   d='Dogs are pets'

Imagine that there are three possible worlds: r (the real one), u (a world like the real one except that snow is green and grass is white), and v (a world like the real one except that dogs aren't pets), Then the assignment function a should award the following truth values:

$$a_r(g)=T \quad a_r(s)=F \quad a_r(d)=T$$
$$a_u(g)=F \quad a_u(s)=T \quad a_u(d)=T$$
$$a_v(g)=T \quad a_v(s)=F \quad a_v(d)=F$$

Now consider the left-hand column in this chart. It keeps track of the values assigned to g in the different possible worlds. This column corresponds to a function $a(g)$ called the intension of g, with the following behavior: to world r it assigns T, to u it assigns F, and to v it assigns T. So $a(g)$ is a function whose domain is W and range is the set of truth values $\{T, F\}$. It gives an account of what the truth value of g is for each of the worlds in W. The intension of g allows us to determine the truth value as soon as a world w is given, for all we have to do is apply the function $a(A)$ to w to obtain the appropriate truth value. In general, the *intension* $a(A)$ (of A on model $<W, R, a>$) is a function that assigns to each member of W a member of the set of truth values {T, F}. The result of applying the function $\mathbf{a}(A)$ to the world $\mathbf{w}$ is a truth value $\mathbf{a_w}(A)$, which is the extension of A at $\mathbf{w}$ on assignment $\mathbf{a}$.

It is a standard tradition in modal semantics to identify the intension of a sentence with its meaning (Carnap, 1947). Though there are problems with this treatment of meaning, many philosophers still find the basic idea an attractive starting point for more sophisticated accounts (Cresswell, 1985).

4

Trees for K

4.1. Checking for K-Validity with Trees

The diagram rules reviewed in the last chapter provide an efficient method for checking whether an argument is K-valid. Let us illustrate the method with a few examples. First, we will show that the argument $\Box(p{\rightarrow}q)$ / $\sim\Box q{\rightarrow}\sim\Box p$ is K-valid. The basic strategy is to assume that the argument is not K-valid and derive a contradiction. So assume that $\Box(p{\rightarrow}q) \nvDash_K \sim\Box q{\rightarrow}\sim\Box p$, that is, that $\Box(p{\rightarrow}q)$ / $\sim\Box q{\rightarrow}\sim\Box p$ has a K-counterexample. Then there must be a K-model $<\mathbf{W}, \mathbf{R}, \mathbf{a}>$ and some world $\mathbf{w}$ in $\mathbf{W}$ where $\mathbf{a_w}(\Box(p{\rightarrow}q))=T$ and $\mathbf{a_w}(\sim\Box q{\rightarrow}\sim\Box p)=F$. Let us diagram that world $\mathbf{w}$.

$$\Box(p{\rightarrow}q) \nvDash_K \sim\Box q{\rightarrow}\sim\Box p$$

$$\boxed{\begin{array}{c} \Box(p{\rightarrow}q) \\ \sim(\sim\Box q{\rightarrow}\sim\Box p) \end{array}}^{\mathbf{w}}$$

Since $\mathbf{a_w}(\sim\Box q{\rightarrow}\sim\Box p)=F$, it follows by ($\rightarrow$F) that $\mathbf{a_w}(\sim\Box q)=T$ and $\mathbf{a_w}(\sim\Box p)=F$.

$$\boxed{\begin{array}{c} \Box(p{\rightarrow}q) \\ \sim(\sim\Box q{\rightarrow}\sim\Box p) \\ \sim\Box q \\ \sim\sim\Box p \end{array}}^{\mathbf{w}} \quad \begin{array}{l} (\rightarrow F) \\ (\rightarrow F) \end{array}$$

But if $\mathbf{a_w}(\sim\Box p)=F$, then by ($\sim$F), we know that $\mathbf{a_w}(\Box p)=T$.

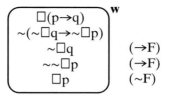

Since $\mathbf{a_w}(\Box q)$=F, we know by ($\Box$F) that there is a world **v** where $\mathbf{a_v}(q)$=F.

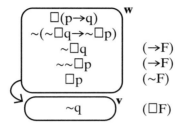

(The arrow between **w** and **v** has been drawn to the side to clarify the structure of the tree and to make for more compact diagrams.) Since $\mathbf{a_w}(\Box p)$=T, and $\mathbf{a_w}(\Box(p{\rightarrow}q))$=T, we know by ($\Box$T) and the fact that **wRv** that $\mathbf{a_v}(p)$=T and $\mathbf{a_v}(p{\rightarrow}q)$=T.

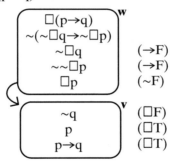

Because $\mathbf{a_v}(p{\rightarrow}q)$=T, we know that either $\mathbf{a_v}(p)$=F or $\mathbf{a_v}(q)$=T by ($\rightarrow$T).

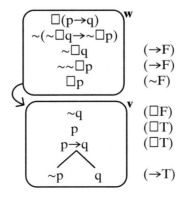

The left-hand branch in **v** indicates that $\mathbf{a_v}(p)=F$. But this alternative is not possible because we already know that $\mathbf{a_v}(p)=T$. We will record that this alternative is impossible by entering the contradiction mark on the left branch. This corresponds to applying the ($\perp$In) rule to that branch, so we label that step with ($\perp$In).

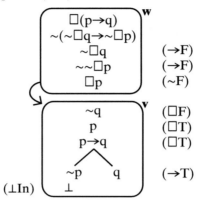

Here is a picture that presents the ($\perp$In) rule for trees:

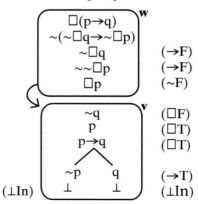

This rule allows us to enter $\perp$ on any branch that contains a contradictory pair in the same world. We will say a branch *is closed* when it contains $\perp$. So the left-hand branch of **v** is closed. The right-hand branch is also closed because it shows that **a** assigns q both T and F in **v**.

Both branches of the tree in world **v** are now closed, which shows that our attempt to find a model where $\mathbf{a_w}(\Box(p{\to}q))=T$ and $\mathbf{a_w}(\sim\Box q{\to}\sim\Box p)=F$

failed. So the argument □(p→q) / ~□q→~□p has no counterexample, and so must be K-valid.

A *tree is closed* when all of its branches are closed. A closed tree indicates that the argument from which it was constructed is K-valid. If every possible step has been carried out and the tree contains a branch that is not closed, the tree is *open* and the argument from which it was constructed is not K-valid. In order to avoid incorrectly diagnosing validity, it is important to have a check-off procedure to make sure that every possible step in a tree has been carried out. Otherwise the tree may appear to be open when there is a step yet to perform that would close it. Crossing out steps as they are performed is a good practice since it makes it easy to see whether all possible steps have been carried out. Any sentence not crossed out, other than a propositional variable p or its negation ~p, has yet to be worked on.

It is important to apply the (□F) and (□T) rules in the right order. For example, it would not be correct to complete the tree for the argument □(p→q) / ~□q→~□p in this manner:

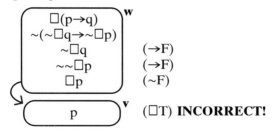

The reason this is wrong has been explained in Section 3.4. Here (□T) has been applied to □p in world **w** to create an arrow and a new world **v**. But the (□T) rule cannot be applied unless the arrow and world **v** *already exist* in the tree. (The same is true of the (◇F) rule.) When sentences of the form □A or ~◇A appear in a world, nothing can be done with them until an arrow pointing to a new world has been added to the tree by some other rule. So it is important that (□F) be applied to ~□q, *first*, to create world **v**, so that (□T) can be correctly applied afterwards.

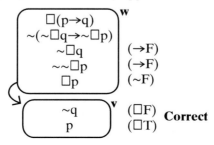

To avoid this kind of problem, the best strategy is to apply all steps one can within a world, then apply (□F) and (◇T), and follow with applications of (□T) and (◇F).

In the argument we just checked, ~, →, and □ were the only logical symbols. So we needed only the basic semantical rules. In the next two examples, we will need to use some of the derived rules. Let us show that □(p&q) / □p&□q is K-valid. We begin by assuming that this argument has a counterexample. So there must be a model with a world **w** such that $a_w(□(p\&q))=T$ and $a_w(□p\&□q)=F$.

$$
\boxed{\begin{array}{l} □(p\&q) \\ \sim(□p\&□q) \end{array}}^{\textbf{w}}
$$

Since $a_w(□p\&□q)=F$, it follows from (&F) that either $a_w(□p)=F$ or $a_w(□q)=F$.

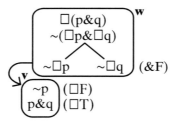

Since $a_w(□p)=F$, it follows by (□F) that there is a world **v** such that **wRv** and $a_v(p)=F$. By (□T) and $a_w(□(p\&q))=T$, it follows that $a_v(p\&q)=T$.

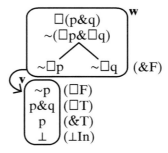

But now world **v** closes because $a_v(p)=T$ follows from (&T).

$$
\boxed{\begin{array}{l} □(p\&q) \\ \sim(□p\&□q) \\ \quad \diagup\diagdown \\ \sim□p \qquad \sim□q \end{array}}^{\textbf{w}} (\&F)
$$
$$
\boxed{\begin{array}{ll} \sim p & (□F) \\ p\&q & (□T) \\ p & (\&T) \\ \perp & (\perp In) \end{array}}^{\textbf{v}}
$$

So the left-hand branch in **w** is closed.

The right-hand branch is also closed by parallel reasoning: If $a_w(\Box q)$ were F, there would have to be a world **u** where **wRu** and $a_u(q)$=F. Then by ($\Box$T) $a_u(p\&q)$=T and $a_u(q)$=T, which is contradictory.

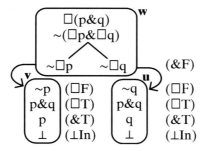

It follows that both alternatives are impossible, and so the assumption that the argument has a counterexample must be rejected. We have discovered that it is impossible for $\Box(p\&q)$ / $\Box p\&\Box q$ to have a K-counterexample, and so we know that it is K-valid.

EXERCISE 4.1 Use diagrams to show that the following arguments are K-valid:

a) $\Box(p\rightarrow q)$ / $\Diamond p\rightarrow\Diamond q$
b) $\Box p\&\Box q$ / $\Box(p\&q)$
c) $\Diamond p \lor \Diamond q$ / $\Diamond(p \lor q)$

In more complex trees it may not be entirely clear how results of applying a rule should be placed on the branches of a tree. To illustrate the problem and its solution, let us work out the tree for the following argument: $\Box((p\&q)\rightarrow r)$, $\Box p \vdash \Box(q\rightarrow r)$. The initial steps of the tree look like this:

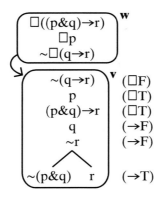

We must now apply (&F) to ~(p&q), and there are two open branches left. The natural (and correct) thing to do at this point is replace the results of applying the rule below ~(p&q), at which point the tree closes.

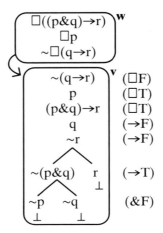

There are two reasons why the results of applying the (&F) rule to ~(p&q) should not go on the right-hand branch that ends with r. First, that branch already contains a contradiction, so there is no need to work there any more. The general principle follows.

There is no need to add new steps to a branch that is already closed.

The second reason is that the results of applying a tree rule are only placed on the open branches **below** the point that a rule is applied. This principle is important, and so worth naming.

The Placement Principle. The results of applying a rule to a tree are placed on every branch below the sentence to which the rule is applied.

There is an important point about arrows between worlds that has yet to be discussed. We will show that the argument □(p∨q), □~p / □q∨□r is valid. Assume that the argument has a counterexample, and apply (∨F) to obtain the following diagram.

$$
\begin{array}{ll}
\fbox{$
\begin{array}{l}
\Box(p\lor q) \\
\Box\sim p \\
\sim(\Box q\lor\Box r) \\
\sim\Box q \\
\sim\Box r
\end{array}
$}^{\,\mathbf{w}} & \begin{array}{l}\\ \\ \\ (\lor F) \\ (\lor F)\end{array}
\end{array}
$$

This indicates that both □q and □r are false at **w**. Since □r is false, it follows by (□F) that there is some world where q is F.

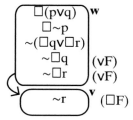

Now (□T) and (vT) can be used to complete work in world **v** leaving an open branch on the right.

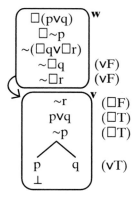

There is still work to be done on this tree because we have yet to apply (□F) to the sentence ~□q in world **w**. So we need to continue the open branch by adding a new world **u** (headed by ~q) to the diagram, with an arrow from **w** to **u**.

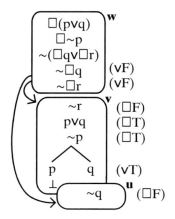

Note that the branch does not close at this point because ~q appears in **u** while q appears in **v**, which is not a contradictory assignment of values to q. Notice also that the fact that ~□r and ~□q were in **w** tells us that there are worlds containing ~r and ~q, but we do *not* know whether q and r are false *in the same* world. So *it is essential to create a new world for each use of (□F)*. When we complete the diagram for world **u**, we discover that the tree closes, which means that the argument was K-valid.

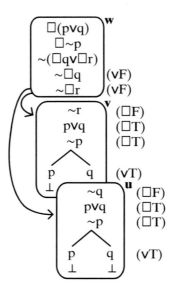

Had (□F) been applied to ~□q before it was applied to ~□r, the tree would have closed much more quickly.

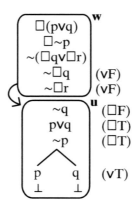

Some students become confused when a tree contains a single open branch and more than one use of (□F) must be applied. There is a tendency for some of them to leave steps "dangling", that is, unattached to any branch. For example, in constructing the above tree, after creating world **v**, some students do this:

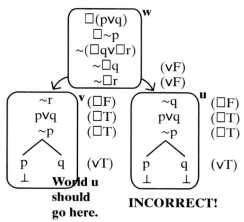

But this tree is **INCORRECT** because it violates the Placement Principle. That principle demands that when (□F) is applied to ~□q, creating world **u**, the results must be placed at the end of an open branch already in the tree. This means that the world **u** and its contents must be placed so that they form an extension of the open branch that ends with q in world **v**. Following the Placement Principle is important in such cases because violating it would cause us to incorrectly diagnose the validity of arguments. The incorrect tree just given would prompt us to diagnose the argument as invalid since there appears to remain an open branch in world **v**; but the argument is in fact valid.

EXERCISE 4.2   Show K-valid with trees.

a) □p, □(p→q) / ◇r→□q

b) ◇p&◇q / ◇(p∨r)

c) ◇~q→□□~~p / □□p∨□q

4.2. Showing K-Invalidity with Trees

Now we will show how the tree method may be used to detect K-invalid arguments. Our first trees will demonstrate that the difference in scope between □(p→q) and p→□q matters. Both of these arguments will be shown invalid: □(p→q) / p→□q and p→□q / □(p→q). Here is the

beginning of the tree diagram for the argument $\Box(p{\to}q) / p{\to}\Box q$. We
have begun by negating the conclusion and applying $(\to F)$.

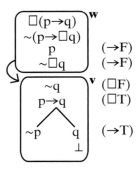

Because $\sim\Box q$ is in **w**, we must apply $(\Box F)$ to create a new world **v**, to
which we add $p{\to}q$ by $(\Box T)$.

We then apply $(\to T)$ in world **v**.

Notice that the right-hand branch in **v** is closed because it contains $\perp$.
However, the left-hand branch is *open*, for it contains no contradiction.
This means the opening segment in world **v** remains open, leaving the
branch in world **w** open as well. (Though p and $\sim$p both appear on the
open branch, this does not represent an inconsistent assignment because
p and $\sim$p are found in different worlds.)

So the tree is open, and this tells us that $\Box(p{\to}q) / (p{\to}\Box q)$ is invalid. In
fact, the tree can be used to construct an explicit K-counterexample to the
argument. Remember, a K-counterexample for $\Box(p{\to}q) / (p{\to}\Box q)$ would
be a K-model $<\mathbf{W}, \mathbf{R}, \mathbf{a}>$, such that for some **w** in **W**, $\mathbf{a_w}(\Box(p{\to}q))=T$ and
$\mathbf{a_w}(p{\to}\Box q)=F$. In order to give such a counterexample, we must say what
W is, we must define **R**, and we must define the assignment function **a**.
W will be the set of worlds we have constructed in our tree diagram. In

this case we have two worlds in **W**, namely, **w** and **v**. The definition of **R** is given by the arrows in the diagram. We see an arrow from **w** to **v**, so we know that **wRv**. Since no other arrows appear, there are no more positive facts about **R**, with the result that the following are all false: **wRw**, **vRv**, **vRw**. Now we are ready to define the assignment function **a**. We note which propositional variables appear (unnegated) in each world on our open branch. If variable p appears in a world **w**, then we let $\mathbf{a_w}(p)=T$, and if it does not appear, we let $\mathbf{a_w}(p)=F$. So, for example, in the tree just completed, $\mathbf{a_w}(p)=T$ (because p appears in **w**), whereas $\mathbf{a_w}(q)=F$ (because q does not appear in **w**). Furthermore, $\mathbf{a_v}(p)=F$ and $\mathbf{a_v}(q)=F$. The values given by **a** for $\perp$, and complex sentences are determined by the standard semantical clauses ($\perp$), ($\rightarrow$), and ($\square$).

The model constructed from a tree in this manner is called the *tree model*. Let us represent the tree model we have just created in a "cleaned-up" version, where we include only the propositional letters or negations of propositional letters in the original tree. Note that although ~q does not appear in **w** in the original tree, we put it in the cleaned-up tree to indicate that our assignment function makes q F in **w**.

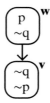

This diagram represents the tree model for our open tree. It is a K-model <**W**, **R**, **a**> for a language with p and q as its only variables, where **W** contains two worlds **w** and **v**, where **wRv**, and where **a** is defined so that $\mathbf{a_w}(p)=T$, $\mathbf{a_w}(q)=F$, $\mathbf{a_v}(p)=F$, and $\mathbf{a_v}(q)=F$. Clearly <**W**, **R**, **a**> satisfies the definition for a K-model (Section 3.6). This model, we claim, is a counterexample to $\square(p{\rightarrow}q)$ / $(p{\rightarrow}\square q)$. To verify that this is so, let us fill in the cleaned-up diagram to represent the values for the complex formulas. For example, $\mathbf{a_w}(\square q)$ must be F according to ($\square$) because q is F in a world **v** such that **wRv**. Since $\mathbf{a_w}(p)=T$, $p{\rightarrow}\square q$ must be F in **w** by ($\rightarrow$).

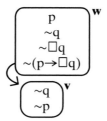

We can see also that since $a_v(p)=F$, $a_v(p \rightarrow q)$ must be T. Since **v** is the only world such that **wRv**, $p \rightarrow q$ is T in all worlds such that **wRv**, and so $\square(p \rightarrow q)$ must be T in **w**.

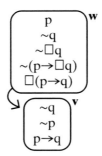

We have verified that the model we have constructed is a counterexample to $\square(p \rightarrow q)$ / $(p \rightarrow \square q)$, for $a_w(\square(p \rightarrow q))=T$ and $a_w(p \rightarrow \square q)=F$. Notice the strategy we have used in verifying the counterexample diagram. We have given reasons for adding back the complex sentences that appeared in the original tree.

Now let us use the same method to find a counterexample for $p \rightarrow \square q$ / $\square(p \rightarrow q)$. Here is the beginning of the tree:

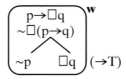

We have begun by applying $(\rightarrow T)$, which means we must draw a fork in world **w**. This represents two possibilities about the values **a** gives at **w**: either $a_w(p)=F$ or $a_w(\square q)=T$. We will need to work out the diagram for each branch. We will start our work on the right.

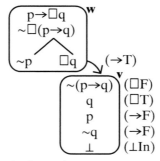

The right-hand branch closes; however, we may still generate an open branch on the left.

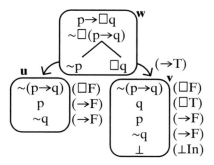

In world **u**, the branch remains open, and so we can construct the following counterexample. Note that the right-hand branch and world **v** are removed from the diagram because they are closed.

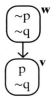

Since q does not appear at **w** in our tree, we place ~q in world **w** in the cleaned-up diagram to indicate that $\mathbf{a_w}(q)=F$.

EXERCISE 4.3   Add formulas to the diagram we just completed to verify that it counts as a counterexample to p→□q / □(p→q).

Using the same technique, a counterexample to □(pvq) / □pv□q can be constructed using the following tree:

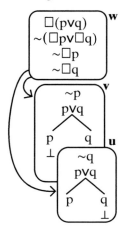

From the open branch in this tree, we may form a counterexample
diagram as follows:

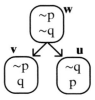

Again, we have filled in values of F for the letters that didn't turn up in
world **w**. Notice that this diagram tells us exactly why we might object to
the validity of □(pvq) / □pv□q. Though □(pvq) may be T in **w** because
either p or q is T in every world related to **w**, it does not follow that
either p is T in all related worlds, or that q is T in all related worlds.
Our counterexample gives us a simple example of this, for it displays a
situation where neither p nor q is T in all worlds related to **w**.

EXERCISE 4.4   Verify that the last diagram is a counterexample to □(pvq) /
□pv□q.

EXERCISE 4.5 Construct counterexamples to the following arguments
using the tree method. Verify that the diagrams you create are counterexamples.

a) □p→□q / □(p→q)
b) ◇p&◇q / ◇(p&q)
c) ~◇~p / ◇p

We need to discuss another complication that may arise in constructing
trees. We will illustrate it with a tree for the argument □p, □~q→□~p / □q.
The diagram might look like this about midway through the construction:

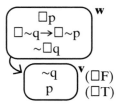

Note that we have yet to apply (→T) to the second line in world **w**. Ordinarily this would be done by placing a fork in world **w** with ~□~q on the
left and □~p on the right. Unfortunately, doing so is not straightforward

since we have already begun a new world **v** using the (□F) rule. We cannot place the result of applying (→T) in the new world **v** because the truth of □~q→□~p in **w** guarantees that either □~q is F or □~p is T *in* **w**, *not* **v**.

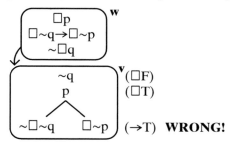

The problem we are facing in applying (→T) would have been avoided if we simply had applied (→T) earlier in the process. This suggests a general strategy for avoiding the problem, namely, to postpone as much as possible any steps that would create new worlds. The idea is to carry out all the propositional logic steps you can in any world before you apply (□F) and (◇T). Reordering the steps in this way so that (→T) is applied before world **v** is created yields the following diagram:

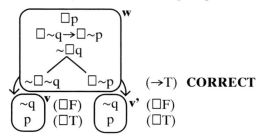

At this point the tree may be completed in the usual way.

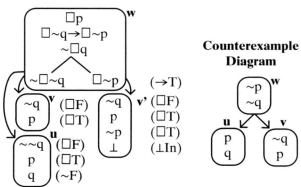

EXERCISE 4.6   Verify that the counterexample diagram just given is indeed
a K-counterexample to □p, □~q→□~p / □q.

Although the reordering strategy resolves the problem in simple propositional modal logics like K, there are modal logics (such as B) where
reordering the steps is not possible. (For more on this point see Section 6.3.) Furthermore, even when working in K, it would be nice to have
a policy that allows us to continue work on a tree when we forget to
postpone use of world-creating steps, rather than redrawing the whole
tree from scratch. For this reason we will introduce a method that allows
work to be continued on worlds that have been "left behind" during tree
construction. To illustrate how the continuation method works, let us
complete the diagram that began our discussion.

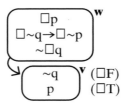

We now need to apply (→T) to world **w**, so we simply draw a new copy of
world **w** (called its *continuation*) and place the results of applying (→T)
to □~q→□~p into it.

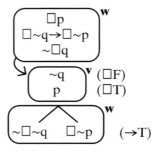

From here the tree may be completed in the usual way.

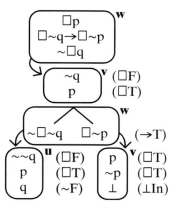

Note that when we returned to **w**, we needed to draw another copy of the arrow from **w** to **v** in order to close world **v**. We also needed to apply (□T) to □p (in the top copy of **w**) to put p in (the second copy of) world **v**. At this point the arrows between worlds, and the contents of the various worlds along the open branch can be collected to create the following counterexample diagram:

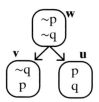

When more than one open branch remains during tree construction, it is very important to follow the Placement Principle correctly. For example, consider the following partially constructed tree diagram for □(p∨q), p∨q / (□p∨□q):

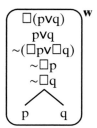

At this point we have two open branches, so when (□F) is applied to ~□p
and ~□q, and (□T) to □(pvq), the corresponding steps must be added to
both of the open branches.

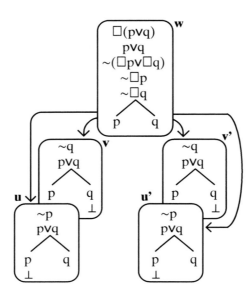

Sometimes, as in this case, tree diagrams specify more than one counterexample for an argument. Notice that there are two open branches
in this tree, one running through p in world **w**, and the other running
through q in world **w**. This means that either of the choices in world **w**
could be used in constructing a counterexample to our argument. However, in order to specify a *single* counterexample, we will have to make a
choice between the two branches. So let us do so by "pruning" our tree to
remove one of the two branches in **w** (say, the right one). When we remove
the closed branches as well, we obtain a pruned tree, which specifies one
counterexample to the argument.

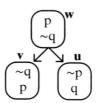

EXERCISE 4.7 Suppose we pruned the left-hand branch in the above tree. What would the counterexample diagram look like?

EXERCISE 4.8 Use the tree method to determine whether the following arguments are K-valid or K-invalid. If an argument is K-invalid create counter-example diagrams, and verify that each diagram is a counterexample. For e) and f) you may use (↔T) and (↔F). Or if you like, you could convert the ↔ into → and & and work the trees from there.

a) ◇(pvq) / ◇pv◇q
b) / □(~□p→(◇~p& ◇q))
c) ◇p / □(◇pv◇q)
d) □q, ◇pv◇q / ◇(p&q)
e) □(p↔q / □p↔□q)
f) □p↔□q / □(p↔q)
*g) □(q→p)v□(~p→q),~□(~pvq) / □(~p→~q)
h) □p / ◇ p (Hint: You may not apply (□T) unless an arrow has been placed in the diagram by some other rule.)

*Note that answers are provided in the back of the book for exercises marked with an asterisk.

4.3. Summary of Tree Rules for K

Basic Truth Rules:

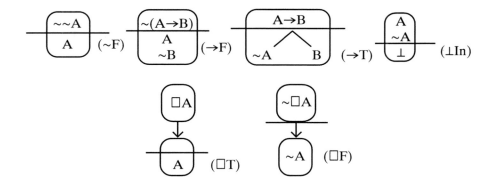

Derived Tree Rules:

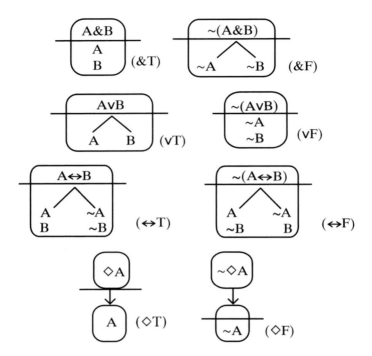

5

The Accessibility Relation

Chapter 3 introduced the accessibility relation **R** on the set of worlds **W** in defining the truth condition for the generic modal operator. In K-models, the frame <**W**, **R**> of the model was completely arbitrary. Any nonempty set **W** and any binary relation **R** on **W** counts as a frame for a K-model. However, when we actually apply modal logic to a particular domain and give $\square$ a particular interpretation, the frame <**W**, **R**> may take on special properties. Variations in the principles appropriate for a given modal logic will depend on what properties the frame should have. The rest of this chapter explains how various conditions on frames emerge from the different readings we might chose for $\square$.

5.1. Conditions Appropriate for Tense Logic

In future tense logic, $\square$ reads 'it will always be the case that'. Given ($\square$), we have that $\square$A is true at **w** iff A is true at all worlds **v** such that **wRv**. According to the meaning assigned to $\square$, **R** must be the relation **earlier than** defined over a set **W** of *times*. There are a number of conditions on the frame <**W**, **R**> that follow from this interpretation. One fairly obvious feature of **earlier than** is transitivity.

Transitivity: If **wRv** and **vRu**, then **wRu**.

When **wRv** (**w** is earlier than **v**) and **vRu** (**v** is earlier than **u**), it follows that **wRu** (**w** is earlier than **u**). So let us define a new kind of satisfiability that corresponds to this condition on **R**. Let a *4-model* be any K-model <**W**, **R**, **a**> where **R** is a *transitive* relation on **W**. Then concepts of satisfiability, counterexample, and validity can be defined in terms of this new

kind of model as you would expect. For example, a list of sentences H
is *4-satisfiable* just in case there is a 4-model <**W**, **R**, **a**> and a world **w**
in **W** where $a_w(H)=T$. An argument H / C has a *4-counterexample* iff H,
~C is 4-satisfiable, and H / C is *4-valid* (in symbols: H $\vDash_4$ C) iff H / C has
no 4-counterexample. We use the name '4' to describe such a transitive
model because the logic that is adequate for 4-validity is K4, the logic that
results from adding the axiom (4): $\Box A \rightarrow \Box \Box A$ to K. (Remember that to
say K4 is *adequate* for 4-validity means that K4 is both sound and complete for 4-validity.) Although (4) is not K-valid, it is 4-valid, and in fact
(4) is all we need to add to K to guarantee proofs of all the 4-valid arguments. Each of the axioms we have discussed in Chapter 2 corresponds
to a condition on **R** in the same way. The relationship between conditions
on **R** and corresponding axioms is one of the central topics in the study
of modal logics. Once an interpretation of the intensional operator $\Box$ has
been decided on, the appropriate conditions on **R** can be determined to
fix the corresponding notion of validity. This, in turn, allows us to select
the right set of axioms for that logic.

The nature of the correspondence between axioms and conditions on
R is difficult for some students to grasp at first. It helps to consider an
example. Consider this instance of the (4) axiom: $\Box p \rightarrow \Box \Box p$. The following tree and counterexample diagram shows that this sentence is
K-invalid.

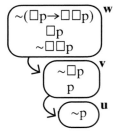

K-Counterexample

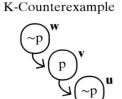

However, this counterexample is not a good reason to reject $\Box p \rightarrow \Box \Box p$
in the case of tense logic, because here the relation **R** is **earlier than**
and this relation is transitive. The K-counterexample given here is not
transitive; there is no arrow from **w** to **u** even though both **wRv** and **vRu**.
In tense logic, the acceptability of $\Box p \rightarrow \Box \Box p$ depends on whether it has
a 4-counterexample, that is, a K-model where **R** is transitive. If we try to
create a 4-counterexample to this sentence by drawing the missing arrow
from **w** to **u** in order to ensure that **R** is transitive, the tree closes. This

is a symptom of the fact that there is no 4-counterexample to □p→□□p, that is, that □p→□□p is 4-valid.

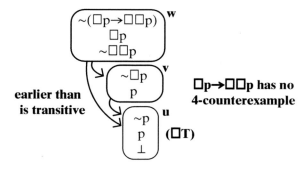

earlier than
is transitive

□p→□□p has no
4-counterexample

I hope this helps you appreciate how conditions on **R** can affect the assessment of validity. The sentence □p→□□p is K-invalid, but it is 4-valid, where models are restricted to those with a transitive **R**.

When discussing properties of frames <**W**, **R**>, it is convenient to have a way of diagramming conditions such as transitivity. We want a diagram for the conditional: if **wRv** and **vRu**, then **wRu**. We may indicate the antecedent *wRv and vRu* by putting two diagrams together.

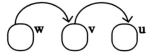

Transitivity says that if

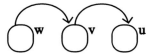

then it follows that

In order to have a *single* diagram for the transitivity condition, we can indicate the situation in the antecedent of the condition with "over" arrows:

and the situation that follows with an "under" arrow below a horizontal line:

Using these conventions, our diagram for transitivity looks like this:

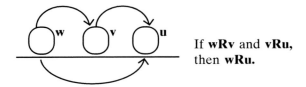

If **wRv** and **vRu**,
then **wRu**.

For simplicity, we will often shrink the worlds to dots:

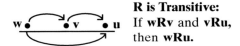

R is Transitive:
If **wRv** and **vRu**,
then **wRu**.

Transitivity is not the only property that we might want to enforce on <**W, R**> if **R** is to be **earlier than** and **W** is a set of times. One condition (which is only mildly controversial) is that there is no last moment of time, that is, that for every time **w** there is some time **v** later than **w**. The diagram of this condition (which is known as seriality) follows:

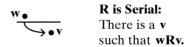

R is Serial:
There is a **v**
such that **wRv**.

This diagram shows that every world has an arrow emerging from it pointing to some other world. Seriality of **R** corresponds to the axiom (D): □A→◇A, in the same way that transitivity corresponds to (4). A D-model is a K-model whose frame <**W, R**> is *serial*, that is, <**W, R**> meets the condition that for any **w** in **W** there is a world **v** in **W** such that **wRv**. From the idea of a D-model, the corresponding notions of D-satisfiability, D-counterexample, and D-validity can be defined just as we did in the case of (4). As you probably guessed from the name 'D', the system that is adequate with respect to D-validity is KD, or K plus (D). Not only that, but the system KD4 (that is K plus (4) and (D)) is adequate with respect to D4-validity, where a D4-model is one where <**W, R**> is *both* serial and transitive.

Another property that might hold for the relation **earlier than** is *density*, the condition that says that between any two times we can always find another.

R is Dense:
If **wRv**,
then for some **u**,
wRu and **uRv**.

This condition would be false if time were atomic, that is, if there were intervals of time that could not be broken down into any smaller parts. Density corresponds to the axiom (C4): $\Box\Box A \rightarrow \Box A$, the converse of (4), so for example, the system KC4, which is K plus (C4), is adequate with respect to models where <**W, R**> is dense, and KDC4 is adequate with respect to models that are serial and dense, and so on.

EXERCISE 5.1 Define validity in the case where <**W, R**> is dense, transitive, and serial. What system do you think is adequate with respect to this notion of satisfiability?
(Hint: Review the opening paragraph of this section. Define first what a C4-D4 model is.)

There are many other conditions we might place on <**W, R**>, depending on the structure of time.

EXERCISE 5.2 Invent two more conditions that could plausibly hold given **R** is **earlier than**. Draw their diagrams.

One important frame condition for modal logics is *reflexivity*. Reflexivity says that every world is accessible from itself.

R is Reflexive:
For all **w** in **W**,
wRw.

However, **earlier than** is not reflexive on the set of times. As a matter of fact, **earlier than** is irreflexive, that is, no time is earlier than itself. (Actually, if the structure of time happens to be circular, then every moment would be earlier than itself and **R** *would* be reflexive.)

R is Irreflexive:
For all **w** in **W**,
not **wRw**.

Note we express **R**'s failing to hold in our diagram by crossing out the arrow. It is interesting to note that the irreflexivity does not correspond to an axiom the way that seriality and transitivity of <**W, R**> do. (For more on this see Section 8.8.) Whether we accept or reject irreflexivity does not affect which arguments are valid, and so the decision has no effect on which axioms must be selected to produce an adequate logic. Reflexivity, on the other hand, corresponds to (M), the characteristic axiom of modal logic: □A→A. By 'corresponds' we mean that a logic that is adequate for a notion of validity defined by models with reflexive frames must contain (M) as a theorem. Clearly we do not want (M) for tense logic. (No time is earlier than itself.) However, there is another reading of □ (and **R**) where reflexivity is acceptable, namely, where □ reads 'is and will always be', and where **R** is interpreted as 'simultaneous to or earlier than'. For this reading, (M) is acceptable, and so there *are* logics of time that adopt (M).

Another condition on **earlier than** that it appears we should reject is symmetry.

R is Symmetric:
If **wRv**,
then **vRw**.

In fact we may want to adopt asymmetry.

R is Asymmetric:
If **wRv**,
then not **vRw**.

The symmetry condition corresponds to the axiom (B): A→□◇A. Just as was the case with irreflexivity, asymmetry corresponds to no axiom.

Actually, there are reasons for rejecting the asymmetry of **R** in temporal logic. If the series of times is circular, then it is possible for both **w** to be earlier than **v**, and **v** to be earlier than **w**. To see why, imagine our times arranged in a circle thus:

We will show you that this diagram, together with transitivity, entails that for each arrow on the diagram there must be a reverse arrow connecting the points in the opposite direction. To show this, consider the arrows from **v** to **u** and **u** to **x**. By transitivity we have an arrow from **v** to **x**.

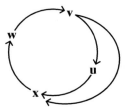

Now we have arrows from **v** to **x** and **x** to **w**, so by transitivity again we obtain an arrow in the reverse direction from **v** back to **w**.

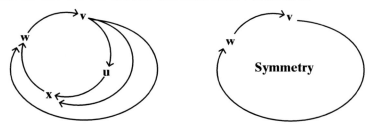

5.2. Semantics for Tense Logics

In tense logic, there are two pairs of intensional operators. **G** and **F** are used for the future tense and **H** and **P** for the past tense. Their English readings are as follows:

G   it always will be the case that
F   it will be the case that
H   it always was the case that
P   it was the case that

G is the strong intensional operator analogous to $\Box$, while **F** is defined from **G** just as $\Diamond$ is defined from $\Box$.

(DefF)   **FA** $=_{df}$ ~**G**~**A**

Similarly, **H** is the strong past tense operator, and **P** is defined by (DefP).

(DefP)   **PA** $=_{df}$ ~**H**~**A**

So far, we have allowed only a single pair of intensional operators, corresponding to $\Box$ and $\Diamond$. However, semantics for a second pair may be easily constructed by introducing a second accessibility relation. In the case of the past tense, the accessibility relation we want is **later than**, which we abbreviate: **L**. A model for tense logic with future and past tense operators is a quadruple $<\mathbf{W}, \mathbf{R}, \mathbf{L}, \mathbf{a}>$, which satisfies all the conditions familiar for K-models $<\mathbf{W}, \mathbf{R}, \mathbf{a}>$, and such that **L** is another binary relation on **W**, and **a** meets the following conditions for **H** and **G**:

(H) $\mathbf{a_W}(\mathbf{HA})$ = T iff for each **v** in **W**, if **wLv**, then $\mathbf{a_v}(A)$=T.
(G) $\mathbf{a_W}(\mathbf{GA})$ = T iff for each **v** in **W**, if **wRv**, then $\mathbf{a_v}(A)$=T.

The logic that is adequate with respect to this semantics is K "doubled"; it consists of the principles of PL plus versions of ($\Box$In) and ($\Box$Out) for both **G** and **H**.

```
 GA          | G           HA           | H
  :          |  :           :           |  :
 | G         | A           | H          | A
 |------     |--------     |------      |--------
 | A (GOut)   GA (GIn)     | A (HOut)    HA (HIn)
```

This system, however, is too weak. There are obvious conditions we will want to place on the relations **L** and **R**, which correspond to axioms that must be added to tense logic. First, as we explained in Section 5.1, **R** and **L** should be transitive, which corresponds to the **G** and **H** versions of the (4) axiom:

(G4)   GA→GGA   (H4)   HA→HHA

Second, **earlier than** and **later than** are related to each other. If **w** is earlier than **v**, then **v** must be later than **w**, and vice versa. So we will want to add the following two conditions:

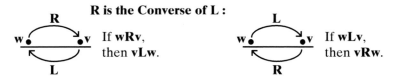

R is the Converse of L :

If **wRv**, then **vLw**.   If **wLv**, then **vRw**.

Since there are two relations **R** and **L** in the model, the arrows in these diagrams are labeled to distinguish **R** from **L**.

The converse conditions look very much like the symmetry condition for a single **R**, so it should not surprise you that their corresponding axioms resemble (B): A→□◇A. If we label the □ and ◇ in (B) with **L** and **R**, the two versions of (B) look like this:

$$A \to \Box_R \Diamond_L A \qquad A \to \Box_L \Diamond_R A$$

If we identify **H** with $\Box_L$, **P** with $\Diamond_L$, **G** with $\Box_R$, and **F** with $\Diamond_R$, you will recognize them (I hope) as two axioms of the system Kt.

(GP)   A→GPA   (HF)   A→HFA

When these axioms were first presented, it was pointed out that some people have a tendency to disagree with (HF) on the grounds that it implies fatalism. However, we have just found out that the axiom corresponds to a perfectly acceptable condition on the relationship between **earlier than** and **later than**. This is a sign that the objection to (HF) rests on a mistake.

Why does (HF) appear to deny that the future is open? The reason is that we often use 'A will be' to say that present facts *determine* that A will happen at some future time, rather than that A just happens to occur at a future time. The old saying 'whatever will be will be' plays off these two meanings of 'will be'. If there weren't two meanings, the saying would amount to a tautology. If we are to think clearly about fatalism and the future, then we must have the resources to distinguish between those things that are merely true of the future and those which are determined to be so. To do this, we should make it clear that **F** is used for the sense of 'will' that has no deterministic overtones, and we should introduce a separate operator **D** for 'it is determined that'. **D** will need its **own** relation R_D, which is not **earlier than**. Instead wR_Dv holds exactly when the facts of **v** are compatible with what is *determined* given the facts of **w**. The proper way to express the mistaken deterministic reading of (HF) in this logic is A→**HDFA**, that is, if A, then it has always been the case that it was *determined* that A will be.

EXERCISE [*]**5.3** Give the truth condition for D.
[*](The answers to this and all other exercises marked with an asterisk are given in the back of the book.)

In the scientific view of the world, especially that of physics, we represent the structure of time with the real numbers. The times are thought of as comprising a linear and dense ordering. This understanding of the nature of time specifically rules out the possibility that times branch toward the future (or the past). A structure like the following:

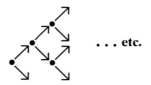

. . . etc.

for example, is inconsistent with the *linear* view of time, which insists that each time is either earlier or later than any other time, so that there are never two times that are alternatives one to the other. The condition on time that rules out this kind of future branching is *connectedness*.

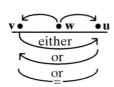

R is Connected:
If **wRv** and **wRu**,
then **vRu** or **uRv** or **v=u**.

The condition that rules out branching toward the past is just the connectedness of **L**.

To illustrate why connectedness rules out forking, let us put the connectedness diagram on its side. The condition insists that whenever we have a potential fork:

then what we have in actuality is a single temporal series with either **v** earlier than **u**:

or **u** earlier than **v**:

or **v** identical to **u**:

Connectedness corresponds to the axiom (L): $\Box(\Box A \rightarrow B) \lor \Box((B \& \Box B) \rightarrow A)$, which means that in a tense logic, **G(GA→B)** ∨

$G((B\&GB)\to A)$ rules out future branching, and $H(HA\to B) \lor$ $H((B\&HB)\to A)$ rules out past branching.

A relation that is both transitive and connected is said to be *linear*. Any linear relation has the property that the set of things that bear the relation can be numbered in such a way that for any two things $\mathbf{w}$, $\mathbf{v}$ such that $\mathbf{w}R\mathbf{v}$, their corresponding numbers $n_\mathbf{w}$ and $n_\mathbf{v}$ are such that $n_\mathbf{w}<n_\mathbf{v}$. So linearity is a crucial condition to adopt for $\mathbf{R}$ if we are to represent the times and their order with numbers.

Some people will feel that the linear approach to time is entirely misguided because it rules out variety in what is possible in the future. Though it is clear that there is no reason to assume branching into the past, the future, they claim, is open, so we should not rule out branching structures toward the future by imposing linearity. I believe this reasoning is confused, though there is something right about it. To help clarify this situation, let us ask ourselves just exactly what it is that we want to branch in order to capture the notion that the future is open. Remember that the issue that concerns tense logic is the nature of the relation **earlier than**. If we reject the connectedness of $\mathbf{R}$, we will allow the possibility that there are two times t and t′ that are incommensurable, that is, such that it makes no sense to say that one or the other is the earlier one. Now that seems an odd thing to say about **earlier than**, and even when we say it, there seems to be a tenuous relationship between this rejection and the rejection of fatalism. On the other hand, it does make perfect sense to insist on the rejection of connectedness for $\mathbf{R_D}$, for it makes perfect sense to say of two situations $\mathbf{v}$ and $\mathbf{u}$ that though their facts are compatible with what is determined by the situation $\mathbf{w}$:

$$\mathbf{R_D}\nearrow\bullet\mathbf{v}$$
$$\bullet\mathbf{w}$$
$$\mathbf{R_D}\searrow\bullet\mathbf{u}$$

nevertheless, the facts of $\mathbf{v}$ and the facts of $\mathbf{u}$ are not compatible with each other. For example, $\mathbf{w}$ might be a situation where I am choosing whether to get married, and $\mathbf{v}$ the situation where I do, and $\mathbf{u}$ the situation where I do not do so. Here, the facts of $\mathbf{v}$ are not compatible with what is determined by the facts of $\mathbf{u}$, and vice versa, and so we must reject the view that $\mathbf{v}R_D\mathbf{u}$ or $\mathbf{u}R_D\mathbf{v}$ or $\mathbf{u}=\mathbf{v}$.

In the end, then, it does make perfect sense to reject the nonbranching condition, but this rejection should be focused on the right relation, namely, the relation $\mathbf{R_D}$ of determination, not the purely temporal relation $\mathbf{R}$ for **earlier than**. The demand for an open future is really a demand for openness in what is **determined** by the present, and should not be treated as a condition on the structure of time. Those who argue for an open "future" are really interested in the structure of determination, not the structure of time.

5.3. Semantics for Modal (Alethic) Logics

Most of the formal concepts needed to understand semantics for modal, deontic, and locative logics have already been developed in discussing tense logic. In this section, we will explain how to apply these concepts to shed light on modal inferences.

In modal (or alethic) logic, the set **W** is understood as the set of possible worlds. If we identify each time with the world as it happens to be at that time, then a time ends up being a possible world. The intuitive appeal of this identification helps us appreciate the strong contacts that exist between tense and modal logic.

> **EXERCISE 5.4** What difficulties might arise in taking times to be identical to their corresponding possible worlds? (Hint: Consider the possibility of eternal recurrence, where the events of the world repeat themselves over and over again.)

Given that **W** is understood as a set of possible worlds, we can go on to ask ourselves how to characterize the semantical behavior of $\Box$, and to identify its corresponding logic. As we said before, there are a number of formal systems that could legitimately claim to be modal logics. The differences arise because there are a number of ways to understand 'necessarily'. So a variety of modal logics may be developed reflecting these differences. Let us begin by trying to characterize a relatively easy concept: that of tautological necessity. The sentence A is tautologically necessary just in case A is a truth-functional tautology, that is, just in case A is true on all rows of its truth table. Each row of a truth table describes the features of a possible world, for it indicates which atomic sentences are true and which are false there. So on this understanding, **W** can be identified with the different possible rows of a truth table.

The truth condition on **a** that we want for $\Box$ on this reading is ($\Box$5).

($\Box$5) $a_w(\Box A)=T$ iff $a_v(A)=T$ for all **v** in **W**.

This says that $\Box A$ is true on truth table row **w** just in case A is true on all rows of its truth table.

Although (□5) appears to be an entirely new truth clause for □, we can obtain exactly its effect by laying down a condition on **R**, namely, that **R** is *universal*, that is, that each world is accessible from any other.

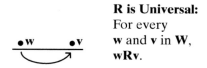

R is Universal:
For every
w and **v** in **W**,
wRv.

EXERCISE 5.5 Show that (□5) is equivalent to (□) when **R** is universal.

So instead of adopting the truth condition (□5), we can use (□) provided we also stipulate that **R** is universal. (Strictly speaking, it is the frame <**W**, **R**> not **R** that is universal.) As you might have guessed from the name '(□5)', universality corresponds to the system S5. The introduction of universality illustrates a basic strategy we will use in working out the semantics of modal logics. We may be tempted to write separate truth conditions (such as (□5)) to handle a given interpretation of a modal operator. But it is more convenient, and more helpful in understanding the relationships between the various systems, to always adopt (□) and to search for some condition on **R** (like universality) that will have the same effect.

Now let us see how things fare when we turn to physical necessity. Here **W** is the set of all possible worlds where the laws of physics hold. There may be some disagreement as to exactly what the laws of physics are, but in any case, we will want our **W** to be some subset of all the logically possible worlds, namely, those that obey the laws of physics. Despite this change, the formal definition for validity is exactly the same as for logical necessity. The only difference is in our intuitive understanding of the contents of **W**. Again we want (□5) or the universality of **R**, and so the appropriate logic is S5.

There are notions of necessity and possibility, however, where universality does not hold. For example, consider the kind of necessity involved when we say "I can't possibly finish my work this term". We might call this personal necessity since it records what a person is capable of bringing about. When I say "I can't possibly finish my work this term," I am not claiming that finishing is either logically or physically impossible. I am saying instead that given all sorts of contingent facts about me, namely, the speed I can work, the amount of time I have left to devote to it, the amount of sleep I need to function, and so forth, there is no way I can finish up. Notice that this kind of necessity is *world relative*, that is, the truth value of □A may change from one world to another. For example, though it is necessary that I fail to finish my work given the facts of the real world, that may be false (say) in a world where I can work effectively with only two hours of sleep, and other things are the same.

In order to do justice to world-relative concepts of necessity we must reject universality of **R**. For example, in the case of personal necessity, **wRv** should hold just in case **v** is a world where abilities I have in **w** also are true of me in **v**, that is, where I can work at the same top speed, need the same amount of sleep, and so on. On this interpretation of □, to say □A is true at **w** is not to say that A is true *in all worlds*, but only that A is true in those worlds properly related to **w**, worlds that hold my relevant abilities the same. So clearly it is not the case that **wRv** for all **w** and **v**.

Though we lose universality, there are still other conditions on **R** worth considering. In modal logic, **wRv** may be read 'world **v** is a possible alternative to **w**'. We clearly want **R** to be reflexive since any world is clearly possible relative to itself. (In the case of personal necessity, for example, it is obvious that my abilities in **w** are the same as my abilities in **w**.) Once we see that **R** must be reflexive under this interpretation, it is clear why the system M for modal logic is an appropriate choice to match our intuitions.

At least two important questions remain about the behavior of <**W**, **R**>. We will want to know whether to adopt the conditions for (4) (transitivity) and (B) (symmetry). Even though we have introduced a world-relative concept of necessity, we may still end up needing the principles of S5. Remember that one way to formulate S5 is to add axioms (4) and (B) to M, so if we have reasons for accepting the transitivity and symmetry of **R**, we will know that S5 is adequate for our semantics.

Given what we have said so far about the nature of <**W**, **R**> for personal necessity, it *does* seem to need both transitivity and symmetry. We wanted **wRv** to hold when **w** and **v** are the same with respect to certain facts about me. But being the same in a certain respect is an equivalence relation, that is, a relation where reflexivity, transitivity, and symmetry all hold. So our concept of personal necessity, which seemed at first to open the door for the modal logics weaker than S5, in fact supports the adoption of S5.

It is beginning to look as if S5 is the only logic that could be adequate for modal logic. Are there any ways of interpreting □ so that the accessibility relation is not transitive or not symmetric? The answer is 'yes' in both cases. We can develop interpretations of these kinds by examining our concept of personal necessity a little more deeply. First, let us see why we might want to reject transitivity. Perhaps we have been too rigid in stipulating what counts as a world accessible from the real world. Suppose, for example, that there are possible situations where I do finish my work on time, but where my motivation to do that work improved by (say) 5 points out of 1,000 on a measure of mental discipline (MD). Do we really want to say that it is impossible for me to finish my work? I think that on some standards of evaluation, you would say that it *is* possible for me to finish. If this is the interpretation we take, then **R** ceases to be transitive, for suppose that we say **wRv** just in case my abilities in **w** and **v** differ by no more than 5 MD points. Then it is possible for my abilities in **w** and **v** to differ by 4, and those in **v** and **u** to differ by 4, while the difference in **w** and **u** is 8. Here **wRv** and **vRu** both hold, but **wRu** does not.

So far the accessibility relation is symmetrical, for if my abilities in **w** differ by 5 points from those in **v**, then my abilities in **v** differ by 5 points from those in **w**. Nevertheless, there are other features of personal necessity that may rule against symmetry as well. If we say that it is possible for me to finish my work on time, we are saying that there is a situation that *I bring about* in which I am doing it on time. For **v** to be accessible from **w**, then **v** must be a situation that could be caused (or at least partly caused) by my actions in **w**. This accessibility relation is not symmetrical because causation operates only in one direction. If my actions of **w** cause events of **v**, then it does not follow that my actions in **v** could cause events in **w**.

Personal necessity, at least under the last understanding of the accessibility relation, provides a motivation for modal logics that reject the transitivity and symmetry of **R**. Our discussion illustrates a method for constructing relations that fail to be transitive and symmetric. Transitivity fails when the relation links two objects within a certain tolerance. For example, **near to** is a nontransitive relation. Symmetry fails when the relation applies in one direction, but not the other. Here **greater than** is a good example.

EXERCISE *5.6 Invent another reading of □ for which the accessibility relation is neither transitive nor symmetric.

What is the upshot of this whole discussion? Which of the various conditions on **R** are correct for modal logic? The question is misguided.

One of the strengths of modal logic is in the variety of systems it offers, each one crafted to a different way of understanding 'necessarily'. There is no one "right" modal logic, nor are the choices between them arbitrary. Given a choice to apply modal logic to evaluate philosophical reasoning, it will be necessary to explicitly examine the concept of necessity in order to locate the appropriate logic.

5.4. Semantics for Deontic Logics

In deontic logics, **W** is again the set of possible worlds or situations. Here **R** is interpreted so that **wRv** iff **v** is a morally acceptable alternative to **w**, that is, given the situation found in **w**, **v** would be a morally correct outcome. If anything is clear about properties of this frame <**W**, **R**>, we certainly do not want symmetry. If **v** is a morally correct alternative to **w**, then **v** is presumably better than (or at least as good as) **w**. However, **as good or better** is an asymmetrical relation.

One condition we clearly *do* want for <**W**, **R**> is seriality: ∃**vwRv**, for this says that there is always a moral alternative to any world. If there were no moral alternative to our world, then there would be nothing coherent we could say about what we ought to do in our world. It is ordinarily thought that if I ought to do something then it follows that I can. Unless seriality holds to ensure that there is a possible world where I do as I ought, I would be unable to act in a morally acceptable fashion. Furthermore, if there is no world related to (say) world **w**, then it turns out that $a_w(O\bot)$=T. That happens because the truth condition for O rates $a_w(O\bot)$=T provided that $a_v(\bot)$=T in every world **v** such that **wRv**, which is vacuously true when there is no world related to **w**. So without seriality, there can be worlds where O⊥ is true, which seems unacceptable since O⊥ says that I ought to bring about a contradiction – something I surely cannot do. You may remember that the axiom that corresponds to seriality is the characteristic axiom of deontic logic: (D) OA→PA. Our examination of semantics with conditions on **R** gives us deeper insight into exactly why we find this principle acceptable.

In deontic logic, we cannot accept reflexivity of **R**, for this would amount to the claim that every world is a morally acceptable alternative to itself. But some worlds will contain deeds that are morally unacceptable. However, there is a property related to reflexivity that seems more palatable. We call it shift reflexivity. This property corresponds to the axiom: O(OA→A). We have recommended this principle in Section 2.6, but we should point out that it corresponds to an assumption about the moral alternatives that can be challenged. The diagram for shift reflexivity follows:

R is Shift Reflexive:
If **wRv**,
then **vRv**.

This says that when a world is a moral alternative to ours, then it is a moral alternative to itself. This can be challenged if we believe that a moral alternative can itself have moral flaws. Then an alternative to our world would not have to have itself as an alternative, as long as we believe that we always have a moral obligation to do better if we can.

The decisions to be made concerning whether $<\mathbf{W}, \mathbf{R}>$ is transitive, symmetric, dense, and so forth are much more difficult to make. Resolving them requires careful study of the details of the concept of morality being dealt with.

There is another variant of possible-worlds semantics for deontic logic that helps explain the intuitions that lead us to accept the iteration principles (OP) and (OO).

(OP)   OPA↔PA
(OO)   OOA↔OA

The idea here is that regardless of the situation in which we find ourselves, there is just one set $\mathbb{M}$ (which is a nonempty subset of **W**) of morally perfect worlds. If we define **R** so that **wRv** iff **v** is in $\mathbb{M}$, then we discover that the standard truth condition for O is equivalent to the following:

(OM) $a_w(OA)=T$ iff $a_v(A)=T$ for all **v** in $\mathbb{M}$.

EXERCISE 5.7   Given that **wRv** iff **v** is in $\mathbb{M}$, show that (O) is equivalent to (OM).

(O) $a_w(OA)=T$ iff   for all **v**, if **wRv** then $a_v(A)=T$.

Notice that (OM) is not the same as (□5) because $\mathbb{M}$ is not the set **W** of all possible worlds. Intuitively it is the much smaller set of worlds that are morally acceptable.

We can easily determine which axioms correspond to the acceptance of this semantic clause by examining what conditions are placed on **R** when

wRv iff **v** is in $\mathbb{M}$. We discover that **R** must be serial, dense, transitive, symmetric, and shift reflexive (at least), and so (D), (OP), (OO), and O(OA→A) are all needed in the corresponding deontic logic.

EXERCISE 5.8   Show that any **R** such that **wRv** iff **v** is in $\mathbb{M}$ is serial, dense, transitive, symmetric, and shift reflexive. Show that such an **R** need not be reflexive or symmetric.

Notice that the concept of obligation is not world relative on condition (**OM**).

EXERCISE 5.9   Show that given (**OM**), O is not world relative, that is, show that for any two **w, u** in **W**, $a_w(OA)$ is $a_u(OA)$.

From this point of view, the facts about a given world (including contracts, laws, and other social arrangements) are irrelevant to determining the correct moral alternatives for that situation. So deontic logics that accept this semantics are limited to systems of morality of this kind (if there are any).

Although (**OM**) is seemingly equivalent to the S5 truth condition (O5), there is an important difference.

(O5) $a_w(OA)=T$ iff $a_v(A)=T$, for any **v** in **W**.

In fact, there had better be a difference since we do not want the principle OA→A, which would follow from S5. Notice that on (**OM**), we do not require that A be true in all worlds in order for OA to be true, but only that A be true in all morally acceptable worlds. So it is possible for OA to be T at a morally imperfect world **u**, where A is F, and so OA→A is invalid on (**OM**).

There is a danger that many moral systems face, one to which Utilitarianism is particularly prone. On the Greatest Happiness Principle, we are obligated to act in such a way as to maximize the greatest common good. So it is highly likely that there is only one truly moral alternative to any world, the world where the Greatest Happiness is brought about. (Chances for a tie between worlds would be vanishingly small.) If the moral course of action requires that we select the best world, then the accessibility relation turns out to be *unique*, that is, there is at most one alternative to any world.

R is Unique:
If **wRv** and **wRu**,
then **v** = **u**.

Uniqueness validates the axiom (CD): PA→OA. This is odd because in the presence of (D), it follows that OA and PA are equivalent. A moral system where permission and obligation are the same strains our concepts beyond what most people will tolerate. This is the price one has to pay for a moral system that lays such strict requirements on what it takes to meet our obligations.

5.5. Semantics for Locative Logic

Uniqueness is probably not appropriate for tense, modal, or deontic logics, but it does make sense in a locative logic, where □ is read 'at position n'. (See Section 2.8.) In fact, a basic semantics for the locative operator Tn stipulates that **R** is both serial and unique. Any relation that is serial and unique is a *function*. When **R** is a function, there is exactly one thing **v** such that **wRv**. The condition that **R** is a function corresponds to the axiom (T~): TnA↔~Tn~A, which ensures the distribution of ~ over Tn. Since there is *exactly one* situation that is accessible from any other, the standard truth clause (T) merely amounts to saying that TnA is true at **w** iff A is T at the one world **v** that **R** picks out for **w**.

(T) a_w(TnA)=T   iff   for all **v**, if **wRv** then a_v(A)=T.

If we use the notation "f" for the function given by **R**, then (Tn) can be rewritten as follows:

(Tf) a_w(TnA)=T   iff $a_{f(w)}$(A)=T.

EXERCISE 5.10   Show that (T) and (Tf) are equivalent when f is the function defined from a serial and unique **R** by f(**w**)=**v** iff **wRv**.

This truth clause (Tf) is exactly what we want in a locative logic that handles such expressions as '5 years ago'. For example, 'there was a depression five years ago' is true in 1940, just in case 'there was a depression' is T in the situation you get by applying the function minus five years to the year 1940, that is, just in case there was a depression in 1935.

Since there are infinitely many operators Ta, Tb, Tc, . . . in locative logic, we will need to set up a separate function f for each. The most convenient way to do this is to let the assignment function assign to each term n a function $\mathbf{a}(n)$ from $\mathbf{W}$ into $\mathbf{W}$. Then our truth clause will read:

(Tn) $\mathbf{a_w}$ TnA=T   iff $\mathbf{a_{a(n)(w)}}(A)=T$.

In case we want to handle such expressions as 'in 1940' that pick out specific situations, rather than picking out one situation relative to another, we may simply add the assumption that $\mathbf{a}$ assigns this expression a constant function, that is, a function that gives the same output for every input. When this condition is added to what we have said about what $\mathbf{a}$ assigns to the terms n, we validate what seems to be the S5 analogue in locative logic.

(TT)   TnA$\leftrightarrow$TmTnA

EXERCISE 5.11   Show that (TT) is valid in a semantics where a model $<\mathbf{W}, \mathbf{F}, \mathbf{a}>$ contains a set $\mathbf{F}$ of constant functions from $\mathbf{W}$ into $\mathbf{W}$, where $\mathbf{a}$ assigns to each term n a member $\mathbf{a}(n)$ of $\mathbf{F}$, and (Tn) is used as the truth clause for Tn.

EXERCISE 5.12   Show that the semantics of Exercise 5.11 is equivalent to one where the truth clause reads: $\mathbf{a_w}(TnA) = T$ iff $\mathbf{a_{a(n)}}(A) = T$, and a model is such that $\mathbf{a}(n)$ is not a function from $\mathbf{W}$ into $\mathbf{W}$, but instead a member of $\mathbf{W}$.

5.6. Relevance Logics and Conditional Logics

Unfortunately this book is already too large to include an adequate discussion of logics where a *binary* modal operator $\Rightarrow$ is introduced for conditional expressions – expressions involving the word 'if'. The best we can do here is whet your appetite for studying these interesting logics on your own. A strong motivation for developing such systems is that material implication (which is symbolized with $\rightarrow$ in this book) provides an inadequate account of many different conditional English expressions, including (most tellingly) 'if A then B'. Although A$\rightarrow$B is true when A is false, this is hardly the way 'if A then B' is understood in natural language. It is false that I am going to live another 1000 years, but that hardly entails the truth of: 'if I am going to live another 1000 years then I will die tomorrow'. When A and B are incompatible with each other as in this case, the normal reaction is to count 'if A then B' false, even when A is false. This illustrates that in English, the truth of 'if A then B' requires some sort of relevant connection between A and B. This demand cannot be captured with $\rightarrow$ or any other binary connective whose truth conditions are given with standard truth tables. Related problems arise in the analysis of strict implication 'if A then necessarily B', nomic conditionals (conditionals that express natural laws), and the counterfactual or subjunctive conditional 'if A were the case, then B would be'. The need for a better analysis is especially clear for subjunctive conditionals. Since the antecedents of such sentences are presumed false, treating these as material implications would require that every counterfactual be true!

Relevance logics are an attempt to define systems that are more faithful to relevance requirements that we normally bring to the use of 'if . . . then' (Dunn, 1986; Mares, 2004). The basic idea is that for 'if A then B' to be true, B must express something relevant to what A expresses. Let us use the symbol ⇒ for the relevant sense of 'if . . . then'. A main concern in relevance logic is to avoid validating the *Paradoxes of Material Implication* – formulas that clearly violate the relevance requirement: A⇒(B⇒A) and A⇒(~A⇒B). (Just because A is true, it does not follow that some other sentence B *relevantly* entails A; moreover, from A and ~A an arbitrary sentence B does not relevantly follow.)

It is a ticklish matter to define a system of rules to block exactly the unwanted cases, and there are some disagreements about which system for ⇒ is best. Part of the problem is that it has been difficult to find an intuitively satisfying semantics for ⇒, especially when negation is to be included in the language. Several truth conditions for ⇒ have been proposed, but one of the most widely known is due to Routley and Meyer, where a three-place relation **R** is defined over a set **W** of situations or sets of information. Situations differ intuitively from possible worlds because they may be incomplete and inconsistent. They might fail to provide information that would decide the truth value of some sentences, and they may also include contradictory information. The truth condition for ⇒ on Routley–Meyer semantics goes as follows:

(⇒) a_w (A⇒B=T iff
for all **v** and **u** in **W**, if **Rwvu** and a_v(A)=T then a_u(B)=T.

Notice how (⇒) is simply a generalization of the standard truth condition (□) for a one-place modal operator □. A number of different conditions (such as Triple Reflexivity: **Rwww**, and Right Hand Symmetry: if **Rwvu** then **Rwuv**) must be added to the definition of a model to validate what intuitively are the right rules for ⇒. The main problem with this semantics is that it is not compatible with the standard truth condition for ~. Further devices must be introduced to prove the semantics for ~, and some people complain that these are not well motivated. Mares (2004) presents a heroic effort to address those objections.

Although relevance logics concern conditionals, the term 'conditional logic' is reserved for systems that address somewhat different concerns (Nute, 1984). Here the aim is not to address the Paradoxes of Material Implication, but to capture other logical behavior of such conditionals as strict implication ('if A then necessarily B'), and counterfactuals ('if A were to hold, then so would B'). A straightforward way to handle strict implication is to define it from material implication using a suitable modal operator $\square$ as follows:

(Def–3) $A \dashv B =_{df} \square(A \rightarrow B)$

The use of the symbol '–3' goes back to C. I. Lewis, who introduced it as a primitive to provide an analysis of logical entailment.

Although (Def–3) is a relatively straightforward way to define a conditional logic, it is not thought to be an adequate system for most of the conditional expressions of English. The problems are clearest in the case of counterfactual conditionals, for which we use the symbol '>'. Here it appears that a number of principles that would be valid given (–3) are no longer acceptable.

Transitivity:	$((A>B)\&(B>C)) > (A>C)$
Contraposition:	$(A>{\sim}B) > (B>{\sim}A)$
Strengthening Antecedents:	$(A>B) > ((A\&C)>B)$

EXERCISE 5.13   Show that the above three formulas are provable from (–3) in M, assuming that –3 is identified with >.

Nute (1984, p. 394) gives counterexamples to all three of these. Transitivity fails because from 'if Carter had died in 1979, then Carter would not have lost the election in 1980' and 'if Carter had not lost the election in 1980, Reagan would not have been president in 1981' it does not follow that 'if Carter had died in 1979, then Reagan would not have been president in 1981'. Contraposition fails because from 'if it were to rain, I would not water the lawn' it does not follow that 'if I were to water the lawn then it would not rain'.

EXERCISE 5.14   Give a counterexample to Strengthening Antecedents.

The best known semantics for > is due to David Lewis (Lewis, 1973). Here a model includes a function **f** that assigns a subset of the set **W** of possible worlds to each world **w** and sentence A. The idea is that **f(w, A)** picks out a set of worlds that are *most similar* to **w** given that A holds in those worlds. People sometimes refer to **f(w, A)** as the (set of) A-worlds closest to **w**. The truth condition for > is given in terms of **f** as follows:

(>) $a_w(A > B) = T$ iff for all **v** in **W**, if **v** is in **f(w, A)** then $a_v(B) = T$.

A number of conditions on **f** are then needed to satisfy our intuitions about closeness of worlds. Lewis's analysis is often employed when philosophical discussion turns on the use of counterfactuals.

5.7. Summary of Axioms and Their Conditions on Frames

In this list of conditions on <**W, R**>, the variables 'w', 'v', and 'u' and the quantifier '∃v' are understood to range over members of **W**. (We use symbols of logic to express the conditions with the understanding that '→' is always the main connective.)

	Axiom	Condition on <W, R>	<W, R> is ..
(D)	□A→◇A	∃v wRv	Serial
(M)	□A→A	wRw	Reflexive
(4)	□A→□□A	wRv&vRu→wRu	Transitive
(B)	A→□◇A	wRv→vRw	Symmetric
(5)	◇A→□◇A	wRv&wRu→vRu	Euclidean
(CD)	◇A→□A	wRv&wRu→v=u	Unique
(□M)	□(□A→A)	wRv→vRv	Shift Reflexive
(L)	□(□A→B)v□((B&□B)→A)	wRv&wRu→vRuvuRvvv=u	Connected
(M)+(5) = S5		wRv	Universal
(C4)	□□A→□A	wRv→∃u(wRu&uRv)	Dense
(C)	◇□A→□◇A	wRv&wRu→∃x(vRx&uRx)	Convergent

EXERCISE 5.15 We have not discussed two conditions that appear on this list: the euclidean condition, and convergence. Draw diagrams for these conditions. Then consider which of them holds when **R** is **earlier than** for various structures of time.

6

Trees for Extensions of K

6.1. Trees for Reflexive Frames: M-Trees

So far we have not explained how to construct trees for systems stronger than K. Trees were used, for example, to show that □(p→q) / p→□q has a K-counterexample, but so far, no method has been given to show that the same argument has an M-counterexample, or a 4-counterexample. It is easy enough to adapt the tree method for M, S4, and other modal logics stronger than K. For example, here is the beginning of an M-tree that generates an M-counterexample to □(p→q) / p→□q.

$$
\begin{array}{ll}
\boxed{\begin{array}{l} \Box(p\rightarrow q) \\ \sim(p\rightarrow\Box q) \\ \quad p \\ \quad \sim\Box q \end{array}}^{\mathbf{w}} & \\
& (\rightarrow F) \\
& (\rightarrow F)
\end{array}
$$

Since the frame <**W**, **R**> is reflexive in M-models, we know that **wRw**, for every member **w** of **W**. So we add an arrow from **w** that loops back to **w** (which we have labeled: M). An M-tree must always include such reflexivity arrows for each of the possible worlds in the tree.

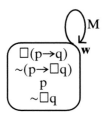

116

This arrow, along with the fact that □(p→q) is true in **w**, means we need to add p→q to **w** by (□T).

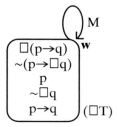

When we apply (→T) to p→q, the world forks, and the left-hand branch closes.

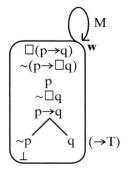

The right branch is still open, and because it contains ~□q, we need to apply (□F) to create a new world **v**. Since we are building an M-model, we must remember to add a reflexivity arrow to this and any other new world we construct.

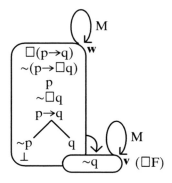

Since □(p→q) is in **w**, we must use (□T) to add p→q to **v**.

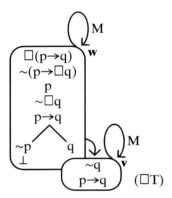

Completing the steps in world **v**, we obtain the following tree:

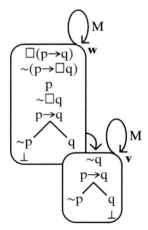

Selecting the open branch, we obtain the following M-counterexample:

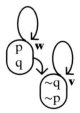

EXERCISE 6.1 Find M-counterexamples to the following arguments:

a) □p→□q / □(p→q)
b) ◇p & ◇q / ◇(p&q)
*c) p→□q / □(p→q)

Construct M-counterexamples for the following axioms:

*d) (4) □p→□□p
*e) (B) p→□◇p
*f) Explain how to construct trees for the system K+(□M), where (□M) is the axiom □(□A→A).

The following M-tree illustrates the case of the argument □(p→q), □~q / ~p, which is M-valid.

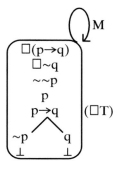

Special care must be taken when arrows are added to a tree in order to ensure that a desired condition on **R** is satisfied. We will illustrate the point by showing that p→q, p→□p / q is M-invalid. After applying (→T) to both premises the tree looks like this:

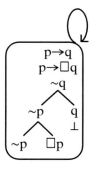

The problem is that the reflexivity arrow together with the (so far) open branch that ends with □p may prompt you to add p at the top of the world. Doing so would cause the tree to close, and you would obtain the incorrect verdict that the argument is M-valid.

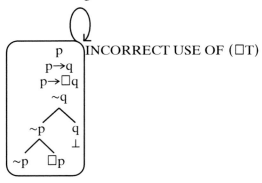

Note that all branches on the left are now closed because ~p contradicts p. The reason that placing p at the top of the world is incorrect is that p follows from □p *only on the middle branch*. The occurrence of □p on this branch indicates that □p is T on *one* of two alternative ways of providing a counterexample for the argument. The other option (indicated by the left branch) is to make ~p T. The fact that p is T *when □p is T* does not mean that ~p might not be T. By entering p at the top of the tree we are (incorrectly) indicating that p is T on all possible assignments, and this is not justified by the information that *one* of the options is to make □p T. This error is easily avoided if you follow the Placement Principle of Section 4.1. It requires that the result of applying a rule is entered on every open branch *below* that line.

According to the Placement Principle, the p that results from (□T) must be entered *below* □p on the same branch. The middle branch then closes. The left-hand branch is still open, however, indicating (correctly) that the argument is M-invalid.

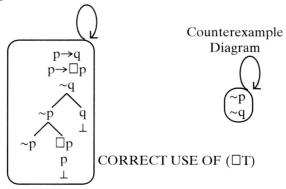

EXERCISE 6.2 Verify that the counterexample above assigns the following values: $a_w(p{\to}q)$=T; $a_w(p{\to}\Box p)$=T; and $a_w(q)$=F, thus demonstrating that p→q, p→□p / q is M-invalid.

EXERCISE 6.3 Check the following arguments for M-validity. Give M-counterexamples for the invalid ones:

a) □□□p / p
b) ◇(pvq) / ◇pv◇q
c) ◇p / □(◇pv◇q)
d) □(p↔q) / □p↔□q (Hint: A good strategy is to convert ↔ to → and &.)
e) □p↔□q / □(p↔q)
f) □(q→p) v □(~p→q), ~□(~pvq) / ~□(~p→~q)

6.2. Trees for Transitive Frames: 4-Trees

In systems with transitive frames, like K4 and S4, extra arrows must be added to a tree to ensure that the relation **R** is transitive. To illustrate the process, here is a K4-tree for the argument □p / □□p. In early stages of tree construction the tree looks like this:

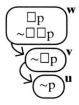

Since there are arrows from **w** to **v** and from **v** to **u**, it follows by transitivity that there should be an added arrow (labeled: **4**) from **w** to **u**.

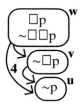

Now it is possible to close the tree using (□T) with the 4-arrow we just added.

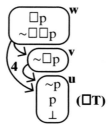

The following 4-tree shows the K4-validity of □p / □~◇◇~p. Here, it was necessary to add several 4-arrows to guarantee transitivity.

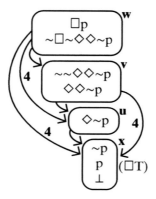

It is a simple matter to check for S4-validity using exactly the same method, except in this case, M-arrows must also be added to the diagram to guarantee reflexivity. What follows is an S4-tree with an S4-counterexample that demonstrates that ◇◇□p / p is S4-invalid:

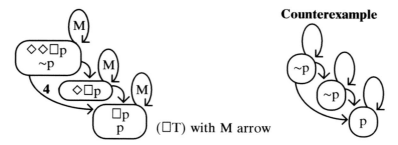

Adding the M- and 4-arrows may lead to complex diagrams. One way to avoid the clutter is to omit the M- and 4-arrows but to modify the (□T) rule so that it applies to those worlds that would have qualified had the arrows been drawn in. In the case of K4, the modified rule, called (□T4), states that when □A is in world **w**, then A may be placed in any world **v**

such that there is a path of one or more arrows leading from **w** to **v**. In the case of S4, we add a rule (□TM) that says that if □A is in **w**, then A can also be added to **w** as well. Diagrams for these modified rules follow:

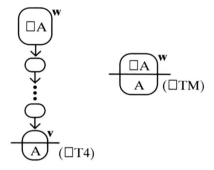

You may work the next set of exercises in two ways, first by drawing in the M- and 4-arrows as necessary, and second using the modified (□T) rules. (In case of invalid arguments, you will need to put the M- and 4-arrows back into the diagram if you used the modified rules.)

EXERCISE 6.4 Check the following arguments for both K4-validity and S4-validity. Give counterexamples for the invalid ones.

a) ◇◇◇p / ◇p
b) ◇(p∨q) / ◇◇p∨◇q
c) ◇◇p / □(◇p∨◇q)
d) □□□p / p
e) □p→□q / □(p→q)
f) □(□p→p) / □p (Hint: You may not be able to perform every step of the tree!)

6.3. Trees for Symmetrical Frames: B-Trees

Unfortunately, the Placement Principle (of Section 4.1) cannot be met in some trees where **R** is symmetric. Let us attempt to show that p / □◇p is KB-valid using trees to illustrate the difficulty. About halfway through the construction, the tree looks like this:

Since KB-models have symmetric frames, and there is an arrow from
w to **v**, we must draw a reverse arrow (labeled 'B' below) from world **v**
back to **w**. Then (◇F) may be used to obtain a contradiction in world **w**.

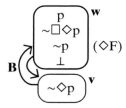

However, this violates the Placement Principle since the result of applying
(◇F) appears *above* the line to which it was applied (namely, the ~◇p in
world **v**). We appear to have no alternative but to violate the Placement
Principle since our goal is to obtain ~p in world **w**, and world **w** lies above
world **v**.

In this example, where there are no forks in the worlds, our reasons
for enforcing the Placement Principle are not operative. In fact, a more
liberal placement principle for trees follows:

Liberal Placement Principle. The results of applying a rule to a step
on a branch may be placed above that step, provided there are no
forks between the point where the rule is applied and the point
where the result of the rule is placed.

Adopting this liberal placement principle, the tree we have just constructed qualifies as a correctly formed B-tree and correctly diagnoses
the argument as valid.

EXERCISE *6.5 Using the Liberal Placement Principle, find a KB-
counterexample to ~(□p→~□□p) / □q.

Now let us illustrate the Liberal Placement Principle with a more complex example. We will show that □◇q→◇□p / q is KB-invalid. About
halfway through the construction the tree looks like this:

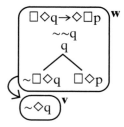

To ensure symmetry, we add an arrow from **v** back to **w**. For simplicity, this can be done by simply converting that arrow into a double-headed one.

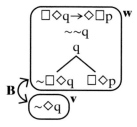

Using the Liberal Placement Principle, (◇F) may be applied to ~◇q in world **v**, to insert ~q on the left branch in **w**, thus closing that branch.

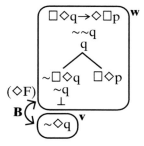

However, work still needs to be done on the right-hand branch, which remains open.

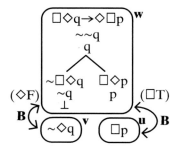

The tree is now complete. When the closed branch is pruned, we obtain the following counterexample.

EXERCISE 6.6 Check these arguments for KB-validity, and give KB-counterexamples for any that are KB-invalid.

a) □□p, ~p / □(pvq) & □(rvp)
b) ◇□p v ◇□q / p

Although the Liberal Placement Principle will work in the case of many arguments, it is not sufficient to correctly manage arguments where forks occur within possible worlds. The following example illustrates the problem. Here we have constructed a B-tree to determine whether □~(□pv□~p) is KB-valid.

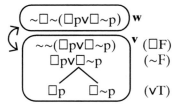

Since there is an arrow from **w** to **v**, (□T) must be applied to □p in world **v**, which would place a p in world **w**. But even the Liberal Placement Principle does not allow this, because there is a fork between the point where □p is found and world **w**. (It is the fork that leads to □~p on the right.) We can not liberalize the Placement Principle further and simply place p into **w**, because if we do, the same privileges would apply to the □~p on the right-hand branch, and that will produce a contradiction in world **w**. This would indicate that ~(□pv□~p) is BK-valid when it is not, as we will soon prove.

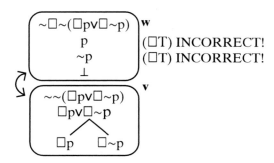

One solution to the problem will be to employ an idea that was introduced in Section 4.2. Instead of drawing the symmetry arrow *upwards*

from **v** towards world **w**, we draw it *downwards* to a new copy of **w** below **v**, where work on **w** may be continued. We will call this second copy of **w** the *continuation* of **w**.

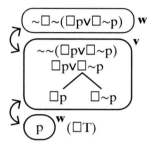

Since we will also need to apply (□Out) to □~p on the right-hand branch, we will need a continuation of **w** there as well.

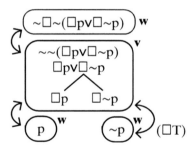

The tree is now complete. It has two open branches so there are two counterexamples. Selecting the right-hand branch, the following KB-counterexample to □~(□pv□~p) can be defined.

EXERCISE 6.7 Double check that the above diagram is a KB-counterexample to □~(□pv□~p). Now select the left-hand branch, produce a second counterexample to □~(□pv□~p), and verify that it is a KB-counterexample.

Given the continuation method, it is never necessary to use the Liberal Placement Principle. Any case where one would copy a step upwards can be duplicated by introducing a continuation and working downwards instead. To illustrate the point, here is a KB-tree that uses continuations to verify the KB-validity of p / □◇p. Applying (◇F) to ~◇p in world **v**, we introduce ~p into the continuation of **w**.

Since p appears in **w** (in the top copy) and ~p appears in the continuation of **w**, it follows that there is a contradiction in world **w** and the tree closes.

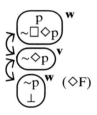

EXERCISE 6.8 Check the following for KB-validity using the continuation method:

a) ~(□p→~□□p) / □q
b) ◇□p / p
c) □□p, ~p / □(pvq) & □(rvp)
d) ◇□p v ◇□q / p
e) ◇□p / □p

It is a simple matter to combine the methods used with M-trees with those used for KB, to construct trees that test for B-validity. Simply add reflexivity arrows to each world in the trees. The following exercise provides practice.

EXERCISE 6.9 Check ~□~(□pv□~p) / p and the problems in Exercise 6.8 for B-validity.

6.4. Trees for Euclidean Frames: 5-Trees

Both the Liberal Placement Principle and continuations may be used to build trees based on (5), which corresponds to the euclidean condition: if **wRv** and **wRu**, then **vRu**. However, special care must be taken in adding extra arrows to trees in order to guarantee the frame <**W, R**> is euclidean. Here we will need to ensure that if **wRv** and **wRu**, then **vRu** for any three worlds **w, v**, and **u** in **W**.

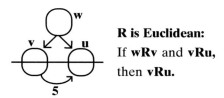

R is Euclidean:
If **wRv** and **vRu**,
then **vRu**.

Note that when **wRv** and **wRu** hold, it follows (trivially) that **wRu** and **wRv**. But by the euclidean condition it follows that **uRv**. So the euclidean condition entails the following one:

For any **w, u**, and **v** in **W**, if **wRv** and **wRu**, then *both* **vRu** and **uRv**.

Therefore a euclidean tree allows *double* arrows to be placed between any worlds **v** and **u** such that **wRv** and **wRu**. Not only that, when **wRv**, it follows (trivially again) that **wRv** and **wRv**, with the result that **vRv**. So there will be reflexive arrows on every world pointed to by an arrow. It follows then that the rule for adding 5-arrows to a diagram looks like this:

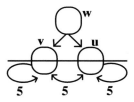

It is easy to overlook 5-arrows that must be added to a tree; however, there is a simple rule about where they go. The euclidean condition guarantees that the tree is *nearly universal*. This means that there are arrows between all worlds except for the one that heads the tree. If we call the set of all worlds other than the world that begins the tree the *body* of the tree, then the body is universal, that is, each world in this set has an arrow

to every other world in the set, and each of those worlds has an arrow
looping back to itself.

EXERCISE 6.10

a) Consider trees with the following three structures:

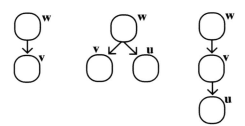

Add all possible 5-arrows to them in order to show that these trees are
nearly universal. Now add a new arrow and world to the second and
third of these trees and repeat the process. Now explain why adding any
arrow to a nearly universal tree results in another tree that is nearly universal. Explain why these considerations show that all 5-trees are nearly
universal.

b) Use mathematical induction to show that any 5-tree is nearly universal.

A problem arises concerning how arrows should be added to a tree
when there is a fork in a world. The situation arises, for example, in the
course of building the K5-tree for ◇□pv◇p / □p, which is K5-invalid,
as we shall see. About halfway through the construction the following
diagram is obtained:

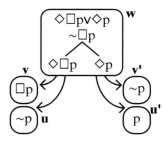

Since we are working in K5, it is necessary to draw in extra arrows to
ensure that <**W**, **R**> is euclidean. A euclidean tree requires *double* arrows
be placed between any worlds **v** and **u** such that **wRv**, and reflexive arrows
as well. So a double arrow must be drawn between **v** and **u**. When (□T)
is applied to this side of the left-hand branch, it closes.

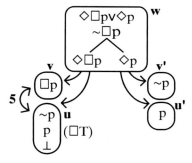

It appears that more 5-arrows must be added to this diagram. Since there are arrows from **w** to **v** and **w** to **v'**, one might expect that there should be a 5-arrow joining these two worlds. However, joining these worlds is fatal since this closes the entire tree, and yet the argument, as we said before, is actually K5-invalid.

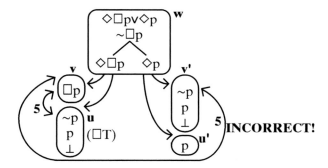

The reason that the placement of this 5-arrow is incorrect is that worlds **v** and **v'** do not belong to the same branch in world **w**. World **v'** lies beneath the branch that contains ◇p, whereas world **v** lies beneath the branch that contains ◇□p. When a fork is created within a world, any 5-arrow to be added to the tree must join *only those worlds that lie along the same branch*.

Arrow Placement Principle. Add arrows to a diagram only between worlds that lie on the same branch.

Another way to diagnose this error is to point out that the use of (□T) violates the Placement Principle, which requires that results of applying a rule must lie on open branches below the point at which the rule is applied. But in this tree, p is placed at a point that does not lie below □p in world **v**.

Notice that a 5-arrow *does* need to be placed between **v′** and **u′** since these worlds are on the same branch. Furthermore, reflexive arrows need to be added to worlds **v′** and **u′**. (Reflexive arrows are not needed for worlds **v** and **u** since this side of the tree is already closed.) The tree is now complete.

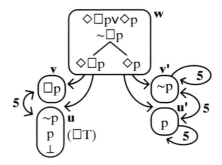

Since the right-hand branch is open, we obtain the following counter-example:

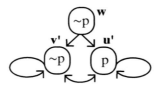

EXERCISE 6.11   Verify that the above diagram is a K5-counterexample to ◇□p∨◇p / □p.

Trees for M5 (better known as S5-trees) differ very little from K5-trees. It is not hard to see that when a relation is reflexive as well as euclidean, it follows that the tree has a universal **R**.

EXERCISE 6.12   Repeat Exercise 6.10 for S5-trees in order to show that M5-trees are universal.

So the only difference between the structure of S5-trees and K5-trees is in the arrow structure for the opening world **w**. World **w** has a reflexive arrow and is fully connected in an S5-tree but not necessarily in a K5-tree. So S5-tree construction is very similar to the process for K5. In both cases, however, the large number of extra arrows in the diagram can be annoying. Instead of adding them, the same effect is obtained by adopting the following variations on the (□T) rule.

(□T5)   If □A is in any world on a branch, then add A to all worlds on that branch other than the opening one.

(□TS5)   If □A is in any world on a branch, add A to all worlds on that branch.

EXERCISE 6.13   Check the arguments in Exercise 6.8 for K5-validity and S5-validity. You may use the (□T5) and (□TS5) rules to simplify your trees if you like.

6.5. Trees for Serial Frames: D-Trees

The deontic logics do not have a reflexive **R**. Instead, the accessibility relation is serial, that is, for each world **w** there is another world **v** such that **wRv**. It is a simple matter to check arguments in deontic logics by simply adding arrows to diagrams to ensure that **R** is serial. To illustrate this, consider the tree for the argument □p / ◇p, which begins as follows:

$$\boxed{\begin{array}{c}\Box p \\ \sim\!\Diamond p\end{array}}^{\mathbf{w}}$$

We have begun the tree, but note that if we were working in K there would be no further step we could do. (Remember that neither the (□T) nor the (◇F) rules can be applied until other rules add arrows to the diagram.) However, now that we are working with a serial **R**, we may simply add an arrow (labeled D) to ensure that there is a world **v** such that **wRv**.

Given the new D-arrow, (□T) and (◇F) can be applied to close the tree.

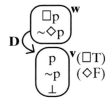

An awkward problem arises when testing D-invalid arguments with trees. For example, consider the following attempt to find a D-counterexample for axiom (4):

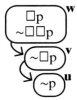

This does not count as a completed D-tree because seriality requires there be an arrow pointing from **u** to another world. If an arrow is added pointing to a new world **x**, there will need to be an arrow pointing from **x** to yet another world.

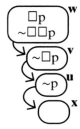

It seems that the process will never terminate. However, there is a simple strategy that can be used to construct a D-counterexample. Eventually there will be worlds (such as **x**) that contain no sentences, and at this point it is safe to simply add a loop arrow to guarantee seriality.

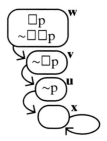

From this diagram, a D-counterexample to (4) is easily constructed.

EXERCISE 6.14   Show that the following axioms are all D4-invalid with trees: (B), (5), and (M).

6.6. Trees for Unique Frames: CD-Trees

In the case of CD-trees, the relation **R** must be unique. That means that when **wRv** and **wRu**, **v** and **u** are the very same world. It is impossible to guarantee this condition using K-tree rules because if ~□p and ~□q ever appear in a world, then when (□F) is applied to each there will be *two* arrows exiting that world. To guarantee uniqueness, we will need to modify the (□F) rule as follows. If an arrow already exits from a world, and we would need to use (□F) to create a new world, use the following rule (U□F) instead:

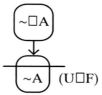

To illustrate how this new rule is applied to CD-trees, here is a tree that demonstrates that ~□p / □~p is CD-valid:

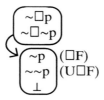

EXERCISE 6.15   Check the following arguments for CD-validity:

a) □(pvq) / □pv□q

b) (□p→□q) / □(p→q)

c) Let c be any of the following connectives: &, v, →. Verify that the following two arguments are CD-valid: □(AcB) / □Ac□B and □Ac□B / □(AcB).

7

Converting Trees to Proofs

7.1. Converting Trees to Proofs in K

Not only is the tree method useful for checking validity in modal logics, but it may also be used to help construct proofs. Trees provide a mechanical method for finding proofs that might otherwise require a lot of ingenuity. If an argument has a proof at all in a system S, the tree method can be used to provide one. The process is easiest to understand for system K, so we will explain that first, leaving the stronger systems for Sections 7.3–7.9. The fundamental idea is to show that every step in the construction of a closed tree corresponds to a derivable rule of K.

It is easiest to explain how this is done with an example, where we work out the steps of the tree and the corresponding steps of the proof in parallel. We will begin by constructing a proof of $\Box(p{\to}q)$ / $\Box p{\to}\Box q$ using the steps of the tree as our guidepost. The tree begins with $\Box(p{\to}q)$ and the negation of the conclusion: $\sim(\Box p{\to}\Box q)$. The first step in the construction of the proof is to enter $\Box(p{\to}q)$ as a hypothesis. In order to prove $\Box p{\to}\Box q$, enter $\sim(\Box p{\to}\Box q)$ as a new hypotheses for Indirect Proof. If we can derive $\bot$ in that subproof, the proof will be finished.

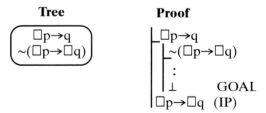

In the tree, we apply ($\to$F) to the second line. Since ($\to$F) was shown to be a derivable rule of propositional logic in Section 1.3, we may enter exactly the same steps in our proof.

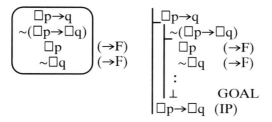

EXERCISE 7.1   Reconstruct the proofs that both versions of (→F) are derivable rules of propositional logic. Version 1: ~(A→B) / A; Version 2: ~(A→B) / ~B. (Hint: See Section 1.3, Exercise 1.5.)

The next step of the tree is to apply (□F) to ~□q, creating a new world containing ~q. This step corresponds to entering a world-subproof, headed by ~q. (A world-subproof, as was explained in Section 1.5, is an abbreviation for the double subproof structure used by (◇Out).)

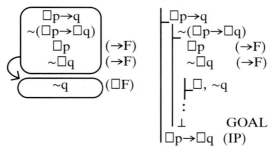

Next, (□T) is applied two times in the tree. These steps correspond to two uses of (□Out) in the proof. (Actually (Reit) is also needed, but we will ignore (Reit) steps in this discussion to simplify the presentation.)

At this point (→T) is applied to the tree creating two branches, one containing ~p, and the other q. In the proof, this corresponds to beginning two subproofs headed by the same two sentences.

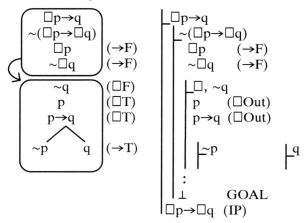

In general, the (→T) rule for trees corresponds to the creation of a pair of side-by-side subproofs of the kind we used with (∨Out).

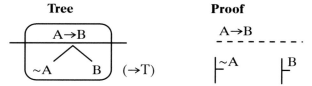

Both branches in the lower world of the tree are closed. Placing ⊥ on these branches corresponds to using (⊥In) (and (Reit)) in the proof to place ⊥ in the subproofs headed by ~p and q.

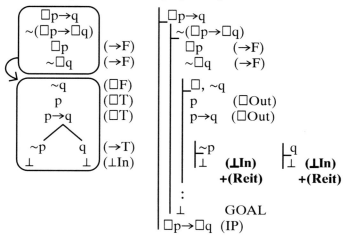

We now have contradictions in the subproofs headed by ~p and q. The next project will be to derive contradictions in all subproofs that enclose these two. The result of that process will place ⊥ in the subproof headed by ~(□p→□q), which was our goal. The first stage of this process will appeal to a derived rule of propositional logic that we will call (→⊥).

$$
\begin{array}{ll}
A{\rightarrow}B & \\
\;\lfloor\,{\sim}A & \quad\lfloor\,B \\
\;\;\vdots & \quad\;\;\vdots \\
\;\;\bot & \quad\;\;\bot \\
\text{-----------} & \\
\quad\bot \quad (\rightarrow\bot) &
\end{array}
$$

EXERCISE 7.2   Show that (→⊥) is a derivable rule of PL. (Hint: From the left subproof derive A, and from the right one derive ~B.)

This rule is similar to (∨Out). It says that when we have a "parent" subproof containing A→B and two side-by-side subproofs, one headed by ~A and the other by B, both of which contain ⊥, then ⊥ may be placed into the parent subproof. In our example, we have p→q, the conditional that caused the fork in the tree, and subproofs headed by ~p and q containing ⊥. When (→⊥) is applied to the proof, we obtain ⊥ in the subproof headed by ~q. In both the tree and the proof, we have shown that the initial segment of the bottom world leads to a contradiction.

$$
\begin{array}{ll}
\Box p{\rightarrow}q & \\
{\sim}(\Box p{\rightarrow}\Box q) & \\
\Box p & (\rightarrow F) \\
{\sim}\Box q & (\rightarrow F) \\
\hline
{\sim}q & (\Box F) \\
p & (\Box T) \\
p{\rightarrow}q & (\Box T) \\
{\sim}p \qquad q & (\rightarrow T) \\
\bot \qquad\;\; \bot & (\bot In) \\
\end{array}
$$

$$
\begin{array}{ll}
\lfloor\Box p{\rightarrow}q & \\
\;\lfloor{\sim}(\Box p{\rightarrow}\Box q) & \\
\quad\Box p & (\rightarrow F) \\
\quad{\sim}\Box q & (\rightarrow F) \\
\quad\lfloor\Box,\,{\sim}q & \\
\quad\; p & (\Box Out) \\
\quad\; p{\rightarrow}q & (\Box Out) \\
\quad\;\lfloor{\sim}p \qquad\qquad \lfloor q & \\
\quad\;\lceil\bot\;(\bot In) \qquad\; \lceil\bot\;(\bot In) & \\
\quad\; \bot & (\rightarrow\mathbf{\bot}) \\
\quad\; \vdots & \\
\quad\; \bot & \text{GOAL} \\
\lfloor\Box p{\rightarrow}\Box q & (IP) \\
\end{array}
$$

In general it is guaranteed that wherever the tree forks, there was a conditional A→B that caused that fork through the use of (→T). The two branches beyond the fork will be headed by ~A and B. In the corresponding proof, the same conditional will be present, which will cause the creation of two subproofs, one headed by ~A and the other by B. When the two subproofs are shown to contain ⊥, (→⊥) may then be applied to the proof to derive ⊥ in the parent subproof, which is, in our case, the world-subproof headed by □, ~q.

The next step in constructing the proof is to derive ⊥ in the subproof headed by ~(□p→□q). This process corresponds to a derivable rule of K that is similar to (◇Out).

$$\sim\Box A$$

$$\left|\begin{array}{l} \Box, \sim A \\ \quad\vdots \\ \quad\bot \end{array}\right.$$

- - - -

$$\bot \qquad (\sim\Box\bot)$$

EXERCISE 7.3   Show that (~□⊥) is a derivable rule of K.

This rule allows us to place ⊥ in the subproof that was headed by ~(□p→□q). Using (IP) on this subproof, we obtain the desired conclusion.

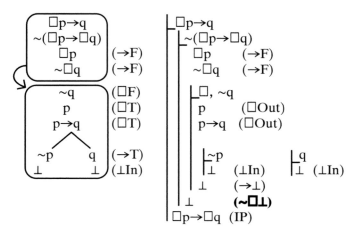

This example demonstrates a general strategy for converting any closed K-tree into a proof in K. Each entry in a tree corresponds (in a proof) to a hypothesis or the result of applying a derivable rule of K. When the tree rules (~F), (→F), and (□T) are used in the tree, we may use corresponding rules of proof – (DN), (→F), and (□Out) (respectively) – to derive the same steps. When (□F) and (→T) are applied in the tree, the corresponding sentences head new subproofs. Since the tree is closed, we can be assured that each of its innermost subproofs contains ⊥. Then (→⊥) and (~□⊥) can be applied repeatedly to drive ⊥ to the parents of those subproofs, then to their parents, and so on. It follows that ⊥ can be proven in the subproof for (IP) headed by the negation of the conclusion. The conclusion can then be proven by (IP).

In the next example, we present the corresponding proof for the tree of the argument ~p→□~□~~p / ~□~□p→p. We leave the justifications for the lines of this proof as an exercise.

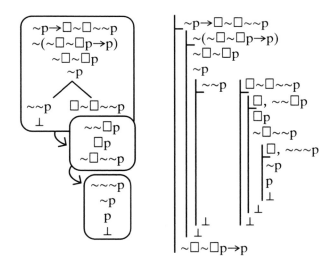

EXERCISE 7.4   Give the rule names for each step of the above proof, using the tree at the left as guidance.

When converting trees to proofs, it is important to let the arrow structure in the tree guide the structure of the subproofs in the corresponding proofs. The tree and corresponding proof for □(p→q), □p / ~□q→□r will illustrate the point.

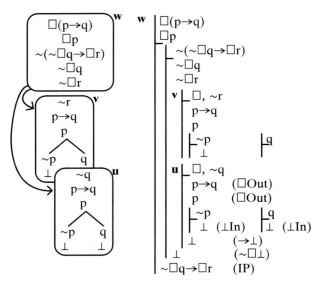

The subproof for the world **v** cannot be completed since the right-hand
subproof headed by q contains no contradiction. (This is why reasons
for the steps in that subproof were omitted.) However, the proof can
be completed nevertheless because the subproof for the world **u** does
contain the needed contradictions, allowing (~□⊥) to be applied to place
⊥ in the main subproof. So none of the steps in the subproof for world
v are needed, and this "failed" subproof may be simply eliminated from
the final solution.

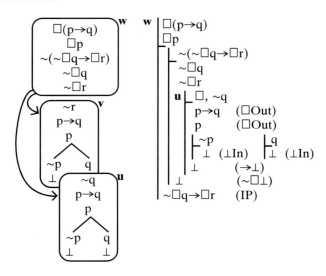

Note how important it was for a successful conversion that the sub-proof for world **u** was placed within the subproof for world **w** rather than within the subproof headed by **v**. The correct choice of subproof layout is guided by the fact that there is no arrow from **v** to **u**, but instead an arrow from **w** to **u**. One feature of trees that can lead to confusion in this example is that it appears that world **u** lies **within** world **v**. So when constructing the corresponding proof, one might be tempted to place the subproof for world **u within** the subproof for world **v**. But that would be a mistake since the proof will be blocked when the subproofs are laid out this way. The difficulty is illustrated in the next diagram.

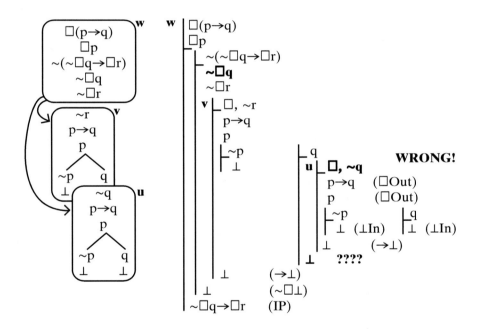

If the subproof for world **u** were placed in the right-hand subproof (headed by q) for world **v**, it would be impossible to apply ($\sim\Box\bot$) correctly since $\sim\Box$q is in the subproof for world **w** rather than in the subproof for world **v**, where it would be needed. (It is not possible to reiterate $\sim\Box$q to place it into the subproof for world **v** because this is a **boxed** subproof so that (Reit) does not apply.)

So when two worlds (such as **v** and **u** in the above example) are "sib-lings" in the arrow structure, it is important that their corresponding

subproofs not be placed one inside the other when the proof is constructed. Instead they should lie "side by side" as illustrated by the original
layout for this proof. The **arrows** determine the subproof layout, not the
order in which worlds appear along a branch.

When sibling worlds appear in a tree along the same branch, it
is always possible to simplify the tree and hence the corresponding
proof. By working first on those steps that produce the world that completely closes, steps for its sibling never have to be performed. The
result is a proof where the "failed" boxed subproof for the other sibling never has to be considered. So for example, the tree we have been
discussing can be simplified by applying ($\Box$F) to ~$\Box$q before applying
($\Box$F) to ~$\Box$r. The result is a shorter tree and quicker discovery of the
proof.

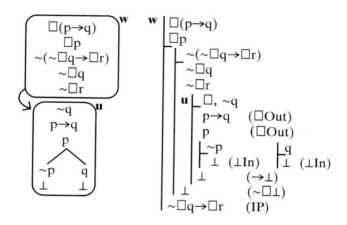

The moral of this example is that whenever sibling worlds appear
along a branch in a closed tree, it is possible to save time and trouble
by deleting parts of a branch that contain any "failed" sibling worlds –
sibling worlds that remain open. The result is a tree where each world
has at most one arrow exiting from it. When the tree is simplified in
this way, the potential confusion concerning subproof layout for sibling worlds will not arise and "failed" subproofs will never occur in the
corresponding proofs. Although it is not always easy to predict which
worlds will end up as failed siblings **during** tree construction, it is possible to simplify a closed tree **after** it is completed and every branch is
closed.

EXERCISE 7.5 Use the conversion process without simplifying to create proofs for the following trees. Then simplify each tree and do the conversion again.

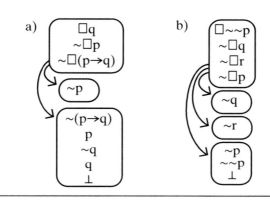

In case a K-tree contains continuations, whether a world counts as a failed sibling depends on how you look at it. For example, consider the following tree:

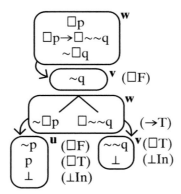

From the point of view of the left branch, world **v** is a failed sibling, but from the point of view of the right-hand branch, **v** is not since the branch is closed by world **v**. To avoid these and other complications introduced by continuations, one should reorder steps in a K-tree so that all continuations are eliminated before the conversion process begins. When this is done to the above tree, the problem does not arise.

> **EXERCISE 7.6** Explore the difficulties raised in attempting to convert the above tree into a proof. Then reorder the steps to eliminate the continuation and convert the tree into a proof.

By performing (→T) before (□F), two separate branches are formed and it is clear that **v** would be a failed sibling on the left branch.

Here is a summary of the tree rules and their corresponding rules of proof:

Tree Rule   **K Rule**

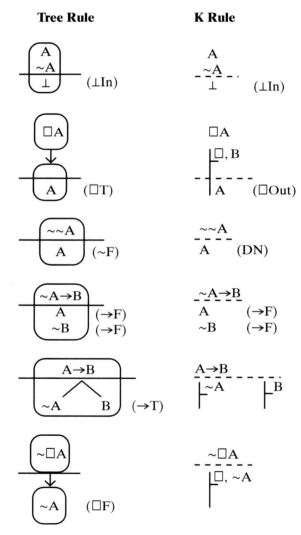

A→B

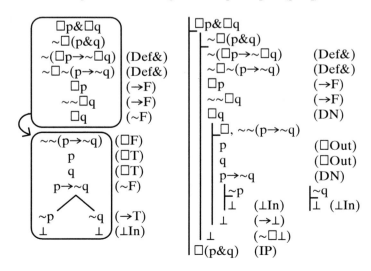

$$\begin{array}{ll} & \sim\!A \qquad\qquad B \\ & \quad\vdots \qquad\qquad \vdots \\ & \quad\bot \qquad\qquad \bot \\ \bot & \qquad (\rightarrow\!\bot) \end{array}$$

$\sim\!\Box A$

$$\begin{array}{ll} & \Box, \sim\!A \\ & \quad\vdots \\ & \quad\bot \\ \bot & \qquad (\sim\!\Box\bot) \end{array}$$

7.2. Converting Trees that Contain Defined Notation into Proofs

Officially, the only tree rules are (→T), (→F), (□T), (□F), and (~F). Since use of these rules corresponds to principles of K, we know that every closed tree corresponds to a proof. However, tree rules for the defined connectives &, ∨, and ◇ were introduced for convenience. These rules were not required because any tree that contains them can be rewritten in favor of ~, →, and □. The new tree can then be closed using the official rules and the proof constructed from that tree using the method explained in Section 7.1. The proofs that result from applying this method are neither obvious nor elegant. However, what matters ultimately is that we are certain to find a proof this way if the tree is closed. To illustrate how this is done, here is a proof for the argument □p&□q / □(p&q) from its tree:

□p&□q	
~□(p&q)	
~(□p→~□q)	(Def&)
~□~(p→~q)	(Def&)
□p	(→F)
~~□q	(→F)
□q	(~F)
~~(p→~q)	(□F)
p	(□T)
q	(□T)
p→~q	(~F)
~p ~q	(→T)
⊥ ⊥	(⊥In)

□p&□q	
~□(p&q)	
~(□p→~□q)	(Def&)
~□~(p→~q)	(Def&)
□p	(→F)
~~□q	(→F)
□q	(DN)
□, ~~(p→~q)	
p	(□Out)
q	(□Out)
p→~q	(DN)
~p ~q	
⊥ (⊥In) ⊥ (⊥In)	
⊥	(→⊥)
⊥	(~□⊥)
□(p&q)	(IP)

Overall, however, the translation technique can be cumbersome. A more convenient alternative is to identify the derived tree rules for &, v, and ◇ with the corresponding derived K rules. The following list explains the correspondence:

Tree Rule   **K Rule**

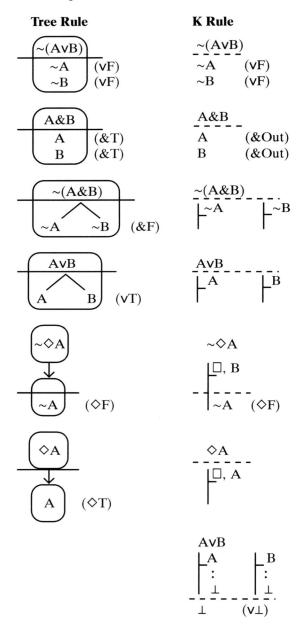

~(A&B)
├─~A   ├─~B
│ :   │ :
│ ⊥   │ ⊥
- - - - - - - - - -
⊥   (~&⊥)

◇A
├─□, A
│   :
│   ⊥
- - - - - - - -·
⊥   (◇⊥)

EXERCISE 7.7   Show that the rules (∨F), (◇F), (∨⊥), (~&⊥), and (◇⊥) are all derivable in K.

With these rules available, the creation of a proof from the tree for □p&□q / □(p&q) is simplified.

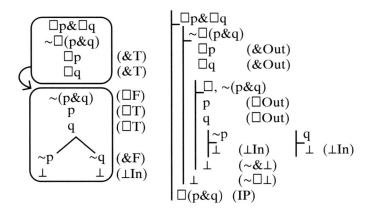

EXERCISE 7.8   Reconstruct tree diagrams for the arguments given in Exercises 4.1 and 4.2, and convert these trees to proofs. Now do the same for Exercise 4.8, problem a).

7.3. Converting M-Trees into Proofs

The previous section shows how to convert any closed K-tree into a proof in K. A variation on the same method may be used to convert trees to proofs for stronger modal logics. The trees we construct for systems stronger than K may contain additional arrows and worlds that were introduced to satisfy the corresponding conditions on frames. These added arrows and worlds introduce new sentences into the tree, usually through the use of ($\Box$T). So the primary issue to be faced in the conversion process for systems stronger than K is to show how these additional steps in the tree can be proven.

In order to pave the way for this demonstration, it helps to consider a variant on the tree method that introduces axioms or rules to the tree rather than extra arrows and worlds. The idea is that any use of ($\Box$T) that added new sentences to the tree because of the addition of an S-arrow could be duplicated by the addition of a derived axiom or rule of S to the tree. So whenever the S-tree is closed, that tree could be reformulated using axioms or rules in place of the additional arrows. Since the new tree will appeal only to steps of K and to derived principles of S, it will be a straightforward matter to convert the reformulated tree into a proof.

Let us start with a simple example in the system M. We will begin with a closed M-tree for the argument $\sim$p / $\sim\Box$p. Notice that ($\Box$T) was used with the M-arrow to obtain p from $\Box$p. Let us use the notation '(M$\Box$T)' to record the idea that this step was applied because of the presence of the M-arrow in this tree.

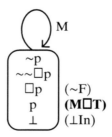

Clearly we could obtain exactly the effect of (M$\Box$T) in a tree that lacked the M-arrow, by applying the (M) rule to the tree instead.

(M) $\Box$A

       A

$$
\begin{array}{ll}
\sim p & \\
\sim\sim\Box p & \\
\Box p & (\sim F) \\
p & \textbf{(M)} \\
\perp & (\perp In)
\end{array}
$$

Clearly any step justified by (M□T) (where (□T) is applied along an M-arrow) can also be duplicated instead using (M). Let us call a tree constructed in this fashion an (M)K-tree, to emphasize that it, like a K-tree, lacks M-arrows but appeals to (M) instead. (M)K-trees can be a convenient alternative to M-trees, especially where excessive numbers of reflexivity arrows clutter up the tree diagram.

Another advantage of (M)K-trees is that it is easy to see how to convert them into proofs. The method is identical to the one used for K, with the exception that there will be appeals to (M) in the proof where they are found in the (M)K-tree. For example, a proof is easily constructed for the (M)K-tree just given as follows:

$$
\begin{array}{ll}
\sim p & \\
\sim\sim\Box p & \\
\Box p & (\sim F) \\
p & \textbf{(M)} \\
\bot & (\bot In)
\end{array}
\qquad
\begin{array}{ll}
\sim p & \\
\sim\sim\Box p & \\
\Box p & (DN) \\
p & \textbf{(M)} \\
\bot & (\bot In) \\
\sim\Box p & (IP)
\end{array}
$$

EXERCISE 7.9   Construct proofs in M from (M)K-trees for valid arguments of Exercise 6.3.

7.4. Converting D-Trees into Proofs

Now let us consider the system D. In D-trees, the frame must be serial, which means that for each world **w** in the tree there must be an arrow from **w** to some world **v**. To guarantee this condition on frames, new D-arrows and worlds may have been added to the tree. So the problem is to explain how to convert this extra structure into corresponding steps of the proof. To handle this kind of case, K-trees for the system D may be constructed that allow an additional step that will guarantee the presence of worlds needed to ensure seriality. It is not difficult to show that the following axiom is derived in D:

($\bot$D) $\sim \Box\bot$

EXERCISE 7.10   Prove $\sim\Box\bot$ in D. (Hint: Use the following instance of (D): $\Box\sim\bot \to \Diamond\sim\bot$, and then show that $\Box\sim\bot$ is provable using (Def$\sim$), (CP), and ($\Box$In).)

(D)K-trees are K-trees (that is, trees that lack D-arrows), but allow instead the introduction of (⊥D) into any world of the tree. When ~□⊥ is added to a world, (□F) must be applied, creating a new world headed by ~⊥. In this way, tree will obey seriality, but without the explicit addition of any D-arrows.

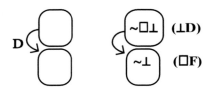

Since (⊥D) constitutes a derived principle in D, converting a (D)K-tree into a proof in D is straightforward.

Here is an illustration of the conversion process. We have presented the (D)K-tree for the argument □(p&q) / ◇(pvq) along with the corresponding proof.

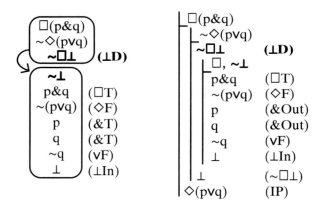

EXERCISE 7.11 Construct a D-tree that shows that the argument □□p / ~□□~p is D-valid. Now convert this tree into a proof in D.

7.5. Converting 4-Trees into Proofs

In the case of 4-trees, extra 4-arrows are added to guarantee that the frame is transitive. This means that (□T) may be used with the added arrows to place new sentences into the tree. Let us use '(4□T)' to notate these steps. Exactly the same effect can be achieved in K-trees that lack the 4-arrows provided that the rule (4) is added to the tree rules.

(4)   □A

□□A

So a (4)K-tree is a K-tree where rule (4) may be applied in any world of the tree. It should be obvious that once the (4)K-tree for an argument is closed, it is a straightforward matter to convert the result into a proof. So to convert any 4-tree to a proof in K4, we need only explain how (4) can be used to duplicate any (4□T) step in the original 4-tree. To illustrate, consider the 4-tree for the argument ~□□p / ~□p, along with the corresponding (4)K-tree.

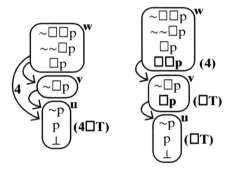

In this case, the (4□T) step was applied to the □p in world **w** along the 4-arrow to place p in world **u**. The same effect may be obtained in the (4)K-tree to the right by applying the (4) rule to □p in world **w**, allowing the placement of p in **u** using (□T) twice with the original K-arrows. Clearly the resulting (4)K-tree can be converted into a proof with the help of (4).

In some 4-trees, many 4-arrows must be added to guarantee transitivity. In cases like this it may be necessary to eliminate (4□T) steps in favor of uses of the (4) rule repeatedly. For example, below on the left is a 4-tree for the argument: □p / □~◇◇~p. To its right, each 4-arrow is eliminated in favor of a use of (4), starting with the 4-arrow last entered into the tree and working in reverse order. The result is a (4)K-tree that contains every step in the original 4-tree but lacks the 4-arrows.

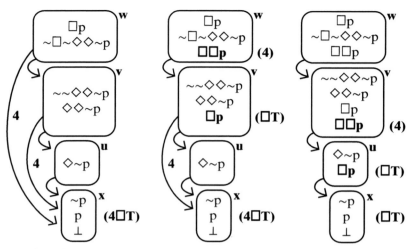

It should be clear that no matter how many 4-arrows have been introduced into a 4-tree, it is possible to use this strategy to create a (4)K-tree
that lacks all 4-arrows, but obtains the same steps using (4). Simply convert each 4-arrow into the corresponding steps in the reverse of the order
in which the 4-arrows are added to the tree.

EXERCISE 7.12   Construct a proof in K4 from the right-most tree of the last
diagram.

This strategy can be easily combined with the strategies used for M-
and D-trees. So it is a straightforward matter to convert D4- and M4-trees
(that is, S4-trees) into (D4)K and (M4)K trees from which proofs in D4
and M4 are easily constructed.

EXERCISE 7.13   Construct trees for the following arguments and convert
them to proofs in the systems mentioned:

a) ◊◊◊(p→q), □p / ◊q in K4
b) □□p / ~□◊◊~p in D4
c) □~~pv□□□q / □□□pv□q in S4

7.6. Converting B-Trees into Proofs

In this section, we will explain how to convert B-trees into proofs in systems that contain (B). Since the strategies for D-trees and M-trees may
be adopted along with the methods we are about to explain, this will

show how to convert trees into proofs for DB and B (=MB) as well. We must explain how to duplicate (B□T) steps (steps introduced using (□T) along B-arrows added to ensure that the frame is symmetric). The result will be a closed (B)K-tree that lacks all the B-arrows but obtains the effect of (B□T) steps by appealing to a derived principle of the system KB. Consider the following closed B-tree for the KB-valid argument □□p / ~p→□p. Here (B□T) has been used to place p in world **w**, by applying (□T) to □p along the B-arrow from world **v** to world **w**.

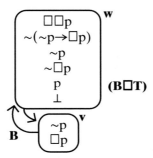

We are hoping to find a principle of B that we can add to trees that will guarantee that p occurs in world **w**, but without the help of the B-arrow. One strategy that works uses the axiom (∨B), which is equivalent to the dual of axiom (B).

(∨B)   □~□A∨A

(By principles of propositional logic □~□A∨A is equivalent to ~□~□A→A, which is the dual of (B): ◇□A→A.) Notice what happens once □~□p∨p is added to world **w** and (∨T) is applied.

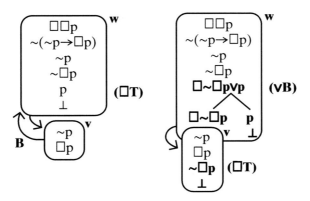

The resulting tree lacks the B-arrow, but it duplicates the original tree in placing p in world **w** on the right-hand branch. This branch closes in the same way it did in the original tree because p was available. But the axiom also produces the branch on the left headed by □~□p, which was not in the original B-tree. One might worry that this branch could stay open so that the new (B)K-tree is no longer closed. Notice, however, that the left branch in world **w** must close, for the presence of □~□p in **w** causes ~□p to be placed in **v**, which contradicts □p.

This suggests a strategy that is guaranteed to replace any closed KB-tree that appeals to (B□T) with a corresponding closed K-tree that lacks B-arrows, but appeals to (vB) instead. The resulting (B)K-tree is easily converted into a proof in B. Consider in general any B-tree where there is a B-arrow from **v** to **w** and a branch that contains □A in **v**.

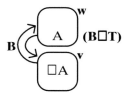

When A is placed in world **w** using (B□T), the same effect can be obtained by placing □~□AvA in world **w**. When (v) is applied to that step, duplicates of world **v** containing □A will be entered below world **w** in each branch, for whatever rules created world **v** and placed □A in it in the K-tree must be applied to create the same structure on both branches of the (B)K-tree. Sentence A will appear in **w** (as desired) on the right-hand branch, which duplicates the effect (B□T), and this branch will therefore close just as it did in the original tree. Furthermore, the left-hand branch (headed by □~□A) will also close, because when (□T) is applied along the K-arrow from **w** to **v**, ~□A will be placed in **v**.

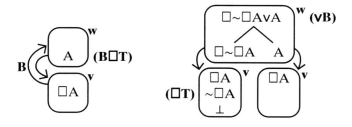

This diagram helps us appreciate that when (∨B) is added to world **w**, any branch that contains □A in world **v** must either close immediately (as in the left-hand branch) or contain A in world **w** and so duplicate the closed branch in the original tree (the right-hand branch). Therefore, the (B□T) steps in a closed B-tree can be duplicated in a corresponding closed (B)K-tree.

There are some occasions where it is necessary to use continuations to correctly construct a B-tree. For example, the following KB-tree for the argument ~q / □((~□q→p)→p)→p) uses (□T) and a B-arrow to place q in a continuation of **w** to close the left-hand branch. This continuation was unavoidable. If q had been placed in the original world **w**, then the Placement Principle would have been violated because of the fork in world **v**.

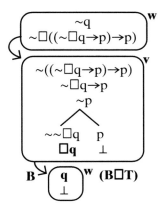

However, the presence of continuations in B-trees requires no modification of the strategy used to convert B-trees into corresponding (B)K-trees. The method works whether the B-arrow points upwards or downwards to a continuation. When an arrow points from world **w** to world **v**, and a sentence A is placed in **w** by applying (B□T) to □A in **v** (in our example the q in the continuation of **w**), simply use (∨B) to place □~□A∨A in the first occurrence of the world **w**. After (∨T) is applied to this step, it will follow that all branches through **w** will either contain □~□A or A. It follows that every branch containing □A in **v** will close immediately by applying (□T) to □~□A or contain A in world **w**, thus duplicating the closed branch in the original tree. To illustrate, the corresponding (∨B)K-tree is added to the right in the next diagram.

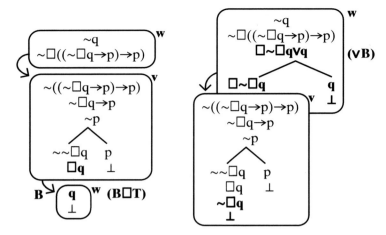

The method for constructing (B)K-trees can become complex when there are multiple cases of (B□T) to deal with. Note, however, that whenever we use (∨B) in world **w**, the left-hand branches that contain □∼□A will all close. Let a simplified (∨B) tree be one that removes any branches that immediately close in this way. It should be clear that it is always possible to construct a simplified (B)K-tree that satisfies the following property:

> (B-Fact)   Whenever there is an arrow from **w** to **v**, then any branch
> that contains □A in **v** also contains A in **w**.

Any simplified (B)K-tree can be expanded into a full-dress (B)K-tree that includes all the steps needed to close the left-hand branches; the result can then be converted into a proof in KB. It is much easier to work with simplified (B)K-trees since they are identical to KB trees, save that B-Fact is appealed to in place of (B□T). For example, here is the simplified (B)K-tree for the first example presented in this section:

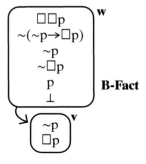

It should be clear then that each B-tree corresponds to a simplified (B)K-tree, which can be converted into a full-dress proof in B.

EXERCISE 7.14 Construct simplified (S)K-trees for the following arguments in the systems S indicated; then construct their (S)K-trees. Finally, convert the (S)K-trees into proofs. You will need to combine B strategies with those for D and M to solve problems c) and d).

a) $\Box\Box p, \sim p$ / $\Box(p \lor q)$ in KB
b) $\Box\Box(p \rightarrow r)$, p, $\sim r$ / $\Box q$ in KB
c) $\Box\Box(p \rightarrow r)$, p / r in DB
d) $\Box\Box(p \rightarrow r)$, $\Box p$ / $\Box\Diamond r$ in B (Hint: You will need to use (vB) twice.)

EXERCISE 7.15 Consider the following strategy for converting KB-trees into proofs: in the **v** subproof containing $\Box A$, use $\Diamond$Out to obtain $\Diamond\Box A$ in **w**, from which A is derived by the dual of (B). Explain why this method is not a general solution to converting KB-trees to proofs. (Hint: Consider the possibility that the tree might have forked in world **v**.)

EXERCISE 7.16 Explain how to convert $\Box$M-Trees into proofs in K+($\Box$M). (Hint: Remember ($\Box$M) is the axiom $\Box(\Box A \rightarrow A)$. $\Box$M-trees obey the property of shift reflexivity, i.e., if **wRv**, then **vRv**. So when an arrow points from **w** to **v**, an arrow looping from **v** back to **v** is added to the tree. Explain how to create (OM)K-trees that allow the introduction of the axiom (OM) into world **w** to obtain the same effect as any use of (OM$\Box$T).)

7.7. Converting 5-Trees into Proofs

A method similar to the one used for KB-trees may be used to generate proofs for closed 5-trees. The secret is to construct corresponding K-trees that avoid uses of (5$\Box$T) (steps that appeal to ($\Box$T) along 5-arrows) in favor of uses of the axiom (v5).

(v5) $\Box\sim\Box A \lor \Box A$

The only difference between (vB) and (v5) is that $\Box A$ (rather than A) appears in the right disjunct. So it should be clear that an analog of the strategy outlined for B can be used to construct corresponding simplified (5)K-trees that satisfy (5-Fact).

(5-Fact)   When there is an arrow from **w** to **v**, then any branch that contains $\Box A$ in **v** also contains $\Box A$ in **w**.

The following diagram illustrates how the application of (v5) guarantees the 5-Fact in the simplified tree:

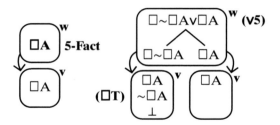

The 5-fact guarantees that (5)K-trees may be used to duplicate any step that results from the use of (5□T). Whenever there are K-arrows from **w** to **v** and **w** to **u**, and a 5-arrow between **v** and **u**, (5□T) allows the placement of A in **u** along any branch that contains □A in **v**. This same step may be duplicated in the simplified (5)K-tree because the 5-Fact guarantees that □A is in **w** on any branch that includes □A in **v**. But if □A is in **v**, (□T) may be used to place A in **u** as desired. An outline of the process appears in the following diagram with the 5-tree on the left, a simplified (5)K-tree in the middle, and all the gory details of the full (5)K-tree on the right:

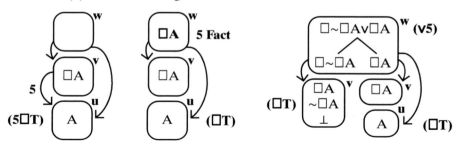

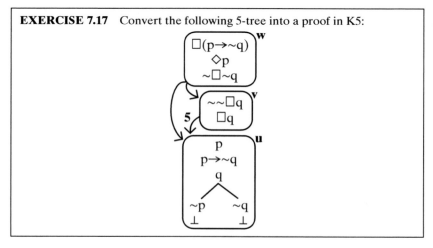

EXERCISE 7.17   Convert the following 5-tree into a proof in K5:

It is easy to combine the strategies for **M**, **D**, **4**, and **B**-arrows with the method just explained for **5**-arrows. Here are some exercises for practice with the idea. All you need to do is to eliminate the arrows from the original tree in the reverse of the order in which they were introduced.

EXERCISE 7.18

a) Construct a simplified (M5)K-tree showing the M5-validity of (B): A→□◇A. Then convert it into a proof.

b) Construct a simplified (45)K-tree for ◇□p /□□p and convert it into a proof in K45.

So far, we have converted only trees that contain a single 5-arrow, but of course, there may be many such arrows in a 5-tree. In this case, it can be difficult to keep track of all the steps needed to complete a conversion. One way to manage the complexity is to create simplified (5)K-trees by eliminating, one by one, each use of (5□T) and the 5-arrow involved in favor of the corresponding 5-Fact. It is important to do this in the reverse order in which the (5□T) steps were entered into the tree. By keeping good records of what sentences were justified by the 5-Fact, it will be easy to determine which instances of (v5) will be needed in the final (5)K-tree. Here is an example to illustrate the idea. On the left is the K5-tree that demonstrates the 5-validity of the axiom (□M): □(□A→A). In the trees to the right, each 5-fact is recorded in turn as the uses of (5□T) are eliminated.

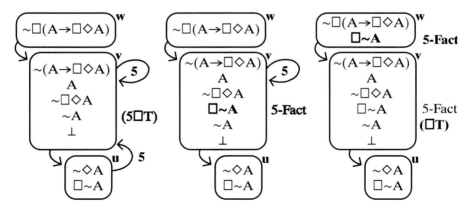

Note that in the tree on the left, the 5-arrow from **u** to **v** was drawn because there were arrows from **v** to **u** and from **v** back to **v**. (□T) was used with this 5-arrow and □~A in **u** to place ~A in **v**. To capture this step in a simplified (5)K-tree, use the 5-Fact to place □~A in **v**, from which ~A follows from (5□T) and the "reflexive" 5-arrow from **v** to **v**. Now it is necessary to eliminate this step and remove this arrow. It was drawn because there was an arrow from **w** to **v** (and an arrow from **w** to **v**), which meant there had to be a 5-arrow from **v** back to **v**. So in this case, the relevant 5-fact is that □~A may be found in world **w**. Once □~A is there, ~A can be placed in **v** by an ordinary use of (□T) following the K-arrow from **w** to **v**. The rightmost simplified (5)K-tree can now be expanded to a (5)K-tree by placing the axiom □~□A∨□A in each world where □A is justified by a 5-Fact.

EXERCISE 7.19   Convert the tree on the right in the last diagram into a (5)K-tree, using the appropriate instance of (v5) at the two locations where a 5-Fact is noted. It is less confusing if you convert each use of (v5) separately. Now convert the result into a K5-proof.

Let us illustrate a final example of the conversion process for 5-trees. In this case we will need to use (v5) three times.

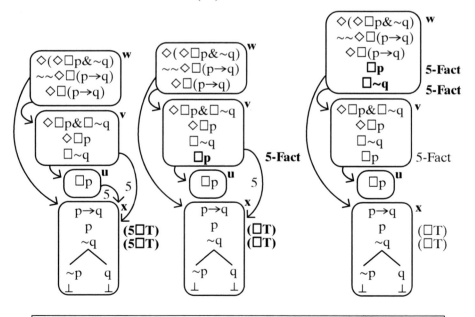

EXERCISE 7.20   Convert the rightmost tree into a K5-proof.

Notice that the 5-arrow last entered into the 5-tree was the "smallest" one from **u** to **x**. When this arrow is removed, the resulting tree uses (□T) *twice* with the remaining 5-arrow, once to place p in **x** and again to place ~q in **x**. So when this arrow is removed, it will be necessary to use the 5-Fact twice to place both □p and □~q in world **w**. When this is done, both p and ~q may be entered into **x** using (□T) with the K-arrow from **w** to **x**. The reason why the arrows should be resolved in reverse order may now be apparent. If the 5-arrow from **v** to **x** had been resolved first, then we would have had trouble seeing that steps for both □p and □~q had to be carried out.

EXERCISE 7.21   Construct trees for the following arguments and convert them into proofs in the systems indicated:

a) ◇p / □□◇p in K45
b) □□p / ◇□◇p in D5
c) □p / ◇□◇p in D45
d) ~□p, □(q→p) / ~□□~□□q in K5 (Hint: This is hard since there will be three 5-arrows in the closed tree. Go slowly resolving each arrow separately.)

7.8. Using Conversion Strategies to Find Difficult Proofs

Strategies for converting trees into proofs are genuinely useful for solving proofs that would otherwise be quite difficult to find. If you suspect an argument is S-valid for a system S that is formed from principles discussed in this chapter, but cannot find the proof in S, simply construct its S-tree. If the tree is open, then you know that the argument is S-invalid, and so not provable after all. If the S-tree is closed, you simply use the methods of this chapter to convert it into a proof in S. Some of the resulting proofs would have been extremely difficult to find without the guidance provided by trees.

EXERCISE 7.22   Show the following facts using a tree and the conversion method:

a) (C4): □□A→□A is provable in K5
b) ◇◇A→◇A is provable in KB5
c) ◇□A→A is provable in M5
d) (M) is provable in D4B (Hint: Make use of seriality to draw an arrow from the opening world. Then use B to construct a continuation of the opening world. Transitivity will then ensure there is an arrow from the opening world to its continuation.)

e) Use the tree method to construct proofs of □(□A→A), □(A→□◇A), and
   □(□A→□□A) in K5 (Hint: Make use of ideas and strategies in the earlier
   problems to help organize your work for later ones. The last of these is
   difficult.)

7.9. Converting CD-Trees into Proofs in CD and DCD

In systems that adopt the (CD) axiom, frames are unique. To guarantee
that CD-trees meet this condition, we adopted a new tree rule (U□F) that
requires that when applying (□F) to a world from which an arrow already
points, a new world should not be created, but the result of applying that
rule is added to the world that already exists.

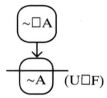

So in converting from CD-trees to proofs, we will need to explain how
the sentence added by (U□F) can be derived. Here is an example to
help illustrate the process. Here we have a CD-tree that demonstrates
the validity of the argument □(pvq) / □pv□q.

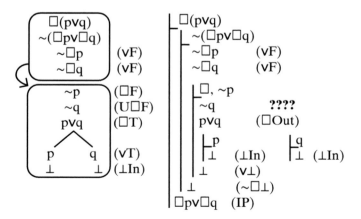

The problem to be faced in constructing the proof is to find a way to derive
the step ~q (at the **????**), which was produced by (U□F) in the CD-tree.

The solution makes use of the (CD) axiom. It is an easy matter to show that the following rule follows in any extension of K that contains (CD):

~□A

□~A   (CD)

EXERCISE 7.23   Demonstrate that ~□A ⊢$_{KCD}$ □~A.

Making use of this rule, the sentence ~□q to which (U□F) was applied in the tree can be transformed to □~q, from which ~q can be derived in the boxed subproof by (□Out).

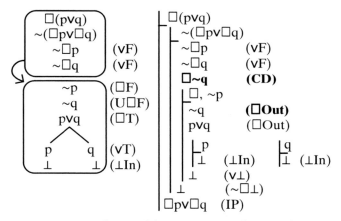

The same strategy may be used in any system that results from adding axioms to KCD, so for example, we may use the same idea to show that DCD-trees can be converted into proofs in DCD.

7.10. A Formal Proof that Trees Can Be Converted into Proofs

A method for converting K-trees into K-proofs was presented in Section 7.1. However, the demonstration given there was informal. One may worry that complications related to failed siblings and continuations might hide some flaw in the reasoning. So it is worthwhile for our peace of mind to give a more careful demonstration that the argument for a closed tree always has a proof in K. Once the result is established, it can be extended to the stronger modal logics S discussed in this chapter. In those cases, note that an (S)K-tree for system S contains only steps for the K-tree plus the use of derived axioms or rules (S). It will follow that any closed (S)K-tree can be converted to a proof in S. In Sections 7.3–7.9, it has been shown that whenever an S-tree is closed, so is the corresponding (S)K-tree. So it follows that any S-tree can be converted into a proof in S.

To simplify what follows, let us presume that all derived notation is removed before the trees are constructed. As a result, each K-tree is built using the basic tree rules (~F), (→F), (→T), (⊥In), (□T), and (□F). The method for showing that arguments with closed K-trees have proofs in K will be to construct a branch sentence *B for each branch B created in the construction of the closed K-tree, and to show that each such *B is K-inconsistent, that is, *B ⊢ ⊥. (Here the subscript 'K' on '⊢' is omitted to save eyestrain. Furthermore, by 'inconsistent', we mean K-inconsistent in what follows.) Since *B for the opening branch (the one that begins the tree-construction process) will consist of the conjunction of the premises with the denied conclusion of the argument H / C being tested, it will follow that H, ~C ⊢ ⊥. It follows immediately by (IP) that the argument has a proof in K.

To construct *B, *w is defined for each world **w** on a branch as follows:

Definition of *w. *w is the conjunction of all sentences appearing in **w** on the branch (including sentences in any continuations of **w**) together with ◇*v, for each world **v** on the branch such that there is an arrow from **w** to **v**.

*B for a branch B is then defined to be *o, where o is the *opening world* on the branch, that is, the one at the top of the tree. So for example, suppose the branch has the following shape:

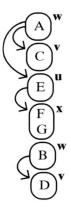

Then *$\mathbf{w}$ is calculated as follows:

$$*\mathbf{w} = A \mathbin{\&} B \mathbin{\&} \Diamond*\mathbf{v} \mathbin{\&} \Diamond*\mathbf{u}$$
$$= A \mathbin{\&} B \mathbin{\&} \Diamond(C\&D) \mathbin{\&} \Diamond*\mathbf{u}$$
$$= A \mathbin{\&} B \mathbin{\&} \Diamond(C\&D) \mathbin{\&} \Diamond(E \mathbin{\&} \Diamond*\mathbf{x})$$
$$= A \mathbin{\&} B \mathbin{\&} \Diamond(C\&D) \mathbin{\&} \Diamond(E \mathbin{\&} \Diamond(F\&G))$$

Let *B be the branch sentence for any branch B created during the construction of a closed K-tree. It will be shown that *B is inconsistent.

Branch Sentence Theorem. *B $\vdash \perp$.

Proof of the Branch Sentence Theorem. Suppose that the result(s) of applying a rule to branch B during the construction of a tree is branch B′ (or branches B′ and B″). Then the branch sentence *B will be called *the parent* of *B′ (and *B″), and *B′ (and *B″) will be known as the *child* (*children*) of *B. Branch sentences for branches that contain $\perp$ will be called *closed*. To prove the branch sentence theorem, we will show two things – first, that all closed branch sentences are inconsistent, and second, that when child (children) *B′ (and *B″) is (are) inconsistent, then so is the parent *B. It will follow from this and the fact that all closed branch sentences are inconsistent that all parents of closed branch sentences are inconsistent. Similarly, parents of those parents are inconsistent, and so on all the way back to the branch sentence for the beginning of the tree. As a result, all branch sentences on the tree are inconsistent. All that remains, then, is to prove the following two lemmas:

Closed Branch Lemma. If *B is closed, *B is inconsistent.

Tree Rule Lemma.
If the children of *B are inconsistent, then so is *B.

For the proofs of these lemmas, it helps to establish some facts about branch sentences *B. Suppose *B contains sentence A. Then *B can be constructed by starting with A and repeatedly adding a conjunct or $\Diamond$ at each step as many times as are necessary to build up *B. Furthermore, by following the same construction procedure, but placing conjuncts to the left of A whenever they would be placed to the right of A in the construction of *B, it is possible to construct a sentence *(A) equivalent to *B such that A is the rightmost sentence in *(A). It follows that the *(A) so constructed has the form:

C_1 & $\Diamond(C_2$ & . . $\Diamond(C_n$&A). .)

A more careful proof of this fact about *(A) is given in the next paragraph. Those who are already convinced may skip to the proof of the Closed Branch Lemma. Define a *&$\Diamond$ sentence* *(A) to be any sentence constructed by starting with A and repeatedly adding $\Diamond$ and conjuncts to the left of the result.

&$\Diamond$ Lemma.   Each branch sentence *w containing A is equivalent to a &$\Diamond$ sentence.

Proof of the &$\Diamond$ Lemma. The proof is by induction on the construction of *w. When A appears in *w, A must be in the conjunction of members of **w**, or in some conjunct $\Diamond$*v where there is an arrow from **w** to **v** on the branch. In the first case, *w is equivalent to the result of conjoining the other members of **w** to the left of A, and this is a &$\Diamond$ sentence. When A is in $\Diamond$*v, then we have by the hypothesis of the induction that *v is equivalent to a &$\Diamond$ sentence **v** and *w is equivalent to the result of adding a conjunct to the left of $\Diamond$v. So *w is equivalent to a &$\Diamond$ sentence in this case as well.

Since *B is *o where o is the top world of the branch, the &$\Diamond$ Lemma guarantees that when *B contains A, it is equivalent to a &$\Diamond$ sentence *(A).

Proof of the Closed Branch Lemma. Assume *B is closed so that $\bot$ appears on B. A sentence *($\bot$) equivalent to *B can be constructed by starting with $\bot$ and repeatedly adding a left conjunct or $\Diamond$ at each step. But (&$\bot$) and ($\Diamond\bot$) are derivable rules of K.

(&$\bot$)	A $\vdash$ $\bot$	($\Diamond\bot$)	A $\vdash$ $\bot$
	------------		-----------
	C&A $\vdash$ $\bot$		$\Diamond$A $\vdash$ $\bot$

So *($\bot$) $\vdash$ $\bot$ may be obtained by repeatedly applying these rules to $\bot \vdash \bot$.

EXERCISE *7.24   Show that (&$\bot$) and ($\Diamond\bot$) are derivable in K. (Hint: for ($\Diamond\bot$): From A $\vdash$ $\bot$ obtain $\vdash$ ~A, and then $\vdash$ $\Box$~A by (Nec). Now use (DN) and (Def$\Diamond$) to obtain $\vdash$ ~$\Diamond$A and you are almost done.)

Tree Rule Lemma.

If the children of *B are inconsistent, then so is *B.

It will be helpful for proving the tree rule lemma to establish some facts about $\&\Diamond$ sentences *(A), that is, sentences of the form:

$$C_1 \& \Diamond (C_2 \& . . \Diamond (C_n \& A) . .)$$

Note first that $\sim(A\&B)$ is equivalent to $A\rightarrow\sim B$, and $\sim\Box A$ is equivalent to $\Diamond\sim A$. So by repeated uses of these equivalences we have the following:

$\sim [C_1 \& \Diamond (C_2 \& . . \Diamond (C_n \& A) . .)]$ is equivalent to
$C_1 \rightarrow \Box(C_2 \rightarrow . . \Box(C_n \rightarrow\sim A) . .)$

But in the light of this equivalence, (Def~), and the rules (CP), (MP), ($\Box$In), and ($\Box$Out), the following Lemma holds.

* Lemma.

$C_1 \& \Diamond(C_2 \& . . \Diamond(C_n \& A). .) \vdash \bot$ iff $C_1, \Box, C_2, . . \Box, C_n, A \vdash \bot$.

EXERCISE *7.25 Prove the * Lemma.

Let '*(A)' abbreviate '$C_1 \& \Diamond(C_2 \& . . \Diamond(C_n \& A). .)$' and '*(A')' abbreviate '$C_1 \& \Diamond(C_2 \& . . \Diamond(C_n \& A'). .)$'.

Entailment Lemma. If $A \vdash A'$, then if *(A') $\vdash \bot$, then *(A) $\vdash \bot$.

Proof of the Entailment Lemma. Suppose $A \vdash A'$ and *(A') $\vdash \bot$. Then *(A') $= C_1 \& \Diamond(C_2 \& . . \Diamond(C_n \& A'). .) \vdash \bot$. Then by the * Lemma $C_1, \Box, C_2, . . \Box, C_n, A' \vdash \bot$, and so $C_1, \Box, C_2, . . \Box, C_n \vdash \sim A'$ by (IP). By $A \vdash A'$ it follows that $\vdash A\rightarrow A'$, from which $C_1, \Box, C_2, . . \Box, C_n \vdash A\rightarrow A'$ follows by (Reit) and (Nec). So $C_1, \Box, C_2, . . \Box, C_n, \vdash \sim A$ by (MT). But $C_1, \Box, C_2, . . \Box, C_n, A \vdash A$, and hence $C_1, \Box, C_2, . . \Box, C_n, A \vdash \bot$ by ($\bot$In). It follows by the * Lemma that $C_1 \& \Diamond(C_2 \& . . \Diamond(C_n \& A). .) \vdash \bot$, and so *(A) $\vdash \bot$.

With the Entailment Lemma in hand, the proof of the Tree Rule Lemma is not difficult.

Proof of the Tree Rule Lemma. It must be shown that when *B′ ⊢ ⊥ (and
*B″ ⊢ ⊥), then *B ⊢ ⊥ when *B is the parent of *B′ (and *B″). The proof
is by cases depending on which rule is applied to B to create B′ (and B″).
In the cases of the rules (~F), (→F), (⊥In), (□T), and (□F), the proof
is an almost immediate consequence of the Entailment Lemma. Assume
*B′ ⊢ ⊥. Cases for (→F) and (□T) are illustrated here, and the others are
left as exercises.

(→F). When this rule is applied to the sentence ~(A→C) on branch B,
A and ~C are added to the branch. Then *B is equivalent to a sentence
with the form: *(~(A→C)) and *B′ equivalent to *(~(A→C)&A&~C).
But ~(A→C) ⊢ ~(A→C)&A&~C. So *B ⊢ ⊥ by the Entailment Lemma.

(□T). In this case, *B is equivalent to *(□A&◇D) and *B′ equivalent
to *(□A&◇(D&A)). But □A&◇D ⊢ □A&◇(D&A), so given that *B′
⊢ ⊥, *B ⊢ ⊥ by the Entailment Lemma.

EXERCISE 7.26   Show that □A&◇D ⊢ □A&◇(D&A).

EXERCISE *7.27   Complete the cases for (~F), (⊥In), and (□F).

The case of (→T) is different because when applied to branch B it cre-
ates two new branches B′ and B″. In this case *B is equivalent to a
sentence with the form C_1&◇(C_2& .. ◇(C_n&(AvD))..). *B′ is equiv-
alent to C_1&◇(C_2& .. ◇(C_n&(AvD)&A)..), and B″ to C_1&◇(C_2& ..
◇(C_n&(AvD)&D)..). Since *B′ ⊢ ⊥ and *B″ ⊢ ⊥, it follows by the *
Lemma that C_1, □, C_2, .. □, C_n, AvD, A ⊢ ⊥ and C_1, □, C_2, .. □,
C_n, AvD, D ⊢ ⊥. It follows from these that C_1, □, C_2, .. □, C_n, AvD
⊢ ~A&~D by (CP), (Def~), and (&In), and so C_1, □, C_2, .. □, C_n,
AvD ⊢ ~(AvD) by (DM). But C_1, □, C_2, .. □, C_n, AvD ⊢ AvD and
so C_1, □, C_2, .. □, C_n, AvD ⊢ ⊥ by (⊥In). By the * Lemma it follows
that C_1&◇(C_2& .. ◇(C_n&(AvD)) ..) ⊢ ⊥. Since *B is equivalent to
C_1&◇(C_2& .. ◇(C_n&(AvD)) ..), it follows that *B ⊢ ⊥, as desired.

This completes the proof that arguments with closed K-trees can always
be proven in K. To obtain the result for stronger modal logics S, all we
need to do is to extend this reasoning to the case of (S)K-trees, where
axioms or rules of S may be added to the tree. But the Entailment Lemma
guarantees the result for these trees as well. In the case of the application
of a rule (such as (M) or (4) or (U□F)), the proofs are easy since the rules

entail their results. When an axiom (S) is applied to branch B, then the parent *B is equivalent to a sentence with the form *(A), and the result *B′ is equivalent to *(A&(S)). But clearly A ⊢$_S$ A&(S), so if *B′ ⊢ ⊥, then *B ⊢ ⊥ as well by the Entailment Lemma.

EXERCISE 7.28 Show the Tree Rule Lemma for systems containing (M), (4), and (U□F).

8

Adequacy of Propositional Modal Logics

The purpose of this chapter is to demonstrate the adequacy of many of the modal logics presented in this book. Remember, a system S is *adequate* when the arguments that can be proven in S and the S-valid arguments are exactly the same. When S is adequate, its rules pick out exactly the arguments that are valid according to its semantics, and so it has been correctly formulated. A proof of the adequacy of S typically breaks down into two parts, namely, to show (Soundness) and (Completeness).

(Soundness)   If H ⊢$_S$ C then H ⊨$_S$ C.
(Completeness)   If H ⊨$_S$ C then H ⊢$_S$ C.

8.1. Soundness of K

Let us begin by showing the soundness of K, the simplest propositional modal logic. We want to show that if an argument is provable in K (H ⊢$_K$ C), then it is K-valid (H ⊨$_K$ C). So assume that there is a proof in K of an argument H / C. Suppose for a moment that the proof involves only the rules of propositional logic (PL). The proof can be written in horizontal notation as a sequence of arguments, each of which is justified by (Hyp) or follows from previous entries in the sequence by one of the rules (Reit), (CP), (MP), or (DN). For example, here is a simple proof in PL of p→q / ~~p→q, along with the corresponding sequence of arguments written in horizontal form at the right.

1.	$p{\to}q$	(Hyp)	1. $p{\to}q$ / $p{\to}q$
2.	$\sim\sim p$	(Hyp)	2. $p{\to}q$, $\sim\sim p$ / $\sim\sim p$
3.	p	2 (DN)	3. $p{\to}q$, $\sim\sim p$ / p
4.	$p{\to}q$	1 (Reit)	4. $p{\to}q$, $\sim\sim p$ / $p{\to}q$
5.	q	3, 4 (MP)	5. $p{\to}q$, $\sim\sim p$ / q
6.	$\sim\sim p{\to}q$	5 (CP)	6. $p{\to}q$ / $\sim\sim p{\to}q$

The usual strategy for showing soundness of *propositional logic* (PL) would be to show that any instance of (Hyp) is valid, and that each of the rules (Reit), (CP), (MP), and (DN) *preserves validity*, that is, if the argument(s) to which the rule is applied is (are) valid, then so is the argument that results. When these two facts are shown, it will follow that every line of a proof in horizontal notation is a valid argument by the following reasoning. Any proof in PL starts with one or more instances of (Hyp), which by the demonstration are valid. For example, the proof in our example begins with two instances of (Hyp) that are valid and so indicated with '⊨' in bold.

1.	$p{\to}q$	(Hyp)	1. $p{\to}q$ **⊨** $p{\to}q$
2.	$\sim\sim p$	(Hyp)	2. $p{\to}q$, $\sim\sim p$ **⊨** $\sim\sim p$
3.	p	2 (DN)	3. $p{\to}q$, $\sim\sim p$ / p
4.	$p{\to}q$	1 (Reit)	4. $p{\to}q$, $\sim\sim p$ / $p{\to}q$
5.	q	3, 4 (MP)	5. $p{\to}q$, $\sim\sim p$ / q
6.	$\sim\sim p{\to}q$	5 (CP)	6. $p{\to}q$ / $\sim\sim p{\to}q$

The next step of the proof (step 3 in our example) must apply one of the other rules to one or more of these valid arguments (in our example to step 2 by (DN)). Since it was assumed that the rules preserve validity, the argument it produces will be valid as well. (So the argument in step 3 is valid in our example.)

1.	$p{\to}q$	(Hyp)	1. $p{\to}q$ ⊨ $p{\to}q$
2.	$\sim\sim p$	(Hyp)	2. $p{\to}q$, $\sim\sim p$ ⊨ $\sim\sim p$
3.	p	2 (DN)	3. $p{\to}q$, $\sim\sim p$ **⊨** p
4.	$p{\to}q$	1 (Reit)	4. $p{\to}q$, $\sim\sim p$ / $p{\to}q$
5.	q	3, 4 (MP)	5. $p{\to}q$, $\sim\sim p$ / q
6.	$\sim\sim p{\to}q$	5 (CP)	6. $p{\to}q$ / $\sim\sim p{\to}q$

The same will be true of the step after that (step 4) since it will apply a validity-preserving rule (in our case (Reit)) to an argument above it in the series that is valid. (In the case of (MP), the rule will be applied to two arguments, both of which will be already known to be valid, so the result will also be valid.) The same reasoning applies again to each step of the proof, including the proof's last line. So the last argument in the sequence is valid.

1.	⌐ p→q	(Hyp)	1. p→q ⊨ p→q
2.	⌐ ~~p	(Hyp)	2. p→q, ~~p ⊨ ~~p
3.	p	2 (DN)	3. p→q, ~~p ⊨ p
4.	p→q	1 (Reit)	4. p→q, ~~p ⊨ p→q
5.	q	3, 4 (MP)	5. p→q, ~~p ⊨ q
6.	~~p→q	5 (CP)	6. p→q ⊨ ~~p→q

But this is the argument being proven. (Consider step 6 in the above example.) So it follows in general that if an argument can be proven in PL (H ⊢$_{PL}$ C), then it is valid (H ⊨$_{PL}$ C). In summary, the soundness of PL can be shown by showing that arguments of the form (Hyp) are valid and that the rules (Reit), (MP), (CP), and (DN) preserve validity.

However, we are interested in demonstrating the soundness of K. In this case, the strategy must be modified in order to accommodate the presence of boxed subproofs and the rules for □. The corresponding horizontal notation for a line of a proof in K has the form L / A, where L might contain one or more boxes. We need some way to deal with the boxes that may appear in L. To employ the basic "preservation of validity" strategy, a more general notion of validity must be defined that applies to arguments whose premises include □. The original definition of K-validity depended on the notion of a set of sentences H being satisfied at a world **w**, which we wrote as follows: **a$_w$**(H)=T. This indicates that every member of H is true at **w**. (When H is empty, the value of **a$_w$**(H) is vacuously T, that is, since there are no members of H at all, there are none to challenge the claim that **a$_w$**(H)=T.) To provide a more general account of K-validity, the notation: **a$_w$**(L)=T must be defined, which says that a list L consisting of sentences *and boxes* is satisfied at a world **w**. The definition may be given as follows:

(L,□)   **a$_w$**(L, □, H)=T iff ∃**v a$_v$**(L)=T and **vRw** and **a$_w$**(H)=T.

The meaning of (L,□) may be appreciated by working out the following example. Let L be the list A, B, □, C, □, D, E. Let us calculate what it means to say **a$_w$**(L)=T in this case.

By definition (L,□), $\mathbf{a_w}$(A, B, □, C, □, D, E)=T iff

$\exists\mathbf{v}\ \mathbf{a_v}$(A, B □, C)=T and $\mathbf{vRw}$ and $\mathbf{a_w}$(D, E)=T.

But by (L,□) again, a_v(A, B, □, C)=T iff

$\exists\mathbf{u}\ \mathbf{a_u}$(A, B)=T and $\mathbf{uRv}$ and a_v(C)=T.

Putting these two together we obtain:

$\mathbf{a_w}$(A, B, □, C, □, D, E)=T iff
$\exists\mathbf{v}\ \exists\mathbf{u}\ \mathbf{a_u}$(A, B)=T and $\mathbf{uRv}$ and $\mathbf{a_v}$(C)=T and $\mathbf{vRw}$ and $\mathbf{a_w}$(D, E)=T.

It is easier to appreciate what this means with a diagram.

$$\boxed{A, B} \xrightarrow{\ \ \mathbf{u}\ \ } \boxed{C} \xrightarrow{\ \ \mathbf{v}\ \ } \boxed{D, E}^{\mathbf{w}}$$

$$\mathbf{a_w}\ (A, B, □, C, □, D, E)=T$$

You can see that each box in L corresponds to an arrow between worlds in this diagram.

In case the list L ends with a box, as in the list: □, A, □, we may work out what $\mathbf{a_w}$(L)=T means using (L, □) by assuming L is preceded and followed by the empty list, which we notate '—'. In this case, the calculation goes as follows:

$\mathbf{a_w}$(—, □, A, □, —)=T iff
$\exists\mathbf{v}\ \mathbf{a_v}$(—, □, A)=T and $\mathbf{vRw}$ and $\mathbf{a_w}$(—)=T iff
$\exists\mathbf{v}\ \exists\mathbf{u}\ \mathbf{a_u}$(—)=T and $\mathbf{uRv}$ and $\mathbf{a_v}$(A)=T and $\mathbf{vRw}$ and $\mathbf{a_w}$(—)=T.

Since the empty list — is automatically satisfied in any world, we may drop the clauses '$\mathbf{a_u}$(—)=T' and '$\mathbf{a_w}$(—)=T', so that the result simplifies to the following.

$\exists\mathbf{v}\ \exists\mathbf{u}\ \mathbf{uRv}$ and $\mathbf{a_v}$(A)=T and $\mathbf{vRw}$.

This would be diagrammed as follows:

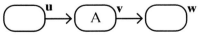

$$\mathbf{a_w}\ (\text{\_}, □, A, □, \text{\_})=T$$

EXERCISE 8.1   Use (L,$\square$) to define the meaning of the following claims and draw the corresponding diagrams:

a) $\mathbf{a_w}$(A, $\square$, B, $\square$, C)=T
b) $\mathbf{a_w}$(A, $\square$, $\square$, B)=T
c) $\mathbf{a_w}$(A, $\square$, $\square$)=T

Now that the definition for $\mathbf{a_w}$(L)=T is in hand, the definition of K-validity for arguments containing boxes is straightforward, for it proceeds from the definition of 'counterexample' just as it did in Section 3.6. Suppose that S is one of the modal logics we have studied. A list L is *S-satisfiable* iff there is an S-model <**W, R, a**> and a world **w** in **W** where $\mathbf{a_w}$(L)=T. Argument L / C has an *S-counterexample* (L $\nvDash_S$ C) iff the list L, ~C is S-satisfiable; and argument L / C is *S-valid* (L $\vDash_S$ C) iff L / C has no S-counterexample. It is a simple matter to verify that this definition amounts to saying that L $\vDash_S$ C iff for all models <**W, R, a**> and all **w** in **W**, if $\mathbf{a_w}$(L)=T then $\mathbf{a_w}$(C)=T, or to put it in English, any world where L is satisfied is one where C is true.

We are now ready to demonstrate the soundness of K by showing that each of its rules preserves K-validity defined for arguments L / C that may include boxes in the hypothesis list L. To show that any instance of (Hyp) is K-valid, we show it has no K-counterexample. Any argument of this form has the shape L, A / A. So to show that such an argument must be K-valid, we assume that L, A / A has a K-counterexample, and derive a contradiction. So let us suppose that L, A / A has a K-counterexample (in symbols: L, A $\nvDash_K$ A). Then there is a K-model <**W, R, a**> such that for some **w** in **W**, $\mathbf{a_w}$(L, A)=T and $\mathbf{a_w}$(A)=F. But $\mathbf{a_w}$(L, A)=T means that $\mathbf{a_w}$(L)=T and $\mathbf{a_w}$(A)=T. We may express this situation as a diagram as follows:

$$
\left.
\begin{array}{c}
\text{L} \\
\text{A} \\
\text{\textasciitilde A} \\
\bot
\end{array}
\right)^{\mathbf{w}}
\quad
\begin{array}{l}
\text{L, A } \nvDash_K \text{ A} \\
\mathbf{a_w}(\text{L})=\text{T} \\
\mathbf{a_w}(\text{A})=\text{T} \\
\mathbf{a_w}(\text{A})=\text{F} \\
\text{impossible}
\end{array}
$$

We see immediately that assuming this commits us to an inconsistent assignment of values to A by **a** at **w**. This contradicts what we know about the assignment function, and so we conclude that (Hyp) has no K-counterexample.

Now let us turn to the rule (Reit). We must show that (Reit) preserves K-validity. The rule allows us to move from an argument of the form L / A to one of the form L, B / A, where a new hypothesis B has been introduced in the hypothesis list. We must show that if L ⊨$_K$ A, then L, B ⊨$_K$ A. So let us assume that L ⊨$_K$ A, that is, that L / A is K-valid. This means that in any model <**W, R, a**> and any **w** in **W**, if **a$_w$**(L)=T, then **a$_w$**(A)=T. Assume for indirect proof that L, B / A has a K-counterexample. Then there must be a K-model <**W, R, a**> where for some **w** in **W**, **a$_w$**(L, B)=T and **a$_w$**(A)=F.

$$\begin{array}{|c|}^{\textbf{w}} L \\ B \\ \sim A \end{array} \quad L, B \nvDash_K A$$

By the K-validity of L / A, we know that any world **w** where L is T is one where A is T. We may express this fact as a diagram rule, which shows that as soon as L is T in world **w**, then so is A.

$$\begin{array}{|c|} L \\ \hline A \end{array} \quad L \vDash_K A$$

Applying this rule to our previous diagram, we have that **a$_w$**(A)=T. But this is a contradiction, since we already said **a$_w$**(A)=F.

$$\begin{array}{|c|}^{\textbf{w}} L \\ B \\ \sim A \\ A \\ \bot \end{array} \quad \begin{array}{l} L, B \nvDash_K A \\ \\ L \vDash_K A \end{array}$$

The indirect proof is complete; we conclude that if L ⊨$_K$ A, then L, B ⊨$_K$ A.

Let us look next at the rule (MP). It allows us to obtain L / B from two arguments L / A and L / A→B. So we must assume that L ⊨$_K$ A and L ⊨$_K$ A→B, and must show that L ⊨$_K$ B. Assume for indirect proof that L ⊭$_K$ B. Then there must be a K-model <**W, R, a**> and a world **w** in **W** such that **a$_w$**(L)=T and **a$_w$**(B)=F.

$$\begin{array}{|c|}^{\textbf{w}} L \\ \sim B \end{array} \quad L \nvDash_K B$$

By the K-validity of both L / A and L / A→B, we have that **a$_w$**(A)=T and **a$_w$**(A→B)=T.

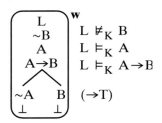

By the truth condition for →, we know that if $\mathbf{a_w}(A{\to}B)=T$, then $\mathbf{a_w}(A)=F$ or $\mathbf{a_w}(B)=T$. So our diagram forks.

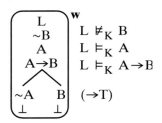

Whether $\mathbf{a_w}(A)$ is F or $\mathbf{a_w}(B)$ is T, we have a contradiction. We conclude that (MP) preserves K-validity.

EXERCISE 8.2   In similar fashion, show that (CP) and (DN) preserve K-validity.

L, A ⊢ B   L ⊢ ~~A

------------   ------------

L ⊢ A→B   (CP)   L ⊢ A   (DN)

The proof of the soundness of K will not be complete until we show that (□In) and (□Out) preserve K-validity. The reasoning makes use of a special case of (L,□). It is easier to see what is going on here to use diagrams, so two useful facts with their diagram rules are recorded here. The two conditionals that make up the definition (L,□) have been separated out and expressed in diagrams.

If $\mathbf{a_w}(L, \square)=T$ then $\exists \mathbf{v}\ \mathbf{a_v}(L)=T$ and $\mathbf{vRw}$.

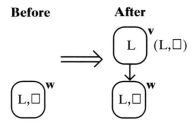

If $\exists$**v** $\mathbf{a_v}(L)=T$ and **vRw** then $\mathbf{a_w}(L, \Box)=T$.

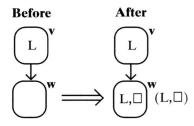

Now we are ready for the demonstration that ($\Box$Out) and ($\Box$In) preserve K-validity. Consider ($\Box$In) first. The rule allows us to move from L, $\Box$ / A to L / $\Box$A, so we must show that if L, $\Box$ $\vDash_K$ A then L $\vDash_K$ $\Box$A. Assume then that L, $\Box$ $\vDash_K$ A, and suppose that L $\nvDash_K$ $\Box$A for indirect proof. Then there must be a world **v** such that $\mathbf{a_v}(L)=T$ and $\mathbf{a_v}(\Box A)=F$.

$$L \nvDash_K \Box A$$
$$\mathbf{a_v}(L)=T$$
$$\mathbf{a_v}(\Box A)=F$$

Since $\mathbf{a_v}(\Box A)=F$, we know by ($\Box$F) that there exists a world **w** such that **vRw** and $\mathbf{a_w}(A)=F$.

$$L \nvDash_K \Box A$$
$$\mathbf{a_v}(L)=T$$
$$\mathbf{a_v}(\Box A)=F$$

vRw

$(\Box F)$

You can see from the diagram that there is a world **v** such that $\mathbf{a_v}(L)=T$ and **vRw**. By definition (L,$\Box$), it follows that $\mathbf{a_w}(L, \Box)=T$.

$$L \nvDash_K \Box A$$
$$\mathbf{a_v}(L)=T$$
$$\mathbf{a_v}(\Box A)=F$$

vRw

$(\Box F)$
$(L,\Box)$

But we know that L, $\Box$ $\vDash_K$ A, which means that since $\mathbf{a_w}(L, \Box)=T$, $\mathbf{a_w}(A)=T$. But this is impossible.

$$L \nvdash_K \square A$$

$$^{v}\mathbf{a}_v(L)=T$$
$$\mathbf{a}_v(\square A)=F$$

$$\boxed{\begin{array}{c} L \\ \sim\square A \end{array}}$$

$$\mathbf{v}\,\mathbf{R}\,\mathbf{w}\ \downarrow$$

$$\boxed{\begin{array}{c} \sim A \\ L,\square \\ A \\ \bot \end{array}}^{w}$$

$$(\square F)$$
$$(L,\square)$$
$$L,\square \vDash_K A$$

EXERCISE *8.3   In similar fashion, show that ($\square$Out) preserves K-validity.

8.2. Soundness of Systems Stronger than K

The soundness of a modal logic S stronger than K can be shown by demonstrating that when the accessibility relation **R** satisfies the corresponding S-conditions, the arguments that correspond to the use of S axioms must be valid. Let us illustrate with the axiom (M): $\square A \rightarrow A$ and its corresponding condition: reflexivity. Note that one is allowed to place axioms anywhere in a proof, so to show that arguments that correspond to such steps are M-valid, we must show that L / $\square A \rightarrow A$ is always M-valid.

We assume for Indirect Proof that L $\nvdash_M$ $\square A \rightarrow A$, that is, that L / $\square A \rightarrow A$ has an M-counterexample. It follows that there is an M-model <**W, R, a**> and a world **w** in **W** where $\mathbf{a_w}(L)=T$ and $\mathbf{a_w}(\square A \rightarrow A)=F$. By ($\rightarrow$F) it follows that $\mathbf{a_w}(\square A)=T$ and $\mathbf{a_w}(A)=F$.

$$\boxed{\begin{array}{c} \sim(\square A \rightarrow A) \\ \square A \\ \sim A \end{array}}$$

$$L \nvdash_M \square A \rightarrow A$$
$$(\rightarrow F)$$
$$(\rightarrow F)$$

Since <**W, R, a**> is an M-model, we know **R** is reflexive: **wRw**, for all **w** in **W**. When we draw the reflexivity arrow into our diagram to express that **wRw**, we may use ($\square$T) with $\mathbf{a_w}(\square A)=T$ to obtain $\mathbf{a_w}(A)=T$. But this is a contradiction.

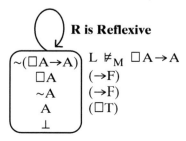

R is Reflexive

$$L \nvdash_M \square A \rightarrow A$$
$$(\rightarrow F)$$
$$(\rightarrow F)$$
$$(\square T)$$

Similarly, we can show that (4) is valid on its corresponding condition: transitivity. Begin by assuming that L / □A→□□A is 4-invalid. Then there is a 4-model <**W, R, a**> and world **w** in **W** where $a_w(L)=T$ and $a_w(□A→□□A)=F$.

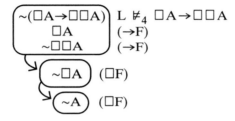

By two uses of (□F) we obtain the following diagram:

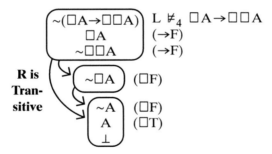

But we know that **R** is transitive, and so by (□T) we have a contradiction.

```
           ~(□A→□□A) ⎞  L ⊭₄ □A→□□A
              □A     ⎟  (→F)
             ~□□A    ⎠  (→F)
    R is    ╱
    Tran-  ╱  ~□A    (□F)
    sitive ╲
            ╲  ~A    (□F)
                A    (□T)
                ⊥
```

Next we will show that arguments for (B) are KB-valid when **R** is symmetrical. Here is the completed diagram. (We have used the Liberalized Placement Principle for simplicity.)

```
          ~(A→□◇A) ⎞  L ⊭_KB A→□◇A
             A     ⎟  (→F)
           ~□◇A    ⎟  (→F)
            ~A     ⎠  (◇F)
             ⊥
   R is    ↖
 Symmetric   ~◇A   (□F)
```

Here is a diagram showing that (5) is 5-valid:

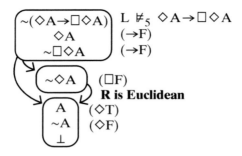

EXERCISE 8.4

a) Show that each of the following axioms is valid on its corresponding condition using diagrams: (D), (CD), (C4), (□M), (C), (L). Consult the chart at the end of Chapter 5 for the corresponding conditions.
b) Show that each of the following principles of S5: (M), (4), (5), and (B), is valid on a semantics where **R** is universal.

8.3. The Tree Model Theorem

The soundness question has now been fully explored. The rest of this chapter will be devoted to proving completeness, along with some related results. At this point, a choice must be made. The completeness proofs to be presented in this chapter depend on properties of the trees we have defined for the various modal logics. In the following chapter, a more standard technique for proving completeness will be covered. It is based on what are called canonical models. The tree method presented here is less powerful because it applies to fewer extensions of K. On the other hand, it has important advantages. First, it is relatively easy to explain. Second, the theorems proven in the course of demonstrating completeness can be used to verify the *adequacy of S-trees*, that is, that an S-tree for an argument is closed iff the argument is S-valid. Third, it is easy to extend the method to systems that include quantifiers, something that cannot be said for the canonical model method. Finally, the tree method is more concrete. When an argument is valid, not only will it follow that there is a proof of the argument, but we will have instructions for actually constructing the proof.

The primary concern in this section is to show what will be called the Tree Model Theorem. This theorem provides one half of what is needed to show the correctness of trees. Once it is established, the completeness of S follows almost immediately.

Assume that S is either K or one of the extensions of K for which we have defined S-trees as explained in Chapters 4 and 6. Assume for simplicity that the defined symbols &, ∨, and ↔ are replaced so that all sentences are written in terms of →, ⊥, and □ alone. We will prove the following theorem:

Tree Model Theorem.
If H / C is S-valid, then the S-tree for H / C is closed.

Before the proof of this theorem is given in detail, it is worth reflecting on the strategies used to prove it. The theorem has the form: if A then B. This is equivalent to the contrapositive: if not B then not A. So to demonstrate the Tree Model Theorem, it will be sufficient to prove (TM) instead.

(TM). If the S-tree for H / C is open (not closed), then H / C is S-invalid.

In Chapters 4 and 6, you learned how to construct counterexamples from open trees for various modal logics. Although you have applied that method many times by now, and have often verified that the method does yield counterexamples of the required kind, no official proof has been given that the method must always yield a counterexample in every case. The proof of (TM) will show just that. Given an open S-tree for H / C, we will demonstrate that the *tree model* that you construct from one of its open branches is an S-counterexample to H / C. It will follow, of course, that H / C is S-invalid. So if an S-tree for H / C is open, then H / C must be S-invalid, and (TM) will be demonstrated.

To begin, an official definition of the tree model constructed for an open branch is needed.

The tree model for an open branch of an S-tree is defined to be the model <**W, R, a**> such that:
W is the set of all worlds on the open branch.
wR**v** iff there is an arrow in the tree from world **w** to **v**.
$a_w(p)=T$ iff p appears (unnegated) in world **w** of the open branch.

The values that **a** assigns to ⊥ and the complex formulas are defined using the conditions (⊥), (→), and (□). Since the arrows in an S-tree ensure that **R** obeys the corresponding conditions for S, we know that the tree model is an S-model.

Now we are ready to prove (TM). The strategy will be to demonstrate something with which you are familiar from the process of verifying that open branches provide counterexamples to arguments. It is that every sentence on the open branch of a tree has the value T in the world in which it is found on the tree model.

Proof of (TM). Let us say that sentence A is *verified* iff whenever A appears in any world **w** in the tree, **a** assigns it true at **w**, (i.e., $a_w(A)=T$). We already know by the definition of **a** on the tree model that all propositional variables are verified. We will now show that the same holds for *all* sentences on the open branch.

Open Branch Lemma.
Every sentence is verified on the tree model.

Once we have shown this Lemma, we will have proven the Tree Model Theorem. The reason is that every tree for H / C begins with a world **w** that contains H and ~C. The Open Branch Lemma will ensure that ~C and all members of H are verified, and so true in **w**. So on the tree model, $a_w(H)=T$ and $a_w(C)=F$, hence the tree model is an S-counterexample to H / C, and H / C is S-invalid. Therefore (TM) (and also the Tree Model Theorem) will follow if we can only prove the Open Branch Lemma.

Proof of the Open Branch Lemma. The proof of this lemma uses the method of *mathematical induction* to show that all sentences are verified. To use mathematical induction, some numerical quantity has to be identified. In our case we will choose the *size* of a sentence, which we define as the number of symbols other than $\perp$ that it contains. (Omitting $\perp$ in the count will make sure that ~B (that is (B→$\perp$)) will always be smaller than (B→C), a fact we need for Case 6 below.) What we hope to show is that whatever size a sentence might have, it will be verified. To do this, we will prove two facts, called the Base Case (BC) and the Inductive Case (IC). The Base Case for this lemma will say that sentences with size 0 are verified. The Inductive Case will say that if all sentences smaller in size than a given sentence A are verified, then it will follow that A is also verified. Here is a list of these two facts for review, where it is understood (of course) that A is any sentence.

(BC) If A has size 0, then A is verified.

(IC) If all sentences smaller in size than A are verified, so is A.

Let us suppose that we succeed in proving these two claims. Then a simple argument can be used to show that A is verified no matter what size A has. To put it another way, it follows that every sentence A is verified. Why is this so? Well, the Base Case shows that all sentences of size 0 are verified. Now consider a sentence A with size 1. Which sentences are smaller than A? Well, sentences with size 0. We know that all those sentences are verified because of the Base Case. But now the Inductive Case ensures that since all sentences smaller than A are verified, A must be verified as well. The same reasoning guarantees that *any* sentence of size 1 is verified. So now we know that sentences of sizes 0 and 1 are all verified. Now consider a sentence A with size 2. Since all sentences of sizes smaller than 2 are now known to be verified, the Inductive Case assures us that A is also verified and so is any other sentence of size 2. Now we know sentences of sizes 0, 1, and 2 are verified. I hope it is now clear that exactly the same argument can be repeated to establish that sentences of sizes 3, 4, and so on are verified. But if A is verified regardless of size, then it follows that every sentence is verified, and this will prove the theorem. So all that remains to prove the Open Branch Lemma is to prove the Base Case (BC) and the Inductive Case (IC) listed above.

Proof of (BC): If A has size 0, then A is verified.
To prove this, suppose that A has size 0. Then A must be ⊥. There is no need to consider this case because ⊥ can never appear in any world of an open branch.

Proof of (IC): If all sentences smaller in size than A are verified, so is A.
To prove this, assume that all sentences smaller in size than A are verified. Let us call this assumption the Inductive Hypothesis (IH).

(IH)   All sentences smaller in size than A are verified.

We must show that A is also verified. The Base Case already tells us that A is verified if it has size 0, so let us now consider the case where A has size 1 or larger. To show that A is verified, we must show that if A is in world **w**, then $a_w(A)=T$. So let us assume (1) and then prove $a_w(A)=T$.

(1)   A is in world **w**.

Since A is size 1 or larger, A must have one of the following four shapes: p, ~C, B→C, or □B. But a sentence of the form ~C must in turn have one of the following four forms: ~p, ~~B, ~(B→C), or ~□B. So let us prove $a_w(A)=T$ in all of the possible seven cases.

Case 1. *A has the form p.* Variables p are verified because the definition of **a** says that $a_w(p)=T$ when p is in **w**.

Case 2. *A has the form ~p.* To show that ~p is verified, we will assume ~p appears in **w**, and demonstrate that $a_w(\sim p)=T$ as follows. Since ~p appears in **w**, p cannot appear in **w**, because the branch was open and having both p and ~p in **w** would have closed the branch. By the definition of the tree model, $a_w(p)=F$. Hence $a_w(\sim p)=T$ by (~).

Case 3. *A has the form ~~B.*

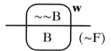

By (1), ~~B appears in world **w**. The tree rules require that (~F) be applied to ~~B so that B is in **w**. By (IH), B is verified because B is smaller in size than A. Since B appears in **w**, it follows that $a_w(B)=T$. By the truth condition (~), we know that $a_w(\sim B)=F$, and by (~) again, $a_w(\sim\sim B)=T$. Hence $a_w(A)=T$ in this case.

Case 4. *A has the form ~(B→C).*

$$\boxed{\begin{array}{c} \sim(B{\rightarrow}C) \\ \hline B \\ \sim C \end{array}}^{\textbf{w}} \quad (\rightarrow F)$$

EXERCISE *8.5   Complete Case 4.

Case 5. *A has the form ~□B.*

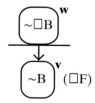

By (1), ~□B appears in **w**. The (□F) rule was applied to ~□B. So on every open branch through **w**, there is a world **v**, with an arrow from **w** to **v**, such that ~B is in **v**. Since ~B is smaller than A, (IH) ensures that ~B is verified. So $a_v(\sim B)=T$ and $a_v(B)=F$ by (~). So there is a world **v**′ such that **wRv**′ and $a_v(B)=F$. By ($\Box$), $a_w(\Box B)=F$, and hence by (~), $a_w(\sim\Box B)=T$. So $a_w(A)=T$ in this case.

Case 6. *A has the form B→C.*

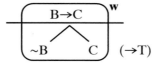

By (1), B→C appears in world **w**. By the (→T) rule, the branch on which B→C is found forks, with the result that either ~B or C is in **w** on the open branch. Suppose it is ~B that appears in **w**. The definition of the size of a sentence guarantees that ~B is smaller in size than A=B→C, so by (IH), ~B is verified. Since ~B is in **w**, $a_w(\sim B)=T$. By the truth condition (~), it follows that $a_w(B)=F$, and so by (→), $a_w(B→C)=T$. Now suppose it is C that appears in **w**. Again by (IH), C is verified and in **w**, so $a_w(C)=T$. It follows by (→) that $a_w(B→C)=T$. So whether ~B or C is in **w**, $a_w(B→C)=T$, and $a_w(A)=T$ in this case.

Case 7. *A has the form $\Box B$.*

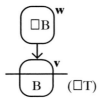

By (1), $\Box B$ appears in **w**. We must show that $a_w(\Box B)=T$. By ($\Box$), this means that we must show that for any world **v**, if **wRv** then $a_v(B)=T$. So let **v** be any world in **W** such that **wRv**. Here is how to show that $a_v(B)=T$. By the definition of **R** on the tree model it follows that there is an arrow pointing from **w** to **v**. So the ($\Box$T) rule was applied to $\Box B$, so as to place B in **v**. B is smaller in size than A, and so by (IH), B is verified, with the result that $a_v(B)=T$. (Note that the same reasoning would apply to any other world **v**′ such that **wRv**′.) It follows that for *any* **v** in **W**, if **wRv** then $a_v(B)=T$, so by ($\Box$), $a_w(\Box B)=T$. Therefore $a_w(A)=T$ in this case.

EXERCISE 8.6 Construct a K-tree for the following K-invalid argument: ~~□(p→q) / □(p→~q). Now construct the tree model for the open branch in the tree. Write an essay explaining how (BC) and (IC) guarantee that each and every sentence on this open branch is verified.

The proof of the Tree Model Theorem is now complete. Not only does this theorem contribute to showing that the tree method is correct, but it will also play an important role in the proof of the completeness of propositional modal logics, a topic we turn to next.

8.4. Completeness of Many Modal Logics

It is a simple matter to use the results of this chapter to show that many modal logics are complete. The proof for K illustrates the basic strategy for all the other systems. To show the completeness of K, we will need to show that every K-valid argument is provable in K. So suppose that argument H / C is K-valid. It follows by the Tree Model Theorem that the tree for this argument is closed. But if the tree for H / C is closed, H / C must have a proof in K because we have explained how to convert each K tree into a corresponding proof in Section 7.1. Exactly the same argument works to show the completeness of any modal logic S for which we can verify the Tree Model Theorem, and for which we can give a method for converting closed trees into proofs. Since the Tree Model Theorem was proven for any given system S, completeness follows for all the modal logics discussed in Chapter 7. A diagram of this reasoning follows:

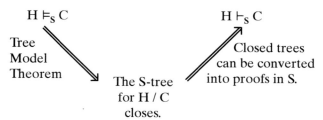

EXERCISE 8.7

a) Demonstrate in detail that M is complete.

b) The solution to Exercise 6.12 guarantees that any S5-tree will have a universal arrow structure. Use this fact to demonstrate that S5 is complete for universal frames.

8.5. Decision Procedures

A *decision procedure* for a system is a method that determines for each argument whether it is valid or invalid in a finite number of steps. The completeness proof given here can be used to show that the tree method serves as a decision procedure for many of the systems discussed in Chapter 7. For example, to determine whether an argument is K-valid, construct its tree. We know that if the tree is open, then the argument must be invalid by the Tree Model Theorem. If the tree is closed, we know that the argument is valid because the tree can be converted to a proof, and any provable argument must be valid because of the soundness of K. So K-trees will serve as a decision procedure for K provided they can always be finished in a finite number of steps. However, it is easy to verify that each step in the construction of a K-tree reduces the number of symbols in the resulting sentences. So the process of applying the rules eventually ends in atoms and the tree is finite. The same reasoning may be applied to show that trees for many systems that are formed from the following axioms serve as a decision method: (M), (B), (5), (CD), and (□M).

However, there are difficulties with systems that involve axioms like (D), (C), and (C4), whose corresponding conditions involve the construction of new worlds in the tree. For example, when trees are constructed for a serial **R**, each world in the tree must have an arrow exiting from it pointing to another world. But that other world must also have another world related to *it*, and so on. As a result, a tree for a serial relation may go on forever, and so the tree method is not a decision procedure since it does not terminate in a finite amount of time. In Section 6.5, a strategy was explained that partly overcomes this problem. It was to add loop arrows to certain worlds to guarantee seriality. This method works, for example, to provide a decision procedure for D.

There is a more serious problem in using trees for solving the decision problem. It can be illustrated by the K4-tree for the following argument, which was given as Exercise 6.4f: □(□p→p) / □p. Here is what the tree looks like in the early stages of its construction:

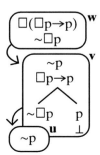

Since this is a K4-tree, it is necessary to add an arrow from world **w** to world **u**, to guarantee transitivity. When this arrow is added, however, (□T) must be applied to □(□p→p) in world **w**, to place □p→p in world **u**. After (→T) and (□F) are applied in world **u**, the tree looks like this:

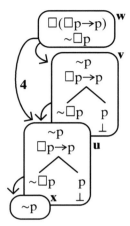

Notice that the contents of worlds **v** and **u** are identical, and that it was necessary to create a new world **x** to satisfy (□F). But now a 4-arrow from **w** must be drawn to this new world, with the result that □p→p must be added there. So the contents of **x** will be identical to those of **v** and **u**, with the result that a new arrow pointing from **x** to yet another new world will be needed. It should be clear that this tree will never terminate. Since a decision procedure requires that we obtain an answer in a finite number of steps, the tree method does not serve as a decision procedure for K4, nor for some other systems that contain (4).

The reader should know that trees are not the only method one might use to show that a modal logic has a decision procedure. A more abstract and powerful method for doing so is called *filtration* (Chellas, 1980, Sections 2.3, 2.8). The basic idea is that to show that whenever an argument H / C has an S-counterexample, then it also has another S-counterexample in a model with a *finite frame*, that is, one where there is a finite number of possible worlds in W. When this occurs, we say that S has the *finite model property*. Filtration is a technique that allows one to reduce an S-counterexample for an argument H / C, by collapsing together into one world all those worlds that agree on the values of sentences that appear in H / C (including sentences that appear as parts of other sentences). Very often filtration produces a model with a finite frame, so it follows that S has the finite model property.

When S has the finite model property, it follows that S has a decision procedure, for to decide the validity of an argument H / C, one may use the following (long-winded and impractical, but effective) procedure. First, order all the finite models for S, and then oscillate between carrying out steps in the following tasks a) and b).

a) Apply all possible sequences of rules of S to H in an attempt to derive C.
b) Calculate the value of members of H and C in each finite model in an attempt to find an S-counterexample to H / C.

If we perform some of task a), followed by some of task b), then some of task a) and so on, we are guaranteed to eventually have an answer after a finite number of steps. For if H / C has a proof in S, it will be found by doing only a finite number of steps of task a), and if H / C has no proof, then it will (by the adequacy of S) have an S-counterexample, which will be found after performing only a finite number of steps in task b).

8.6. Automatic Proofs

The tree method has another use. Suppose H / C is provable in any modal logic S that we have been able to show is sound and complete by the reasoning in this chapter. Then the S-tree for H / C must close, for if it were open, it would have an S-counterexample by the Tree Model Theorem, and this conflicts with the soundness of S. It follows that the tree method can be used to construct a proof of H / C in S. This means that if H / C has any proof at all in S, the tree method is guaranteed to find a such a proof. So there is never any need for creative abilities in proof finding for the modal logics covered in Chapter 7. If a proof is possible at all, you can automatically construct a proof by building a tree and converting it to a proof by the methods of Chapter 7.

8.7. Adequacy of Trees

So far, there is no guarantee that the tree method is adequate, that is, that S-trees identify exactly the S-valid arguments. By putting together facts that have already been demonstrated, it is a simple matter to show that S-trees are indeed *adequate*, that is, that the S-tree for H / C is closed iff H / C is S-valid (H $\vDash_S$ C). The demonstration depends on the reasoning used to prove the completeness of S together with the fact that S is sound. The structure of the reasoning is illustrated in the following diagram:

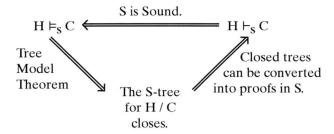

We must show the following:

(S-Tree Adequacy) The S-tree for H / C closes   iff   H ⊨$_S$ C.

The Tree Model Theorem provides a proof for one direction of the iff, namely, that if H ⊨$_S$ C then the S-tree for H / C closes. (See the arrow from the top left to the bottom center of the diagram.) To show the other direction (namely, that if the S-tree for H / C closes, then H ⊨$_S$ C), the reasoning goes in two steps. Suppose that the S-tree for H / C closes. (See the bottom center of the diagram.) Section 7 explained how to convert an S-tree into a proof in S. So H ⊢$_S$ C. (See the top right part of the diagram.) But the soundness of S was shown in Sections 8.1–8.2. So it follows that H ⊨$_S$ C. It should be obvious now that three basic concepts introduced in this book all coincide: S-validity, closure of an S-tree, and provability in S. This provides strong confirmation that we have been on the right track in formulating the various propositional modal logics.

8.8. Properties of Frames that Correspond to No Axioms

We know that certain axioms correspond to conditions on frames, in the sense that by adding these axioms to K we can create a system that is sound and complete with respect to the notion of validity where frames meet those conditions. For example, we showed axiom (M) corresponds to reflexivity, (4) to transitivity, and (B) to symmetry. In this section we ask a new question. Is it always possible to find an axiom that corresponds to a given frame condition? It turns out that the answer is "No". For example, there are no axioms that correspond to such "negative" conditions as irreflexivity, intransitivity, and asymmetry, because any such axioms would already be derivable from the principles of K alone.

The methods developed to show the Tree Model Theorem may be used to prove this. The proofs depend on features of the frame defined by the tree model of any K-tree. The accessibility relation **R** defined by such a tree model is such that **wRv** iff there is an arrow from **w** to **v** in the K-tree. But the arrows in a K-tree diagrams have the structure of an upside down tree.

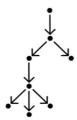

Each arrow is entered into the diagram using the (□F) rule, which places that arrow so that it points to a new world in the tree. It follows that no arrows loop back on themselves, that is, none of them point from world **w** back to world **w**, and so the frame for the K-tree model is irreflexive.

This fact may be used to show that there is no axiom that corresponds to irreflexivity. To do that, let us assume that there is an axiom (I) that corresponds to irreflexivity, and derive a contradiction. Let I-models be K-models with irreflexive frames. Then the system K + (I) must be sound and complete for I-validity, for that is what it means to say that (I) corresponds to irreflexivity. Since (I) is provable in K + (I), it follows that (I) must be I-valid. Now consider the K-tree headed by ∼(I), the negation of the axiom (I). If the tree is open, then by the proof of the Tree Model Theorem we can construct a K-model <**W, R, a**> such that $a_w(I)$=F. But note that the tree model so constructed is irreflexive, so it would follow that (I) has an I-counterexample, which is impossible, since (I) was I-valid. So the K-tree for ∼(I) must be closed, which means that it can be converted into a proof of (I) in K. Since all modal logics we discuss are extensions of K, (I) is provable in all modal logics, and so there is no need for adding (I) as an independent axiom to K. It follows that K is already adequate for I-validity, so no new axiom is required.

The proof that no axiom corresponds to either asymmetry or intransitivity is similar. Simply show that each K-tree is asymmetric and intransitive, and rehearse the same argument to show that these conditions correspond to no axioms. Here is why the frame for each K-tree is asymmetric. Whenever an arrow is introduced in a K-tree by (□F), the arrow always points to a new world introduced with that arrow. So no new arrow points back to any previously introduced world during tree construction. As a result, the frame defined by a K-tree can never have **wRv** and **vRw** since any arrow exiting from world **v** must point to a new world different from **w** (or **v**).

A similar argument works to show that the frame for each K-tree is intransitive. In this case, it must be shown that if **wRv** and **vRu**, then not **wRu**. So suppose that **wRv** and **vRu**. Then worlds **w** and **u** must be distinct because otherwise **wRw**, and this conflicts with irreflexivity, which was proven above. But in K-trees, the introduction of new arrows and worlds by (□F) guarantees that no more than one arrow points to a world. So **wRu** does not hold, for otherwise there would have to be two distinct arrows pointing to world **u**, one for world **w** and the other for world **v**.

EXERCISE 8.8   Give proofs in detail that asymmetry and intransitivity correspond to no axioms.

9

Completeness Using Canonical Models

Not all the systems mentioned in this book have been shown to be complete, only the ones for which a method has been described for converting trees into proofs. In this section, a more powerful strategy for showing completeness will be presented that applies to a wider range of propositional modal logics. It is a version of the so-called Henkin or canonical model technique, which is widely used in logic. This method is more abstract than the method of Chapter 8, and it is harder to adapt to systems that include quantifiers and identity, but a serious student of modal logic should become familiar with it. The fundamental idea on which the method is based is the notion of a maximally consistent set. Maximally consistent sets play the role of possible worlds. They completely describe the facts of a world by including either A or ~A (but never both) for each sentence A in the language.

9.1. The Lindenbaum Lemma

A crucial step in demonstrating completeness with such maximally consistent sets is to prove the famous Lindenbaum Lemma. To develop that result, some concepts and notation need to be introduced. When M is an infinite set of sentences, 'M, A' indicates the result of adding A to the set M, and 'M $\vdash_S$ C' indicates that there is a finite list H formed from some of the members of M, such that H $\vdash_S$ C. Set M' *is an extension of* M, provided that every member of M is a member of M'. We say that set M *is consistent in* S iff M $\nvdash_S \perp$. M *is maximal* iff for every sentence A, either A or ~A is in M. M is *maximally consistent for* S (or mc for short) iff M is both maximal and consistent in S. When it is clear from the context what system is at issue, or if the results being discussed are general with respect to S, the subscript 'S' on '⊢' will be dropped, and we will use 'consistent' in place of 'consistent for S'. It should be remembered, however, that what counts as an mc set depends on the system S. We are now ready to state the Lindenbaum Lemma.

Lindenbaum Lemma. Every consistent set has an mc extension.

This means that it is always possible to add sentences to a consistent set so that consistency is preserved and the result is maximal. The proof of the Lindenbaum Lemma depends on displaying a method for doing just that.

Proof of the Lindenbaum Lemma. Let M be any consistent set, that is, $M \nvdash \bot$. We will explain how to construct an mc set m that is an extension of M. First, order all the sentences of the language in an infinite list: A_1, A_2, .. A_i, .. The notation 'A_i' stands for the ith sentence in the list. Here is a method for adding sentences to M in stages so as to create m, the desired mc set. First we create a whole series of sets: M_1, M_2, .. M_i, .. in the following manner. Let M_1 be the set M, and consider the first sentence A_1. If M_1, A_1 would be a consistent set, then let M_2 be identical to this set, but if M_1, A_1 would be an inconsistent set, then let M_2 be M_1, ~A_1. In short, add A_1 to M_1 if doing so leaves the result consistent, otherwise add ~A_1. So M_2 is defined officially as follows:

$$M_2 = M_1, A_1 \qquad \text{if } M_1, A_1 \nvdash \bot.$$
$$M_2 = M_1, \sim A_1 \qquad \text{if } M_1, A_1 \vdash \bot.$$

Now consider the next sentence A_2, and create M_3 from M_2 in the same fashion. You add A_2 to M_2 if doing so would make the result consistent, and you add ~A_2 otherwise.

$$M_3 = M_2, A_2 \qquad \text{if } M_2, A_2 \nvdash \bot.$$
$$M_3 = M_2, \sim A_2 \qquad \text{if } M_2, A_2 \vdash \bot.$$

Continue this construction for each of the sentences A_i.

$$M_{i+1} = M_i, A_i \qquad \text{if } M_i, A_i \nvdash \bot.$$
$$M_{i+1} = M_i, \sim A_i \qquad \text{if } M_i, A_i \vdash \bot.$$

This process of constructing $M_1, M_2, .., M_i, ..$ begins with the consistent set M, and at each stage i, it either adds a sentence A_i if doing so would be consistent, otherwise it adds ~A_i. Either way, as we will soon see, each set in this series is a new consistent set.

Now we can define the mc set m, which is the desired extension of M. Let m be the set containing the members of M and each of the sentences (either A_j or $\sim A_j$) that was added in the construction of any of the M_j. So the set m is the infinite set that would result from adding each sentence (or its negation) to M according to the recipe for constructing the sets M_j. By definition, m is an extension of M. So to prove the Lindenbaum Lemma, we need only show that m is a maximally consistent set. Clearly the construction of m ensures that it is maximal. So it remains to show that m is consistent.

Proof that m is consistent. We will show first that the process of constructing the M_j preserves consistency, that is, that if M_i is consistent, then so is M_{i+1}. So suppose that M_i is consistent. Consider A_i. If A_i was added to M_i, then $M_i, A_i \nvdash \perp$, and M_{i+1} is consistent. If $\sim A_i$ was added to M_i, then $M_i, A_i \vdash \perp$, and we have $M_i \vdash \sim A_i$ by (IP). Suppose for a minute that M_{i+1} is not consistent. Then $M_i, \sim A_i \vdash \perp$, and so by (IP), $M_i \vdash A_i$, which means that $M_i \vdash \perp$ by ($\perp$In). But this is incompatible with the assumption that M_i is consistent. So M_{i+1} must be consistent. We have just shown that the process of constructing M_{i+1} from M_i preserves consistency. Since this process begins with the consistent set M, it follows that M_j is consistent for each j.

We still need to demonstrate that m is consistent, which is not (quite) the same thing as showing that $M_j \nvdash \perp$ for each j. However, the consistency of m follows from the following general lemma concerning the consistency of sets of the kind we have constructed.

M Lemma. Suppose that $M_1, M_2, \ldots M_i, \ldots$ is a series of consistent sets each of which adds sentences to M, and each one an extension of its predecessor. If m is the set containing all sentences in M and all sentences added to any of the M_i, then m is consistent.

Proof of the M Lemma. Let $M_1, M_2, \ldots M_i, \ldots, M$, and m be as described in the Lemma. We will show m is consistent by supposing the opposite and deriving a contradiction. So suppose that $m \vdash \perp$ (m is not consistent). It follows by the definition of $\vdash$ for sets that there is a finite list H of members of m that are sufficient for the proof of $\perp$. So there is a finite subset M' of m such that $M' \vdash \perp$. Since M' is finite, there must be a largest j such that the sentence A_j is a member of M'. Since the sets $M_1, M_2, \ldots M_i, \ldots$ grow larger with larger index j, each of the sentences of M' must have been already added by the time M_j was constructed, and so all members of M' are already in M_{j+1}. Since $M' \vdash \perp$, and M_j includes all members of M', it follows that $M_{j+1} \vdash \perp$. But that conflicts with the fact that each M_i in the series is consistent. Therefore we must conclude that m is consistent.

This completes the proof of the Lindenbaum Lemma.

9.2. The Canonical Model

The next stage in the completeness method based on mc sets is to define what is called the canonical model. Let S be any system obtained by adding axioms described in this book to K=PL+($\square$In)+($\square$Out). The *canonical model* <**W**, **R**, **a**> for S is defined as follows:

W contains each and every mc set for system S.
(Def**a**) $\mathbf{a_w}(A)=T$ iff $\mathbf{w} \vdash_S A$.
(Def**R**) $\mathbf{wRv}$ iff for all sentences B, if $\mathbf{w} \vdash_S \square B$ then $\mathbf{v} \vdash_S B$.

It is important to prove that the canonical model just defined is a K-model. So the rest of this section is devoted to showing just that. We drop the subscript 'S' in what follows to save eyestrain.

Canonical Model Theorem.
The canonical model for S is a K-model.

Proof of the Canonical Model Theorem. If <**W**, **R**, **a**> is a K-model, **W** must be nonempty, **R** must be a binary relation on **W**, and **a** must obey the clauses for an assignment function. **R** is clearly a binary relation on **W**. **W** is nonempty by the following reasoning. The system S has been proven consistent in Chapter 8, Sections 1.2–1.3. Since every provable sentence is valid in S, and since the sentence $\perp$ is invalid, we know that $\perp$ is not provable. So the empty set {} has the feature that {} $\nvdash_S \perp$. Since {} is consistent, it follows by the Lindenbaum Lemma that {} can be extended to an mc set **w** in **W**. To complete the demonstration that the canonical model is a K-model, we must show that **a** obeys ($\perp$), ($\rightarrow$), and ($\square$).

*Proof that **a** obeys ($\perp$).* We must show that $\mathbf{a_w}(\perp)=F$. According to (Def**a**), this means we must show that $\mathbf{w} \nvdash \perp$, that is, that **w** is consistent. But that follows from the fact that **w** is an mc set.

*Proof that **a** obeys ($\rightarrow$).* To show ($\rightarrow$), it will be sufficient to show ($\rightarrow$T) and ($\rightarrow$F).

($\rightarrow$T)   If $\mathbf{a_w}(A \rightarrow B)=T$ then $\mathbf{a_w}(A)=F$ or $\mathbf{a_w}(B)=T$.
($\rightarrow$F)   If $\mathbf{a_w}(A \rightarrow B)=F$ then $\mathbf{a_w}(A)=T$ and $\mathbf{a_w}(B)=F$.

By (Def**a**) this amounts to showing ($\rightarrow\vdash$) and ($\rightarrow\nvdash$).

($\rightarrow\vdash$)   If $\mathbf{w} \vdash$ A$\rightarrow$B then $\mathbf{w} \nvdash$ A or $\mathbf{w} \vdash$ B.
($\rightarrow\nvdash$)   If $\mathbf{w} \nvdash$ A$\rightarrow$B then $\mathbf{w} \vdash$ A and $\mathbf{w} \nvdash$ B.

To establish ($\rightarrow\vdash$), assume $\mathbf{w} \vdash$ A$\rightarrow$B. Since $\mathbf{w}$ is maximal, we know that either A or ~A is in $\mathbf{w}$. If A is in $\mathbf{w}$, it follows by the rule (MP) that $\mathbf{w} \vdash$ B. On the other hand, if ~A is in $\mathbf{w}$, then $\mathbf{w} \nvdash$ A, since $\mathbf{w}$ is consistent. So it follows that either $\mathbf{w} \nvdash$ A or $\mathbf{w} \vdash$ B.

To establish ($\rightarrow\nvdash$), assume $\mathbf{w} \nvdash$ A$\rightarrow$B. So A$\rightarrow$B is not in $\mathbf{w}$. By the fact that $\mathbf{w}$ is maximal, it follows that ~(A$\rightarrow$B) is in $\mathbf{w}$. It is a simple exercise in propositional logic to show that ~(A$\rightarrow$B) entails both A and ~B. (See Exercise 7.1.) So both $\mathbf{w} \vdash$ A and $\mathbf{w} \vdash$ ~B. Since $\mathbf{w}$ is consistent, it follows that $\mathbf{w} \nvdash$ B.

*Proof that **a** obeys* ($\square$). To establish ($\square$), it will be sufficient to show ($\square$T) and ($\square$F).

($\square$T)   If $\mathbf{a_w}(\square$A$)$=T then for all $\mathbf{v}$ in $\mathbf{W}$, if $\mathbf{w}R\mathbf{v}$, then $\mathbf{a_v}($A$)$=T.
($\square$F)   If $\mathbf{a_w}(\square$A$)$=F then for some $\mathbf{v}$ in $\mathbf{W}$, $\mathbf{w}R\mathbf{v}$, and $\mathbf{a_v}($A$)$=F.

By (Def**a**), this amounts to showing ($\vdash\square$) and ($\nvdash\square$).

($\vdash\square$)   If $\mathbf{w} \vdash \square$A, then for all $\mathbf{v}$ in $\mathbf{W}$, if $\mathbf{w}R\mathbf{v}$, then $\mathbf{v} \vdash$ A.
($\nvdash\square$)   If $\mathbf{w} \nvdash \square$A, then for some $\mathbf{v}$ in $\mathbf{W}$, $\mathbf{w}R\mathbf{v}$, and $\mathbf{v} \nvdash$ A.

Proof of ($\vdash\square$). Suppose $\mathbf{w} \vdash \square$A, and let $\mathbf{v}$ be any member of $\mathbf{W}$ such that $\mathbf{w}R\mathbf{v}$. By (Def**R**), for any sentence B, if $\mathbf{w} \vdash \square$B, then $\mathbf{v} \vdash$ B. So $\mathbf{v} \vdash$ A.

The following lemmas will be used in the proof of ($\nvdash\square$).

Extension Lemma.
If M$'$ is an extension of M, then if M $\vdash$ A then M$'$ $\vdash$ A.

Proof of the Extension Lemma. This should be obvious. If M $\vdash$ A, then H $\vdash$ A where H is a finite list of some members of M. Since M$'$ is an extension of M, H is also a finite list of some members of M$'$ such that H $\vdash$ A. Therefore M$'$ $\vdash$ A.

Let V be a list of sentences that result from removing $\square$ from those members of $\mathbf{w}$ with the shape $\square$B. So set V is defined by (V), where the symbol '$\in$' means 'is a member of'.

(V)   B $\in$ V iff $\square$B $\in$ $\mathbf{w}$.

Let □V be the set that results from adding □ to each member of V. So for example, if **w** is the set {A, □C, ~□B, □D, □A→E}, then V is {C, D}, and □V is {□C, □D}. This example illustrates a general feature of □V, namely that all its members are in **w**.

V-Lemma. **w** is an extension of □V.

Proof of V-Lemma. Consider any member C of □V. Then C is □B for some sentence B in V. By (V), □B (that is C) is in **w**. It follows that any member of □V is in **w**.

Consistency Lemma. If **w** ⊬ □A, then V, ~A is consistent.

Proof of the Consistency Lemma. Suppose **w** ⊬ □A. We will prove that V, ~A is consistent by assuming the opposite and deriving a contradiction. So suppose that V, ~A ⊢ ⊥. Then H, ~A ⊢ ⊥, where H, ~A is some finite list of members of V, ~A. By (IP), H ⊢ A. We proved that the rule of General Necessitation (GN) is derivable in K (Section 1.8), so it follows that □H ⊢ □A. But □V is an extension of □H, since V is an extension of H. The V-Lemma tells us that **w** is an extension of □V, so **w** is an extension of □H and by the Extension Lemma it follows that **w** ⊢ □A. This conflicts with our first assumption, so V, ~A ⊬ ⊥ and V, ~A must be consistent.

R Lemma. If **v** is an extension of V, ~A then **wRv**.

Proof of the R Lemma. Assume **v** is an extension of V. According to (DefR), **wRv** holds iff for any B, **w** ⊢ □B then **v** ⊢ B. So to show **wRv**, let B be any sentence, suppose **w** ⊢ □B and show **v** ⊢ B as follows. From **w** ⊢ □B, we know that □B ∈ **w**, because otherwise it would follow from the fact that **w** is maximal that ~□B ∈ **w**, and so **w** ⊢ ~□B, which conflicts with the consistency of **w**. Since □B ∈ **w**, it follows by (V) that B ∈ V. But **v** is an extension of V, ~A so B ∈ **v**. It follows that **v** ⊢ B.

We are finally ready to prove (□⊬).

Proof of (□⊬). Suppose **w** ⊬ □A. The Consistency Lemma guarantees that V, ~A is consistent. By the Lindenbaum Lemma, we can extend the set V, ~A to an mc set **v** in **W**. By the R Lemma, **wRv**. Since **v** is an extension of V, ~A, it also follows that ~A ∈ **v**, and hence by the consistency of **v** that **v** ⊬ A. We have now found a mc set **v** with the feature that **wRv** and **v** ⊬ A, which finishes the proof of (□⊬).

9.3. The Completeness of Modal Logics Based on K

The canonical model may now be used to show the completeness of many systems built on K. To demonstrate completeness of one of these systems S, we must show that if H / C is S-valid, then H ⊢$_S$ C. It is easier to show the contrapositive, that is, if H ⊬$_S$ C, then H / C is S-invalid. So assume H ⊬$_S$ C. It follows by (IP) that H, ~C ⊬$_S$ ⊥. Since H, ~C is consistent, the Lindenbaum Lemma ensures that the set containing members of H, ~C can be extended to a mc set **w**. Now consider the canonical model <**W**, **R**, **a**>. Since **w** is an mc set, it is in **W**. By (Def**a**), and the fact that every member B in H, ~C is such that **w** ⊢ B, we have **a$_w$**(H)=T and **a$_w$**(~C)=T. So **a$_w$**(C)=F. By the Canonical Model Theorem, the canonical model is a K-model. So the canonical model is a K-counterexample to H / C. If we can show that the frame <**W**, **R**> of the canonical model obeys the corresponding properties for system S, then it will follow that the canonical model is a S-counterexample, and so H / C is S-invalid. It would then follow that S is complete.

So the only thing that remains for the proof of completeness is to show that the canonical model's frame obeys the properties corresponding to system S. For example, when S is system M, then we must show **R** is reflexive. It will follow that the canonical model is an M-counterexample to H / C so that H / C is M-invalid.

In preparation for demonstrations of this kind, we will first show a useful fact about **R** on the canonical model. We present it with its diagram.

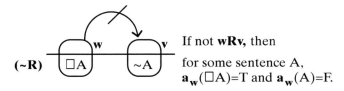

(~R)   If not **wRv**, then for some sentence A, **a$_w$**(□A)=T and **a$_w$**(A)=F.

EXERCISE *9.1   Prove (~R). (Hint: (~R) can be proven from the contrapositive of one side of (Def**R**) along with (Def**a**)).

It also helps to prove a second fact. Let us say that an mc set **w** is *(deductively) closed* iff if H ⊢ C and **a$_w$**(H)=T, then **a$_w$**(C)=T. A closed set **w** has the feature that when the argument H / C is provable in S, **a** will assign its conclusion T in **w** as long as its hypotheses were also assigned T in **w**.

Closed Lemma.   In any model that obeys (Def**a**), **w** is closed.

Proof of the Closed Lemma. Suppose H ⊢ C and $\mathbf{a_w}$(H)=T. Let B be any member of H. Then $\mathbf{a_w}$(B)=T and by (Def**a**) **w** ⊢ B. So each member of H is provable from **w**. This, along with H ⊢ C, ensures that **w** ⊢ C, and so by (Def**a**), it follows that $\mathbf{a_w}$(C)=T.

Now we are ready to show that **R** meets the corresponding condition for a wide range of axioms of modal logic. Let us take (M) first. We want to show that **R** is reflexive on the canonical model when (M) (that is, □A→A) is provable in S. To do so, we assume the opposite and derive a contradiction. Assume, then, that **R** is not reflexive. So for some world **w**, not **wRw**, which is expressed with the following diagram.

By (~**R**), we have that $\mathbf{a_w}$(□A)=T and $\mathbf{a_w}$(A)=F, for some sentence A.

But we know that (M) is provable in S, so □A ⊢ A, by (MP). Since every world **w** in **W** is closed, it follows from $\mathbf{a_w}$(□A)=T that $\mathbf{a_w}$(A)=T.

However, this conflicts with (~), the truth condition for ~: $\mathbf{a_w}$(~A)=T iff $\mathbf{a_w}$(A)=F. Since a contradiction was obtained from the assumption that **R** is not reflexive, it follows that **R** is reflexive on the canonical model.

Let us give the same kind of proof in the case of axiom (4): □A→□□A. Here we want to show that **R** is transitive on the canonical model given that (4) is provable in S. We begin by assuming that **R** is not transitive, which means that there are worlds **w**, **v**, and **u** such that **wRv**, and **vRu**, but not **wRu**.

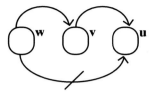

We apply (~**R**) to introduce sentences □A and ~A into the diagram.

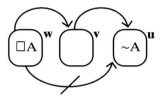

We then use the presence of (4) in S and the fact that **w** is closed to obtain $a_w(\Box\Box A)=T$, from which we obtain a contradiction with two uses of (□T).

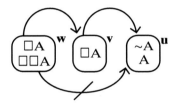

EXERCISE 9.2

a) Show that **R** is shift reflexive on the canonical model when (□M) is provable. (Hint: Assume **wRv** and not **vRv**. Since **w** is closed and □(□A→A) is provable, $a_w(\Box(\Box A\to A))=T$. Now produce a contradiction.)

b) Similarly, show **R** is serial when (D) is provable. (Hint: There are many ways to do this, but a quick method is to note that (⊥D): ~□⊥ is derivable in D. (See Exercise 7.10.) By closure of **w**, it follows that $a_w(\sim\Box\bot)=T$. Now use the fact that the canonical model obeys (□) to argue that **wRu** for some **u**.)

To obtain the relevant results for (B) and (5), it is useful to show the following fact about **R** on the canonical model:

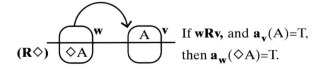

(**R◇**) If **wRv,** and $a_v(A)=T$, then $a_w(\Diamond A)=T$.

The condition (**R◇**) makes sense, for if A is T in a world accessible from **w**, then this means that A must be possible in **w**.

Now let us turn to the proof for (B). We assume that **R** is not symmetric, and then apply both (~**R**) and (**R◇**).

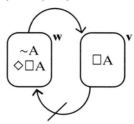

We then use the dual of (B) (namely, ◇□A→A) to argue that any world where ◇□A is T also assigns T to A. This provides a contradiction.

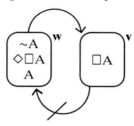

EXERCISE 9.4
   a) Show that **R** is euclidean on the canonical model in the presence of (5).
   b) Show that **R** is unique on the canonical model when (CD) is present. (Hint: Use the fact that if two worlds differ, then there must be some sentence A such that A is in one world and ~A is in the other.)
   *c) Show that **R** is connected when (L): □(□A→B) v □((B&□B)→A) is provable. (Hard.)

EXERCISE 9.5   (Project) Prove that S5 is complete for models with universal frames. (Hint: Assume H ⊬ C, and use the Lindenbaum Lemma to find an mc set **o** such that **a₀**(H)=T and **a₀**(C)=F. Adjust the definition of **W** in the canonical model so that **w** ∈ **W** iff **oRw**. **R** is then defined in the usual way for members of **W**. Establish that <**W, R**> is reflexive and euclidean and use reflexivity to prove that **o** is in **W**. Then show <**W, R**> is universal as follows. Let **w** and **v** be members of **W**. Then **oRw** and **oRv**. Since <**W, R**> is euclidean, **wRv**. Take special care with the proof that **a** obeys (□F).)

EXERCISE 9.6 (Project) Show the completeness of TL. TL is a tense logic that is a strengthening of system Kt mentioned in Section 2.7. TL has two intensional operators **G** and **H**. The weak modal operators **F** and **P** are defined from **G** and **H** on analogy with $\Box$ and $\Diamond$.

(DefF) $FA =_{df} {\sim}G{\sim}A$ (DefP) $PA =_{df} {\sim}H{\sim}A$

The rest of the notation of TL consists of the propositional connectives $\to$ and $\bot$, and all other notation is defined in the usual way. The rules of TL consist of the rules of propositional logic, together with (HIn), (HOut), (GIn), and (GOut), and four axioms:

(FH)   **FHA$\to$A**   (PG)   **PGA$\to$A**
(G4)   **GA$\to$GGA**   (H4)   **HA$\to$HHA**

The semantics for TL is based on the one found in Section 5.2, and defined as follows. A TL-model is a quadruple: **<W, R, L, a>** satisfying the following conditions:

W is not empty.
R and **L** are binary relations on **W**.
R and **L** are both transitive, and they obey **wRv** iff **vLw**.
a is an assignment function that satisfies ($\bot$), ($\to$), (G), and (H).

(G) $\mathbf{a_w(GA)}$=T iff for all **v** in **W**, if **wRv** then $\mathbf{a_v(A)}$=T.
(H) $\mathbf{a_w(HA)}$=T iff for all **v** in **W**, if **wLv** then $\mathbf{a_v(A)}$=T.

EXERCISE 9.7 (Project) Show a locative logic is complete. (See Sections 2.8 and 5.5.)

So far, completeness has been demonstrated only for systems for which completeness was already shown in Chapter 8. The true power of the canonical model method becomes apparent when it comes to the more difficult cases of systems that include (C4) (density) and (C) (convergence). We will show next that **R** is dense on the canonical model when (C4): $\Box\Box A\to\Box A$ is provable. For this proof it will be convenient to prove the following fact, which is the "converse" of **(R$\Diamond$)**.

(CR$\Diamond$)   **uRv** provided that if $\mathbf{a_v(A)}$=T then $\mathbf{a_u(\Diamond A)}$=T for all wffs A.

To prove (CR$\Diamond$) let us assume:

If $\mathbf{a_v(A)}$=T, then $\mathbf{a_u(\Diamond A)}$=T, for all wffs A, which we may express in the form of a diagram rule.

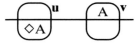

Now let us assume not **uRv** for Indirect Proof. By (~**R**), we know that for some sentence A, $a_u(\square A)=T$ and $a_v(A)=F$.

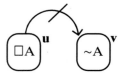

By the diagram rule for our assumption, $a_u(\lozenge\sim A)=T$. But $\lozenge\sim A \vdash \sim\square A$ by ($\lozenge\sim$) of Exercise 1.10b. Since **u** is closed, it follows that $a_u(\sim\square A)=T$.

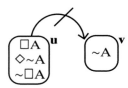

This is impossible because of (~) and $a_u(\square A)=T$. Since assuming that not **uRv** led to this contradiction, we conclude that **uRv**.

We are ready to prove **R** is dense in the canonical model when (C4): $\square\square A\rightarrow\square A$ is provable. We must show for any **w** and **v** in **W**, that if **wRv**, then there is an mc set **u** in **W** such that both **wRu** and **uRv**. So let **w** and **v** be any members of **W**, and assume that **wRv**. We will give instructions for actually constructing an mc set **u** for which **wRu** and **uRv**. Let us define two sets W and V as follows, where the symbol '∈' abbreviates 'is a member of'.

(W)   A ∈ W   iff $a_w(\square A)=T$.
($\lozenge$V) $\lozenge$A ∈ V   iff $a_v(A)=T$.

Let U be the union of W with V, namely the set containing all the members of W and all the members of V. We want to establish first that any mc set **u** such that $a_u(U)=T$ obeys both **wRu** and **uRv**.

(U)   If $a_u(U)=T$ then **wRu** and **uRv**.

Proof of (U). Suppose that $a_u(U)=T$. To show **wRu**, we will assume that B is any sentence such that **w** $\vdash \square$B and show that **u** $\vdash$ B. By (Defa), $a_w(\square B)=T$ and so it follows by (W) that B ∈ W, and hence B ∈ U. Since $a_u(U)=T$, $a_u(B)=T$; hence **u** $\vdash$ B by (Defa). To show **uRv**, we make use of (CR◇). Assume that A is any sentence such that $a_v(A)$=T. Then by (◇V), ◇A ∈ V and ◇A ∈ U. Since $a_u(U)$=T, a_u(◇A)=T. We have shown that if $a_v(A)$=T, then a_u(◇A)=T, for any wff A, and so **uRv** follows by (CR◇).

Now suppose that we could show that U ⊬ ⊥. By the Lindenbaum Lemma, there would be a member **u** of **W** such that $a_u(U)$=T. It would follow by (U) that **wRu** and **uRv**, which will ensure the density of **R** on the canonical model. So to complete the proof we must show only that U is consistent.

Proof that U is consistent. Suppose for Indirect Proof that U ⊢ ⊥. Then by the definition of ⊢, there is a finite portion U′ of U such that U′ ⊢ ⊥. Let W′ contain the members of W that are in U′, and let ◇V_1, .. , ◇V_i be the members of V that are in U′. Remember that we assumed that **wRv**. We also know by the definitions of W and V that a_w(□W′)=T and $a_v(V_1, .. , V_i)$=T. Let us summarize this information in the following diagram.

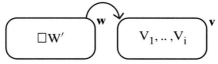

Since U′=W′,◇V_1,..,◇V_i, we know that W′,◇V_1,..,◇V_i ⊢ ⊥. It follows that W′ ⊢ ~(◇V_1 & .. & ◇V_i). But ~(◇V_1 & .. & ◇V_i) ⊢ □~(V_1 & .. & V_i), as you will show in the next exercise.

EXERCISE 9.8 Show ~(◇V_1 & .. & ◇V_i) ⊢ □~(V_1 & .. & V_i) (Hint: Show ◇(V_1 & .. & V_i) ⊢ ◇V_1 & .. & ◇V_i using (◇Out).)

It follows from this that W′ ⊢ □~(V_1 & .. & V_i), from which we obtain □W′ ⊢ □□~(V_1 & .. & V_i) by (GN). By (C4): □□A→□A, it follows that □W′ ⊢ □~(V_1 & .. & V_i), and since a_w(□W′)=T, it follows by the closure of **w** that a_w(□~(V_1 & .. & V_i))=T.

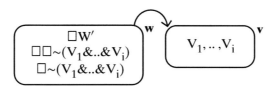

We also know that **wRv**, so by ($\Box$T), it follows that $\mathbf{a_v}(\sim(V_1\&..\&V_i))$=T.

But we also know that $\mathbf{a_v}(V_1,..,V_i)$=T, and so by (&) that $\mathbf{a_v}(V_1\&..\&V_i)$=T.

This contradicts the fact that **v** is an mc set that obeys ($\sim$). We have derived a contradiction from U ⊢ ⊥, and so we conclude that U ⊬ ⊥. This completes the proof for the density condition.

The proof for (C) uses some of the same methods we used for (C4). In this case we want to show that **R** is convergent given that (C): $\Diamond\Box A\rightarrow\Box\Diamond A$ is provable in S. Given that **wRv** and **wRu**, we must show that there exists an mc set **x** in **W** such that **vRx** and **uRx**. To prove this, let us construct two sets V and U as follows:

$$A \in V \quad \text{iff} \quad \mathbf{a_v}(\Box A)=T.$$
$$A \in U \quad \text{iff} \quad \mathbf{a_u}(\Box A)=T.$$

Let X be the union of V and U. It is a simple matter to show that if any mc set **x** satisfies X (i.e., if $\mathbf{a_x}(X)$=T), then **vRx** and **uRx**.

EXERCISE 9.9   Show that if $\mathbf{a_x}(X)$=T, then **vRx** and **uRx**.

If we can show X ⊬ ⊥, then it will follow by the Lindenbaum Lemma that there is an mc set **x** in **W** that satisfies X and the proof for convergence will be done.

Proof that X is consistent. To prove X ⊬ ⊥, we will assume H ⊢ ⊥ and derive a contradiction. So assume X ⊢ ⊥. Then we have V', $U_1, \ldots, U_n$ ⊢ ⊥, where V' is a finite portion of V, and $U_1, \ldots, U_n$ is a list of sentences in U. But then by many uses of (&Out), it follows that V', $(U_1\& .. \&U_n)$ ⊢ ⊥. So V' ⊢ $\sim(U_1\& .. \&U_n)$ by (IP), and hence $\Box$V' ⊢ $\Box\sim(U_1\& .. \&U_n)$

by (GN). By the definition of V, it follows that $\mathbf{a_v}(\Box V')$=T. Since $\mathbf{v}$ is closed, $\mathbf{a_v}(\Box\sim(U_1 \& \,.\,.\, \& U_n))$=T. By the definition of U, we know that $\mathbf{a_u}(\Box U_1,\,.\,.\,,\Box U_n)$=T. The following diagram summarizes what we have established so far:

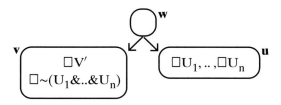

Now by $(\mathbf{R}\Diamond)$, and $\mathbf{a_v}(\Box\sim(U_1 \& \,.\,.\, \& U_n))$=T, it follows that $\mathbf{a_w}(\Diamond\Box\sim(U_1 \& \,.\,.\, \& U_n))$=T. By the presence of axiom (C), $\Diamond\Box A$ $\vdash \Box\Diamond A$ and the closure of $\mathbf{w}$, it follows that $\mathbf{a_w}(\Box\Diamond\sim(U_1 \& \,.\,.\, \& U_n))$=T.

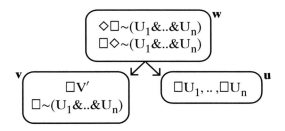

By $(\Box T)$, we know that $\mathbf{a_u}(\Diamond\sim(U_1 \& \,.\,.\, \& U_n))$=T, and this, as you will show, is not consistent with $\mathbf{a_u}(\Box U_1,\,.\,.\,,\Box U_n)$=T.

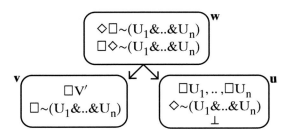

EXERCISE 9.10 Show $\Box U_1,\,.\,.\,,\Box U_n, \Diamond\sim(U_1 \& \,.\,.\, \& U_n) \vdash_K \bot$, and use this to explain why it is impossible that both $\mathbf{a_u}(\Diamond\sim(U_1 \& \,.\,.\, \& U_n))$=T and $\mathbf{a_u}(\Box U_1,\,.\,.\,,\Box U_n)$=T. (Hint: Given $\Box U_1,\,.\,.\,,\Box U_n$, prove $\Box(U_1 \& \,.\,.\, \& U_n)$. From $\Diamond\sim(U_1 \& \,.\,.\, \& \Box U_n)$ obtain $\sim\Box(U_1 \& \,.\,.\, \& \Box U_n)$ by $(\Diamond\sim)$ of Exercise 1.10b.)

EXERCISE 9.11 (Difficult Project) The basic provability logic GL results from adding axiom (GL) to K.

(GL) $\square(\square A \to A) \to \square A$

A corresponding condition on frames for GL-validity is that the frame be transitive, finite and irreflexive. Prove the adequacy of GL with respect to GL-validity. You may assume without proof that (4) $\square A \to \square\square A$ is provable in GL.

9.4. The Equivalence of PL+(GN) and K

We have just shown completeness of many logics based on K. Note that the proof requires only that (GN) (General Necessitation), rules of PL, and the appropriate axioms be available in the system at issue. So this shows that a whole host of modal logics based on PL+(GN) (rather than K=PL+($\square$In)+($\square$Out)) are also complete. In particular we have the completeness of PL+(GN) with respect to K-validity. This fact provides an easy proof that K is equivalent to PL+(GN), a fact we noted in Section 1.8, but one we have yet to prove. To show this equivalence, we must show two things:

Fact 1.   If H / C has a proof in PL+(GN), then H / C has a proof in K.
Fact 2.   If H / C has a proof in K, then H / C has a proof in PL+(GN).

Fact 1 was already shown in Section 1.8, because (GN) was derived in K. Fact 2 can be shown as follows. Suppose H / C has a proof in K. By the consistency of K, it follows that H / C is K-valid. By completeness of PL+(GN), H / C has a proof in PL+(GN).

10

Axioms and Their Corresponding Conditions on R

10.1. The General Axiom (G)

So far, the correspondence between axioms and conditions on **R** must seem a mystery. Although the diagram technique may be used to help decide what condition it would take to validate a given axiom, or to determine which condition the axiom will cause **R** to obey on the canonical model, no rigorous account has been given concerning the relationships between axioms and their corresponding conditions on **R**. In this section, we will prove a theorem that may be used to determine conditions on **R** from axioms (and vice versa) for a wide range of axioms (Lemmon and Scott, 1977). (For a more general result of this kind see Sahlqvist, 1975.)

The theorem concerns axioms that have the form (G).

(G) $\Diamond^h \Box^i A \rightarrow \Box^j \Diamond^k A$

The notation '$\Diamond^n$' represents n diamonds in a row, so, for example, '$\Diamond^3$' abbreviates: $\Diamond\Diamond\Diamond$. Similarly, '$\Box^n$' represents a string of n boxes. When the values of h, i, j, and k are all 1, we have axiom (C).

(C) $\Diamond \Box A \rightarrow \Box \Diamond A$ is $\Diamond^1 \Box^1 A \rightarrow \Box^1 \Diamond^1 A$.

The axiom (B) results from setting h and k to 0, and letting j and k be 1.

(B) $A \rightarrow \Box \Diamond A$ is $\Diamond^0 \Box^0 A \rightarrow \Box^1 \Diamond^1 A$.

To obtain (4), we may set h and k to 0, set i to 1 and j to 2.

(4) $\Box A \rightarrow \Box\Box A$ is $\Diamond^0 \Box^1 A \rightarrow \Box^2 \Diamond^0 A$.

211

EXERCISE 10.1   Give values for h, i, j, and k for the axioms (M), (D), (5), (C4), and (CD).

Although axioms such as ($\Box$M) and (L) do not have the shape (G) for any values of h, i, j, and k, the other axioms we have discussed all have the shape (G).

Our next task will be to give the condition on **R** that corresponds to (G) for a given selection of values for h, i, j, and k. In order to do so, we will need a definition. The *composition* of two relations **R** and **R'** is a new relation **RoR'** which is defined as follows.

(Defo)   **wRoR'v** iff for some **u**, **wRu** and **uR'v**.

For example, if **R** is the relation of being a brother, and **R'** is the relation of being a parent, then **RoR'** is the relation of being an uncle (because **w** is the uncle of **v** iff for some person **u**, both **w** is the brother of **u** and **u** is the parent of **v**).

A relation may be composed with itself. For example, when **R** is the relation of being a parent, then **RoR** is the relation of being a grandparent, and **RoRoR** is the relation of being a great-grandparent. It will be useful to write '$\mathbf{R}^n$' for the result of composing **R** with itself n times. So $\mathbf{R}^2$ is **RoR**, and $\mathbf{R}^4$ is **RoRoRoR**. We will let $\mathbf{R}^1$ be **R**, and $\mathbf{R}^0$ will be the identity relation, that is, $\mathbf{wR}^0\mathbf{v}$ iff **w=v**.

EXERCISE 10.2   Let S be the relation **sister of**, let C be the relation **child of**, and let M be **mother of**. Define the following relations using composition of relations: aunt, great-great-grandmother.

We may now state the condition on **R** that corresponds to an axiom of the shape (G).

(hijk-Convergence)
If $\mathbf{wR}^h\mathbf{v}$ and $\mathbf{wR}^j\mathbf{u}$, then for some x in **W**, $\mathbf{vR}^i\mathbf{x}$ and $\mathbf{uR}^k\mathbf{x}$.

Let us adopt the notation:

to represent $\mathbf{R}^n$. Then the diagram for hijk-convergence is a generalization of the diagram for convergence.

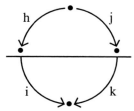

This is to be expected, since convergence is hijk-convergence when h=i=j=k=1.

It is interesting to see how the diagrams for the familiar conditions on **R** result from setting the values for h, i, j, and k according to the values in the corresponding axiom. We have explained that $\mathbf{R}^0$ is the identity relation. So if we see a zero arrow between two worlds, we know they are identical, and we can collapse them together in the diagram. To illustrate this idea, consider the diagram for (5). In this case i=0, and h=j=k=1.

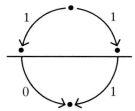

When we shrink together the two dots joined by the zero arrow on the bottom left of this diagram, we obtain the diagram for the euclidean condition.

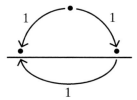

The same thing works for the axiom (B). Here h=i=0, while j=k=1.

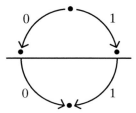

When we resolve the zero arrows, we obtain the diagram for symmetry, just as we would hope.

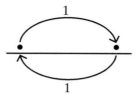

In the case of axiom (4), we begin with the following diagram:

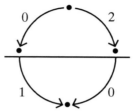

Resolving the zero arrows, we obtain:

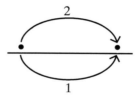

The 2 arrow at the top of this diagram represents the composition of **R** taken twice, so this arrow resolves to a series of two arrows. So we obtain the familiar transitivity diagram.

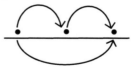

The case of axiom (D) involves a slight complication. We begin with the following diagram:

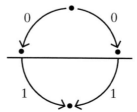

which resolves to:

This diagram indicates that for every world **w**, there is another world **v** such that **wRv** and **wRv**. But this just amounts to saying in a stuttering way that for every world **w** there is a world **v** such that **wRv**. Clearly, the second arrow is superfluous, and we obtain the diagram for seriality.

EXERCISE 10.3   Derive diagrams for (M), (C4), and (CD) by setting values for h, i, j, and k in the diagram for hijk-convergence, and then resolving the arrows.

10.2. Adequacy of Systems Based on (G)

The rest of this chapter will present an adequacy proof for any system that results from adding axioms of the form (G) to K. To show soundness, it will be proven that regardless of which values h, i, j, and k are chosen for an axiom with shape (G), the axiom is valid when **R** is hijk-convergent. To show completeness, a demonstration will be given that when an axiom of the shape (G) is available in a system, then the canonical model's relation **R** must be hijk-convergent for the appropriate values of h–k.

It will be helpful to have the four general diagram rules that follow:

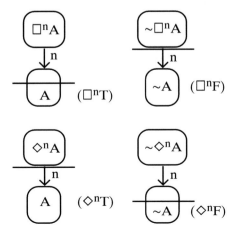

The arrows with n on them in these diagrams represent $\mathbf{R}^n$. From the point of view of diagrams, the arrow:

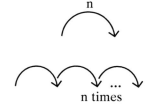

abbreviates:

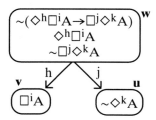

n times

The correctness of these four rules is easily shown. For example, $(\Box^n T)$ may be proven using n applications of $(\Box T)$, and similarly for the others.

> **EXERCISE 10.4** Prove $(\Box^3 T)$, $(\Box^3 F)$, $(\Diamond^3 T)$, and $(\Diamond^3 F)$. Then explain why $(\Box^n T)$, $(\Box^n F)$, $(\Diamond^n T)$, and $(\Diamond^n F)$ hold for any value of n.

We are ready to show that (G) is valid when $\mathbf{R}$ is hijk-convergent. We assume that (G) has a counterexample and derive a contradiction. If (G) has a counterexample, then there is a model with a world where (G) is false. From $(\rightarrow F)$, $(\Diamond^h T)$ and $(\Box^j F)$, we obtain the following diagram.

Since $\mathbf{R}$ is hijk-convergent, there is a world $\mathbf{x}$ such that $\mathbf{v}\mathbf{R}^i\mathbf{x}$ and $\mathbf{u}\mathbf{R}^k\mathbf{x}$. Using $(\Box^i T)$ and $(\Diamond^k T)$, we obtain a contradiction in world $\mathbf{x}$, and so (G) cannot have a counterexample when $\mathbf{R}$ is hijk-convergent.

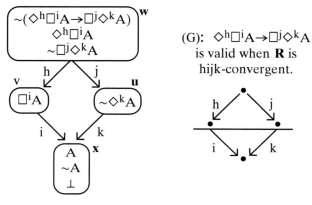

(G): $\Diamond^h\Box^i A \rightarrow \Box^j\Diamond^k A$
is valid when $\mathbf{R}$ is
hijk-convergent.

To prove completeness for a system that extends K using axioms of the form (G), we will first demonstrate the following fact about the canonical model:

($\mathbf{R^n}$) $\mathbf{wR^n v}$ iff   if $\mathbf{a_w}(\Box^n A) = T$, then $\mathbf{a_v}(A) = T$, for all sentences A. The proof for ($\mathbf{R^n}$) when n=0 requires that we show ($\mathbf{R^0}$),
($\mathbf{R^0}$) $\mathbf{wR^0 v}$ iff   if $\mathbf{a_w}(\Box^0 A) = T$, then $\mathbf{a_v}(A) = T$, for all sentences A. This amounts to showing that
      $\mathbf{w}$ is $\mathbf{v}$ iff   if $\mathbf{a_w}(A) = T$, then $\mathbf{a_v}(A) = T$, for all sentences A.

The proof from left to right is obvious, and the proof from right to left requires the following argument. Suppose that if $\mathbf{a_w}(A) = T$, then $\mathbf{a_v}(A) = T$ for all sentences A, and suppose for indirect proof that $\mathbf{w}$ is not identical to $\mathbf{v}$. By the latter assumption, there must be a sentence B for which $\mathbf{w}$ and $\mathbf{v}$ differ. This means that either $\mathbf{a_w}(B) = T$ and $\mathbf{a_v}(B) = F$, or $\mathbf{a_w}(B) = F$ and $\mathbf{a_v}(B) = T$. In the first case, where $\mathbf{a_w}(B) = T$ and $\mathbf{a_v}(B) = F$, it follows by ($\sim$) that $\mathbf{a_v}(\sim B) = T$. Since every sentence true in $\mathbf{w}$ is true in $\mathbf{v}$, we have $\mathbf{a_v}(B) = T$. But this is impossible since the assignment $\mathbf{a}$ must obey ($\sim$). The proof of the case where $\mathbf{a_w}(B) = F$ and $\mathbf{a_v}(B) = T$ is similar.

EXERCISE 10.5   Complete the proof of ($\mathbf{R^0}$).

To show that ($\mathbf{R^n}$) holds for n > 0, notice first that ($\mathbf{R^n}$) for n=1 is exactly the truth condition ($\Box$), so this case is easy. To show ($\mathbf{R^n}$) for n > 1, we will use the strategy of mathematical induction by establishing ($\mathbf{R^{next}}$).

($\mathbf{R^{next}}$)   For any value of k, if ($\mathbf{R^k}$) holds, then ($\mathbf{R^{k+1}}$) also holds.

This will guarantee that ($\mathbf{R^n}$) holds for all values of n. The reason is that we have already shown ($\mathbf{R^0}$) and ($\mathbf{R^1}$). But ($\mathbf{R^{next}}$) guarantees that since ($\mathbf{R^1}$), it follows that ($\mathbf{R^2}$). By applying ($\mathbf{R^{next}}$) again to this last result, ($\mathbf{R^3}$) follows. By continuing this argument as many times as we need, ($\mathbf{R^n}$) can be established for any value of n.

So all that remains is to show ($\mathbf{R^{next}}$). To do this, let k be any value of n and assume ($\mathbf{R^k}$). We will now show ($\mathbf{R^{k+1}}$) as follows. (For your reference we have written out ($\mathbf{R^k}$) and ($\mathbf{R^{k+1}}$) below, applying the fact that $\Box^{k+1} A = \Box^k \Box A$.)

($\mathbf{R^k}$) $\mathbf{wR^k v}$ iff   if $\mathbf{a_w}(\Box^k A) = T$ then $\mathbf{a_v}(A) = T$ for all sentences A.
($\mathbf{R^{k+1}}$) $\mathbf{wR^k oRv}$ iff   if $\mathbf{a_w}(\Box^k \Box A) = T$ then $\mathbf{a_v}(A) = T$ for all sentences A.

First (R^{k+1}) is shown from left to right. We assume $\mathbf{w}R^k\mathbf{oRv}$, and $\mathbf{a_w}(\Box^k\Box A)=T$ for a given sentence A, and show that $\mathbf{a_v}(A)=T$, as follows. By $\mathbf{w}R^k\mathbf{oRv}$ and the definition of $\mathbf{o}$, it follows that for some mc set $\mathbf{u}$, both $\mathbf{w}R^k\mathbf{u}$ and $\mathbf{uRv}$. By $\mathbf{a_w}(\Box^k\Box A)=T$, and ($R^k$), it follows that $\mathbf{a_u}(\Box A)=T$, and so $\mathbf{a_v}(A)=T$ follows from $\mathbf{uRv}$ by ($\Box T$) and the definition of $\mathbf{a}$.

To complete the proof, (R^{k+1}) must be shown from right to left given (R^k). Let us suppose that ($R^{k+1}R$).

($R^{k+1}R$) If $\mathbf{a_w}(\Box^k\Box A)=T$, then $\mathbf{a_v}(A)=T$ for all sentences A.

We will show that there is an mc set $\mathbf{u}$ such that $\mathbf{w}R^k\mathbf{u}$ and $\mathbf{uRv}$. The proof that such a $\mathbf{u}$ exists is similar to the completeness proof for the density axiom (C4). We define the set U as the union of two sets W and $\Diamond$V defined in turn as follows.

$A \in W$ iff $\mathbf{a_w}(\Box^k A)=T$.

$\Diamond A \in \Diamond V$ iff $\mathbf{a_v}(A)=T$.

We then show that any assignment that satisfies U obeys $\mathbf{w}R^k\mathbf{u}$ and $\mathbf{uRv}$.

(U) If $\mathbf{a_u}(U)=T$ then $\mathbf{w}R^k\mathbf{u}$ and $\mathbf{uRv}$.

(U) is proven as follows. Assume $\mathbf{a_u}(U)=T$. Since W contains A whenever $\mathbf{a_w}(\Box^k A)=T$, and all members of W are in U, it follows from $\mathbf{a_u}(U)=T$ that $\mathbf{a_u}(A)=T$. So for any sentence A, if $\mathbf{a_w}(\Box^k A)=T$ then $\mathbf{a_u}(A)=T$, with the result that $\mathbf{w}R^k\mathbf{u}$. Since $\Diamond A \in \Diamond V$ whenever $\mathbf{a_v}(A)=T$, it follows that $\mathbf{a_u}(\Diamond A)=T$ whenever $\mathbf{a_v}(A)=T$ for any wff A. By ($CR\Diamond$) it follows that $\mathbf{uRv}$.

To complete the proof, we need show only that $U \nvdash_S \bot$, for then by the Lindenbaum Lemma it will follow that there is an mc set $\mathbf{u}$ that satisfies U, and hence $\mathbf{w}R^k\mathbf{u}$ and $\mathbf{uRv}$ by (U). This is done by assuming $U \vdash_S \bot$ and deriving a contradiction. If we assume $U \vdash_S \bot$, it follows that W' $\vdash \sim(\Diamond V_1 \& .. \& \Diamond V_i)$, where W' is a finite subset of W and $\Diamond V_1, ..$ $\Diamond V_i$ are members of $\Diamond$V. By the solution to Exercise 9.8, we have W' $\vdash_S$ $\Box\sim(V_1 \& .. \& V_i)$, from which we obtain $\Box^k$W' $\vdash_S \Box^k\Box\sim(V_1 \& .. \& V_i)$ by k applications of General Necessitation (GN). We know $\mathbf{a_w}(\Box^k$W'$)=T$, so $\mathbf{a_w}(\Box^k\Box\sim(V_1 \& .. \& V_i))=T$ by the Closed Lemma. We have assumed ($R^{k+1}R$), that is, that if $\mathbf{a_w}(\Box^k\Box A)=T$ then $\mathbf{a_v}(A)=T$, so it follows that $\mathbf{a_v}(\sim(V_1 \& .. \& V_i))=T$. But this is impossible since $\mathbf{a_v}(V_1, ..., V_i)=T$ with the result that $\mathbf{a_v}(V_1 \& .. \& V_i)=T$. We have the required contradiction, and so the proof of (R^n) is complete.

We are ready to show that when (G) is provable in a system, then the standard model is hijk-convergent. The proof is similar to the proof of completeness for axiom (C) with respect to convergence, the only difference being the presence of superscripts. Along the way, the following generalization of ($\mathbf{R}\Diamond$) will be useful:

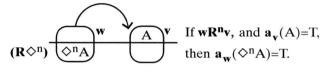

$(\mathbf{R}\Diamond^n)$ $\Diamond^n A$ | w | A | v   If $\mathbf{wR^nv}$, and $\mathbf{a_v}(A)=T$, then $\mathbf{a_w}(\Diamond^n A)=T$.

The proof is easy using ($\mathbf{R}\Diamond$) n times.

EXERCISE 10.6   Prove ($\mathbf{R}\Diamond^n$) by showing that if ($\mathbf{R}\Diamond^k$) holds for any value k, then so does ($\mathbf{R}\Diamond^{k+1}$).

Now suppose that $\mathbf{wR^hv}$ and $\mathbf{wR^ju}$. We must show that there is an mc set $\mathbf{x}$ in $\mathbf{W}$ such that $\mathbf{vR^ix}$ and $\mathbf{uR^kx}$. Let V and U be defined as follows:

$A \in V$ iff $\mathbf{a_v}(\Box^i A)=T$.
$A \in U$ iff $\mathbf{a_u}(\Box^k A)=T$.

Let X be the union of V and U. It is a straightforward matter to show for any mc set $\mathbf{x}$ that if $\mathbf{a_x}(X)=T$, then both $\mathbf{vR^ix}$ and $\mathbf{uR^kx}$.

EXERCISE 10.7   Show that if $\mathbf{a_x}(X)=T$, then $\mathbf{vR^ix}$ and $\mathbf{uR^kx}$.

Now we will show that X is S-consistent, from which it follows from the Lindenbaum Lemma that there is an mc set $\mathbf{x}$ such that $\mathbf{a_x}(X)=T$. As usual, we assume $X \vdash_S \perp$ and derive a contradiction. Assuming $X \vdash_S \perp$, it follows that $V', U_1, \ldots, U_n \vdash_S \perp$, where V' is a finite subset of V and $U_1, \ldots, U_n$ is a list of sentences of U. So $V' \vdash_S \sim(U_1 \& \ldots \& U_n)$, and hence $\Box^i V' \vdash \Box^i \sim(U_1 \& \ldots \& U_n)$ by i applications of (GN). By the definition of V, $\mathbf{a_v}(\Box^i V')=T$, and so $\mathbf{a_v}(\Box^i \sim(U_1 \& \ldots \& U_n))=T$ by the Closed Lemma. By the definition of U, we know that if $A \in U$ then $\mathbf{a_u}(\Box^k A)=T$, hence $\mathbf{a_u}(\Box^k U_1, \ldots, \Box^k U_n)=T$.

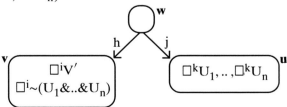

Now $\mathbf{w}\mathbf{R}^h\mathbf{v}$ and $\mathbf{a_v}(\Box^i\sim(U_1\&..\&U_n))=T$, so it follows by $(\mathbf{R}\Diamond^h)$ that $\mathbf{a_w}(\Diamond^h\Box^i\sim(U_1\&..\&U_n))=T$. By the presence of (C): $\Diamond^h\Box^iA\to\Box^j\Diamond^kA$ in S and the Closed Lemma, it follows that $\mathbf{a_w}(\Box^j\Diamond^k\sim(U_1\&..\&U_n))=T$.

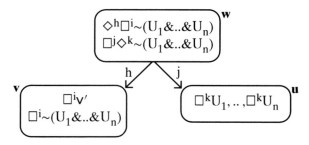

From this and $(\mathbf{R}^j)$, we know that $\mathbf{a_u}(\Diamond^k\sim(U_1\&..\&U_n))=T$. But this is not consistent with $\mathbf{a_u}(\Box^kU_1,\ldots,\Box^kU_n)=T$.

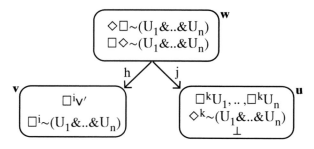

EXERCISE 10.8 Show $\Box^kU_1,\ldots,\Box^kU_n\vdash_K \sim\Diamond^k\sim(U_1\&..\&U_n)$. (Hint: Use (GN) k times.)

11

Relationships between the Modal Logics

Since there are so many different possible systems for modal logic, it is important to determine which systems are equivalent, and which ones distinct from others. Figure 11.1 lays out these relationships for some of the best-known modal logics. It names systems by listing their axioms. So, for example, M4B is the system that results from adding (M), (4), and (B) to K. In boldface, we have also indicated traditional names of some systems, namely, S4, B, and S5. When system S appears below and/or to the left of S′ connected by a line, then S′ is an *extension* of S. This means that every argument provable in S is provable in S′, but S is *weaker* than S′, that is, not all arguments provable in S′ are provable in S.

11.1. Showing Systems Are Equivalent

One striking fact shown in Figure 11.1 is the large number of alternative ways of formulating S5. It is possible to prove these formulations are equivalent by proving the derivability of the official axioms of S5 (namely, (M) and (5)) in each of these systems and vice versa. However, there is an easier way. By the adequacy results given in Chapter 8 (or Chapter 9), we know that for each collection of axioms, there is a corresponding concept of validity. Adequacy guarantees that these notions of provability and validity correspond. So if we can show that two forms of validity are equivalent, then it will follow that the corresponding systems are equivalent. Let us illustrate with an example.

We will show that K4B (i.e., K+(4)+(B)) is equivalent to K4B5 (K=(4)+(B)+(5)) by showing that K4B-validity is equivalent to K4B5-validity. That will follow from a demonstration that a relation is transitive

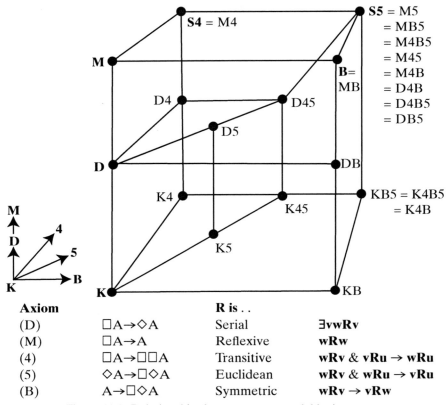

Axiom		R is . .	
(D)	□A→◇A	Serial	∃v**wRv**
(M)	□A→A	Reflexive	**wRw**
(4)	□A→□□A	Transitive	**wRv & vRu → wRu**
(5)	◇A→□◇A	Euclidean	**wRv & wRu → vRu**
(B)	A→□◇A	Symmetric	**wRv → vRw**

Figure 11.1. Relationships between some modal logic systems.

and symmetric if and only if it is transitive, symmetric, and euclidean. Clearly if a relation is transitive, symmetric, and euclidean, it must be transitive and symmetric. So to show equivalence of the two kinds of validity, we need only show that whenever a relation is transitive and symmetric, it is also euclidean. We begin by assuming that **R** is transitive and symmetric. To show that **R** is also euclidean, assume that **wRv** and **wRu** and prove that **vRu**. The assumption that **wRv** and **wRu** may be presented in a diagram as follows:

Since **wRv**, it follows by the symmetry of **R** (which corresponds to the axiom (B)) that **vRw**.

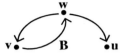

But this with **wRu** and the transitivity of **R** (which corresponds to (4)) yields **vRu**, the desired result.

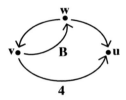

It follows that whenever a relation is symmetric and transitive, it is already euclidean. This means that the requirement that **R** be symmetric and transitive is equivalent to the requirement that **R** is transitive, symmetric, and euclidean. It follows that K4B-validity is identical to K4B5-validity and so theorems of K4B and K4B5 are identical. By the same reasoning, we may prove also that any serial, transitive, and symmetric relation is euclidean. So it follows that D4B-validity is identical to D4B5-validity and the systems D4B and D4B5 are equivalent as well.

EXERCISE 11.1

a) Prove that M4B is equivalent to M4B5.
b) Prove that any symmetric euclidean relation is transitive. Use this result to show that (4) is provable in KB5, DB5, and MB5. Now show KB5 and K4B5 are equivalent. Use this with previous results to show K4B and KB5 are equivalent.
c) Use these results to show that D4B = D4B5 = DB5, and that M4B = M4B5 = MB5.

Let us give a second illustration of the method for showing equivalence. It is perhaps surprising that D4B is equivalent to M4B, for the axiom (D) is quite a bit weaker than (M). However, this may be proven by showing that every serial, transitive, and symmetric relation is also reflexive as follows. Let **w** be any world in **W**. By seriality, (D), we know that there is a world **v** such that **wRv**.

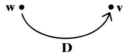

By symmetry (B), it follows that **vRw**.

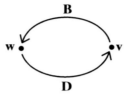

We now have both **wRv** and **vRw**, so **wRw** follows from transitivity (4).

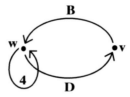

EXERCISE *11.2 Using diagrams show that (B) is provable in M5. Use this and previous results to show that the following are all equivalent to S5: M5, MB5, M4B5, M45, M4B, D4B, D4B5, DB5.

11.2. Showing One System Is Weaker than Another

Next we will explain how to use facts about the accessibility relation to prove that one system is weaker than another, and that one is an extension of the other. How do we know, for example, that (B) is not already a theorem of M, so that M is equivalent to B? To show that M is really weaker than B, it is necessary to show that (B) is not a theorem of M. This may be proven by showing that p→□◇p (an instance of (B)) is not M-valid. The demonstration of invalidity may be carried out by showing that the tree for the argument with no premises and p→□◇p as a conclusion has an open branch. By the Tree Model Theorem (Section 8.3), it follows that p→□◇p is invalid on the tree model and so ⊭ₘ p→□◇p. It follows from this by the adequacy of M that $\nvdash_M$ p→□◇p. What follows is the open tree that indicates the M-invalidity of p→□◇p.

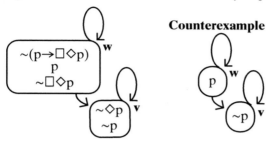

Counterexample

> **EXERCISE 11.3**   Verify that the model defined in the above counterexample diagram is such that a_w(p→□◇p)=F.

Now that we know that M cannot prove (B), it follows that B is an extension of M, for anything provable in M is provable in B=MB, and yet there is a theorem of B that cannot be proven in M (namely, p→□◇p).

Another result follows from the fact that M cannot prove (B), namely, that no weaker system can. Therefore, neither D nor K can prove (B), which shows that DB is an extension of D and KB is an extension of K. The same diagram may also be used to establish that (B) cannot be proven in S4. Note the accessibility relation in this diagram is transitive. Transitivity amounts to the claim that any journey following two arrows in succession may also be completed by following a single arrow.

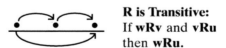

R is Transitive:
If **wRv** and **vRu**
then **wRu**.

One two-hop journey in the counterexample diagram above is from **w** to **w** followed by **w** to **v**. But obviously this may be accomplished in one step by simply going from **w** to **v**. The only other two-hop journey is **w** to **v** followed by **v** to **v**, which can also be done by simply going from **w** to **v**. Since the diagram is transitive, it shows that $\nvdash_{S4}$ (B), and so we know that (B) is not provable in S4. It follows from this that S4 must be weaker than S5, because S5 can prove (B).

> **EXERCISE 11.4**   Show that (4) is not provable in B, and hence that S5 is an extension of B.

Given the last exercise, we know that B cannot prove (4). We also showed that S4 cannot prove B. This means that these systems are *incommensurable*, meaning that neither system is an extension of the other.

The fact that (4) is not provable in B may be used to obtain many results about which systems are extensions of others. If B cannot prove (4), neither can any system with fewer axioms than B. This includes M, D, K, DB, and KB. So the following facts about extensions hold, where we use '>' to abbreviate 'is an extension of':

M4>M
D4>D
K4>K
K4B>K4.

Not only that, but the same considerations used to show that S4 and B are incommensurable can be used to show that D4 and DB (and K4 and KB) are incommensurable.

> **EXERCISE 11.5** Show that D4 is incommensurable with DB and K4 is incommensurable with KB.

Now let us show that K4B5 and D4B5 are extensions of K45 and D45, respectively. The last counterexample diagram will not demonstrate this because the relation there is not euclidean (**wRv** and **wRw**, but not **vRw**). A slight change in this diagram will prove what we want. Here we create a counterexample to p→□◇p in a D-tree.

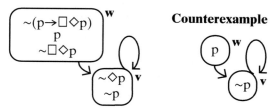

Counterexample

Although the accessibility relation in this diagram is not reflexive, it is serial since there is an arrow exiting each world. Note that the relation is both transitive and euclidean in this diagram. For transitivity, note there is only one two-hop journey in the diagram (**w** to **v** and **v** to **v**), and this can be done in one hop by going from **w** to **v**. To show that the relation is euclidean, we must show that whenever two arrows exit the same world, there is a third arrow between the two. But there is no world with two arrows exiting it, so the euclidean condition is trivially satisfied. So this diagram shows that (B) is not provable in D45, which establishes that D4B5 (alias S5) is an extension of D45. It also follows that (B) is not provable in K45, so K4B5=K4B=KB5 is an extension of K45.

The fact that S5 is an extension of D45 may be used to establish further results. D4 could not prove (M) because if it did, then D45 would also prove (M), and so D45 would be equivalent to M45=S5. But we just showed that S5 is an extension of D45, and so they are not the same. Since (M) is not provable in D4, it follows that M4 is an extension of D4. It also follows that D could not prove (M) either, for again this would entail the equivalent of D45 and S5. So we also learn that M is an extension of D.

Now let us show that (D) is not provable in K4B. This can be done with a very simple diagram.

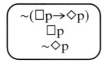 **Counterexample**

Note that if there were an arrow exiting the diagram, then ($\Box$T) and ($\Diamond$F) rules could be applied to $\Box$p and $\sim\Diamond$p to obtain a contradiction in that world. However, this diagram indicates that **R** holds for no worlds, and so ($\Box$T) and ($\Diamond$F) rules do not apply. Since there are no atoms in the world at the left, and no variables other than p, the counterexample diagram contains $\sim$p. Notice that since **R** holds for no worlds, **R** is trivially transitive and symmetric. So this diagram serves as a 4B-counterexample to (D). It follows that K4B=KB5=K4B5 cannot prove (D). So (D) is also not provable in any of the K systems: K, K4, K5, KB, and K45. It follows that each of the D systems is an extension of its K counterpart: K<D, K4<D4, K5<D5, K45<D45, K4B<S5, KB<DB.

EXERCISE 11.6

a) Show the following with diagrams: $\nvdash_{D4}$ (5), $\nvdash_{D5}$ (4), and $\nvdash_{DB}$ (M).

b) Use these results to demonstrate the remaining extension facts indicated on the diagram at the beginning of this chapter, namely, the following: D4<D45, K4<K45, D5<D45, K5<K45, DB<B.

c) Show that the following pairs are incommensurable: D4, D5; DB, D5.

12

Systems for Quantified Modal Logic

It would seem to be a simple matter to outfit a modal logic with quantifiers. You would simply add the standard (or classical) rules for quantifiers to the principles of some propositional modal logic. Although systems of this kind can be constructed, the combination of classical quantifier rules and modality has unexpected consequences. Logicians interested in a more general treatment of names and definite descriptions have invented alternative systems for the quantifiers called free logics. I believe that free logics allow a more natural fit between quantifiers and the underlying propositional modal logics. So the treatment of quantified modal logic in this book begins with a discussion of the differences between classical quantification and free logic. To prepare the way for everything that follows, languages for quantified modal logic need to be defined.

12.1. Languages for Quantified Modal Logic

All the quantifier systems to be discussed in this book result from adding the universal quantifier $\forall$ to the language of propositional logic. The existential quantifier $\exists$ is defined by (Def$\exists$).

$$(\text{Def}\exists) \quad \exists xA =_{df} {\sim}\forall x{\sim}A$$

Besides $\forall$, the symbols of a quantifier language include an unlimited supply of *variables* x, y, z, x′, y′, z′, . . . , a set of *constants* c, b, c′, b′, c″ . . , a set of *predicate letters* P, Q, R, P′, Q′, R′, . . . , the propositional logic symbols $\perp$ and $\rightarrow$ (the symbols ${\sim}$, &, v, and $\leftrightarrow$ are defined), the intensional operator $\Box$, the identity sign $\approx$, and finally parentheses and the comma. For the moment, the only *terms* are the constants. In sections to come, the collection t, s, u, t′, s′, u′, . . of terms will be expanded to include terms other than the constants and complex expressions for definite descriptions. Officially, all systems will include a predicate letter E for existence. However, in most cases, Et ↔ ∃xx≈t is provable, and so the existence predicate may be eliminated by the following definition.

(DefE)   Et $=_{df}$ ∃xx≈t

For more on this issue see Section 12.12.

Now let us define the *sentences* of the language of quantified modal logic. The *atomic sentences* have the forms ⊥, s≈t, and Pl, where s and t are terms, P is any predicate letter, and l is any list of terms. The official notation for a list requires parentheses and commas. So a list of terms has the form $(t_1, t_2, . . . , t_i)$. This means that an English sentence such as 'Joe loves Mary' is symbolized by placing a list of constants (j, m) to the right of the predicate letter L like this: L(j, m). Although the official notation requires that terms in an atomic sentence appear in a list, writing the extra parentheses and commas can become tiresome. So we will write 'Lj,m', or even 'Ljm' in place of 'L(j, m)' when no ambiguity will arise. This practice conforms to a convention used throughout this book. Although the official notation for a list has the form $(o_1, o_2, . . . , o_i)$, we drop the parentheses: $o_1, o_2, . . . , o_i$ and even the commas: $o_1 o_2 . . o_i$ when this is convenient.

The identity sign ≈ is considered to be a predicate letter, and so officially, the notation to indicate (for example) that Jim is identical to Dan is: '≈(j, d)'. However, we will abbreviate '≈(j, d)' to the more familiar notation: 'j≈d' when this is convenient. Strictly speaking, the constants fall alphabetically from 'b' through 'c', and predicate letters (other than ≈) from 'P' through 'R'. However, a wider range of lower case and upper case letters will be used for constants and predicate letters when this is convenient (as has just been done for 'John loves Mary').

In order to keep the definition of atomic sentences uniform, predicate letters followed by the empty list () (for example, 'P()') will be used in place of propositional variables. However, the parentheses will usually be dropped to obtain the more ordinary notation: ('P', 'Q', etc.).

On the standard account, predicate letters are classified by the number of term places they contain. For example, 'is green' is a one-place predicate, since it takes only a subject, whereas 'loves' is a two-place predicate taking both a subject and object. However, the definition of atoms given here allows term lists of varying lengths to follow the same predicate letter. So, for example, P(n) and P(n, m) may both be atomic sentences. This liberal policy reflects the fact that some verbs of English have both transitive and intransitive forms; for example, consider 'obeys' in 'John obeys', and 'John obeys Mary'. The result is a notational system that offers a closer match with the form of ordinary language (Grandy, 1976; Garson, 1981).

In quantificational logic, the idea of an *instance* of a universal sentence is central. For example, if every *p*hilosopher is *m*ortal (in symbols: $\forall x(Px \rightarrow Mx)$), it follows that if *S*ocrates is a *p*hilosopher, then *S*ocrates is *m*ortal: Ps$\rightarrow$Ms. Here, Ps$\rightarrow$Ms is an instance of $\forall x(Px \rightarrow Mx)$. A notation for instances will be needed in order to present the quantifier rules. '$[A]^t/x$' will be used to indicate the instance that results from $\forall xA$ when $\forall x$ is dropped and t is replaced for all those occurrences of the variable x in A that were bound by $\forall x$. So, for example, $[P(x, t)]^t/x$ is P(t, t), and $[P(x, x)]^t/x$ is also P(t, t). Note that when an instance $[A]^t/x$ is formed, t may replace only occurrences of x bound by the initial quantifier $\forall x$ in $\forall xA$. For example, a correct instance $[Px \rightarrow \forall xQx]^t/x$, for $\forall x(Px \rightarrow \forall xQx)$, is Pt$\rightarrow\forall xQx$. It would be illegal to replace t for the occurrences of x in $\forall xQx$ as well since this yields Pt$\rightarrow\forall tQt$, which is ill formed. (A technical definition of $[A]^t/x$ is given in Section 15.12.)

A less formal notation is commonly used to indicate instances. It is to write '$\forall xAx$' for the quantifier sentence, and 'At' for the corresponding instance. A problem with this scheme is that when 'At' is viewed out of context, it is impossible to tell which variable was replaced by t in forming the sentence At. On rare occasions, that is important information that cannot be recovered from the context. Despite this technical failing, the informal notation has its attractions. Visually, '$\forall x(Px \rightarrow Mx)$' and 'Pt$\rightarrow$Mt' resemble '$\forall xAx$' and 'At', respectively; furthermore, the notation '$[A]^t/x$' introduces annoying clutter. So this book will use the informal notation for the most part, and resort to the more formal style only when technical requirements demand it.

Now we are ready to define the set of sentences of quantified modal logic (QML). A string of symbols is a *sentence of QML* iff it can be generated by the following rules:

Atomic sentences are sentences.
If A is a sentence, then $\Box$A is a sentence.
If A and B are sentences, then (A$\rightarrow$B) is a sentence.
If Ac is a sentence, then $\forall xAx$ is a sentence.

Notice that the last clause constructs the universal sentence $\forall xAx$ from one of its *instances* Ac. This way of defining the sentences ensures that variables are always bound by a quantifier. According to this definition, the open formula Px is not a sentence because variables such as x do not count as terms. The quantifier clause is the only way in which variables can be introduced into sentences, and so all variables in sentences end up bound by a quantifier. A more liberal account of sentences would include the open formulas among the sentences. Then the quantifier clause could be simplified to read: if A is a sentence, then ∀xA is a sentence. However, the more narrow definition has been chosen to avoid tedious complications that crop up in proofs concerning substitution of terms for variables.

From time to time, we will talk of the expressions of a language. An *expression* is simply any predicate, term, list of terms, or sentence. In this book, systems written in different languages for QML will be considered. Usually the languages will differ only with respect to their terms and predicate letters. In some cases, a given language may be extended by adding to it a new set of terms, or additional predicate letters. We will even consider languages where the *objects* of the domain of quantification are treated as if they were terms of the language. (See Section 13.5.) Since languages vary in the course of the discussion, no fixed language will be defined for this book. For most of the discussion to come, it will be assumed that some language for quantified modal logic has been provided.

12.2. A Classical System for Quantifiers

You are probably familiar with predicate logic (or quantificational logic or first order logic, which is the same thing). So a good place to begin a discussion of modal quantification will be to start with set of standard rules for quantifiers. A natural deduction system QL- for *classical quantificational logic without identity* may be given by adding the following two rules to PL (propositional logic):

System QL- = PL + (Q∀Out) + (Q∀In).

Q∀Out	**Q∀In**	
∀xAx	Ac	
-------	-------	
Ac	∀xAx	where c is not in ∀xAx nor in any of its hypotheses

It is understood that these rules, and rules to be presented in the future, may be applied within any subproof and that when applied, all lines appear in the same subproof.

The rule (Q∀Out) reflects the principle (sometimes called universal instantiation) that when ∀xAx holds, so does the instance Ac for any constant c. A more standard instantiation rule for quantifiers applies to all terms and not just the constants. For the moment, the constants are the only terms, so the difference does not matter. However, it will be important that (Q∀Out) has been restricted to constants in this book, because universal instantiation for all terms is invalid in some systems.

The rule (Q∀In) may appear to be unacceptable, for it seems to warrant the invalid inference from a single instance Pc to the general claim that all things have property P. The restriction on this rule is crucial. When the constant c does not appear in ∀xPx nor in any of the hypotheses under which ∀xPx lies, then it turns out that a deduction of Pc provides a recipe for proving Pb for *any* choice of constant b. The fact that Pb holds for any choice of b *does* support the conclusion ∀xPx.

Most readers of this book will already have had some exposure to the process of finding proofs in some version of classical quantificational logic. However, it is still useful to discuss briefly the methods for discovering proofs in QL-. Here is a proof of the argument ∃xPx, ∀x(Px→Q) / Q, to help illustrate some useful strategies. The proof begins by converting ∃xPx to ~∀x~Px by (Def∃).

```
1. │  ∃xPx
2. └  ∀x(Px→Q)
3. │  ~∀x~Px        (Def∃)
   │  ???
   │  Q
```

At this point, it is not a particularly good strategy to apply (∀Out) to line 2. It is best to delay the application of (∀Out) until the proof is better developed. Since there seems little else one can do, a good plan would be to try to obtain the conclusion by Indirect Proof (IP). Note that the order in which the proof is developed is recorded with 'discovery numbers' in square brackets to the right.

```
1. │  ∃xPx
2. └  ∀x(Px→Q)
3. │  ~∀x~Px        (Def∃)   [1]
4. │   │ ~Q                   [2]
   │   │ ???
   │   │ ⊥          (⊥In)     [3]
   │  Q             (IP)
```

The problem now is to derive some contradiction (a pair of the form A and ~A) in the new subproof so as to obtain ⊥ by (⊥In). Since step 3 is the only negation available, it is best to assume that the desired contradiction will be ~∀x~Px and its opposite: ∀x~Px. So what remains is to find a proof of ∀x~Px, which in all likelihood will be obtained by (Q∀In).

1.	∃xPx		
2.	∀x(Px→Q)		
3.	~∀x~Px	(Def∃)	[1]
4.	~Q		[2]
	???		
	∀x~Px	(Q∀In)	[5]
	~∀x~Px	(Reit)	[4]
	⊥	(⊥In)	[3]
	Q	(IP)	

To create a proof of ∀x~Px, we will need to prove an instance Pc, choosing c so that it does not appear in any hypothesis or in ∀x~Px. Luckily any constant will do, since no constant appears anywhere so far. The proof can then be completed by applying (Q∀Out) to step 2 and using MT.

1.	∃xPx		
2.	∀x(Px→Q)		
3.	~∀x~Px	(Def∃)	[1]
4.	~Q		[2]
5.	Pc→Q	2 (Q∀Out)	[7]
6.	~Pc	4 5 (MT)	[6]
7.	∀x~Px	6 (Q∀In)	[5]
8.	~∀x~Px	3 (Reit)	[4]
9.	⊥	7, 8 (⊥In)	[3]
10.	Q	9 (IP)	

It will be helpful to develop derivable rules for QL- to simplify proofs involving ∃. Here is a useful pair of rules:

Q∃In   Q∃Out

Ac   ∃xAx

------   ⌐ Ac

∃xAx   :

              B

              B   where c is not in B, ∃xAx or any hypothesis for ∃xAx

---

EXERCISE 12.1   Show (Q∃In) and (Q∃Out) are derivable in QL-. (Hint: In the case of (Q∃Out) apply (CP) and (∀In) to the subproof headed by Ac. Then use strategies discussed above.)

Given the derived rules, the proof of ∃xPx, ∀x(Px→Q) / Q can be simplified as follows:

1. | ∃xPx
2. └ ∀x(Px→Q)
3. | └ Pc
5. | | Pc→Q   (Q∀Out)
6. | | Q   (MP)
7. | Q   (Q∃Out)

To make sure that you can find proofs in QL- smoothly, complete the following exercise.

EXERCISE 12.2   Prove in QL-. You may use derivable rules.

a) ∀x(Px&Qx) ↔ (∀xPx & ∀yQy)
b) ∀x(Px→Qx), ∃xPx / ∃xQx
c) ∀x(Px→Q) / ∃xPx→Q
d) ∀x(Px→Qx) / ∀x(∃y(Px&Rxy)→∃z(Qx&Rxz))
e) ∀x∀yLxy / ∀y∀xLxy
f) ∀xPx ∨ ∀yQy / ∀x(Px∨Qx)
g) ∀xPx ↔ ~∃y~Py
h) ∀xPx / ∃xPx

12.3. Identity in Modal Logic

A system QL for identity can be constructed by adding the following pair of rules to QL-:

System QL = QL- + (≈In) + (≈Out).

≈In   **≈Out**

------   s≈t

t≈t   P(l, s, l′)

                P(l, t, l′)   where P is a predicate letter (including ≈)

The rule (≈In) has no premises, so it indicates that t≈t may be added to any subproof whenever we like. As in propositional modal logic, such premise-free rules are called *axioms*. The rule (≈Out) is designed to allow substitution of one term t for another s when s≈t is available. P(l, s, l′) is an atomic sentence composed of the predicate letter P followed by the list of terms (l, s, l′). As you can see, this list contains an occurrence of s. The list (l, t, l′) that appears in the conclusion of the rule results from replacing the t for the occurrence of s in the list (l, s, l′). In the special case where l is the empty list, the rule allows the substitution of (t, l′) for (s, l′), and when both l and l′ are empty, it warrants substitution of (t) for (s).

The rule explicitly allows the substitution into other identity sentences (sentences of the form s≈u). So when s≈t has been proven (officially ≈(s, t)), t may be replaced for s in s≈u (i.e., in ≈(s, u)) to obtain t≈u (i.e., ≈(t, u)). This means that the following is a special case of (≈Out):

s≈t

s≈u

------

t≈u   (≈Out)

Another instance of (≈Out) is the following:

s≈t

s≈s

----

t≈s   (≈Out)

Here t is replaced for s in the first occurrence of s in s≈s. Since s≈s is provable in QL by (≈In), this shows that QL also guarantees the symmetry of ≈, and from that it is easy to show that ≈ is transitive.

(Symmetry)   t≈s / s≈t
(Transitivity)   t≈s, s≈u / t≈u

EXERCISE 12.3   Prove the following in QL.

a) ∃xx≈c
b) t≈s / s≈t
c) t≈s, s≈u / t≈u
d) s≈t, ~Ps / ~Pt
e) s≈t, Ps→Q / Pt→Q
f) s≈t, ~(Ps→Q) / ~(Pt→Q)
g) (Hard.) (Pc&∀y(Py→y≈c)) ↔ ∀y(Py↔c≈y)

The rule ($\approx$Out) may appear to be overly restrictive since it allows substitution of identical terms only in *atomic* sentences. The ordinary rule of substitution familiar from classical predicate logic allows replacement of identical terms in complex sentences as well. However, the failure of the principle of the substitution of identities is a characteristic feature of modal logics. Since substitution fails in the scope of modal operators like $\Box$, the $\approx$ rules should be formulated so that substitution is not possible in those contexts. The rule ($\approx$Out) embodies this restriction by allowing substitution of identicals only in atomic sentences. To apply the rule, one must have both s$\approx$t and an *atomic* sentence P(l, s, l'), from which P(l, t, l') follows. Obviously an atom like P(l, s, l') cannot contain the modal operator $\Box$.

The fact that ($\approx$Out) does not warrant substitution of identities in all contexts allows us to explain the invalidity of a number of famous philosophical arguments. Consider the following example concerning the author of Waverley, which was presented by Russell in 'On Denoting' (1905):

(1)	Scott is the author of Waverley.	s$\approx$w
(2)	<u>King George knows Scott is Scott.</u>	<u>Kg s$\approx$s</u>
(3)	King George knows Scott is the author of Waverley.	Kg s$\approx$w

(1) and (2) were presumably true, yet (3) was false, for King George famously asked who the author of Waverley was. The problem is to explain what is wrong with reasoning from (1) and (2) to (3). From the point of view of this book, the answer is this. Since 'King George knows' is treated as a modal operator, we may deny that (3) follows from (1) and (2). Although (3) results from replacing the second s in (2) with w on the basis of the identity (1), the substitution is blocked because (2) is not atomic. A similar diagnosis handles Quine's (1961) famous example.

(4)	9 is the number of planets.	9$\approx$n
(5)	<u>Necessarily 9 is greater than 7.</u>	<u>$\Box$9>7</u>
(6)	Necessarily the number of planets is greater than 7.	$\Box$n>7

Here again the premises are true and the conclusion is false. An explanation of this is that the substitution of n for 9 occurs in the nonatomic sentence (5).

These two examples illustrate the problems that arise in applying the law of substitution of identicals beneath a modal operator. However, the law of substitution has seemed to many philosophers to be beyond reasonable doubt. They would argue that there is no need to restrict ($\approx$Out) in any way. On the view that substitution of identicals is legal in all contexts, some other way of explaining the errors in (1)–(3) and (4)–(6) must be found. In fact, some have claimed that the failure of the rule of substitution for an expression in *any* context is a sign that what was substituted is not really a term.

This was Russell's technique for analyzing the error in the argument about King George. He claimed that the description 'the author of Waverley' is not to be treated as a term, and must be translated into the notation of QL using his theory of descriptions. His strategy has the advantage that no adjustments to the classical rules for quantifiers or identity need to be made. Once the theory of descriptions is applied to (1)–(3), the argument no longer appears to have the form of a substitution of identical terms. If Russell's method for eliminating descriptions is thoroughly applied, one need not place restrictions on ($\approx$Out) because any argument that would be a purported violation of the unrestricted rule of substitution of identities would show that substitution of *terms* did not occur.

The details of Russell's descriptions strategy, and some complaints against it, will be presented in the next section, but one objection bears mentioning here. Russell's method forces us to treat even proper names of English as if they were descriptions. For example, consider (7)–(9).

(7) Cicero is Tully. $c \approx t$
(8) <u>King George knows Cicero is Cicero.</u> <u>Kg $c \approx c$</u>
(9) King George knows Cicero is Tully.   Kg $c \approx t$

The above argument is invalid, and yet there is no explicit description to unpack in (7) or (8). A Russellian reaction to this would be to claim that the argument shows that 'Cicero' and 'Tully' are not really names, and so should be represented in the formal theory with descriptions for 'the thing with Cicero's properties' and 'the thing with Tully's properties' which may then be unpacked using the theory of descriptions. Since arguments like (7)–(9) can be constructed for any pair of names, the consequence of the Russellian strategy is to deny that proper names (or any other denoting expressions) count as terms of the formal language.

A reluctance to abandon the law of substitution of identicals, tied with the influence of Russell's theory of descriptions, has led many to deny that expressions like 'the number of planets' and 'Cicero' should be represented with terms in logic. Although this is a consistent way to deal with apparent failures of substitution, this book takes a more general approach. By restricting the rule of substitution to atoms, systems that include terms for proper names and definite descriptions may be included directly, without reliance on Russell's theory of descriptions. This will allow a much simpler process of translation from English to the formal language. Those who prefer Russell's strategy may use those systems to be developed here that lack the extra terms.

We have explained why substitution beneath $\square$ is restricted, but the restriction actually used in ($\approx$Out) appears stronger, for it allows substitution only in atomic sentences. This may seem too harsh. For example, s$\approx$t and Ps$\rightarrow$Qs do not yield Pt$\rightarrow$Qt by ($\approx$Out) because Ps$\rightarrow$Qs is not atomic. However, it is possible to show that a rule ($\approx$Out+) allowing substitution of identities outside the scope of modal operators is a derivable rule in fS.

($\approx$Out+)

s$\approx$t

As

At   where At is the result of replacing an occurrence of s in As that is
        not in the scope of $\square$

Note, however, that the following argument is *not* available in K, nor any of the other modal logics we have studied:

   s$\approx$t, $\square$Ps / $\square$Pt

So it is not possible to show that substitution in *modal* contexts is a derived rule.

EXERCISE 12.4   (Project for more advanced students.) Prove that ($\approx$Out+)
is a derived rule of QL. Use mathematical induction on the length of At.
(Hint: It is convenient to show first that the following rules are derivable.)
s$\approx$t / As$\leftrightarrow$At, when As is atomic
As$\leftrightarrow$At / $\sim$As$\leftrightarrow$$\sim$At
As$\leftrightarrow$At / (As$\rightarrow$B)$\leftrightarrow$(At$\rightarrow$B)
Bs$\leftrightarrow$Bt / (A$\rightarrow$Bs)$\leftrightarrow$(A$\rightarrow$Bt)
As$\leftrightarrow$At / $\forall$y[Ay]^s/x$\leftrightarrow$$\forall$y[Ay]^t/x

---

The fact that substitution of identities fails in modal contexts does not mean that such substitutions are never warranted. Since ($\approx$Out) may be applied in any subproof, it follows that arguments of the following form are derivable:

$$\square s \approx t \qquad \square\square s \approx t \qquad \square\square\square s \approx t$$
$$\square Ps \qquad \square\square Ps \qquad \square\square\square Ps$$

-------   -------   -------

$$\square Pt \qquad\quad \square\square Pt \qquad\quad \square\square\square Pt$$

EXERCISE 12.5   Prove each of the above arguments.

Notice that in general, the identity $\square^n s \approx t$, (i.e., $s \approx t$ prefixed by n boxes) warrants the substitution of t for s in any term position that lies beneath exactly n boxes.

$$\square^n s \approx t$$
$$\square^n Ps$$

$$\square^n Pt$$

12.4. The Problem of Nondenoting Terms in Classical Logic

One puzzling feature of the classical system QL for the quantifiers is that it allows us to prove sentences that apparently claim the existence of God, Pegasus, and anything else for which we have a name. As you saw in the solution to Exercise 12.3a, the identity $g \approx g$ (for 'God is God') is provable by ($\approx$In). From this it is possible to obtain $\exists x x \approx g$ ('there exists something identical to God') by the rule ($\exists$In). However, God's existence is surely not something one should expect to prove on the basis of logic alone. The fact that $\exists x x \approx g$ is a theorem of QL corresponds to an assumption traditionally included in the semantics for classical quantification, namely, that each constant has a referent in the quantifier's domain. So if 'God' counts as a constant, it would seem that it must refer to something that exists. The problem with this is that we commonly use names to refer to things that do not exist, such as Pegasus, or things that might not exist, such as God.

A standard way of resolving the problem that $\exists x x \approx g$ is provable in QL is to deny that 'God' is to be translated using a constant. Since the constant g must refer to an existing object, its use presupposes that what it refers to is something real. Therefore, in a philosophical context where God's existence is in question, some other way must be found to express the English: 'God exists'. One alternative is to choose a predicate letter G for 'is Godlike', or 'has all the properties of God', and then express God's existence with ∃xGx. Using this translation tactic, 'God exists' is no longer classified a logical truth because ∃xGx is not a theorem of QL.

There are a number of difficulties with this strategy. First, it maintains the classical principles for the quantifiers at the expense of complicating the process of translation from English to logic, for it must deny that certain English names are to be treated as terms in logic. Second, it yields strange consequences for sentences that mention mythical creatures. On this scheme, 'Pegasus does not exist' translates to ~∃xPx. Now how do we notate such claims as 'Pegasus is a winged horse' and 'Pegasus is a hippopotamus'? One way is to use ∀x(Px→Wx) for 'Everything that is a Pegasizer is a winged horse' and ∀x(Px→Hx) for 'Everything that is a Pegasizer is a hippopotamus'. The trouble with this is that both ∀x(Px→Wx) and ∀x(Px→Hx) follow from ~∃xPx in QL. (In general, when ∀x(Ax→Bx) holds because there are no things with property A, the quantification is said to be *vacuous* and the sentence is called a vacuous truth.)

EXERCISE 12.6   Prove ~∃xPx / ∀x(Px→Hx) in QL.

So QL forces us to conclude that Pegasus is both a winged horse and a hippopotamus (and anything else for that matter) merely on the grounds that Pegasus does not exist.

One might reply that this odd result is caused by an incorrect method of translation. Let us try again, this time using Russell's theory of descriptions. (For more on descriptions, see Chapter 18.) Let us introduce the abbreviation 1Px, which is read: 'only x is a Pegasizer'.

$$1Px =_{df} Px \ \& \ \forall y(Py \rightarrow y \approx x)$$

The abbreviation 1Px says that only x is a Pegasizer because it says that x is a Pegasizer, and that anything that is a Pegasizer is identical to x. According to Russell's theory of descriptions 'the Pegasizer is a winged horse' is to be translated as follows:

$$\exists x(1Px \& Wx)$$

This says that there is a thing that is the only Pegasizer that is a winged horse. Now presuming that 'Pegasus is a winged horse' has the same meaning as 'The Pegasizer is a winged horse', the translation for 'Pegasus is a winged horse' comes to ∃x(1Px&Wx). This looks more promising because ~∃x(1Px&Hx) follows from ~∃xPx, and so from the nonexistence of Pegasus you obtain that Pegasus is not a hippopotamus, which seems correct. However, ~∃xPx *also* entails ~∃x(1Px & Wx), and so according to the description tactic, one must conclude that Pegasus is not a winged horse, which seems wrong.

EXERCISE 12.7   Prove in QL that ~∃xPx entails ~∃x(1Px & Wx).

Even if we could solve the problem concerning Pegasus and other mythical beings, there is another difficulty to face with the view that names that fail to refer should be dealt with according to Russell's theory of descriptions. The sentence 'Jim was happy' is presumably translated Hj, as long as Jim exists. But when Jim dies, we may not use j for 'Jim' any longer, and our translation of 'Jim was happy' becomes ∃y(1Jy&Hy). It seems odd that what counts as the correct translation of an English sentence should depend on the facts of the world in this way. To avoid embarrassment, defenders of classical logic tend to deny that most proper names in English are translated using terms in logic. In the extreme, one will take the view that all proper names need to be treated as descriptions.

There is a second tactic for resolving the difficulty posed by the fact that QL seems to support the existence of God or Pegasus in theorems of the form ∃xx≈g. On this approach, 'God' is treated as a term, but it is denied that ∃xx≈g claims that He really exists. Instead, the domain of the quantifier is understood to contain all *possible* objects, not just the real ones. On this interpretation, ∃xx≈g claims only that God is possible. To translate the claim that God really exists, you write: Eg, where E is a predicate letter for 'exists'. Since Eg is not a theorem of QL, you are not forced into accepting God's existence.

This strategy raises some important philosophical issues. In the first place, it treats existence as a predicate, a view that has been hotly debated in the history of philosophy. We will not take up the controversy here, but it might be better to choose a logical system that does not force us to take sides in the matter. A second problem raised by this approach is that the domain of quantification contains items that do not exist, and yet many philosophers consider the quantifier domain the best measure of what there is. Assuming that we want to avoid having possible objects in our ontology (in the set of things we count as real), we are forced into the position that the existential quantifier does not mean what it says. This will seem an especially unacceptable conclusion to philosophers like Quine

(1963) who consider the existential quantifier the paradigm expression for making clear what really exists. If the symbol ∃x really means 'there *might* exist an x such that', then we will still be interested in working out the logic of some other symbol (say *∃*) that really *does* carry the ontological implications expected of the phrase 'there *is* an x such that'. A third problem is that even if the domain of quantification is understood to contain only possible objects, the fact that ∃xx≈g is a theorem forces one into the position that God is possible *as a matter of logic alone*. However, for all we know, the concept of God may be contradictory, and so God is not even a possible object. In any case, a logic that allows us to debate the issue should not count as a theorem the translation of a claim in dispute.

The problems just mentioned do not provide a knock-down, drag-out demonstration that classical quantification must be abandoned. However, they do provide motivations for considering an alternative system that avoids counting ∃xx≈g as a theorem. In free logic, the quantifier ∃x may carry strong ontological commitment if we like. At the same time it is possible to use the constant g for 'God' instead of having to employ a predicate letter G and a complex and unsatisfying translation strategy. Free logic solves the problems we have been discussing at the cost of giving up the standard rules of QL. However, the rules of free logic are not difficult, and they have the added attraction that they allow room for important flexibility when modal operators are added to the logic.

12.5. FL: A System of Free Logic

The rules of free logic (FL for short) are similar to the QL rules, except the quantifier rules are restricted to block unwanted inferences, for example, the inferences from g≈g (God is God) to ∃xx≈g (God exists) and from ∀xRx (everything is real) to Rp (Pegasus is real). (For more details on free logic see Bencivenga, 1986). A correct pair of rules for free logic may be formulated by prefixing instances in the standard rules with 'Ec→', where E is the special predicate for 'exists'. For those who object to the idea that existence should be expressed by a predicate letter, note that in most of the systems to be defined, Et may be eliminated in favor of ∃xx≈t.

System FL = PL + (∀Out) + (∀In) + (≈In) + (≈Out).

∀Out	∀In	
∀xAx	Ec→Ac	
-----	--------	
Ec→Ac	∀xAx	where c is not in ∀xAx nor in any of its hypotheses

According to (∀Out), it is no longer possible to deduce that Pegasus is real (Rp) given that everything is real (∀xRx). In order to conclude Rp, one must also have that Pegasus exists (Ep). The *system FL* is the result of adding (∀Out), (∀In), (≈In), and (≈Out) to PL (propositional logic). In FL, the proof of ∃xx≈g, which claims God's existence, is no longer possible, because from g≈g, ∃xx≈g cannot be derived.

EXERCISE 12.8   Attempt to derive ∃xx≈g in FL. How is the proof blocked?

In order to prove ∃xx≈g (God exists) from g≈g (God is God) in free logic, one must already have a proof of Eg (God exists). One difficulty with QL is that 'God is God' appears to entail 'God exists' even though our intuitions rule that 'God exists' is a stronger claim. In free logic, 'God is God' is weaker since it does not entail 'God exists'.

Some useful derivable rules for ∃ follow. As you can see, they are just like the classical rules except that instances are prefaced by 'Ec&'.

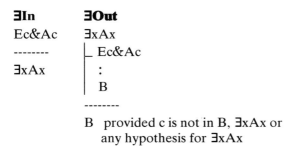

∃In   ∃Out
Ec&Ac   ∃xAx
--------   ⌐ Ec&Ac
∃xAx | :
             | B

             B   provided c is not in B, ∃xAx or
                 any hypothesis for ∃xAx

EXERCISE 12.9   Show (∃In) and (∃Out) are derivable in FL.

The addition of 'E' in the FL rules has surprisingly little effect on which arguments are provable. Most of the standard properties of the quantifiers in QL carry over to FL.

EXERCISE 12.10   Prove the following in FL.

a) ∀x(Px&Qx) ↔ (∀xPx & ∀yQy)
b) ∀x(Px → Qx), ∃xPx / ∃xQx
c) ∀x(Px → Q) / ∃xPx → Q
d) ∀x(Px → Qx) / ∀x(∃y(Px&Rxy) → ∃z(Qx&Rxz))
e) ∀x∀yLxy / ∀y∀xLxy
f) ∀xPx ∨ ∀yQy / ∀x(Px∨Qx)
g) ∀xPx ↔ ~∃y~Py

FL has the nice feature that the principles of classical logic can be restored by adding Et as an axiom for every term t. So an alternative way of formulating QL is to add the axiom (Q) to FL.

(Q)   Et

EXERCISE 12.11   Show that any argument provable in QL is also provable in FL + (Q). (Hint: Show that the rules of QL are derivable in FL + (Q).)

Since classical principles may be easily restored using this axiom, there is no need to fret over whether to adopt classical or free logic rules. The most general choice is to use free logic. Those who believe that classical quantification is a better choice may simply add (Q) to FL. In this respect, FL will play something like the role of K in propositional modal logics. K is rather weak, but acceptable modal logics may be constructed for various purposes by adding the right selection of additional axioms. The approach in this book, then, will be to concentrate on FL and to develop a number of special axioms and/or rules to capture alternative assumptions about quantification.

Notice that in FL, the universal instantiation principle (∀Out) applies to the constants and not to other terms. For the moment, the constants are the only terms so far included in the language, so the difference does not matter. However, in the future, new terms will be introduced, including complex terms for the definite descriptions. In that case, we will need to consider a more general statement (t∀) of the instantiation principle.

∀xAx

Et→At   (t∀)

When (t∀) is available, it is easy to see that the more general rule of existential instantiation (t∃) is provable.

Et&At

∃xAx   (t∃)

Unfortunately, (t∀) is not correct in some quantified modal logics. (See Section 13.6 for the details.) So (t∀) should not be in the foundational system from which all other systems of quantified modal logic are constructed.

Although most theorems of QL that lack any term are also theorems of FL, the following QL theorem is not provable in FL: ∀xPx→∃xPx. Perhaps this is a good thing, for ∀xPx→∃xPx is invalid if the domain of discourse of the quantifiers happens to be empty. (In that case ∀xPx is vacuously true, but ∃xPx is false.) So acceptance of ∀xPx→∃xPx depends on the assumption that at least one thing exists. There are those who believe that the fact that there is at least one thing in the universe is an empirical accident, and so not a proper assumption to make in logic. These people will find FL attractive. When reasoning is evaluated in the normal case where something exists, one may simply list ∃xEx as a premise for the argument. For more adventurous logicians who tire of constantly adding this assumption, ∃xEx may be added as an axiom to FL.

(∃E)   ∃xEx

When this is done, ∀xPx→∃xPx becomes provable.

EXERCISE 12.12   Show that ∀xAx→∃xAx is a theorem of the system that results from adding (∃E) to FL. Now show that if you add ∀xAx→∃xAx as an axiom to FL, (∃E) is provable. (Hint: For the proof from ∀xAx→∃xAx to ∃xEx, show ∀xEx and use a special case of ∀xAx→∃xAx.)

12.6. fS: A Basic Quantified Modal Logic

The simplest way to formulate a quantified modal logic is to add to a given propositional modal logic S the rules of free logic FL forming a system called fS. For example, fK, the quantified modal logic based on K, includes all the rules of K and the four rules of FL. fK is the foundation for all the systems in this book since all the other systems are generated from it by adding principles of propositional modal logic or additional principles having to do with the interactions between the quantifiers, E, ≈, and □. For example, if a classical treatment of quantification is desired, one may simply add (Q) as an axiom to fS, so that (Q∀In) and (Q∀Out) become derivable rules. The resulting system is called qS. To illustrate some strategies for finding proofs in these systems, we will work out a proof of the following argument in qK and fK: □∀x(Px→Qx), ∼□∀x∼Px / ∼□∀x∼Qx. The proof in qK will be presented first. Since the conclusion is a negation, the Indirect Proof strategy comes to mind.

1. | □∀x(Px→Qx)
2. |_ ∼□∀x∼Px
3. | |_ □∀x∼Qx   [1]
   | ???
   | ⊥
   | ∼□∀x∼Qx   (IP)

Since ~□∀x~Px is the only negative sentence available, it is a good bet that ⊥ can be obtained by proving the contradictory pair: □∀x~Px, ~□∀x~Px. So all that remains is to construct a proof of □∀x~Px.

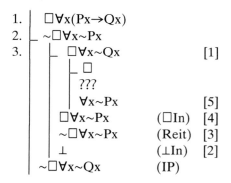

1.	□∀x(Px→Qx)		
2.	~□∀x~Px		
3.	□∀x~Qx		[1]
	???		
	□∀x~Px		[4]
	~□∀x~Px	(Reit)	[3]
	⊥	(⊥In)	[2]
	~□∀x~Qx	(IP)	

Since this step begins with □, the best strategy is to try to obtain it with (□In).

1.	□∀x(Px→Qx)		
2.	~□∀x~Px		
3.	□∀x~Qx		[1]
	□		
	???		
	∀x~Px		[5]
	□∀x~Px	(□In)	[4]
	~□∀x~Px	(Reit)	[3]
	⊥	(⊥In)	[2]
	~□∀x~Qx	(IP)	

Now (□Out) may be applied to steps 1 and 3. What remains is a simple proof in quantificational logic to be completed inside the boxed subproof.

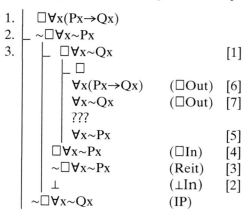

1.	□∀x(Px→Qx)		
2.	~□∀x~Px		
3.	□∀x~Qx		[1]
	□		
	∀x(Px→Qx)	(□Out)	[6]
	∀x~Qx	(□Out)	[7]
	???		
	∀x~Px		[5]
	□∀x~Px	(□In)	[4]
	~□∀x~Px	(Reit)	[3]
	⊥	(⊥In)	[2]
	~□∀x~Qx	(IP)	

The remaining steps can be solved using the classical quantifier rules and the derivable rule Modus Tollens (MT).

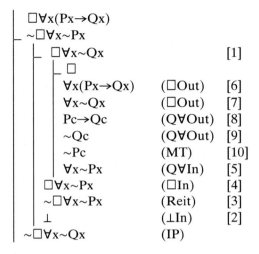

□∀x(Px→Qx)		
~□∀x~Px		
□∀x~Qx		[1]
□		
∀x(Px→Qx)	(□Out)	[6]
∀x~Qx	(□Out)	[7]
Pc→Qc	(Q∀Out)	[8]
~Qc	(Q∀Out)	[9]
~Pc	(MT)	[10]
∀x~Px	(Q∀In)	[5]
□∀x~Px	(□In)	[4]
~□∀x~Px	(Reit)	[3]
⊥	(⊥In)	[2]
~□∀x~Qx	(IP)	

The same strategy can be used to prove □∀x(Px→Qx), ~□∀x~Px / ~□∀x~Qx in fK. The only difference comes in the quantifier steps in the boxed subproof.

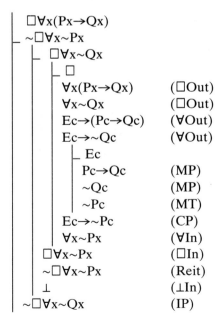

□∀x(Px→Qx)	
~□∀x~Px	
□∀x~Qx	
□	
∀x(Px→Qx)	(□Out)
∀x~Qx	(□Out)
Ec→(Pc→Qc)	(∀Out)
Ec→~Qc	(∀Out)
Ec	
Pc→Qc	(MP)
~Qc	(MP)
~Pc	(MT)
Ec→~Pc	(CP)
∀x~Px	(∀In)
□∀x~Px	(□In)
~□∀x~Px	(Reit)
⊥	(⊥In)
~□∀x~Qx	(IP)

The following exercises will help you practice proof strategies in qK and help you appreciate the differences between qK and fK.

EXERCISE 12.13   Prove that the following sentences are theorems of qK. Then attempt proofs of the same sentences in fK to appreciate how the proof of each is blocked.

a) □∃xx≈c
b) ∀y□∃xx≈y
c) □∀xPx → ∀x□Px
d) ∀x□Px → □∀xPx
e) ◇∃xAx ↔ ∃x◇Ax

12.7. The Barcan Formulas

An important issue posed by the introduction of quantifiers to modal logic is how the quantifiers should interact with □ and ◇. The best-known principles governing this interaction are the Barcan Formula (BF) and its converse (CBF).

(BF)   ∀x□Ax→□∀xAx
(CBF)   □∀xAx→∀x□Ax

(The principles are named in honor of Ruth Barcan Marcus, who first considered them in print (Barcan, 1946).) These two axioms are often referred to together as the *Barcan Formulas*. Adopting them commits us to the view that ∀x and □ may be exchanged.

If the classical rules for the quantifiers are adopted, there is no choice but to accept *both* Barcan Formulas, since they are provable in qK as follows. (These are solutions to parts c) and d) of the previous exercise.)

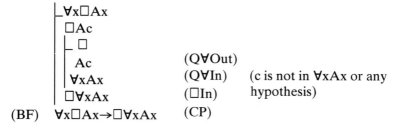

	∀x□Ax		
	□Ac		
	□		
	Ac	(Q∀Out)	
	∀xAx	(Q∀In)	(c is not in ∀xAx or any
	□∀xAx	(□In)	hypothesis)
(BF)	∀x□Ax→□∀xAx	(CP)	

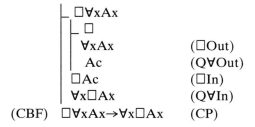

□∀xAx	
□	
∀xAx	(□Out)
Ac	(Q∀Out)
□Ac	(□In)
∀x□Ax	(Q∀In)
(CBF) □∀xAx→∀x□Ax	(CP)

The *traditional formulation* TK of propositional modal logic K does not used boxed subproofs. Instead, Necessitation (Nec) and Distribution (Dist) are used in place of (□In) and (□Out). (TK was discussed in Section 1.7.) The propositional modal logics TK and K are equivalent in the sense that any modal logic S built from K proves exactly the same arguments as the corresponding logic TS constructed from TK. It is easy to prove the converse Barcan Formula (CBF) in qTK, the system that results from adding classical quantifier rules to TK.

EXERCISE *12.14   Prove (CBF) in qTK. (Hint: Prove □∀xAx→□Ac first.)

Although (BF) is provable in systems as strong as qTB, it is (strangely) *not* provable in qTS for many modal logics S weaker than B, such as qTM and qTS4 (Hughes and Cresswell, 1996, Ch. 15). The traditional formulation has the awkward feature that although intuitions that support (CBF) tend to support (BF) as well, (BF) needs to be added to qTS as a separate axiom for weaker modal logics S. So there is an odd asymmetry in the status of (BF) and (CBF) using the traditional rule set. Although the *propositional* logics TS and S are equivalent, the systems differ once quantifier rules are added. (BF) is provable in qS (and not qTS) because the natural deduction rules (□In) and (□Out) are somewhat stronger than (Nec) and (Dist) in systems that contain quantifiers. The strange asymmetry induced by the classical quantifier rules in the traditional formulations for modal logic is an important motive for adopting the subproof formulations used in this book.

Another advantage of the subproof formulation is that it simplifies statement of the rules in some quantified modal logics. For example, the system Q3 (Thomason, 1970, p. 63) includes a complex rule (G∀In) of universal instantiation.

(G∀In)   ⊢ □(A$_1$→□(A$_2$→ .. □(A$_n$→(Ec→Ac)) ..))

⊢ □(A$_1$→□(A$_2$→ .. □(A$_n$→∀xAx) ..)) where c is not in
the conclusion

However, when boxed subproof notation is used, the effect of this rule is already obtained without the mention of complex sequences of boxes and conditionals found in (G∀In). The reason is that the ability to apply our rule (∀In) within boxed and unboxed subproofs captures exactly the effect of those sequences.

It is important to note that although classical quantifier rules entail both of the Barcan Formulas, the principles of free logic entail neither one. It will be argued below that (BF) and (CBF) should be rejected for many applications of modal logic, so this provides another reason to build quantified modal logic around free logic rules. In Exercises 12.13c and 12.13d you showed that attempts to prove instances of (BF) and (CBF) are blocked in fK. It is worth reviewing here why this occurs in the case of (BF). Here is a sample proof attempt:

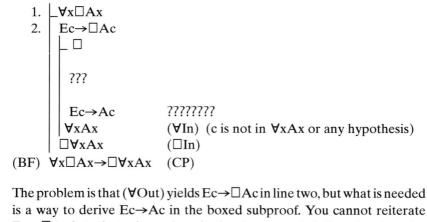

The problem is that (∀Out) yields Ec→□Ac in line two, but what is needed is a way to derive Ec→Ac in the boxed subproof. You cannot reiterate Ec→□Ac into that subproof to obtain what is needed: Ec→Ac, since the box in Ec→□Ac is not the main connective.

12.8. Constant and Varying Domains of Quantification

Since the classical quantified modal logic qK entails the Barcan Formulas, reasons for rejecting the Barcan Formulas would appear to be reasons for abandoning classical quantification. Are the Barcan Formulas acceptable? It is easier to assess the situation by considering (◇BF), which is derivable in qK, as you showed in Exercise 12.13e.

(◇BF)   ◇∃xAx↔∃x◇Ax

On at least some interpretations of ◇ and ∃, it appears that (◇BF) should be rejected. For example, suppose that ◇ reads 'it was the case that', and we read the quantifier ∃x in the present tense: 'there (now) exists an x such that'. Let Sx read 'x signs the Declaration of Independence'. Under this interpretation ◇∃xSx claims that at some time in the past, someone existed who signed the Declaration of Independence, which is true. On the other hand, ∃x◇Sx says that there *now* exists someone who signed the Declaration of Independence, which is false.

EXERCISE 12.15.   Invent an interpretation of (◇BF) where the left side is false and the right side is true. Invent interpretations of (◇BF) to show that it fails (in both directions) when ◇ reads 'John believes that'.

The tense logic reading of ∃ and ◇ illustrates a general issue concerning how the quantifiers should be treated in modal logic. Two basic options concerning the quantifier domains have been proposed. The simpler of the two, the *constant domain* approach, presupposes a single domain of quantification. Assuming constant domains is compatible with the Barcan Formulas. The *varying domain* option, on the other hand, assumes that the domain of quantification changes from world to world, and contains only the objects that exist *in a given* world. On this understanding, ∃xPx would be true in a world **w** iff there is an object *that actually exists in w* that has property P. This is sometimes called the *actualist interpretation* of the quantifier. The constant domain approach is attractive to many logicians just because it dovetails so nicely with classical quantifier rules. However, we have reviewed reasons in Section 12.4 for rejecting the classical principles – reasons that were independent of any worries about how to deal with modality. Apart from their familiarity, classical rules have no decided advantage over free logic.

In intensional languages, there are further objections to classical principles. On ordinary interpretations of 'there is . .' in everyday language, the domain of quantification depends on the context at which it is evaluated. For example, 'There is a severe economic depression' is (at the time of this writing) false, and yet it was once true, for example, in the 1930s. So the domain of the present-tense expression 'there is . .' changes to reflect what exists at different times. Quantifier domains vary along many other dimensions as well. Place, speaker, and even topic of discussion play a role in determining the domain in ordinary communication. If I say to a class 'everyone must turn in Exercise 4 tomorrow', it is clear from the context that I do not mean to include the president of the USA, the president of the university, or even myself in the domain of quantification. When we begin a fairy tale with the words 'once upon a time there was a king', we are establishing a new possible world and peopling the domain with a new character. If later we say 'everyone feared the king', it is clear that we do not mean all real people, or even all presently existing people, feared that mythical king, but only that some relevant set of characters *in our story* did so. It is a standard feature of storytelling that the domain for the story and the domain for the real world differ.

The same point extends from storytelling to communication in more practical settings. It is commonplace in planning, decision making, and even scientific theorizing to consider (counterfactual) alternatives to our own possible world that feature "ideal" objects – objects that do not exist in reality (for example, objects totally isolated from external forces in Newtonian mechanics). It is also a standard assumption that objects in the real world need not exist in others. I exist in the real world, but it does not follow that my existence is necessary. There are clearly possible worlds where I never existed, for example, ones where my parents did not meet, or ones where humans never evolved on Earth. So 'Jim Garson existed' varies in truth value from one possible world to the next. It seems to be a fundamental feature of our ordinary understanding of possibility that our existence is contingent and that different objects exist in different possible worlds. The only thing that has been widely thought to exist necessarily is God, but even God's existence is of course highly controversial. So it is far from clear that we could find even *one* thing that exists in all possible worlds. Yet the constant domain approach to the quantifiers would appear to claim that *everything* in the domain of one world exists in all the others.

It is interesting to explore the relationships between the Barcan Formulas and sentences that express conditions on the quantifier domains more directly. Since the truth of Ec in a world says that the referent of c exists in that world, sentence (ED) says that when the referent of c exists in a world, it also exists in all accessible worlds.

(ED) $Ec \rightarrow \Box Ec$

It should not be too surprising then that adoption of (ED) as an axiom corresponds to a condition on models (ED) (for *expanding domains*), which says that the domains never shrink as we move from one world to another accessible world.

(ED)   If **wRv**, then everything in the domain of **w** is in the domain of **v**.

It turns out that adoption of (ED) is equivalent to adopting the converse Barcan Formula (CBF) in fK. Whether (CBF) or (ED) is added to fK as an axiom, the resulting system proves exactly the same arguments. Since (ED) is an instance of ∀x□Ex, and (ED) yields ∀x□Ex by (∀In), it also follows that the effect of the (CBF) may be obtained by using the axiom ∀x□Ex instead.

EXERCISE 12.16

a) Prove that systems fK+∀x□Ex and fK+(ED) prove exactly the same arguments. That is, prove Ec→□Ec in fK+∀x□Ex, and then prove ∀x□Ex in fK + the axiom Ec→□Ec.

*b) Show that fK+(CBF) and fK+(ED) prove exactly the same arguments. (Hint: Prove (ED) in fK+(CBF) and prove (CBF) in fK+(ED). To prove (ED) in fK+(CBF), first prove ∀xEx in a boxed subproof, from which □∀xEx follows by (□In). Then use (CBF) and (∀Out) to obtain the desired result. To prove (CBF) in fK+(ED), obtain □Ec→□Ac from □∀xAx. Then use (ED) to obtain Ec→□Ac, from which ∀x□Ax follows by (∀In).)

It follows then that the converse of the Barcan Formula (CBF) expresses the expanding domain condition (ED). The "mirror image" of domain condition (ED) is (CD) (for *contracting domains*). This says that the domains never include new objects as we move to new accessible worlds.

(CD)   If **wRv** then everything in the domain of **v** is in the domain of **w**.

This condition corresponds to (CD), which asserts that if c fails to exist in a world then it does not exist in any accessible world.

(CD)   ~Ec→□~Ec

You might guess that (CD) is equivalent to (BF).

(BF)   ∀x□Ax→□∀xAx

However, this guess is only partly right. Although (CD) yields (BF) in fK, there are some quantified modal logics where (BF) does not entail (CD). (For more on this point, see Garson, 2005.)

EXERCISE 12.17 (Hard.) Show that (BF) is derivable in fK+(CD). (Hint: From ∀x□Ax obtain Ec→□Ac, from which ◇Ec→□Ac may be proven with the help of (CD). Now show that ◇Ec→□Ac entails □(Ec→Ac). (That is difficult, but it may be solved constructing a tree in propositional logic and converting the result to a proof using the method given in Section 7.1.) Once □(Ec→Ac) is in hand it is not difficult to prove □∀xAx by starting a boxed subproof and using (□Out), (∀In), and (□In).)

When the conditions (ED) and (CD) hold together, it follows that the domains are constant across accessible worlds. This is essentially the semantical effect of adopting the two Barcan Formulas. The problem with accepting these conditions is that they validate ◇Et→□Et, the counterintuitive claim that if something possibly exists, then it exists of necessity.

Notice also that the adoption of axiom (Q) (that is, Et) entails the classical quantifier rules. But this immediately yields both (ED) and (CD).

EXERCISE 12.18 Prove (ED) and (CD) in qK = fK+(Q).

12.9. A Classicist's Defense of Constant Domains

Defenders of the constant domain interpretation respond to the counterintuitive nature of the Barcan Formulas by proposing the *possibilist* account of the role of the quantifier domain (Linsky and Zalta, 1994). They claim that the domain of quantification contains all the *possible* objects, and not the objects that actually exist in a given world or context. So the sentence ∃xSx does not claim that there is an actual thing (now) that signed the Declaration of Independence, but only that some possible object did so. English quantifier expressions with an actualist reading can still be defined using possibilist quantifiers and special predicate letters. For example, the present tense quantifier ∃p can be defined using ∃ and a predicate letter P that reads 'presently exists' as follows.

∃pxA =df ∃x(Px&A)

To express the present-tense sentence 'there is now a thing that signed the Declaration of Independence', one would write: ∃x(Px&Sx), which says that there is a possible object that presently exists who signed the Declaration of Independence.

The possibilist response has the advantage that it preserves the standard quantifier rules. Since the domain contains all *possible* objects, and since there are presumably the same possible objects for each possible world, there is no need to distinguish domains for each world. So acceptance of the Barcan Formulas makes perfect sense. A workable possibilist logic with classical quantifier rules and both Barcan Formulas can be formulated by adding the axiom Ec to fS.

However, this book presents a full variety of weaker systems to accommodate alternatives to the possibilist interpretation. A problem with the possibilist reading is that it strips the quantifier ∃x of its ontological commitment – it no longer indicates what is really there. *Actualists*, who wish to preserve the ontological implications of ∃x, will want to develop a logic where ∃x is reserved to pick out what is actual (in a given world or context) rather than what is merely possible. Of course it does not matter whether the symbol ∃x is appropriated for the actualist or the possibilist reading. The actualist is free to donate the symbol ∃x to the possibilist, and use another one (say ∃*x* or ∃px) for the actualist interpretation. The point is that the actualist is interested in developing the logic of the actualist quantifier (however it is to be notated) because this is the reading normally given to the expression 'there is' in English. Even if that quantifier is to be defined from the possibilist quantifier by (Def∃p), one will still want to work out the logical rules for the actualist quantifier. It is interesting to note that the rules determined by (Def∃p) are exactly the principles of free logic. Far from undermining interest in free logic, the possibilist vindicates it in this way.

Linksy and Zalta (1994) have argued that the constant domain quantifier has an interpretation that is perfectly acceptable to actualists. Any actualists who employ possible-worlds semantics routinely quantify over *abstracta* (abstract objects) such as possible worlds in formulating semantics for modal logic. So some abstracta are actual by these actualists' lights. By cleverly outfitting the domain with abstracta no more objectionable than the ones actualists accept, Linsky and Zalta show that the Barcan Formula and classical quantifier rules can be accepted. Note, however, that this demonstration does nothing to establish that actualists must adopt for ∃x the specific interpretation of the quantifier domain Linsky and Zalta have discovered. It is open to actualists (and non-actualists as well) to investigate the behavior of quantifiers with more robust domains, for example, domains containing only the (nonabstract) material objects, or the things present at a given time or place. Under interpretations of this kind, a varying domain approach will still be needed. To keep our options open, then, it would be better to explore a full range of possible quantified modal logics.

Cresswell (1991) makes the interesting observation that varying quantification has limited expressive power relative to constant domain quantification. Varying domain quantification can be defined with constant
domain quantifiers and E, but there is no way to fully express constant
domain quantifiers with varying ones. When ∀x is given the actualist reading, there is no way to say that all the possible objects have a certain property. One response to this objection is to note that one can easily create
classical quantification within free logic when one wishes by adopting the
axiom Et. Better yet, one can introduce two different quantifiers into the
language, one with actualist and the other with possibilist readings. Either
way, no reason has been given for abandoning the project of working out
the logics of the actualist quantifier expressions that are so common in
natural language. The advantage of doing so is that a logic appropriate
for possibilist quantification can always be obtained when needed as a
special case.

12.10. The Prospects for Classical Systems with Varying Domains

We have good reasons to want to develop an actualist quantified modal
logic with varying domains. Once this decision is made, major difficulties
arise for classical quantification theory. There *are* systems that use classical
rules with the varying domain quantifiers; however, an examination of
their limitations reveals the advantages to be gained from employing free
logic.

If quantifiers have varying domains, then it should be possible for something to exist in one world and not another. However, if classical rules
for quantifiers are used with a modal logic as strong as K, it is possible
to prove $\Box\exists xx \approx c$ for any constant c. (This is the solution to Exercise
12.13a.) $\Box\exists xx \approx c$ reads: 'necessarily there is something identical to c', or
more simply: 'c exists necessarily'. If this sentence is to be a theorem,
all constants in such a logic must refer to things with the (God-like) feature that they exist of necessity. One response to this difficulty is to deny
that names like 'God' and 'Pegasus' count as terms in logic. Pressures in
this direction already exist when classical rules are adopted in nonmodal
logic. In classical logic, every term must refer to something that exists,
with the result that terms like 'Pegasus', and (possibly) 'God' may not be
treated as terms. In modal logic with classical quantification, the criteria
for termhood are even harder to meet. Now the only terms are those that
refer to objects that exist *necessarily*. Since it is unclear that anything at
all so qualifies, it follows that no expressions of natural language may

be translated as terms. It will be necessary to employ some translation strategy using predicate letters instead. Kripke (1963) gives an example of a system in this spirit. It uses the varying domain interpretation for quantifiers and still manages to preserve the classical rules by eliminating terms from the language.

Even if one is prepared to pay this cost, there is a second problem to be faced. There remain theorems of qK that are incompatible with the intuitions behind varying domains. We already showed that (CBF) is provable in any system that uses the principles of classical logic with K. But Exercise 12.16b shows that (CBF) entails $\forall x \Box Ex$, which claims that *everything* necessarily exists. This is in direct conflict with the desire to interpret the quantifier with varying domains. We wanted to allow there to be accessible possible worlds where one of the things in our world fails to exist. Just because I exist in the real world, it should not follow that I also exist in all accessible worlds. However, any varying domain semantics that accepts $\forall x \Box Ex$ or (CBF) must satisfy the expanding domain condition (ED).

(ED)   If **wRv**, then everything in the domain of **w** is in the domain of **v**.

However, (ED) conflicts with the whole point of introducing varying domains, namely, to accommodate the intuition that things in the real world need not exist in related possible worlds The difficulty becomes even more acute in modal logics as strong as B. Those systems have symmetric frames, and it follows from (ED) that all worlds accessible from a given world contain exactly the same objects. This is in direct conflict with our intention to distinguish the domains.

Supposing that some way is found to make (ED) palatable, further adjustments must be made to preserve classical logic in any system that contains terms. The sentence Pc→∃xPx, for example, is classically provable, but it is not valid for varying domains. If Pc is true at world **w**, but c refers to an object that does not exist in **w**, then ∃xPx can be false at **w**. It follows that any system that uses classical quantifier principles will be unsound since Pc→∃xPx will be provable but not valid.

One way to recapture the validity of Pc→∃xPx is to add to the definition of a model that the *terms are local*, that is, that the extension of a term at a world must always be in the domain of that world. However, there are serious problems with this requirement. First, it will mean that nondenoting expressions such as 'Pegasus' and 'the present king of France' cannot count as terms since their extensions are not in the real world. This objection may not impress the classicist, who must deny the "termhood" of nonreferring expressions in any case.

A more serious problem arises for rigid terms. *Rigid terms* are terms that refer to the same object in every possible world. It is commonly held that proper names are rigid terms. But if terms are local, there cannot be any rigid terms at all because locality entails that the referent of any rigid term must exist in *all* the possible worlds. It follows that the referent of any proper name not only must exist, but also must exist necessarily. I have already explained why there is reason to doubt that there is even one object that exists in all possible worlds. So there may be no suitable targets to which rigid terms can refer, and even if there are, the local-terms condition has the odd consequence that objects that exist in some worlds and not others cannot be given proper names.

For these reasons, the requirement that terms be local faces serious difficulties. There is a related idea, however, that appears to work better. It is to guarantee the validity of Pc→∃xPx by stipulating in the definition of a model that *predicate letters are local*. This means that their extensions at a world must contain only objects that exist at that world. The reason this entails the validity of Pc→∃xPx is that from the truth of Pc, it follows that c refers to an existing object, and so ∃xPx must be true as well. But this idea does not work as things stand, because the local-predicate condition does not validate all instances of the classical rules. For example, consider ~Pc→∃x~Px. From the truth of ~Pc, it does not follow that the extension of c is an existing object, and so it does not follow that ∃x~Px is true. So the local-predicate condition does not manage to rescue classical quantification.

These problems can be mitigated somewhat by using a semantics with truth value gaps. Strawson (1950) argued that uses of sentences that contain nonreferring terms do not express statements, and so they lack truth values. Adapting this idea to modal logic, we could allow terms to refer to objects outside of the domain of a given world, with the provision that sentences containing such terms lack truth values. Valid sentences are then defined as sentences that are never false. On this understanding, Ac→∃xAx is valid since any assignment that gives c an extension outside the domain of a world leaves the whole conditional without a value, and assignments that give t an extension inside the domain will make ∃xAx true if Ac is true.

The introduction of truth-value gaps, however, results in new problems. Several choices are available concerning the truth clause for the modal operator □. Truth value gaps interest us because they appear to provide a way to free ourselves from the expanding domain condition (ED). (See Gabbay, 1976, pp. 75ff.) However, there are technical problems that pressure us into accepting (ED). Suppose we hope to calculate the value of □Ac at world **w** and the referent of c is in the domain of **w**. Then □Ac should receive a truth value that depends on the values Ac has in the worlds accessible from **w**. But there is no guarantee that c refers to an existing object in all those accessible worlds, and so Ac may be undefined in some of them. Adopting (ED) would ensure that whenever the referent of c is in the domain of **w**, it is also in the domain of all the accessible worlds so that the values of Ac in all those accessible worlds would be defined, and the determination of the value of □Ac can be carried out in the standard way.

If (ED) is dropped, however, the truth clause for □ must be revised. There are two ways to determine the value of □Ac at **w** depending on whether the failure of Ac to be defined in an accessible world should make □Ac false or undefined. On the first option (Gabbay, 1976, system GKc), the necessitation rule must be restricted so that (CBF) is no longer derivable. On the second option (Gabbay, 1976, system GKs), (CBF) is derivable, but the truth of (CBF) in a model no longer entails (ED). Either way, the principles of the underlying modal logic are nonstandard.

For these reasons, the more popular choice for truth-value-gap theories with local predicates has been to assume (ED) (Hughes and Cresswell, 1996, Ch. 15). This approach is attractive from a purely formal point of view. There are relatively simple completeness proofs for classical systems based on the major propositional modal logics, provided the language omits ≈. Proofs are available, for example, for M and S4. In case the modality is as strong as B, the domains become rigid, and completeness can be established using methods developed for systems that validate the Barcan Formula (Garson, 2001, Section 2.2.4).

Those technical results should not cause us to overlook the problems with the expanding domains condition (ED). (ED) conflicts with the same intuitions that prompt the use of varying domains, and in stronger modal systems such as S5, it is flatly incompatible with those ideas. Although there are semantics for classical logics without (ED), they require truth value gaps and awkward formal principles. Our conclusion is that there is little reason to preserve the classical rules in formulating systems with varying domains. As we will see in coming sections, the semantics for systems based on free logic is both general and natural, and the formal results are as easily obtained as those for classical quantified modal logic. Furthermore, whenever classical quantification is desired, it may be obtained by simply adding Et as an axiom to fS. For both technical and philosophical reasons, the varying domain interpretation of the quantifiers provides good motives for exploring systems based on free logic.

12.11. Rigid and Nonrigid Terms

Kripke's famous paper "Naming and Necessity" (1972) lays out the important distinction between rigid and nonrigid terms. According to him, rigid terms (also known as rigid designators) include proper names like 'Saul' and natural kind terms such as 'water' and 'gold'. A *rigid term* picks out exactly the same object in all possible worlds. (Kripke's definition is actually more complicated since he counts a term rigid if it picks out the same object in all worlds *where that object exists*. That refinement will not be explored here until the last paragraph of Section 19.4.) Definite descriptions such as 'the inventor of bifocals' are assumed to be nonrigid terms since the referent of this term varies from one possible world to another. In the real world, it refers to Benjamin Franklin, but in other possible worlds it refers to other individuals, for example, Thomas Edison or Saul Kripke.

Whether a term is rigid or not depends on how the modal operator (and hence the set of possible 'worlds') is understood. For example, in a tense logic, where **W** is taken to contain instantaneous states of the universe, one might treat proper names as nonrigid terms, which pick out instantaneous time slices of objects (Garson, 1987). In such a logic, the proper name 'Saul Kripke' could pick out different instantaneous states of Kripke – a different one for each instant of time.

The logical behavior of rigid and nonrigid terms is different, and the issue turns on the rule of substitution for identities. Let us assume for a moment that the constants are rigid terms. When b≈c holds in a possible world, it follows that the referents of the constants b and c are the same there. But since b and c are rigid, it follows that b and c refer to the same object in *all* the possible worlds. It follows that if b≈c holds, then so does □b≈c. Furthermore, if ~b≈c holds, then □~b≈c holds as well. So *r*igid *c*onstants obey the axiom (RC).

(RC)   (b≈c→□b≈c) & (~b≈c→□~b≈c)

When (RC) is available, it follows that a rule (R≈Out) of full substitution for (rigid) constants is derivable.

(R≈Out)   b≈c, Ab / Ac

Note that there is no restriction on the substitution in this rule. The constant c may be replaced for b in any context, even within the scope of □. The proof that this principle holds will be left to Exercise 12.19 below.

The introduction of rigid constants is helpful in solving a technical problem to be faced in formulating correct principles for some of the quantified modal logics. In Section 13.5 a standard treatment of the quantifier will be introduced called the objectual interpretation. Here the domain of quantification consists of a set of existing objects. A problem with this approach is that the following instance of the general instantiation rule (t∀) is *invalid* when t is not rigid:

(t∀)   ∀x□Px / Et→□Pt

(The full details of the matter are explored in Section 13.6.) Attempts to formulate an adequate system for the objectual interpretation appropriate for a full range of underlying modal systems has led to the introduction of very complicated quantifier rules. One costly way to solve the problem is simply to eliminate nonrigid terms from the language. In that case, an adequate system can be formulated using the system rS consisting of the free logic system fS with (RC).

System rS = fS + (RC).

EXERCISE 12.19   (Project for advanced students) Using mathematical induction, prove that (R≈Out) is derivable in the system rS.

However, the lack of nonrigid terms in the system is a major failing since such nonrigid expressions are so common in natural language. A contribution of this book is to show that an adequate system for the objectual interpretation with nonrigid terms can be formulated with the help of a rule (∃i) that controls the interaction between the rigid constants c and the other terms t.

(∃i)   L ⊢ ~t≈c

L ⊢ ⊥   where c is a constant not in L or t

The system oS that is adequate for the objectual interpretation results from adding (∃i) to rS.

System oS = rS + (∃i).

It was shown in Section 12.8 (Exercise 12.17) that Ec→□Ec is provable in fK when (CBF) or ∀x□Ex is present, so Ec→□Ec is also provable when one of these is in oS. The result is that all three of these formulas are equivalent in oS. It was remarked there that ~Ec→□~Ec does not follow from (BF) in fK, so that ~Ec→□~Ec is not equivalent to (BF) there. However, in oS, ~Ec→□~Ec does follow, with the result that it is equivalent to (BF) in oS.

(CBF)   □∀xAx→∀x□Ax
(BF)   ∀x□Ax→□∀xAx

EXERCISE 12.20   Show that ~Ec→□~Ec is a theorem of oK+(BF). (Hint: It will suffice to show ◇Ec→Ec. Assume ◇Ec and obtain ◇∃xx≈c, since Ec↔∃xx≈c is provable in oS (Exercise 12.22 below). The dual of (BF) yields ◇∃xAx→∃x◇Ax, so ∃x◇x≈c can now be derived from (BF). Now assume Eb&◇b≈c, in order to perform (∃Out). Obtain b≈c by (RC), and use (≈Out) to obtain Ec. Since Ec contains no occurrence of b, (∃Out) yields Ec outside the subproof headed by Eb&◇b≈c.)

12.12. Eliminating the Existence Predicate

Philosophers who reject the idea that existence is a predicate will be uncomfortable with those systems based on free logic that include E as a primitive predicate of the language. Many people presume that free logic requires that E be a primitive predicate. That is not the case. In fact for most systems developed in this book, E may be eliminated from the language using (DefE).

(DefE)   Et =$_{df}$ ∃xx≈t

Understood this way, the sentence Et does not contain a predicate letter at all, but merely abbreviates ∃xx≈t. To verify that the use of this definition is legitimate, it must be shown that Et and ∃xx≈t are equivalent in the system at issue. With this equivalence in hand it is safe to reformulate the system by eliminating E from the language and using (DefE) instead. The equivalence proof is straightforward in case the only terms are the constants, for then what needs to be proven is Ec↔∃xx≈c.

EXERCISE 12.21 Prove Ec↔∃xx≈c in FL. (Hint: For the proof from left to right, obtain Ec&Ec from Ec and use (∃In). For the other direction, use (∃Out) with ∃xx≈c. Assume Eb and b≈c, use (≈Out) to obtain Ec, and apply (∃Out).)

However, when there are terms in the language beyond the constants, the method used to solve Exercise 12.21 will not work. If the more general instantiation principle (t∀) is available, Et↔∃xx≈t may be obtained using a parallel strategy to the solution of Exercise 12.21. In systems like oS that lack (t∀), but include the rule (∃i), Et↔∃xx≈t can be proven in a different way.

EXERCISE *12.22 Prove Et↔∃xx≈t in oS. (Hint: The hard part is proving Et ⊢ ∃xx≈t. To do that, first establish Et, ~∃xx≈t ⊢ ~c≈t, using (Def∃), (∀Out), and (≈Out). Then apply (∃i) and Indirect Proof.)

So the only systems for which (DefE) is not available will be those that include terms that are not constants and contain neither (t∀) nor (∃i). I cannot think of any useful application for such systems, but in order to present quantified modal logic in the most general way possible, this book assumes that the language contains E as a primitive predicate. The reader with qualms about existence as a predicate may safely reformulate all systems to be discussed below using (DefE), save for the few exceptions explicitly mentioned.

12.13. Summary of Systems, Axioms, and Rules

QL- = PL + (QOut) + (QIn).

(Q∀Out) ∀xAx / Ac
(Q∀In) Ac / ∀xAx, where c is not in ∀xAx nor in any of its hypotheses

QL= QL- + (≈In) + (≈Out).

(≈In) t≈t
(≈Out) t≈s, P(l, t, l') / P(l, s, l'), where P is a predicate letter or ≈

FL = PL + (∀Out) + (∀In) + (≈In) + (≈Out).

fS = S + (∀Out) + (∀In) + (≈In) + (≈Out).

(∀Out) ∀xAx / Ec→Ac
(∀In) Ec→Ac / ∀xAx, where c is not in ∀xAx nor in its hypotheses

rS = fS + (RC).

(RC)   (b≈c→□b≈c) & (~b≈c→□~b≈c)

oS = rS + (∃i).

(∃i)   L ⊢ ~t≈c / L ⊢ ⊥, where c is a constant not in L or t

Quantifier Domain Axioms

(∃E)	∃xEx	(Nonempty Domain)
(Q)	Et	(Classical Quantification)
(CBF)	□∀xAx → ∀x□Ax	(Expanding Domains)
(∀□E)	∀x□Ex	(Expanding Domains)
(ED)	Ec→□Ec	(Expanding Domains)
(BF)	∀x□Ax→□∀xAx	(Contracting Domains)
(CD)	~Ec→□~Ec	(Contracting Domains)

13

Semantics for Quantified Modal Logics

There are a number of different approaches one can take to giving the semantics for the quantifiers. The simplest method uses truth value semantics with the substitution interpretation of the quantifiers (Leblanc, 1976). Although the substitution interpretation can be criticized, it provides an excellent starting point for understanding the alternatives since it avoids a number of annoying technical complications. For students who prefer to learn the adequacy proofs in easy stages, it is best to master the reasoning for the substitution interpretation first. This will provide a core understanding of the basic strategies, which may be embellished (if one wishes) to accommodate more complex treatments of quantification.

13.1. Truth Value Semantics with the Substitution Interpretation

The substitution interpretation is based on the idea that a universal sentence ∀xAx is true exactly when each of its instances Aa, Ab, Ac, .., is true. For classical logic, ∀xAx is T if and only if Ac is T for each constant c of the language. In the case of free logic, the truth condition states that ∀xAx is T if and only if Ac is T for all constants that *refer to a real object*. Since the sentence Ec indicates that c refers to a real object, the free logic truth condition should say that Ac is T for all those constants c such that Ec is also true.

Semantics for quantified modal logic can be defined by incorporating these ideas into the definition of a model for propositional modal logic. When S is one of the propositional modal logics we have studied, a truth value model for S, or a *tS-model* <**W**, **R**, **a**> contains the familiar items: a

265

frame <**W**, **R**> containing a set of possible worlds **W** and an accessibility relation **R** that obeys the conditions for the modal logic S, and an assignment function **a**, which gives truth values at each world for each sentence of a language of quantified modal logic. The assignment function **a** must obey all the requirements we introduced for propositional logic, namely, ($\bot$), ($\rightarrow$), and ($\Box$).

($\bot$) $\mathbf{a_W}(\bot)$=F.
($\rightarrow$) $\mathbf{a_W}(A{\rightarrow}B)$=T   iff $\mathbf{a_W}(A)$=F or $\mathbf{a_W}(B)$=T.
($\Box$) $\mathbf{a_W}(\Box A)$=T   iff   for each **v** such that **wRv**, $\mathbf{a_v}(A)$=T.

Furthermore, **a** must obey the relevant truth conditions for $\forall$ and $\approx$. The more general truth condition for the quantifier is the one for free logic, which may be spelled out as follows.

($\forall$) $\mathbf{a_W}(\forall xAx)$=T iff for every constant c, if $\mathbf{a_W}(Ec)$=T then $\mathbf{a_W}(Ac)$=T.

EXERCISE 13.1   Using ($\forall$) and (Def$\exists$), show that the truth clause for $\exists$ is ($\exists$).

($\exists$) $\mathbf{a_W}(\exists xAx)$=T iff for some constant c, $\mathbf{a_W}(Ec)$=T and $\mathbf{a_W}(Ac)$=T.

In case the semantics for classical quantification is desired, (Q) can be added to the definition of a model.

(Q) $\mathbf{a_W}(Et)$=T for all terms t.

When (Q) holds, the truth clause ($\forall$) entails (Q$\forall$).

(Q$\forall$) $\mathbf{a_W}(\forall xAx)$=T iff for every constant c, $\mathbf{a_W}(Ac)$=T.

EXERCISE 13.2   What would be the classical truth condition (Q$\exists$) for $\exists$?

Truth value semantics defines truth conditions that explain how to assign truth values to sentences given the truth values of the sentences from which they are constructed. However, it does not attempt to explain how truth values of sentences of the forms Pl, Et, and s$\approx$t depend on the values of the predicate letters and terms from which they are constructed. The sentence-based orientation of truth value semantics leads to difficulties in providing a natural semantics for $\approx$. One would want to say that the sentence s$\approx$t is T provided that s and t refer to the same thing; and yet truth value semantics does not have the resources to develop the notion of the reference of terms. A richer account designed to provide a better treatment of ≈ will be developed in the next section. For the moment, however, the truth behavior of *sentences* containing ≈ can be regulated by insisting that the assignment function **a** obey the following condition (t≈), which reflects the rules (≈In) and (≈Out) introduced in the previous chapter:

(t≈) $\mathbf{a_w}(t{\approx}t)=T$ and if $\mathbf{a_w}(s{\approx}t)=T$ then $\mathbf{a_w}(Plsl')=\mathbf{a_w}(Pltl')$.

Although (t≈) is not ideal, it at least makes some sort of sense. The requirement is that t≈t never be false and that the substitution of identities hold for atomic sentences.

It is time to summarize the discussion and provide an official definition of a truth value (or tS) model. A *tS-model* <**W**, **R**, **a**> is defined for a language that contains a primitive existence predicate E. It contains a frame <**W**, **R**> that obeys the conditions for the modal logic S, and an assignment function **a** that obeys (⊥), (→), (□), (∀), and (t≈). (The reason the language must include E as a primitive will be explained in the next section.)

A variety of stronger conditions on models will be introduced later. However, most of what we have to say will not depend on which selection of additional conditions is made. To simplify such general discussion, 'S' will be used to indicate not only conditions on frames for propositional modal logic, but any of a selection of further conditions to be introduced concerning the quantifier, such as (Q). It will be understood from the context that a tS-model obeys those extra conditions. Once the notion of a tS-model is in place, corresponding notions of satisfiability, counterexample, and validity are defined just as they were in propositional logics. Here is a review. When H is a list of sentences, $\mathbf{a_w}(H)=T$ means that $\mathbf{a_w}(A)=T$, for every sentence A in H. A tS-model <**W**, **R**, **a**> *satisfies* the set of sentences H at **w** iff $\mathbf{a_w}(H)=T$. A list H of sentences is *tS-satisfiable* just in case there is a tS-model for a language containing sentences of H that satisfies H at some world. An argument H / C has a tS-counterexample iff H, ~C is tS-satisfiable. A tS-counterexample to H / C is a tS-model whose assignment function gives all members of H the value T, and assigns the conclusion C the value F at some world. An argument H / C is *tS-valid* iff H / C has no counterexample. Whenever we define new varieties of model in the future, the corresponding notions of satisfiability, counterexample, and validity are assumed to be given in exactly the same way.

13.2. Semantics for Terms, Predicates, and Identity

The truth values semantics just presented is relatively simple. It is not too difficult to demonstrate that the basic system fS is adequate for tS-validity in the case of most of the modal logics S discussed in this book. However, tS-semantics is problematic in two ways. First, it does not give a fine analysis of the semantical behavior of the terms and predicates that make up atomic sentences. This limitation causes an inadequate treatment of the semantical behavior of $\approx$. Second, tS-semantics requires that E be a primitive predicate of the language, for otherwise the attempt to define truth values by ($\forall$) would be circular. To see why, note that according to ($\forall$), the truth value of $\forall x A x$ depends on the value of Ec, for each constant c. If each sentence Ec is defined by $Ec = \exists x x \approx c = \sim \forall x \sim x \approx c$, then Ec is a complex sentence containing $\forall$, and so by ($\forall$), its value also depends on the values of all sentences with the form Ec, including itself. The only way to break out of this vicious circle and guarantee that the values of the Ec sentences are fixed in a model is to assume that E is primitive so that values of sentences with the form Ec are given directly by the assignment function.

A more satisfying analysis of terms, predicates, and $\approx$ can be given by introducing quantifier domains and defining the referents of terms and predicate letters with their help. A *domain structure* $\mathbb{D}$ consists of a nonempty set **D** of possible objects and a subset **Dw** of **D** for each world **w**. A substitution or *sS-model* <**W**, **R**, $\mathbb{D}$, **a**> includes a domain structure $\mathbb{D}$ and an assignment function **a** that gives appropriate extensions to the expressions of the language, including terms and predicate letters, and meets the truth conditions governing the behavior of the logical symbols. We will describe these conditions in a minute, but first we must say what an appropriate extension of an expression is. An *appropriate extension of a term* is a member of **D**, an *appropriate extension for a list of terms* is a list of members of **D**, an *appropriate extension of a sentence* is a truth value (either T or F), and an *appropriate extension of a predicate letter* is a set containing lists of members of **D**. (For example, the extension of a predicate letter G for 'greater than' would be a set containing two member lists (n, m) such that n is greater than m.) We will also need to define the *intensions* for terms and predicates. This is done on analogy with the way intensions were defined for propositional modal logics in Section 3.8. There the *appropriate extension of a sentence* was a truth value, whereas the intension of a sentence was a function that takes us from a world (member of $\mathbf{W}$) to a truth value. By analogy, the *appropriate intension of any expression e* is a function that takes members of $\mathbf{W}$ into appropriate extensions for e. As a result, the intension of a term is a function from worlds to objects, and the intension of a predicate letter is a function that takes each world into a set of lists of objects.

Let us spell this out more carefully. The *intension $a(t)$ of term* t on assignment $\mathbf{a}$ is a function from $\mathbf{W}$ into $\mathbf{D}$ (the set of objects). Following Carnap (1947), we will call the intension $\mathbf{a}(t)$ of a term an *individual concept*. It follows from this definition that the extension $\mathbf{a_w}(t)$ of t at $\mathbf{w}$ on $\mathbf{a}$ is an object in $\mathbf{D}$. The intension $\mathbf{a}(P)$ of a predicate letter P is a function from $\mathbf{W}$ into the set containing all sets of lists of objects, and the extension $\mathbf{a_w}(P)$ of P at $\mathbf{w}$ on $\mathbf{a}$ is a set containing lists of objects. We use the notation '$\mathbf{a_w}((t_1, \ldots, t_n))$' to abbreviate the list $(\mathbf{a_w}(t_1), \ldots, \mathbf{a_w}(t_n))$ of the extensions of the terms $t_1, \ldots, t_n$.

(t_i) $\mathbf{a_w}((t_1, \ldots, t_n)) = (\mathbf{a_w}(t_1), \ldots, \mathbf{a_w}(t_n))$.

An *assignment function* is any function $\mathbf{a}$ that is defined over the expressions of the language that gives each expression an appropriate intension and that obeys the truth conditions $(\bot)$, $(\rightarrow)$, $(\Box)$, and $(\forall)$, along with the following:

(E) $\mathbf{a_w}(E) = \mathbf{Dw}$.

(The extension of the existence predicate at $\mathbf{w}$ is the domain for $\mathbf{w}$.)

$(\approx)$ $\mathbf{a_w}(s \approx t) = T$ iff $\mathbf{a_w}(s) = \mathbf{a_w}(t)$.

(The sentence $s \approx t$ is T iff the terms s and t have the same extension.)

(Pl) $\mathbf{a_w}(Pl) = T$ iff $\mathbf{a_w}(l) \in \mathbf{a_w}(P)$.

The symbol '$\in$' in (Pl) is read 'is a member of'. The condition says, for example, that 'Loves(John, Mary)' is true iff the extension of the list formed of the extensions of 'John' and 'Mary' is a member of the extension of 'Loves'.)

The notions of sS-satisfiability, sS-counterexample, and sS-validity are defined from the notion of an sS-model in the usual way.

It has been assumed so far that E is a primitive predicate, so values of sentences of the form Et are given by (Pl). But given that the assignment function assigns values to terms and predicate letters, it is possible to eliminate the predicate letter E and define Et by (DefE).

(DefE)   Et$=_{df}$ $\exists x x \approx t$.

When E is a predicate letter of the language, it follows by (Pl) that $\mathbf{a_w}(Et)=T$ iff $\mathbf{a_w}(t) \in \mathbf{a_w}(E)$. But in the light of (E), this comes to (Et).

(Et) $\mathbf{a_w}(Et)=T$ iff $\mathbf{a_w}(t) \in \mathbf{Dw}$.

It follows that the substitution truth clause ($\forall$) can be rewritten in a way that avoids any mention of E.

($\forall$Dw) $\mathbf{a_w}(\forall xAx)=T$ iff for every c, if $\mathbf{a_w}(c) \in \mathbf{Dw}$ then $\mathbf{a_w}(Ac)=T$.

Therefore, no problem of circularity can possibly arise in using (DefE) with this semantics. All that is needed to guarantee that the use of (DefE) is correct is to verify (E∃).

(E∃) $\mathbf{a_w}(Et)=\mathbf{a_w}(\exists x x \approx t)$.

For the moment it is easy to verify that (E∃) holds, given that constants are the only terms of the language. Therefore, it will not matter whether we include a primitive existence predicate and use truth condition ($\forall$) or eliminate it using (DefE) and ($\forall$Dw). Since it won't matter which choice is made, 'sS-model' will indicate models that adopt either method of dealing with the quantifier. Note, however, that when new terms are added to the language, use of (DefE) will depend on being able to show (E∃). (Exercise 13.5 of Section 13.5 illustrates a demonstration of this kind.)

EXERCISE *13.3   Show (E∃) holds for any sS-model for a language whose terms include only the constants. What problems with the argument might arise when there are terms other than constants?

13.3. Strong Versus Contingent Identity

There are two ways to give the truth clause for identity in modal logics. On the *strong interpretation* ($\equiv$), s$\approx$t says that the *intensions* of s and t are identical.

($\equiv$) $a_w(s \approx t) = T$ iff $\mathbf{a}(s) = \mathbf{a}(t)$.

For the sS-models defined in the previous section, the *contingent interpretation* ($\approx$) was chosen, where $s \approx t$ asserts that the *extensions* of s and t agree at the world **w**.

($\approx$) $a_w(s \approx t) = T$ iff $a_w(s) = a_w(t)$.

The purpose of this section is to explain why contingent identity was preferred over the strong interpretation. (One could introduce symbols for both kinds of identity into the language. However, we will leave that project for another day.)

In ordinary speech, we almost always give identity the contingent interpretation. For example, in 1984 people would have claimed that 'Ronald Reagan is the president' is true even though the terms 'Ronald Reagan' and 'the president' did not refer to the same object at other times. It is enough for this sentence to be true in 1984 that the extensions of these two terms are the same in 1984. Similarly, we count 'nine is the number of planets' true, even though there are possible worlds where the referents of 'nine' and 'the number of planets' differ.

Some would object that it is wrong to treat 'Ronald Reagan is the president' as having the form $s \approx t$. Instead they would opt for an analysis using Russell's theory of descriptions where 'the president' does not count as a term. Instead, 'the president' is translated away in favor of the existential quantifier and a predicate letter for being a president. In Sections 12.3 and 12.4 it was explained why this book has chosen to leave open the possibility that definite descriptions like 'the president' and 'the number of planets' count as genuine referring expressions. Given this choice, an analysis of contingent identity is in order.

Notice that on the strong interpretation, the truth values of identities are not world-varying. Since 'w' does not appear on the right side of ($\equiv$), it follows that whether $s \approx t$ is true at **w** does not depend on the value of **w**.

EXERCISE 13.4   Show that $a_w(s \approx t) = a_v(s \approx t)$, for any two worlds **w** and **v**, given ($\equiv$).

For this reason, the strong interpretation validates the rule of substitution of identical terms in all contexts, whether beneath a modal operator or not.

EXERCISE 13.5   Show that s≈t, □Fs / □Ft is ≡S-valid, where an ≡S-model
is a sS-model that obeys (≡) instead of (≈).

This feature is attractive to those who believe that substitution of identicals is correct in all contexts. However, the strong interpretation has a
price. The substitution of identicals in all contexts guarantees that the
argument s≈t, □s≈s / □s≈t is valid. It is clear that □s≈s is valid on any
interpretation of ≈, and so s≈t / □s≈t must also be valid on the strong
interpretation. As a result, *all* true identities are necessary on the strong
interpretation; in fact, the distinction between contingent and necessary
identities collapses from this point of view. The examples of 'the president'
and 'the number of planets' should make it clear that the strong interpretation is acceptable only under very special circumstances. It would hold,
for example, in a language where all the terms are rigid, but given the
decision that descriptions are to count as terms, many terms of ordinary
language are not rigid.

Given the contingent interpretation, it is possible to show officially that
the substitution of identities fails in the scope of modal operators. Here
for example is a sS-model <**W**, **R**, $\mathbb{D}$, **a**> that is a sS-counterexample to the
following instance of that principle: s≈t, □Ps / □Pt. The frame <**W**, **R**>
of the model and the values **a** assigns to sentences will be given by the
following diagram:

EXERCISE 13.6   Verify that $\mathbf{a_w}(\Box Ps)=T$ and $\mathbf{a_w}(\Box Pt)=F$ on the above
diagram.

Notice that **R** in this diagram has the property that **wRv** for all **w** and **v**
in **W**. A relation of this kind has all of the properties we have studied for
modal logics except uniqueness. To obtain a counterexample for a unique
R, simply remove the two reflexivity (loop) arrows. If we can be assured
that **a** can be successfully defined so as to give the values shown in the

diagram, then we will know that substitution of identicals is invalid for all the modal logics we have studied.

In order to convince you that a model can be defined that assigns to sentences the values in the above diagram, let us give a more detailed definition of the countermodel $<W, R, \mathbb{D}, a>$ depicted above. W contains the two worlds w and v that are found in the diagram. In the language of set theory this is written: $W=\{w, v\}$, that is, W is the set containing the objects w and v. R is defined so that wRv for all w and v in W. The domain structure has domains that all contain two objects: 1 and 2. So $D=Dw=\{1, 2\}$. The assignment function a is defined so that $a_w(s)=1$, $a_v(s)=1$, $a_w(t)=1$, $a_v(t)=2$, $a_w(P)=\{1\}$, $a_v(P)=\{1\}$. Since $a_w(s)=a_w(t)$, we know by ($\approx$) that $a_w(s\approx t)=T$. Because $a_w(s) \in a_w(P)$, $a_w(t) \in a_w(P)$, and $a_v(s) \in a_v(P)$, it follows that $a_w(Ps)=T$, $a_w(Pt)=T$, and $a_v(Ps)=T$. However $a_v(t)$ is not a member of $a_v(P)$, so $a_v(Pt)=F$. Since a model has been defined whose assignment function gives the values shown in the diagram, we have a counterexample to the principle of substitution of identities in all contexts. Notice, however, that substitution is valid when it is properly restricted, as in ($\approx$Out). (See Section 15.2.) (Strictly speaking, $a_w(P)$ must be a *list*, so the correct value on this model would be $a_w(P)=\{(1)\}$, which is the set containing the *list* containing the single member 1. Furthermore, we should have written: $(a_w(s)) \in a_w(P)$. Here and in the future, the extra parentheses are omitted to save the reader eyestrain.)

It is rather cumbersome to specify an assignment to terms and predicates in the language of set theory as we have just done. It will be more convenient to show how an assignment gives intensions to terms and predicate letters using diagrams. In order to do so, we set up a chart with the situations listed on one dimension and the objects listed on the other. Then the intension of a term may be indicated by a line in the chart. For example, the diagonal line in the following chart represents an intension that takes situation w into object 1, and situation v into object 2. The label $a(t)$ shows that this is the intension that a assigns to the term t.

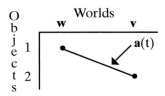

To read the value of a function that is represented as a line on this sort of graph, simply follow the dotted lines thus:

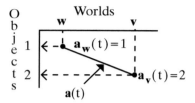

It is also possible to represent the intensions of 1-place predicate letters on the same kind of diagram. We simply draw a boundary that includes the region for an object and world just in case the extension of the predicate letter includes the object in that world. For example, the region indicated in the following diagram indicates that the intension $\mathbf{a}(Q)$ is defined so that $\mathbf{a_w}(Q)$ includes both objects 1 and 2, $(\mathbf{a_w}(Q)=\{1,2\})$, whereas $\mathbf{a_v}(Q)$ includes only object 1, $(\mathbf{a_v}(Q)=\{1\})$:

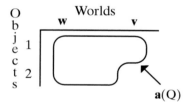

Now we may present in a single diagram all the information we have on the model we used to invalidate the substitution of identities.

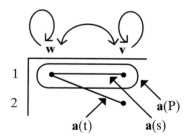

It is not difficult to "read off" values of simple formulas using this kind of diagram. For example, we can see immediately that $\mathbf{a_w}(s{\approx}t)$ is T because the two lines for $\mathbf{a}(s)$ and $\mathbf{a}(t)$ converge at world $\mathbf{w}$. We can also see that

$\mathbf{a_v}$(Ps) is T and $\mathbf{a_v}$(Pt) is F because the line for $\mathbf{a}$(s) lies inside the region $\mathbf{a}$(P) at world $\mathbf{v}$, whereas the line for $\mathbf{a}$(t) lies outside $\mathbf{a}$(P) at $\mathbf{v}$. Checking the value of □Ps at $\mathbf{w}$ is also easily done. We first locate all worlds that may be reached from $\mathbf{w}$ following an arrow. The worlds in question are $\mathbf{w}$ and $\mathbf{v}$. So for □Ps to be true at $\mathbf{w}$, Ps must be T in both $\mathbf{w}$ and $\mathbf{v}$. Since the line for $\mathbf{a}$(s) lies within the boundary for $\mathbf{a}$(P) at both worlds, we know that $\mathbf{a_w}$(□Ps) is T. Similarly, the truth of □Pt at $\mathbf{w}$ requires that the line for $\mathbf{a}$(t) lie within the boundary for $\mathbf{a}$(P) at both $\mathbf{w}$ and $\mathbf{v}$. Since that line is outside this boundary in $\mathbf{v}$, we know that $\mathbf{a_w}$(□Pt) is F. For convenience, the values for sentences that we calculate may be represented by entering them into the worlds of the diagram.

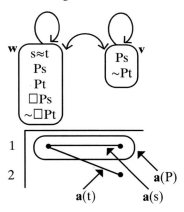

In the future, we will (where possible) present models in the form of diagrams so that values of sentences may be more easily calculated. There is no inaccuracy or ambiguity in doing so since it is always possible to convert any diagram into a complete description of the model in the notation of set theory.

EXERCISE 13.7

a) Express the following models as diagrams:

1. $\mathbf{W}$={w, v, u}, $\mathbf{R}$={<w, v>, <v, w>, <u, u>}, $\mathbf{D}$=$\mathbf{Dw}$={1, 2, 3}
   $\mathbf{a_w}$(t)=1, $\mathbf{a_v}$(t)=1, $\mathbf{a_u}$(t)=1, $\mathbf{a_w}$(s)=2, $\mathbf{a_v}$(s)=2, $\mathbf{a_u}$(s)=3,
   $\mathbf{a_w}$(P)=$\mathbf{a_v}$(P)=$\mathbf{a_u}$(P)={1, 2, 3}, $\mathbf{a_w}$(Q)={1, 2}, $\mathbf{a_v}$(Q)={2, 3},
   $\mathbf{a_u}$(Q)={3}.

2. $\mathbf{W}$={w, v, u}, $\mathbf{R}$={<w, v>, <v, u>}, $\mathbf{D}$=$\mathbf{Dw}$={2, 3}
   $\mathbf{a_w}$(t)=2, $\mathbf{a_v}$(t)=3, $\mathbf{a_u}$(t)=2, $\mathbf{a_w}$(s)=3, $\mathbf{a_v}$(s)=2, $\mathbf{a_u}$(s)=3,
   $\mathbf{a_w}$(P)={2, 3}, $\mathbf{a_v}$(P)={3}, $\mathbf{a_u}$(P)={}, $\mathbf{a_w}$(Q)={}, $\mathbf{a_v}$(Q)={2},
   $\mathbf{a_u}$(Q)={2, 3}.

b) Express the following diagrams in the notation of set theory:

1.

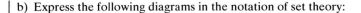

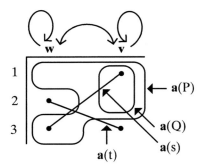

2.

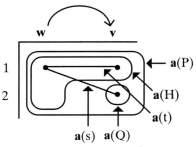

c) Calculate the following truth values for the model depicted in diagram b)2 above: $a_w(\Box Ht)$, $a_v(\Box Hs)$, $a_w(\exists x \Diamond Qx)$, $a_w(\forall x \Box Px)$, $a_w(\Diamond \forall x Hx)$, $a_v(\Diamond \forall x Hx)$.

13.4. Rigid and Nonrigid Terms

As we explained in Section 12.11, a rigid term or designator is a denoting expression that picks out the same object in every world, whereas the referents of nonrigid expressions may vary from one possible world to another. In some modal languages, we will want to use the constants to abbreviate rigid terms only. In order to guarantee that the constants are rigid, the following condition may be placed on models (where c is any constant and **w** and **v** are any two worlds in **W**):

(RC) $a_w(c) = a_v(c)$.

The condition (RC) says that the extension of a constant is the same thing in every possible world. When this condition holds, there is no longer a need to include the world subscripts, so they can be dropped. In this case,

a(c) would not indicate a function from possible worlds to objects, but instead an object (or member of **D**).

This more direct notation has the merit of simplicity, and it conforms to the position that a rigid term refers directly to objects. It also corresponds nicely to the notion that such terms have referents (extensions) but no meanings (intensions) apart from the objects they pick out.

Some philosophers object that talk of the identity of objects across possible worlds is misguided or incoherent. Given these qualms, it is disturbing to describe the intension of a rigid term as a term whose referent is the *same* in all possible worlds; in fact, the very use of the term 'rigid' would seem out of place. For all of these reasons it might be better to define the referents of rigid constants so that **a**(c) is a member of **D**, rather than a function from **W** into **D**.

(CR)   **a**(c) is a member of **D**.

To keep our presentation as general as possible, (RC) will be the official way to indicate that the constants are rigid in this book. However, the alternative approach (CR) may be used whenever constants are rigid, and it will come in handy for proving a general theorem about substitution in Section 15.12.

An important question in the design of quantified modal logics is whether all the terms in the language ought to be rigid. So far, we have simply assumed that at least some terms are nonrigid. There are good reasons for this choice. It is clear, for example, that definite descriptions are nonrigid. The term 'the inventor of bifocals' refers to Benjamin Franklin in the real world, but we can easily imagine a possible world where someone else was the inventor of bifocals. The fact that descriptions are nonrigid does not conclusively prove that languages for modal logic ought to have nonrigid terms. Some would argue that descriptions should not be treated as terms but should be translated away instead according to Russell's theory of descriptions. This attitude motivates the development of modal logics where all terms are rigid. An advantage of those systems is that no restrictions need to be placed on the substitution of identities.

EXERCISE 13.8   Show that b≈c, □Pb / □Pc is valid, assuming that both b and c are rigid.

In Section 12.4, complaints were lodged against the thoroughgoing application of Russell's theory of descriptions to eliminate the terms of ordinary language for the result is a logical language that lacks any terms

at all. It is better to allow nonrigid terms in the language and so to reject
the substitution of identities in all contexts. The price is the restriction
to atomic sentences in the substitution rule ($\approx$Out), but the benefit is a
much more natural translation between natural and logical languages.

13.5. The Objectual Interpretation

In the previous sections, semantics for the quantifiers was developed using
the substitution interpretation. The substitution interpretation has the
merit of simplicity, but it is superficial. Ordinarily $\exists$xPx (something is
P) means that there is an *object* with the property P, not that there is
some instance Pt that is true for some term t. So it will be interesting to
examine ontological interpretations of the quantifier, where the truth of
$\exists$xPx commits us to the *existence* of things, rather than merely to the truth
of other sentences (namely, the instances of $\exists$xPx).

Furthermore, there are reasons for thinking that the substitution inter-
pretation is simply incorrect. Consider a sS-model $<\mathbf{W}, \mathbf{R}, \mathbb{D}, \mathbf{a}>$ with
the following features: $\mathbf{D}=\mathbf{D}\mathbf{w}=\mathbf{a_w}(E)=\{1, 2\}$, $\mathbf{a_w}(P)=\{1\}$, and $\mathbf{a_w}(c)=1$
when c is any constant $c', c'', c''', \ldots$ The diagram at world $\mathbf{w}$ for this model
follows:

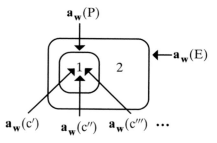

Intuitively $\forall$xPx should be false at $\mathbf{w}$ on this model, because there is an
object (namely, 2) that exists at $\mathbf{w}$ but does not satisfy the predicate P. However, the value of $\mathbf{a_w}(\forall xPx)$ is T according to ($\forall$) because $\mathbf{a_w}(Pc)=T$ for
every constant c, and so if $\mathbf{a_w}(Ec)=t$, then $\mathbf{a_w}(Pc)=T$. The difficulty with
the substitution interpretation is that there can be models with objects
(such as 2) that are unnamed. Since the truth value of $\forall$xPx depends on
its instances, the presence of an unnamed object will not affect it, even if
this object would intuitively serve as a reason to reject $\forall$xPx.

One may repair this defect by stipulating that a model must contain no
unnamed objects. However, this will only go so far. In case the domain
contains as many objects as there are real numbers, it will be impossible
to name every object. Despite the fact that there are infinitely many

integers, Cantor famously proved that there are still more real numbers than there are integers, and so more reals than names in our language (Boolos, Burgess, and Jeffrey, 2002). It is hard to measure how serious a problem this poses. It depends on whether one needs to quantify over such immensely large domains as the reals. For safety, however, let us explore an alternative.

Consider a truth clause for the quantifier where the truth value of ∀xAx depends on the features of objects, and not the truth values of instances of ∀xAx. There are a number of ways to give quantifier truth clauses along these lines. One of these uses the notion of satisfaction of an open sentence by an infinite sequence of terms, and another the notion of a valuation of the variables. We will employ a different strategy due to Smullyan (*First Order Logic*, 1968), where we substitute *objects* (not their names) directly into sentences. This approach combines the technical simplicity of the substitution interpretation, with a solution to the problem of unnamed objects. The idea is to introduce what we will call *hybrid* sentences. These sentences are instances of ∀xAx that result from replacing the *object* d for each free occurrence of x in Ax. This may sound odd at first, so let me define it clearly. Suppose d is an *object* in the domain **D**, and let P be any predicate letter. The hybrid sentence P(d) is composed of the predicate letter P followed by a list containing *object* d. P(d) is not a sentence because predicate letters are normally followed by lists of *terms*, not objects. Nevertheless, we may introduce such hybrids and give rules for evaluating their truth values. Officially, *A is a hybrid* iff A is $[B]^d/x$, the instance of ∀xBx that results from replacing an object d for those instances of x bound by ∀x in ∀xBx. The hybrid P(d) asserts that the object d has the property P, so we expect $\mathbf{a_w}(Pd)$ to be true just in case (d) $\in \mathbf{a_w}(P)$. In the case of a sentence involving a binary relation symbol R, we want to be sure that $\mathbf{a}(R(d_1, d_2))=T$ iff the list of objects (d_1, d_2) is a member of the extension $\mathbf{a}(R)$ of R.

One simple method of ensuring this is to adopt a notational ruse, namely, to treat objects in the domain as if they were honorary terms, and to stipulate that the notation '$\mathbf{a_w}(d)$' means d.

(d) $\mathbf{a_w}(d)$ is d for each d $\in \mathbf{D}$.

This together with abbreviation (t_i) entails that the extension of a list of objects will be that list itself.

(t_i) $\mathbf{a_w}((t_1, \ldots, t_i))=(\mathbf{a_w}(t_1), \ldots, \mathbf{a_w}(t_i))$.

This will guarantee that $\mathbf{a_w}(P(d_1, .., d_i))=T$ just in case the list $(d_1, ..,$ $d_i)$ is a member of $\mathbf{a_w}(P)$, by the following reasoning:

$\mathbf{a_w}(P(d_1, .., d_i))=T$
iff $\mathbf{a_w}((d_1, .., d_i)) \in \mathbf{a_w}(P)$ (by (Pl))
iff $(\mathbf{a_w}(d_1), .., \mathbf{a_w}(d_i)) \in \mathbf{a_w}(P)$ (by (t_i))
iff $(d_1, .., d_i) \in \mathbf{a_w}(P)$ (by (d))

Condition (d) will also ensure the correct truth behavior for hybrid sentences containing terms as well as objects, as can be seen in the next example:

$\mathbf{a_w}(R(t, d))=T$
iff $\mathbf{a_w}((t, d)) \in \mathbf{a_w}(R)$
iff $(\mathbf{a_w}(t), \mathbf{a_w}(d)) \in \mathbf{a_w}(R)$
iff $(\mathbf{a_w}(t), d) \in \mathbf{a_w}(R)$

We are now ready to define semantics using the hybrid approach. An objectual or *oS-model* $<\mathbf{W}, \mathbf{R}, \mathbb{D}, \mathbf{a}>$ for a quantified modal language contains a frame $<\mathbf{W}, \mathbf{R}>$ for a propositional modal logic S, a *domain structure* $\mathbb{D}$ consisting of a set $\mathbf{D}$ (of possible objects) and subsets $\mathbf{Dw}$ of $\mathbf{D}$ to serve as domains for each world $\mathbf{w}$, and an assignment function $\mathbf{a}$ (defined over sentences and hybrid sentences), which obeys $(\approx)$, (Pl), $(\perp)$, $(\rightarrow)$, and $(\square)$, along with $(o\forall)$, the *objectual truth clause* for the quantifier, the condition (RC) to guarantee that constants are rigid, and (E) to ensure that E indicates existence. To save eyestrain, '$\mathbf{a_w}(Ad)=T$' abbreviates '$\mathbf{a_w}([A]^d/x)=T$' in condition $(o\forall)$.)

$(o\forall)$ $\mathbf{a_w}(\forall x Ax)=T$ iff for all $d \in \mathbf{Dw}$, $\mathbf{a_w}(Ad)=T$.
(RC) $\mathbf{a_w}(c)=\mathbf{a_v}(c)$.
(E) $\mathbf{a_w}(E)=\mathbf{Dw}$.

It is a simple matter to show that the following derived truth condition follows:

$(o\exists)$ $\mathbf{a_w}(\exists x Ax)=T$ iff for some $d \in \mathbf{Dw}$ and $\mathbf{a_w}(Ad)=T$.

EXERCISE 13.9   Using (Def∃), and $(o\forall)$, show that $(o\exists)$ holds.

At the end of Section 12.2 it was pointed out that (DefE) can be used to eliminate the existence predicate provided that (E∃) can be proven.

(E∃) $a_w(Et)=a_w(\exists xx\approx t)$.

On the substitution interpretation, the proof of (E∃) depended on the terms including only the constants. However, on the objectual interpretation, (E∃) can be proven regardless of which terms are in the language. As a result, we may always eliminate E in oS-models.

EXERCISE 13.10   Show that $a_w(Et)=a_w(\exists xx\approx t)$ for any oS-model.

13.6. Universal Instantiation on the Objectual Interpretation

The importance of allowing nonrigid terms in languages for quantified modal logic has already been argued in Section 13.4. Unfortunately, systems that use nonrigid terms with the objectual interpretation face a serious difficulty. The problem is that the rules for quantifiers (whether classical *or free*) are no longer valid (Hintikka, 1970). In classical logic, the principle (Qt∀Out) of universal instantiation is accepted, which means that existential generalization over terms (Qt∃In) is a derivable rule.

(Qt∀Out)   ∀xAx / At
(Qt∃In)   At / ∃xAx

Now consider (∃□).

(∃□)   □t≈t / ∃x□x≈t

This is a special case of (Qt∃In). Since t≈t is provable, □t≈t follows by (□In), and so ∃x□x≈t is a theorem of any classical quantified modal logic. However, ∃x□x≈t is not valid on the objectual interpretation. To see this intuitively, let t read 'the inventor of bifocals'. Then ∃x□x≈t says that someone exists who is necessarily the inventor of bifocals. This claim is at best questionable. Even Benjamin Franklin (bright as he was) was not *necessarily* the inventor of bifocals.

It is not difficult to support this informal objection to ∃x□x≈t with a formal counterexample. Consider the following oK-model:

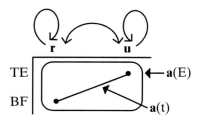

The diagram shows that $\mathbf{a_r}(t)$ is BF (Benjamin Franklin is the inventor of bifocals in the *r*eal world), and that $\mathbf{a_u}(t)$ is TE (Thomas Edison is the inventor of bifocals in an *u*nreal world). Now consider the hybrid sentence BF≈t. This is false in **u** (Benjamin Franklin is not the inventor of bifocals in the unreal world), and so □BF≈t is F at **r**. Similarly, □TE≈t is F at **r**, because TE≈t is F at **r**. The domain **Dr**=$\mathbf{a_r}$(E) for this model contains the objects BF and TE, and so ∃x□x≈t is T at **r** provided that either □BF≈t or □TE≈t is T at **r**. But we showed that neither of these hybrids is T at **r**, and so ∃x□x≈t is F at **r**.

The reason that ∃x□x≈t is refuted on this diagram is that the truth of ∃x□x≈t requires that there is *one* object that is identical to the referent of t in both worlds **r** and **u**. However, no one object so qualifies since the value of t shifts from one object to the other as we move from one world to the other. These reflections help explain why we resist the inference from □t≈t to ∃x□x≈t. We want to say that it is necessary that the inventor of bifocals is identical to the inventor of bifocals, but it does not follow that there is some one *object* that is necessarily the inventor of bifocals. True, there is "something" that is necessarily the inventor of bifocals, namely, the inventor of bifocals. But the inventor of bifocals has different manifestations in different worlds. To put it differently, the inventor of bifocals does not count as a unified *object* the way BF and TE do, and for this reason the truth of 'the inventor of bifocals is necessarily the inventor of bifocals' does not support the *ontological* claim that *some one thing* exists that is necessarily the inventor of bifocals.

We have shown that the classical rule of Existential Instantiation is incorrect for the objectual interpretation, but the same problem arises with the free logic rules. In FL + (t∀), Et & □t≈t / ∃x□x≈t is provable as a special case of the derivable rule (t∃).

(t∀)   ∀xAx / Et→At
(t∃)   Et & At / ∃xAx

Since $\Box t \approx t$ is a theorem of fK, Et / $\exists x \Box x \approx t$ is provable there as well. However, this argument can be shown to be oK-invalid, using virtually the same model we used in the case of $\exists x \Box x \approx t$.

EXERCISE 13.11 Show that Et / $\exists x \Box x \approx t$ is oK-invalid.

So the problem we are facing does not depend on the treatment of the quantifier domain. A quantified modal logic that is sound with respect to (o$\forall$) must not use the free logic instantiation rule (t$\forall$).

The quantifier rules that specify which instances are correct for nonrigid terms t are not easy to formulate. Although the inference Et & Ft / $\exists x$Fx is valid when $\exists x$Fx contains no intensional operators, we have just shown that Et & $\Box$Ft / $\exists x \Box$Fx is invalid. The reason is that the truth of Et does not ensure that there is *one* object d for which $\Box$Fd holds. Notice, however, that the truth of $\exists x \Box x \approx t$ at world **r** does guarantee that there is an object d identical to the referent of t in all worlds related to **r**. For this reason, the argument $\exists x \Box x \approx t$ & $\Box$Ft / $\exists x \Box$Fx is oK-valid, and in general so is $\exists x \Box^n x \approx t$ & $\Box^n$Ft / $\exists x \Box^n$Fx.

EXERCISE 13.12 Show that $\exists x \Box^n x \approx t$ & $\Box^n$Ft / $\exists x \Box^n$Fx is oK-valid when n=2 and n=3. Now explain why this holds for any value of n. (You may use mathematical induction if you are familiar with it.)

It appears we have made some progress. Let us reformulate this principle with $\forall$ in place of $\exists$ in hopes of defining a correct quantifier rule for the objectual interpretation. The result is the following:

($\forall^n$Out) $\forall x \Box^n Ax, \exists x \Box^n x \approx t$ / $\Box^n At$

Unfortunately, even this complicated rule is not fully adequate. Consider the argument $\forall x \Box$(Px & $\Box$Qx), $\exists x \Box x \approx t$ / $\Box$(Pt & $\Box$Qt). Here t lies beneath one box in the conclusion in its first occurrence and beneath two boxes in its second occurrence. Although $\exists x \Box x \approx t$ warrants the inference from $\forall x \Box$Px to $\Box$Pt, and $\exists x \Box \Box x \approx t$ warrants the inference from $\forall x \Box \Box$Qx to $\Box \Box$Qt, neither $\exists x \Box x \approx t$ nor $\exists x \Box \Box x \approx t$ by itself is sufficient for deducing $\Box$(Ft & $\Box$Gt) from $\forall x \Box$(Fx & $\Box$Gx). What we need is the conjunction $\exists x \Box x \approx t$ & $\exists x \Box \Box x \approx t$.

EXERCISE 13.13 Show that ($\forall^n$Out) is oK-invalid. (Hint: Let At in ($\forall^n$Out) be (Ft & $\Box$Gt).)

A correct instantiation rule for the objectual interpretation with non-rigid terms is difficult to summarize. $\forall x A x$ entails $A t$ provided that for each occurrence of x in Ax, $\exists x \Box^n x \approx t$ is provable, where n is the number of boxes under which that occurrence lies. If many occurrences of x in Ax lie beneath varying numbers of boxes, we will need to establish many different sentences of the form $\exists x \Box^n x \approx t$ in order to warrant the inference from $\forall x A x$ to $A t$. In modal logics as strong as S4, the ($\forall$Out) rule may be simplified a great deal. Since $\exists x \Box^n x \approx t$ is equivalent to $\exists x \Box x \approx t$ in S4 (and since $\exists x \Box x \approx t$ entails $\exists x x \approx t$), the ($\forall$Out) rule may be given in the form: $\forall x A x, \exists x \Box x \approx t$ / $A t$.

The difficulties to be faced in allowing nonrigid terms with the objectual interpretation has exerted strong pressure on researchers to consider systems where only rigid constants are allowed in the language. On that assumption, the formulation of a logic for the objectual interpretation is fairly straightforward. For most underlying modal logics S, an adequate system rS may be constructed by adding (RC) to fS.

(RC) $(b \approx c \rightarrow \Box b \approx c)$ & $(\sim b \approx c \rightarrow \Box \sim b \approx c)$

EXERCISE 13.14   Show that $\forall x A x$ / $A c$ is qoK-valid.

Systems of this kind are appealing to those who dislike restrictions on the substitution of identity. When the only terms are constants and constants are rigid, it turns out that the substitution of identical terms is valid in all contexts.

EXERCISE 13.15   (Advanced Project.) Use mathematical induction to prove that substitution of identical terms is oK-valid in all contexts when terms are all rigid.

However, it seems fainthearted for logicians to abandon the project of accommodating the nonrigid terms in logic simply because complications arise in dealing with them. Perhaps we can do better. It is truly difficult to formulate quantified modal logic for the objectual interpretation if all of the terms (including the constants) are nonrigid. However, supplying the language with a rank of rigid constants simplifies matters immensely, for then adequate systems can be based on the standard free logic rule ($\forall$Out), which instantiates to constants only.

This point may have been missed in the literature on quantified modal logic because it appears that a stronger instantiation principle is needed to handle the instantiation of nonrigid terms t. Luckily, nothing more is required. (∀Out) is strong enough by itself to guarantee the derivability of all the valid instantiation principles that we have just discussed. It is interesting to explore how the correct rules for instantiating ∀xAx are already derivable within fK. For example, it is not difficult to show that the following argument can be proven in fK: ∀xPx / ∃xx≈t→Pt as follows:

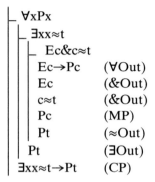

```
 ⎮ ∀xPx
 ⎮ ⎮ ∃xx≈t
 ⎮ ⎮ ⎮ Ec&c≈t
 ⎮ ⎮ ⎮ Ec→Pc      (∀Out)
 ⎮ ⎮ ⎮ Ec          (&Out)
 ⎮ ⎮ ⎮ c≈t         (&Out)
 ⎮ ⎮ ⎮ Pc          (MP)
 ⎮ ⎮ ⎮ Pt          (≈Out)
 ⎮ ⎮ Pt            (∃Out)
 ⎮ ∃xx≈t→Pt        (CP)
```

Now consider the proof of ∀x□Px / ∃x□x≈t→□Pt where the instantiation occurs beneath a single box.

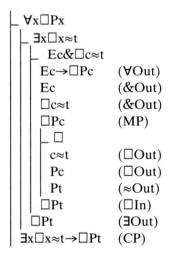

```
 ⎮ ∀x□Px
 ⎮ ⎮ ∃x□x≈t
 ⎮ ⎮ ⎮ Ec&□c≈t
 ⎮ ⎮ ⎮ Ec→□Pc       (∀Out)
 ⎮ ⎮ ⎮ Ec           (&Out)
 ⎮ ⎮ ⎮ □c≈t         (&Out)
 ⎮ ⎮ ⎮ □Pc          (MP)
 ⎮ ⎮ ⎮ ⎮ □
 ⎮ ⎮ ⎮ ⎮ c≈t        (□Out)
 ⎮ ⎮ ⎮ ⎮ Pc         (□Out)
 ⎮ ⎮ ⎮ ⎮ Pt         (≈Out)
 ⎮ ⎮ ⎮ □Pt          (□In)
 ⎮ ⎮ □Pt            (∃Out)
 ⎮ ∃x□x≈t→□Pt        (CP)
```

EXERCISE 13.16

a) Prove in fK: ∀x(□Px&□□Qx), ∃x□x≈t, ∃x□□x≈t / □Pt&□□Qt.

b) Prove in fS4: ∀x(□Pxv□□Qx), ∃x□x≈t / □Ptv□□Qt.

These examples illustrate the surprising power of (∀Out) to guarantee proofs of valid instantiation principles for nonrigid terms. The secret is to let the process of instantiation depend on the substitutions allowed by (≈Out) to generate all and only the right instances.

Of course a few examples do not prove that a system based on (∀Out) is correct. In fact, completeness requires that the new rule (∃i) be added to govern the interaction between rigid constants and nonrigid terms t.

(∃i) $\underline{L \vdash \sim t \approx c}$ where c is a constant not in L or t

      L ⊢ ⊥

Fortunately this is the only addition needed for a complete system. (See Sections 16.3 and 17.8.) So the system oS = rS + (∃i) provides a relatively simple solution to the problem of formulating rules for the objectual interpretation with nonrigid terms.

13.7. The Conceptual Interpretation

Let us investigate another approach to avoiding the complications that arise for the objectual interpretation. It depends on choosing a more general interpretation of the quantifier. Difficulties with the objectual interpretation arose because we allowed terms to have *intensions* (which is another way to say that they may be nonrigid) while at the same time we quantified over term *extensions*, that is, the domain of quantification was a set of *objects* in the domain **Dw**. If we were to quantify over term *intensions* or individual concepts, then there would be a better match between the treatment of quantification and the treatment of terms.

In the *conceptual interpretation* of the quantifier, the domain of quantification is the set of all term *intensions* (individual concepts), rather than the set of all term extensions (objects). For constant domains, the truth clause is would be (cQ∀).

(cQ∀) $a_w(\forall x Ax) = T$ iff $a_w(Af) = T$ for every individual concept f.

Remember that an individual concept (or term intension) is a function from the set **W** of worlds into the set **D** of objects. Notice also that Af is a new kind of hybrid sentence, one that is the result of replacing the *function* f for occurrences of x bound by ∀x in ∀xAx. We will need to explain how such hybrid sentences are evaluated. In the case of the atomic hybrid Pf, we want $a_w(Pf)$ to be T when $f(w) \in a_w(P)$. To obtain the more general definition we need for all hybrids, the strategy used for the objectual interpretation may be generalized. Let us treat functions as honorary members of the set of terms, and use (f) to define the notation '$a_w(f)$'.

(f) $a_w(f)=f(w)$.

In the truth condition for atomic sentences (Pl), we understand that the list l includes terms and/or functions.

The conceptual interpretation promises to simplify the quantifier rules and to allow a more general understanding of the quantifier domain. Unfortunately, there are a number of difficulties with it. In the first place, this interpretation validates the classical quantifier rules. The problem is that $\exists x\Box x\approx t$ is valid on the conceptual interpretation because there is an individual concept f (namely, $a(t)$) such that $a_w(\Box f\approx t)=T$ for any choice of a and w. On the conceptual interpretation, 'there is something which is necessarily the inventor of bifocals' is true because the inventor of bifocals counts as *something* that is necessarily the inventor of bifocals. Since we quantify over *all* individual concepts on the conceptual interpretation, and since the intension of 'the inventor of bifocals' counts as an individual concept, we have no reason to reject $\exists x\Box x\approx t$.

The conceptual interpretation has another tantalizing consequence, namely, that $\exists x\Box\exists yy\approx x$ is valid. Using (DefE), this amounts to $\exists x\Box Ex$, the claim that something necessarily exists, a conclusion that will gladden the hearts of those who hope for an ontological proof of the existence of God. Closer analysis of the meaning of $\exists x\Box Ex$ on the conceptual interpretation reveals that its validity is cold comfort to the theist. To show that $\exists x\Box Ex$ is true under all interpretations, we may pick any individual concept f we like, for the hybrid $\Box Ef$ is T on any assignment in any world. (The reason is that the hybrid $f\approx f$ is true in all worlds, and so by the conceptual interpretation, $\exists yy\approx f$ is T in all worlds. This means that $\Box\exists yy\approx f$ [i.e., $\Box Ef$] is true on any given world.) An arbitrarily chosen individual concept, however, does not reflect the Deity, for it may pick out Jim Garson in one world, Richard Nixon in another, and Adolph Hitler (or even a stone) in yet another. The sentence 'something necessarily exists' is interesting to those investigating God's existence only when it is interpreted to mean that there is some *one* thing that exists in all possible worlds, and this is not the interpretation given to it by the conceptual interpretation. So the conceptual interpretation does not correspond to the usual interpretation we give to sentences in quantified modal logic, with the consequence that it is not the proper tool for analyzing philosophical controversies such as whether God exists.

The conceptual interpretation suffers from technical problems as well. As long as the underlying propositional modal logic is S4.3 or less, the semantics that uses the conceptual interpretation cannot be formalized. (S4.3 is the system S4 plus the axiom: $\Box(\Box A{\to}\Box B)v(\Box B{\to}\Box A)$, which is appropriate for a tense logic where time is a continuous series of moments.) This means that there is no finite set of axioms or rules that is adequate (sound and complete) with respect to the brand of validity defined by the conceptual interpretation. In short, the conceptual interpretation has no logic. This result is proven by showing that there are sentences in conceptual semantics that express the basic concepts of arithmetic. Godel's famous incompleteness theorem showed that arithmetic is not formalizable, and so it follows that neither is conceptual semantics (Garson, 2001, Section 3.4). These difficulties remain even when the truth clause for varying domains is used. On a varying domain version of the conceptual interpretation (c∀), ∀xAx should be true at **w** only if Af is true for an individual concept f such that f(**w**) *exists* in the domain for **w**.

(c∀) $\mathbf{a_w}(\forall xAx)$=T iff for all f, if f(**w**) $\in$ **Dw**, then $\mathbf{a_w}(Af)$=T.

To define semantics for the conceptual interpretation, let a cS-model <**W, R, $\mathbb{D}$, a**> contain a frame <**W, R**> for a propositional modal logic S, a domain structure $\mathbb{D}$, and an assignment function **a** that obeys ($\approx$), (Pl), ($\bot$), ($\to$), ($\Box$), (E), and (c∀). cS-validity is defined in the usual way.

Unfortunately, the restriction to varying domains does nothing to solve the problem. The resulting semantics is *still* not formalizable, and although $\exists x\Box Ex$ is no longer cK-valid, $\exists x\Box Ex$ still does not receive its intuitive meaning, for it is enough for the cK-validity of $\exists x\Box Ex$ merely that some object exist in each domain **Dw**.

EXERCISE 13.17   Show that if **Dw** is not empty for each **w** $\in$ **W**, then $\mathbf{a_w}(\exists x\Box Ex)$=T in every cK-model.

13.8. The Intensional Interpretation

Let us survey the situation. A simple truth value semantics for quantified modal logic using the substitution interpretation was presented. We explained that it can be formalized with system fS, using free logic rules. Difficulties, however, have arisen with interpretations of the quantifier that involve ontological commitment. If we choose the objectual interpretation, then either very complex rules must be adopted, or the system must contain rigid constants along with the rules (RC) and ($\exists$i). If we quantify over individual concepts, the result is a semantics that cannot be formalized and that interprets sentences in counterintuitive ways. Is there some way around these complications? The answer is "Yes". A simple modification of the conceptual interpretation results in a definition of validity that picks out exactly the basic system fS. The result is an ontological approach to quantifiers that is general and validates exactly the arguments valid on the substitution interpretation. For these reasons, it provides a framework within which the other systems can be formulated and understood.

To present the new interpretation, it helps to revisit what may have gone wrong with the conceptual approach. Our rejection of the inference from 'necessarily the inventor of bifocals is the inventor of bifocals' to 'something is necessarily the inventor of bifocals' was prompted not by the fact that the inventor of bifocals does not exist in the real world, but by the fact that the intension of 'the inventor of bifocals' across possible worlds does not count as a unified substance. Our intuitions rule that there are only certain individual concepts that count in supporting existential claims. To reflect this idea, let us introduce a set **I** of individual concepts (functions from **W** into **D**) that count as substances, that is, that are unified in the proper way. Let us work out this idea more carefully by defining what we call intensional models.

A *intensional model* or *iS-model* $<$**W**, **R**, $\mathbb{D}$, **I**, **a**$>$ contains a frame $<$**W**, **R**$>$ for a propositional modal logic S, a domain structure $\mathbb{D}$, a set **I** of individual concepts for the substances, and an assignment function **a** that obeys ($\approx$), (Pl), ($\perp$), ($\rightarrow$), ($\square$), and (E), along with (cI) and (i$\forall$).

(cI) $\mathbf{a}(c) \in \mathbf{I}$.

(i$\forall$) $\mathbf{a_w}(\forall x A x) = T$ iff for all $i \in \mathbf{I}$, if $i(\mathbf{w}) \in \mathbf{Dw}$ then $\mathbf{a_w}(Ai) = T$.

Note that (cI) matches the intuition that constants should pick out substances. It is needed to guarantee the validity of ($\forall$Out). In the next exercise, you may verify that the derived truth condition for $\exists$ comes to (i$\exists$).

(i$\exists$) $\mathbf{a_w}(\exists x A x) = T$ iff for some $i \in \mathbf{I}$, $i(\mathbf{w}) \in \mathbf{Dw}$ and $\mathbf{a_w}(Ai) = T$.

EXERCISE 13.18 Show that (i$\exists$) holds.

The intensional interpretation of the quantifier has a number of important advantages. First, $\exists x \Box x \approx t$ and $\exists x \Box Ex$ are iK-invalid, which conforms to our intuitive readings of these sentences. $\exists x \Box x \approx t$ will be true at **w** only if we can find a function i in **I** that matches the intension **a**(t) of t in related worlds. If **a**(t) is not unified in the right way, then there will not be such a function. Similarly, $\exists x \Box Ex$ is iK-invalid because in order for $\Box Ei$ to be true in **w**, i(**v**) must exist in all worlds **v** related to **w**. A model where i(**v**) fails to be in the domain **Dv** at some world **v** related to **w** will make $\Box Ei$ false in **w**. So all it takes to invalidate $\exists x \Box Ex$ is to build a model so that for every function i in **I**, there is a world **v** such that i(**v**) is not in **Dv**.

EXERCISE 13.19   Construct iK-counterexamples to both $\exists x \Box x \approx t$ and $\exists x \Box Ex$.

A second advantage of the intensional interpretation is that it may be easily formalized. It is possible to modify the relatively straightforward completeness results for the substitution interpretation to show completeness of systems based on fS. So the intensional interpretation is the ontological approach that exactly matches the concept of validity generated by the substitution interpretation. The strong kinships between the truth value, substitution, and intensional interpretations will play an important role in simplifying the adequacy proofs to be presented in future chapters.

A final advantage of the intensional interpretation is its generality and flexibility. We have incorporated a notion of substance into the semantics without laying down any conditions on what the substances are. They might be the constant functions, but they needn't be (and in fact it might turn out that no substances correspond to constant functions). The objectual and conceptual interpretations are less general. Each of them can be treated as special cases of the intensional interpretation when special assumptions are made about the set of substances **I**.

On the conceptual interpretation, it is assumed that *all* individual concepts count as substances, that is, **I** is the set of all functions from **W** into **D**. The formal problems that arise for the conceptual interpretation are the result of difficulties in capturing this stipulation with rules. The objectual interpretation corresponds to the assumption that substances are reflected by constant functions, for quantification over objects is formally equivalent to quantification over constant functions that pick out the same objects. This idea will be exploited in Section 15.6 to show that the objectual interpretation can be exactly captured within intensional models by adding the extra condition (o) that **I** contains all and only the

constant functions defined over **D**. So adequacy for the objectual interpretation falls out as a special case of the adequacy for the intensional
interpretation once it is shown that the additional rules (RC) and (∃i)
correspond to condition (o). As a result, the intensional interpretation
provides an excellent basis for viewing and comparing a variety of treatments of the quantifier in a unified way (Garson, 2005).

EXERCISE 13.20   Show that ∃x□x=t is iK-invalid, even assuming that t is
rigid.

The reader may wonder if there is any independent reason for preferring the intensional interpretation over the objectual interpretation. The
notion that substances are the same thing or one thing across possible
worlds seems to be built into our ordinary interpretation of modal sentences, so perhaps the objectual interpretation, less general as it is, is the
proper approach to take in quantified modal logic.

However, there are positive reasons, apart from its technical generality, for preferring the intensional interpretation. A particularly clear case
where the intensional interpretation is necessary arises in tense logic.
Let the worlds in **W** be times, and the members of **D** be time slices of
things. A time slice for time **w** is an object "frozen" as it is at the instant
w. The objects of the real world are thought of as being made up of
time slices; in fact they are represented in the semantics as functions
from times into time slices. The function orders the slices into a "time
worm", which gives a history of the thing through time. Now imagine that
we adopt the objectual interpretation so that our substances (or things)
are represented by constant functions. Then things would never change
since the function for a thing would give the same time slice for each
moment of time. Since things *do* change, we need the flexibility of the
intensional interpretation and must reject the objectual interpretation.
Notice that part of the reason for this rejection is that the objects of
our *ontology*, the enduring things, are not the members of **D**. The members of **D** are time slices and so are not the things we would ordinarily
say exist. The items in our semantics that correspond to real enduring
objects of our everyday ontology are represented in the semantics by
term *intensions*, not by the term extensions or "objects" that are members
of **D**.

Although it is clear that the intensional interpretation is needed in tense
logic, one might still argue that the objectual interpretation is the only correct one for a logic of necessity. Insistence on the objectual interpretation
in modal logic, however, begs the question against certain theories about

possible objects. The theory of *world-bound individuals* (Lewis, 1968) claims that it never makes sense to say that the *same* object exists in two possible worlds on the grounds that there is no way to make sense of identity conditions across possible worlds. On this view, the sentence 'Jim Garson could have been the inventor of bifocals' is not true because Jim Garson in some other possible world is the inventor of bifocals. By the theory of world-bound individuals, there *is* no Jim Garson in any world other than the real one. The world-bound individualist takes 'Jim Garson could have been the inventor of bifocals' to be true because a *counterpart* of Jim Garson (something like him in the relevant ways, but not identical to him) is the inventor of bifocals in some other world. On this view, the notion of a counterpart of an object is used to bind together non-identical manifestations of Jim Garson into a substance. The term intension for 'Jim Garson', then, must pick out different objects in different worlds.

Even if you are not a defender of the theory of world-bound individuals, it is important to note that the objectual interpretation conflicts with a consistent view about possible objects held by at least some philosophers. If the semantical theory for quantified modal logics is to serve as a neutral device for exploring alternative views about possible objects and substance, it is crucial that it not beg the question against a view that has had able defenders.

The reader may not be very happy at the prospect of a semantics where the quantifier domain, the set of *real* things, contains individual *concepts*. *Concepts* have a very poor claim to existence in any sense. One of the advantages of the objectual interpretation appears to be that there we quantify over *objects*, whose claims to existence cannot be disputed. This rejoinder may be rebutted by pointing out that the words 'object' and 'individual concept' are used as convenient labels for items in our semantical theories, and the meanings we ordinarily attribute to these labels may mislead us when we try to determine the ontological claims of a semantical theory.

Notice first that the use of the word 'object' for the domain **D** is misleading because **D** must contain *possible* objects that do not exist in the real world. The members of **D** have no better claim to ontological respectability by being called objects. In fact, in the tense logic example we used to motivate the intensional interpretation, the members of **D** were ontologically suspect (they were time slices of things), whereas the members of **I** (the so called individual concepts or world lines) turned out to represent the objects of daily life. On this application, term *intensions* correspond to what is real, whereas term *extensions* are abstract, or conceptual.

A similar argument may be made in the case of the logic of necessity, though it is bound to be more controversial. If we have to choose between what we call objects in the semantics, and substances, I would think it is substances that correspond to what is truly real. In the temporal case, we insisted that real things have a temporal dimension; they are not mere slices. I think that real things also have a modal dimension. A real thing would be less real if its possibilities were not included. A chair is what it is partly because it could not possibly be a desk. Part of what makes the chair what it is is that it ceases to exist though radical change (for example, if its wood were used to build a desk). I claim that for something to be real, it must have a modal "history" as well as a temporal one. In the same way that certain properties such as changing do not apply to time slices, the notion of what is possible for a thing does not apply to members of **D**, the things we paradoxically call *possible* objects. The members of **D** are modally bare particulars, in the sense that though they may have actual properties, it makes no sense to talk of what is possible or not possible for them. On the other hand the members of **I**, the substances, have a modal history, which reflects the nature of things we take to be fully real. On this account, it is the objectual interpretation that is ontologically mistaken, for it quantifies over "things" that are shorn of their modal aspects, and so have no more reality than do time slices. For more on this point see Garson (1987).

13.9. Strengthening Intensional Interpretation Models

A number of special conditions on quantifier domains may be added to form stronger kinds of iS-models. Here is a list of so-called *domain rules* (most mentioned in Chapter 12) with their corresponding conditions on iS-models. The first five of these are axioms, but we will refer to them as rules since the rule in question is that one may add instances of the axiom to any subproof.

Domain Rules		**Corresponding Domain Conditions**
(∃E)	∃xEx	For some $i \in \mathbf{I}$, $i(\mathbf{w}) \in \mathbf{Dw}$.
(Q)	Et	$\mathbf{Dw=D}$.
(ED)	Ec→□Ec	If $\mathbf{wRv}$ and $\mathbf{a_w}(c) \in \mathbf{Dw}$, then $\mathbf{a_v}(c) \in \mathbf{Dv}$.
(CD)	~Ec→□~Ec	If $\mathbf{wRv}$ and $\mathbf{a_v}(c) \in \mathbf{Dv}$, then $\mathbf{a_w}(c) \in \mathbf{Dw}$.
(RC)	(b≈c→□b≈c) &(~b≈c→□~b≈c)	$\mathbf{a_w}(c)\mathbf{=a_v}(c)$.
(∃i)	L ⊢ ~t≈c / L ⊢ ⊥, no c in L, t	For some $i \in \mathbf{I}$, $i(\mathbf{w})\mathbf{=a_w}(t)$.

The rules (RC) and (∃i) *together* correspond to the condition (o) that **I** contain all and only the constant functions whose values are in **D**. It will be shown in Section 15.6 that the objectual interpretation for the quantifier is obtained by adding condition (o) to iS-models. So the objectual interpretation can be seen as a special case of the intensional interpretation where (o) holds.

(o)=(RC)+(∃i)   **I** is the set of all constant functions with values in **D**.

As a result, the adequacy of systems for the objectual interpretation can be proven as a special cases of the proof for the intensional interpretation.

When (o) is satisfied, the conditions for (∃E), (ED), and (CD) may be simplified as follows:

(∃E)	∃xEx	(o∃E)	**Dw** is not empty.
(ED)	Ec→□Ec	(oED)	If **wRv**, then **Dw** ⊆ **Dv**.
(CD)	~Ec→□~Ec	(oCD)	If **wRv**, then **Dv** ⊆ **Dw**.

(In conditions (oED) and (oCD), the symbol '⊆' is used for 'is a subset of'. So '**Dw** ⊆ **Dv**' means that every member of **Dw** is a member of **Dv**.)

In system oS, it turns out (ED) and (CD) are equivalent (respectively) to the Barcan Formulas, (CBF) and (BF). (See the discussion preceding Exercises 12.16a and 12.20.)

(BF)	∀x□Ax→□∀xAx
(CBF)	□∀xAx→∀x□Ax

Therefore, systems that adopt the objectual interpretation and any of these domain conditions can be viewed as special cases of the intensional interpretation where (o) and the domain conditions hold. In case a system with a constant domain is desired, an adequate system may be formulated using axiom (Q). Since (Q) clearly entails both (ED) and (CD), it follows that the Barcan Formulas are derivable in that system.

13.10. Relationships with Systems in the Literature

A wide variety of systems for quantified modal logic have been presented in this book. It is worth exploring how these systems are related to the logics that have been presented in the literature over the years. For a more thorough discussion of this, see the taxonomy of quantified modal logics developed in Garson (2001).

Kripke's historic paper (1963) set the stage for introducing quantifiers into modal logic. Kripke adopted the objectual interpretation with the varying domains approach (oS-models), employing a wide domain **D** of possible objects and separate domains **Dw** for objects that exist in each world **w**. Kripke showed that the Barcan Formulas ((BF) and (CBF)) fail on this semantics and pointed out that their validity can be restored by stipulating the corresponding conditions on the domains.

		Corresponding Condition	
(BF)	$\forall x \Box Ax \rightarrow \Box \forall x Ax$	(oCD)	If **wRv**, then **Dv** $\subseteq$ **Dw**.
(CBF)	$\Box \forall x Ax \rightarrow \forall x \Box Ax$	(oED)	If **wRv**, then **Dw** $\subseteq$ **Dv**.

Kripke considered M, S4, B, and S5 as suitable choices for the underlying propositional modal logic S. It is implicit from his discussion that if one were to prefer the possibilist or constant domain approach, one could stipulate **Dw=D**, and the logic could be formulated in a system where both Barcan Formulas are derivable. Kripke used the traditional formulation TK for the underlying modal logics. (See the discussion in Section 12.7.) He noted (as we have) that (CBF) can be derived from classical quantifier rules, and that (BF) follows when the underlying modality is B or stronger.

So Kripke made it clear that using classical quantifier rules with logics built from TK is not compatible with varying quantifier domains. Although he considered introducing an existence predicate E, and noted that Et may be defined by $\exists xx \approx t$ in a system that includes identity, Kripke, oddly, did not resolve the conflict by choosing the free logic rules for the quantifiers. Free logics were not well developed in his day, so perhaps he saw no alternative to classical rules. As we noted in Sections 12.4 and 13.6, the classical principle of universal instantiation (Q∀Out) is invalid when varying domains are used.

(Q∀Out) $\forall x Ax$ / Ac

Kripke's solution for the problem was to require that *variables* be the only terms of the language and to stipulate that open sentences receive the *closure interpretation*, where an open sentence Ax is presumed to be universally bound: $\forall x Ax$. On this approach, $\forall x Ax \rightarrow Ay$ is considered

oS-valid because it is equivalent in content to the oS-valid closed sentence
∀y(∀xAx→Ay).

EXERCISE 13.21   Prove that ∀y(∀xAx→Ay) is oK-valid.

In this book, sentences containing free variables are not even well formed,
but a comparison can be made to Kripke's logic by assuming that our *constants* play the role of variables and are to be given the closure interpretation. That would mean that Ac is understood to assert ∀xAx. Allowing
only constants of this kind is a serious limitation on the expressive power
of the language. In the case of ordinary terms t of natural language, we
expect that At should not entail ∀xAx. For example, it should not follow
from 'Bush is president' that 'everyone is president'. However, in Kripke's
system there are no terms of this kind.

Kripke adopted the universal closures of classical predicate logic principles to formulate his logic, but a further restriction was still needed to
avoid deriving the Barcan Formulas. His rule of Necessitation applied
only to closed sentences. From our point of view, that amounts to the
requirement that Necessitation applies to no sentence containing a constant. Although logics based on Kripke's systems can be shown to be
complete (Corsi, 2002), they are not able to give a reasonable account of
terms. There have been two different reactions to the problem. One has
been to modify varying domain models in some way to preserve classical
rules, and the other has been the path taken in this book, namely, to adopt
free logic.

Thomason's influential paper (1970) explores both of these options.
His system Q1 adopts the *possibilist* approach, namely, to use a single
domain of quantification, or equivalently, to stipulate that **D**=**Dw** for
each world **w**. However, the classical principle of universal instantiation
(Q∀Out) is invalid on this semantics if c is a nonrigid term, so Thomason
simply presumed that all terms are rigid. It is not difficult to show that
Thomason's Q1 is equivalent to our system qrS when constants are the
only terms of the language. System qrS, remember, is the result of adding
(Q) and (RC) and modal axioms of S to the basic logic fK.

(Q)   Et
(RC)   (b≈c→□b≈c) & (~b≈c→□~b≈c)

This system has been widely adopted in the literature on quantified modal
logic. It has been argued that it is either superior to other logics (Cresswell,

1991; Linsky and Zalta, 1994) or the only coherent system (Williamson, 1998). We have explained in Section 12.9 why a preference for this system is shortsighted.

Thomason (1970) was one of the first people to use free logic to formulate a system Q3 for *actualist* quantification, a system with varying domains and nonrigid terms. Some of the problems he faced were discussed in Section 13.6. The main difficulty was that even the free logic rule ($\forall$Out) is not valid.

($\forall$Out) $\forall x A x$ / $Ec \rightarrow Ac$

Thomason solved the problem by requiring that his variables (our constants) be rigid terms; but even so, it appeared that the rule of universal instantiation for nonrigid terms would have to be quite complicated, for reasons discussed in Section 13.6. To formulate a manageable system, he presumed the underlying modal logic was as strong as S4, so that $\forall x A x$, $\exists x \Box x \approx t$ / At could be adopted as a valid instantiation rule. Thomason also noted the need to adopt what amounts to the rule ($\exists i$) in order to obtain a complete system.

($\exists i$) $L \vdash \sim t \approx c$ / $L \vdash \perp$, where c does not appear in L, or t

One contribution of this book is to show that there is no need to adopt complex instantiation principles to manage nonrigid terms. When constants are rigid, ($\forall$Out) is valid, and it is sufficient to allow the deduction of exactly the correct principles for instantiation of the nonrigid terms. The completeness results in this book, and those given by Thomason, show that his Q3S4 generates exactly the same provable arguments as our system oS4. Furthermore, our systems oS are both sound and complete for Thomason's Q3 models (our oS-models), for a wide variety of propositional modal logics S, including many weaker than S4.

Before Thomason's paper was published, Hughes and Cresswell (1968, Ch. 10) had presented a different way to preserve classical rules for quantified modal logic in a semantics with varying domains. Systems of this kind have resurfaced in many places. They have been attractive because they are built from classical predicate logic and their completeness is relatively easy to prove. The essential insight is that (Q$\forall$Out) would be valid on varying domain semantics provided that whenever sentence Ac is T in a world $\mathbf{w}$, the referent $\mathbf{a_w}(c)$ of c must be an existing object, that is, a member of $\mathbf{Dw}$. Under these circumstances, $\mathbf{a_w}(Ac) = T$ will always entail that

$\mathbf{a_w}(Ec)=T$, and from this it will follow that $\mathbf{a_w}(\exists xAx)=T$. Hence (Q∃In), which is equivalent to (Q∀Out), will turn out valid.

(Q∃In)   Ac / ∃xAx

The success of this approach depends on finding a way to secure (AE), the principle that when a sentence involving c is true in a world, the referent of c exists in that world.

(AE)   If $\mathbf{a_w}(Ac)=T$ then $\mathbf{a_w}(c) \in \mathbf{Dw}$.

(AE) seems counterintuitive because from 'Superman does not exist' (~Es) it should not follow that 'Superman' refers to something real. Nonetheless, (AE) can be made plausible if we introduce the idea that sentences lack truth values when terms they contain do not refer to existing things. Consider for example, Russell's famous example: 'The present king of France is bald'. Strawson (1950) argues that since there is no present king of France, a present use this sentence does not make any statement, and so lacks a truth value. If the assignment function is *partial* so that sentences may be undefined, the plausible principle (Undefined) will provide a good basis for accepting (AE).

(Undefined)   If $\mathbf{a_w}(c) \notin \mathbf{Dw}$, then $\mathbf{a_w}(Ac)$ is not defined.

EXERCISE 13.22   Explain why (Undefined) entails (AE).

Using partial assignment functions is an initially attractive solution to the problem of validating the classical rules with variable domains. Unfortunately, in formulating the truth condition for □, Hughes and Cresswell felt compelled to adopt (oED), which they called the *inclusion requirement*.

(oED)   If $\mathbf{wRv}$ then $\mathbf{Dw} \subseteq \mathbf{Dv}$.

That is not too surprising, for (oED) corresponds in oS to the Converse Barcan Formula (CBF), which we know follows from classical quantifier rules and principles of K. The problem is that (oED) undermines the whole motivation for varying domains, namely, to accommodate the intuition that things in the real world need not exist in related possible worlds. (See the discussion in Section 12.10.)

Since Hughes and Cresswell adopted the traditional formulation TK for their underlying modal logic, the adoption of classical rules did not entail the Barcan Formula (BF). So their system can at least accommodate the idea that new objects may come into existence in accessible worlds. In this book, we have adopted the boxed subproof approach to formulating modal principles. So in our systems, adopting the classical rules (adopting Et) forces acceptance of both (CBF) and (BF). Therefore, Hughes and Cresswell's logic cannot be identified with any system formulated here, with the exception that when the modal logic S is B or stronger, (BF) is obtained, and the logic comes to our qS.

In Garson (1984, 2001), a semantics similar to the intensional interpretation of Section 13.8 was presented called the *substantial interpretation*. The basic idea was that the problems faced in working out a rule of universal generalization in a system with nonrigid terms and the objectual interpretation could be solved if the domain of quantification were generalized so that it "matched" the treatment of terms. Since nonrigid terms have individual concepts as their intensions, the domain of quantification should contain *individual concepts* rather than objects. (Remember that individual concepts are functions from the set of possible worlds $\mathbf{W}$ to the set of possible objects $\mathbf{D}$.) To accommodate systems with varying domains, a separate domain $\mathbf{Iw}$ of individual concepts was introduced for each world $\mathbf{w}$, and an intentional existence predicate E was defined so that Et was true in a world $\mathbf{w}$ just in case the *intension* of t was a member of E in $\mathbf{w}$. So the truth conditions for $\forall$ and E on this semantics read as follows:

(iw$\forall$) $\mathbf{a_w}(\forall xAx)=T$ iff for every $i \in \mathbf{Iw}$, $\mathbf{a_w}(Ai)=T$.

(iE) $\mathbf{a_w}(Et)=T$ iff $\mathbf{a}(t) \in \mathbf{Iw}$.

The effect of (iE) is that E becomes and *intensional* predicate. That is, the rule (eE) of substitution of identicals no longer holds behind E.

(eE) $s \approx t\ /\ Es \rightarrow Et$

However, it can be shown that the (iE), which allows substitution of *provable* identities, does preserve validity on this semantics.

(iE) $\vdash s \approx t\ /\ \vdash Es \rightarrow Et$

When E is intensional, the ($\approx$Out) rule must be restricted so that it does not apply to sentences of the form Et. Otherwise (eE) will be obtained.

This semantics validates (t∀), universal generalization for all terms, including nonrigid terms.

(t∀) $\forall xAx / Et \rightarrow At$

Because this semantics validates (t∀), and the objectual interpretation does not, it does not qualify as a system from which all the other logics can be constructed by laying down extra conditions on the domains and frames of the models. So it does not serve as a good foundation for quantified modal logic. To provide such a general starting point, Garson (2005) introduced a global domain **I** of individual concepts and proposed the following more general truth condition in place of (iw∀):

(ii∀) $a_w(\forall xAx)$=T iff for every $i \in \mathbf{I}$, if $i \in \mathbf{Iw}$, $a_w(Ai)$=T.

In this semantics, the effect of (iw∀) may be obtained by assuming that every member of **Iw** is in **I**, and the effect of the objectual interpretation is obtained by stipulating that **I** is the set of all constant functions, and that E is *extensional*, in the sense that (eE) holds.

(eE)   If $a_w(s)=a_w(t)$ and $a_w(Es)$=T then $a_w(Et)$=T.

When E is extensional, it is possible to define an extensional domain **Dw** from **Iw** by letting d be in **Dw** iff for some i in **Iw**, i(**w**)=d. Under these circumstances the truth condition (ii∀) reduces to the intensional interpretation used in this book.

(i∀) $a_w(\forall xAx)$=T iff for every $i \in \mathbf{I}$, if $i(\mathbf{w}) \in \mathbf{Dw}$ then $a_w(Ai)$=T.

By working with an extensional domain **Dw**, instead of **Iw**, this book avoids complications both in exposition and in the completeness results. However, the reader who wants to explore a fully general quantified modal logic will want to consider systems that not only treat E as an intensional predicate, but include other intensional predicates as well. (For the merits of introducing intensional predicates in general, see Thomason's Introduction to (Montague, 1974) and Bressan (1973).)

13.11. Summary of Systems and Truth Conditions

What follows is a table of different quantified modal logics, their model conditions, and the corresponding rules (including axioms) to be added to system fS. Basic truth conditions are listed first, followed by definitions of the different kinds of models and their special truth conditions. All models meet the basic truth conditions $(\bot)$, $(\rightarrow)$, $(\Box)$. It is also assumed that $<\mathbf{W}, \mathbf{R}>$ is a frame for a given propositional modal logic S and that $\mathbb{D}$ is a *domain structure* consisting of a nonempty set $\mathbf{D}$ (of possible objects) and a subset $\mathbf{Dw}$ of $\mathbf{D}$ for each world $\mathbf{w}$. It is presumed that $\mathbf{a_w}(e)$ is the appropriate extension of expression e, where an *appropriate extension of a term* is a member of $\mathbf{D}$, an *appropriate extension for a list of terms* is a list of members of $\mathbf{D}$, an *appropriate extension of a sentence* is a truth value (either T or F), and an *appropriate extension of a predicate letter* is a set containing lists of members of $\mathbf{D}$.

Basic Truth Conditions

$(\bot)$	$\mathbf{a_w}(\bot)=F.$
$(\rightarrow)$	$\mathbf{a_w}(A{\rightarrow}B)=T$　iff　$\mathbf{a_w}(A)=F$ or $\mathbf{a_w}(B)=T.$
$(\Box)$	$\mathbf{a_w}(\Box A)=T$　iff　for each $\mathbf{v}$ such that $\mathbf{wRv}$, $\mathbf{a_v}(A)=T.$
$(t\approx)$	$\mathbf{a_w}(t{\approx}t)=T$ and if $\mathbf{a_w}(s{\approx}t)=T$ and $\mathbf{a_w}(Plsl')=T$ then $\mathbf{a_w}(Pltl')=T.$
$(\approx)$	$\mathbf{a_w}(s{\approx}t)=T$　iff　$\mathbf{a_w}(s)=\mathbf{a_w}(t).$
(Pl)	$\mathbf{a_w}(Pl)=T$　iff　$\mathbf{a_w}(l) \in \mathbf{a_w}(P).$
(E)	$\mathbf{Dw}=\mathbf{a_w}(E).$

Abbreviations

(t_i)	$\mathbf{a_w}((t_1, .., t_i))=(\mathbf{a_w}(t_1), .., \mathbf{a_w}(t_i)).$
(d)	$\mathbf{a_w}(d)=d.$
(f)	$\mathbf{a_w}(f)=f(\mathbf{w}).$

Substitution Interpretation

A *tS-model* $<\mathbf{W}, \mathbf{R}, \mathbf{a}>$ obeys and $(t\approx)$ and $(\forall)$.

A *sS-model* $<\mathbf{W}, \mathbf{R}, \mathbb{D}, \mathbf{a}>$ obeys $(\approx)$, (Pl), (E) and $(\forall)$, or equivalently, it obeys $(\approx)$, (Pl), and $(\forall Dw)$.

$(\forall)$	$\mathbf{a_w}(\forall xAx)=T$ iff for every c, if $\mathbf{a_w}(Ec)=T$ then $\mathbf{a_w}(Ac)=T.$
$(\forall Dw)$	$\mathbf{a_w}(\forall xAx)=T$ iff for every c, if $\mathbf{a_w}(c) \in \mathbf{Dw}$ then $\mathbf{a_w}(Ac)=T.$

Objectual Interpretation

A *oS-model* $<\mathbf{W}, \mathbf{R}, \mathbb{D}, \mathbf{a}>$ obeys $(\approx)$, (Pl), (E), $(o\forall)$, and (RC).

$(o\forall)$	$\mathbf{a_w}(\forall xAx)=T$ iff for $d \in \mathbf{D}$, if $d \in \mathbf{Dw}$ then $\mathbf{a_w}(Ad)=T.$
(RC)	$\mathbf{a_w}(c)=\mathbf{a_v}(c)$ for all $\mathbf{w}$, and $\mathbf{v}$ in $\mathbf{W}.$

Conceptual Interpretation

A *cS-model* $\langle \mathbf{W}, \mathbf{R}, \mathbb{D}, \mathbf{a} \rangle$ obeys ($\approx$), (Pl), (E), and (c$\forall$). IC is the set of all functions from $\mathbf{W}$ into $\mathbf{D}$.

(c$\forall$) $\mathbf{a_w}(\forall xAx)=T$ iff for all $f \in IC$, if $f(\mathbf{w}) \in \mathbf{Dw}$ then $\mathbf{a_w}(Af)=T$.

Intensional Interpretation

An *iS-model* $\langle \mathbf{W}, \mathbf{R}, \mathbb{D}, \mathbf{I}, \mathbf{a} \rangle$ contains a subset $\mathbf{I}$ of the set of *individual concepts* (functions from $\mathbf{W}$ into $\mathbf{D}$) and obeys ($\approx$), (Pl), (E), (cI), and (i$\forall$).

(cI) $\mathbf{a}(c) \in \mathbf{I}$.
(i$\forall$) $\mathbf{a_w}(\forall xAx)=T$ iff for every $i \in \mathbf{I}$, if $i(\mathbf{w}) \in \mathbf{Dw}$ then $\mathbf{a_w}(Ai)=T$.

Stronger systems may be captured within the intensional interpretation as follows:

Domain Rules		**Corresponding Domain Conditions**
($\exists$E)	$\exists xEx$	For some $i \in \mathbf{I}$, $i(\mathbf{w}) \in \mathbf{Dw}$.
(Q)	Et	$\mathbf{Dw}=\mathbf{D}$.
(ED)	$Ec \rightarrow \Box Ec$	If $\mathbf{wRv}$ and $\mathbf{a_w}(c) \in \mathbf{Dw}$, then $\mathbf{a_v}(c) \in \mathbf{Dv}$.
(CD)	$\sim Ec \rightarrow \Box \sim Ec$	If $\mathbf{wRv}$ and $\mathbf{a_v}(c) \in \mathbf{Dv}$, then $\mathbf{a_w}(c) \in \mathbf{Dw}$.
(RC)	$(b\approx c \rightarrow \Box b\approx c)$ & $(\sim b\approx c \rightarrow \Box \sim b\approx c)$	$\mathbf{a_w}(c)=\mathbf{a_v}(c)$.
($\exists i$)	$L \vdash \sim t\approx c \,/\, L \vdash \bot$, no c in L, t	For some $i \in \mathbf{I}$, $i(\mathbf{w})=\mathbf{a_w}(t)$.
(o)=(RC)+($\exists i$)		$\mathbf{I}$ is the set of all constant functions with values in $\mathbf{D}$.
(o$\exists$E)=(o)+($\exists$E)		(o) + $\mathbf{Dw}$ is not empty.
(oED)=(o)+(ED)		(o) + if $\mathbf{wRv}$, then $\mathbf{Dw} \subseteq \mathbf{Dv}$.
(oCD)=(o)+(CD)		(o) + if $\mathbf{wRv}$, then $\mathbf{Dv} \subseteq \mathbf{Dw}$.

14

Trees for Quantified Modal Logic

14.1. Tree Rules for Quantifiers

In order to calculate whether an argument is valid or invalid, it is useful to formulate the truth conditions for $\forall$ in the form of tree rules. For example, the substitution truth clause $(\forall)$ supports the following pair of rules:

$(\forall)$ $a_w(\forall x Ax)=T$ iff for every c, if $a_w(Ec)=T$ then $a_w(Ac)=T$.

where c is new to the tree

fS-trees will be trees that use these two quantifier rules, together with the tree rules for a given propositional modal logic S. (Two additional rules for fS-trees will be given in the next section to manage identity.) In constructing fS-trees, it is important to pay attention to the difference in the position of the horizontal line in $(\forall T)$ and $(\forall F)$. The $(\forall T)$ rule requires that both $\forall x Ax$ *and* Ec be in a world before the rule can be applied to place Ac in the same world. On the other hand, $(\forall F)$ indicates that whenever $\sim\forall x Ax$ is in a world, then one may add *both* Ec and $\sim$Ac to the same world, provided c is a constant new to the tree. The restriction requiring that c be new to the diagram is very important. Given $a_w(\forall x Ax)=F$, the substitution clause $(\forall)$ entails that there is some constant c such that $a_w(Ec)=T$ and $a_w(Ac)=F$. Since we have no information about which

constant this is, we may not identify it with any other term found already
in the tree. If a term already in the tree is chosen, it is possible to close
a tree even though the argument being tested is tS-invalid. For safety, a
brand new constant must be chosen instead. One might worry that ($\forall$F)
is not safe enough, for neither Ec nor ~Ac follows from ~$\forall$xAx, even
given that c is new. This worry is reasonable, but it will be laid to rest in
Section 16.5 where the correctness of trees will be proven.

There is a final worry to contend with concerning ($\forall$F). Although trees
are normally constructed from finite arguments, it will be useful to consider the case where the opening world of a tree contains infinitely many
sentences. In this situation, all of the constants of the language may already
appear in the tree before any step is applied. But then it will be impossible
to find a constant c that is new to the tree when applying ($\forall$F). This problem may be overcome by assuming that before tree construction takes
place, the language is expanded (if necessary) so that there are infinitely
many constants that do not appear in the tree.

In case trees for classical quantification are desired, qS-trees can be
defined by adding to the rules for fS-trees a new rule (Q) that says that Et
should be added to every world of the tree, for each term t that occurs in
it. The effect of (Q) is that whenever $\forall$xAx appears in a world, Et will be
available to warrant the deduction of At. Furthermore, since Ec may be
placed in any world, there is never any need to derive Ec using ($\forall$F). So
the procedures for the quantifiers may be simplified in qS-trees by using
the following derived tree rules:

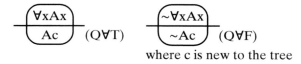

where c is new to the tree

Here is an fK-tree for the argument $\forall$x(Px→Qx), $\forall$xFx / $\forall$xQx to
illustrate the use of these rules:

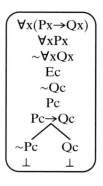

> **EXERCISE 14.1**   Fill in the rule names for each step of this tree.

Notice that (∀T) could not be applied to the first two steps until Ec was introduced to the tree by applying (∀F) to the third step. This illustrates a useful ordering strategy: consider applying (∀F) steps before (∀T) steps wherever possible. This idea is important for another reason. Consider the following attempt to construct a qK-tree for the same argument. In the classical case, Ec is not needed for the (Q∀T) rule, and so it is legal to apply (Q∀T) to the first two steps. But though that is legal, it is a bad idea because it leads to a violation of the restriction on (Q∀F) when that rule is finally applied.

$$
\begin{array}{c}
\forall x(Px{\rightarrow}Qx) \\
\forall xPx \\
{\sim}\forall xQx \\
Pc \\
Pc{\rightarrow}Qc \\
{\sim}Qc
\end{array}
\quad (Q\forall F)
$$

Illegal use of (Q∀F)!

The restriction on (Q∀F) is violated because the constant c appeared in the tree when (Q∀F) was used. The correctly constructed tree applies (Q∀F) as soon as possible, before the letter c appears.

$$
\begin{array}{c}
\forall x(Px{\rightarrow}Qx) \\
\forall xPx \\
{\sim}\forall xQx \\
{\sim}Qc \\
Pc \\
Pc{\rightarrow}Qc \\
\end{array}
$$

$$
\begin{array}{cc}
{\sim}Pc & Qc \\
\perp & \perp
\end{array}
$$

Using (Def∃), it is not difficult to show that the following rules for ∃ are derivable principles for fS-trees:

$$
\begin{array}{c}
{\sim}\exists xAx \\
Ec \\
\hline
{\sim}Ac
\end{array}
\ (\exists F)
\qquad
\begin{array}{c}
\exists xAx \\
\hline
Ec \\
Ac
\end{array}
\ (\exists T)
$$

where c is new to the tree

In the case of qS-trees the rules for ∃ may be simplified to the following ones:

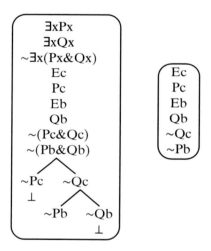

where c is new to the tree

EXERCISE 14.2   Using (Def∃), show that (Q∃T) and (Q∃F) follow from (Q∀T) and (Q∀F). Now do the same for (∃T) and (∃F).

Here is a fK-tree for the tK-invalid argument ∃xPx, ∃xQx / ∃x(Px&Qx) to illustrate the use of these rules:

This tree has an open branch ending with ~Pb, so a diagram for a truth value model (or tK-model) that is a counterexample to the argument has been constructed to the right. It simply lists the atomic sentences that appear on this open branch. This corresponds to a tK-counterexample where $a_w(Ec)=a_w(Pc)=a_w(Eb)=a_w(Qb)=T$, and $a_w(Qc)=a_w(Pb)=F$. It is worth taking a moment to check that this assignment qualifies as a tK-counterexample to ∃xPx, ∃xQx / ∃x(Px&Qx) by verifying that $a_w(∃xPx)=a_w(∃xQx)=T$ and $a_w(∃x(Px&Qx))=F$. Notice that to obtain the correct counterexample, every possible step must be applied to the tree. It was especially important that (∃F) was applied *twice* to ~∃x(Px&Qx) to obtain instances for both the constant c and the constant b. In general you should check carefully that an instance has been obtained for every term in the tree for those steps to which (∃F) and (∀T) apply.

EXERCISE 14.3 Check the following arguments for tK-validity and qK-validity with trees, where a qK-model is a tK-model that satisfies (Q): $a_w(Et)=T$. Construct tK- or qK-counterexample diagrams for each invalid argument and verify that the models you constructed are indeed counterexamples.

a) $\forall x(Px \rightarrow Qx), \exists xPx \,/\, \exists xQx$

b) $\forall x(Px \& Qx) \,/\, \forall xPx \& \forall yQy$

c) $\forall x(Px \rightarrow Q) \,/\, (\exists xPx \rightarrow Q)$

d) $\forall xPx \rightarrow \forall xQx \,/\, \forall x(Px \rightarrow Qx)$

e) $\forall x\forall yRxy \,/\, \forall y\forall xRxy$

f) $\forall x(Px \lor Qx) \,/\, \forall xPx \lor \forall yQy$

g) $\forall xPx \leftrightarrow \sim\exists y\sim Py$

h) $\forall x(Px \rightarrow Qx) \,/\, \forall x(\exists y(Px \& Rxy) \rightarrow \exists z(Qx \& Rxz))$

i) (Hard.) $(Pc \& \forall y(Py \rightarrow y \approx c)) \leftrightarrow \forall y(Pc \leftrightarrow c \approx y)$

14.2. Tree Rules for Identity

The tree rules for $\approx$ are the same as the rules for proofs in fS.

To illustrate the use of these rules, here is a fK-tree demonstrating that $\forall y\exists xx \approx y$ is tK-valid:

There are two points worth mentioning about this tree. Once Ec is introduced by applying ($\forall$F) to the first step, it becomes possible for ($\exists$F) to be applied to obtain the instance $\sim c \approx c$. This is legal because there is no restriction on the ($\exists$F) rule and $\sim c \approx c$ is an instance of the right kind. To check this, note that $\sim\exists xx \approx c$ abbreviates $\sim\sim\forall x \sim x \approx c$, which comes to $\forall x \sim x \approx c$. Note that $\sim c \approx c$ is truly an instance of $\forall x \sim x \approx c$ because $\sim c \approx c$ results from replacing c for x in $\sim x \approx c$. Finally, note the introduction of $c \approx c$ by ($\approx$In) in the last step to close the tree. A simpler rule would be to simply close any branch immediately when it contains a sentence of the form $\sim t \approx t$.

Here is a fK-tree for the argument Pc / ∀y(c≈y→Py):

$$
\begin{array}{c}
\text{Pc} \\
\sim\forall\text{y}(\text{c}\approx\text{y}\rightarrow\text{Pc}) \\
\text{Eb} \\
\sim(\text{c}\approx\text{b}\rightarrow\text{Pb}) \\
\text{c}\approx\text{b} \\
\sim\text{Pb} \\
\text{c}\approx\text{c} \\
\text{b}\approx\text{c} \\
\sim\text{Pc} \\
\perp
\end{array}
$$

Notice that c≈b and ~Pb were obtained in the fifth and sixth steps, but (≈Out) does not, strictly speaking, warrant the replacement of c for b in ~Pb to obtain ~Pc to close the tree. The rule (≈Out) says only that s≈t and warrants the replacement of t for s in atomic sentences. That is why it was necessary to introduce c≈c with (≈Out) to reverse c≈b, so that the substitution could be correctly accomplished. This may be excessively finicky. To save annoyance of such extra steps, it is safe enough to adopt a more liberal policy that simply assumes symmetry (and transitivity) of ≈.

EXERCISE 14.4   Use a fK-tree to show 1Pc / ∀y(Py↔c≈y) is tK-valid, where 1Pc is defined by: Pc & ∀y(Py→y≈c). Now use a fK-tree to check whether ∀y(Py↔c≈y) / 1Pc is tK-valid. Try the same one with a qK-tree. Can ∀y(Py↔c≈y) be used as the definition for 1Pc in free logic?

It is worth making clear how these instantiation principles apply to fK-trees for arguments such as ∀xPx / ∃xPx where no sentences of the form Ec appear in the tree. In this case, the fK-tree begins with ∀xPx and ~∃xPx. Once (Def∃) and (~F) are applied to the second line to obtain ∀x~Px, no further rule may be applied, for no sentence of the form Ec is available to warrant the use of (∀T). The result is a tK-counterexample to the argument with the feature that Ec is false for every choice of constant c, that is, nothing exists in any world of the model. However, when the qK-tree is constructed, there is no restriction on the instantiation principle, so any instance Ac of ∀xAx may be placed in the tree using (Q∀T).

> **EXERCISE 14.5** Complete fK- and qK-trees for $\forall xPx$ / $\exists xPx$ noting the differences.

In the interest of efficient tree construction, it is worth noting that it is never necessary to take an instance of $\forall xAx$ with respect to a constant that fails to appear in the tree, with the one exception that in the case of qK-trees an instance of $\forall xAx$ is needed if no constant appears so far in the tree.

14.3. Infinite Trees

In order to construct a completed diagram for an invalid argument, it is important to make sure that every step that can be applied is in fact applied in the tree. Otherwise the model constructed from an open branch of the tree may not qualify as a counterexample. Completing every possible step in a fS-tree requires that if $\forall xAx$ appears in world **w**, then there must be an instance Ac in **w** for every constant c such that Ec is in **w**. For qS-trees the requirement is that whenever $\forall xAx$ appears in world **w**, an instance Ac must appear in **w** for *every constant c that appears in the tree*. (If none appears, an instance is taken for an arbitrarily selected constant.)

Satisfying these requirements can cause some trees to become infinite, as the following qK-tree for $\exists x \forall y x \approx y$ illustrates. The tree opens by applying (Q∃F) to obtain an instance for the constant c. But then (Q∀F) must be applied to introduce a new letter c′ into the tree.

$$\begin{array}{c} \sim\exists x\forall yx\approx y \\ \sim\forall yc\approx y \\ \sim c\approx c' \end{array}$$

But now it is necessary to apply (Q∃F) to the first line to form a new instance with respect to c′, and this will cause the introduction of yet a new constant c″ into the tree. Clearly the process will go on forever.

$$\begin{array}{c} \sim\exists x\forall yx\approx y \\ \sim\forall yc\approx y \\ \sim c\approx c' \\ \sim\forall yc'\approx y \\ \sim c'\approx c'' \\ \sim\forall yc''\approx y \\ \sim c''\approx c''' \\ \vdots \end{array}$$

Trees may become infinite because sentences with shapes ∀xAx, and ~∃xAx cannot be "crossed off" when (Q∀T) or (Q∃F) is applied to them, for it may be necessary to apply these rules again if new letters are later introduced into the tree. For this reason, trees do not serve as a decision procedure for quantificational logic since it is possible that a tree may cycle infinitely between creating new terms and applying (Q∀T). In that case, it will not be possible to determine whether the argument being tested is valid in a finite numbers of steps. Trees do provide a *quasi-decision procedure*, in the sense that, if the argument is valid, the tree will eventually close after finitely many steps. However, because of the possibility of infinite trees, one may work forever on an invalid argument and never find out that it is invalid in a finite amount of time.

EXERCISE 14.6   There is an important difference between the claim that everything has a cause: ∀x∃yCxy and there is a cause of everything: ∃y∀xCxy. Some causation-based arguments for the existence of God blur this important distinction by proceeding from the idea that each thing has a cause to the idea that there must be one thing that is the cause of everything. Check the following arguments with qK-trees: ∀x∃yCxy / ∃y∀xCxy and ∃y∀xCxy / ∀x∃yCxy. What happens? What is the result in the case of fK-trees? Would the results change if we were to add ∃xEx as an axiom? How do these results bear on arguments for the existence of God?

14.4. Trees for Quantified Modal Logic

So far we have explained the tree rules using arguments that did not contain the modal operator. When rules for □ and ∀ are applied in the same tree, new issues arise concerning the ordering of steps during tree construction. To illustrate the point, here is a tree that shows the qK-validity of □∀xPx / ∀x□Px. You may think of this as an "argument" version of the Converse Barcan Formula (CBF): □∀xPx→∀x□Px. The order in which the steps were applied is indicated with circled numerals.

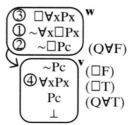

Note that the rules for □ require that (□T) not be applied to □∀xPx until a new world **v** is formed. So before (□T) could be used, it was necessary that (Q∀F) be applied to ~∀x□Px, and (□F) applied to the result: ~□Pc to create world **v**. After these steps, (□T) and (Q∀T) can be used to close the tree. This illustrates a general strategy for ordering the construction of a tree. It is best to apply (Q∀F) (or (∀F) in the case of free logic) before applying (Q∀T) (or (∀T)). This is reminiscent of the modal logic principle that it is better to apply (□F) before (□T).

An important issue arises during the construction of a qK-tree that shows (BF) is qK-valid. Here is the tree about halfway through its construction:

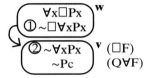

As we explained, (□F) is applied first, and (Q∀F) is immediately applied to the result in world **v**. Now it is necessary to return to world **w** and apply (Q∀T) to the first line, after which (□T) can be applied to close the tree.

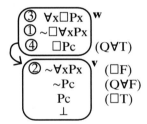

It is very important that the steps be carried out in this order to guarantee that the restriction on the (Q∀F) rule is honored. If, for example, (Q∀T) had been applied before (Q∀F), then the restriction would require that the instance for ~∀xPx chosen not involve the letter c. So the following tree would be illegal because here the instance ~Pc chosen for ~∀xPx contains a letter that has already been introduced into the tree (in the third step of world **w**).

Illegal Use of (Q∀F)!

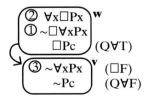

To satisfy the restriction on (Q∀F), it was necessary to delay the application of (Q∀T) until after (Q∀F) was applied.

You may wonder whether returning to work in world **w** violates the
Placement Principle. (See Section 4.1.) Actually it does not, because all
that principle requires is that the result of applying a rule be placed on
every open branch below the step to which it is applied, and that holds
in this case. However, it can become inconvenient to find room to place
steps in a world that has already been completed. To avoid the problem
you might want to use the continuation method described in Section 6.3.
Using it, we may construct a tree where each step is added to the bottom
of the tree as follows.

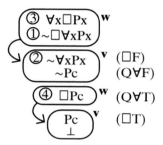

Our next project will be to use fK-trees to show that "argument" versions of the Barcan Formulas are tK-invalid. We will construct open trees
for ∀x□Px / □∀xPx and □∀xPx / ∀x□Px, and then explain how to convert
them into counterexamples. We begin with (BF).

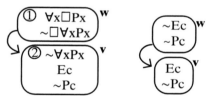

Notice that we are unable to apply (∀T) to ∀x□Px in world **w** because
Ec is not available there.

The tree is open, and so we are ready to construct a tK-counterexample
to (BF). The diagram to the right of the tree illustrates the basic features
of the open branch model. We choose for the tK-model a language where
P is the only predicate letter and c is the only term. We then define the
tK-model <**W, R, a**> for that language so that the frame <**W, R**> contains the worlds **w** and **v** of our tree, and where **R** is given by the arrow
structure found in the tree. (In this case the only fact that holds for **R** is
that **wRv**.) Since neither Pc nor Ec appear in **w**, we follow the principle
for constructing counterexamples in propositional logic and assign to the
absent atoms the value F. So $a_w(Ec)=F$ and $a_w(Pc)=F$. In world **v**, we
have Ec but not Pc, so **a** gives the following values in **v**: $a_v(Ec)=T$ and

$a_v(Pc)=F$. All other sentences are assigned values by **a** according to the truth conditions ($\bot$), ($\rightarrow$), ($\Box$), and ($\forall$).

Let us verify that the model we have just defined represents a counterexample to (BF). Remember, the model is defined for a language that contains c as its only term. We know that $a_w(Ec)=F$. By ($\forall$) we also know that if $a_w(\forall x\Box Px)=F$, there must be some constant c such that $a_w(Ec)=T$ and $a_w(\Box Pc)=F$. Since c is the only constant in the language of our model and $a_w(Ec)=F$, this condition cannot be satisfied. It follows that $a_w(\forall x\Box Px)$ cannot be F, and so it is T. Now consider world **v**. Here $a_v(Ec)=T$ and $a_v(Pc)=F$, so it follows that $a_v(\forall xPx)=F$. By ($\Box$), $a_w(\Box\forall xPx)=T$ only if $a_v(\forall xPx)=T$. Since the latter is not so, it follows that $a_w(\Box\forall xPx)=F$. In summary, $a_w(\forall x\Box Px)=T$ and $a_w(\Box\forall xPx)=F$. So the tK-model we have just defined is truly a tK-counterexample to (BF) as we have claimed. Notice that this model corresponds to the intuitive reason one has for rejecting the Barcan Formula, for it proposes the possibility that a constant may refer to something in one world **w** that does not exist, but that does exist in some accessible world **v**. If the contracting domain condition (CD) were to hold, it would have been impossible to construct such a counterexample.

In the next tree, the tK-invalidity of an instance of (CBF) is shown:

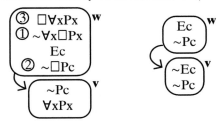

Here ($\forall$T) may not be applied to $\forall xPx$ in world **v** because Ec does not appear there. When we construct the tK-counterexample, Ec is false at **v**. Since c is the only term of the language, and $a_v(Ec)=F$, it follows that for every constant c such that $a_v(Ec)=T$, $a_v(Pc)=T$ insuring that $a_v(\forall xPx)=T$. Since **v** is the only world such that **wRv**, and $\forall xPx$ is T there, the premise $\Box\forall xPx$ is T in **w**.

EXERCISE 14.7 Explain why $\forall x\Box Px$ is false in **w** on the above tK-counterexample diagram.

This tK-model illustrates why (CBF) is fK-invalid, namely, that it is possible for an object that exists in one world to fail to exist in an accessible world. In models that meet the expanding domain condition (ED), a counterexample of this kind is not possible.

EXERCISE 14.8 Practice using diagrams by showing the following are qK-valid, using the classical rules (Q∀T) and (Q∀F). Then determine which of the following is tK-valid, using the rules (∀T) and (∀F). Create counterexamples for the tK-invalid arguments. You may use the derived tree rules for ∃ if you like.

a) ∀x(□Px&□Qx) / □(∀xPx & ∀xQx)
b) □(∀xPx & ∀xQx) / ∀x(□Px&□Qx)
c) □∀x(Px→Qx), ∃x◇Px / ∃x◇Qx
d) ∀x□(Px→Q) / ∃x◇Px→◇Q
e) □□∀x∀yLxy / □□∀y∀xLxy
f) ∀x□Px ∨ ∀x□Qx / □∀x(Px∨Qx)
g) □∀xPx / ~∃x◇~Px
h) ~∃x◇~Px / □∀xPx
*i) □∀x(Px→Qx), ~□∀x~Px / ~□∀x~Qx
j) □s≈t, □Ps / □Pt
k) ∃x□x≈t, ∀x□Px / □Pt

14.5. Converting Trees into Proofs

It is possible to convert closed fS-trees into proofs in fS, and the same is true when domain rules to be discussed later are included in fS. This result is important for two reasons. It will provide a method for locating proofs that might be otherwise quite difficult, and it serves as a crucial step in the proof of the completeness of the various systems. The method for converting trees to proofs in QML is a variant of the method used for propositional modal logics. The idea is that for each rule applied in a tree, there is a corresponding step to apply in the proof. For fS, the additional tree rules are (∀T), (∀F), (≈In), and (≈Out). But (∀T) is just (∀Out), and the identity rules are the same for trees and proofs. So the only remaining problem is to explain how to get the effect of (∀F) in a proof. To mimic the effect of (∀F), it is useful to prove the following derived rule:

$$
\begin{array}{l}
\sim\forall xAx \\
\quad\vert\!\!\!-\; Ec\&\sim Ac \\
\qquad\vdots \\
\quad\vert\!\!\!-\; \bot \\
\text{------} \\
\quad\bot \qquad (\sim\forall\bot)
\end{array}
$$

where c is not in ~∀xAx nor in any hypothesis under which ~∀xAx lies.

EXERCISE 14.9   Show ($\sim\forall\bot$) is a derivable rule of fK. What would be the derived rule needed to manage the derived tree rule ($\exists$T)?

In the case of classical quantification, the following derived rule may be used for (Q$\forall$F). It has strong kinships with the (Q$\exists$Out) rule introduced in Section 12.2.

$$\sim\forall xAx$$
$$\left|\underset{}{\raise2pt\hbox{---}}\ \sim Ac\right.$$
$$\vdots$$
$$\bot$$
$$\text{------}$$
$$\bot \quad (Q\sim\forall\bot)$$

where c is not in $\sim\forall xAx$ nor in any hypothesis under which $\sim\forall xAx$ lies.

EXERCISE 14.10   Show (Q$\sim\forall\bot$) is a derivable rule of qK.

It is simpler to illustrate the conversion method for QML with classical rules first. Once that method is made clear, the method for the free logic rules should be obvious. Here is the closed qK-tree for the "argument" version of (CBF) from which the proof will be constructed in stages. The first step in the tree applies (Q$\forall$F) to $\sim\forall x\square Px$ to obtain $\sim\square Pc$. The corresponding line of the proof will be to add $\sim\square Pc$ to the proof *as a new hypothesis*.

$$
\begin{array}{ll}
\left.\begin{array}{c}\square\forall xPx\\ \textcircled{1}\ \sim\forall x\square Px\\ \sim\square Pc\end{array}\right)^{\mathbf{w}} &
\begin{array}{l}
\left|\raise2pt\hbox{---}\ \square\forall xPx\right.\\
\quad\left|\raise2pt\hbox{---}\ \sim\forall x\square Px\right.\\
\qquad\left|\raise2pt\hbox{---}\sim\square Pc\right.\\
\qquad\quad\text{???}\\
\qquad\quad\bot\\
\qquad\bot\quad (Q\sim\forall\bot)\\
\quad\forall x\square Px\quad (IP)
\end{array}
\\
(Q\forall F)
\end{array}
$$

The plan for solving the problem is to prove $\bot$ in the subproof headed by $\sim\square Pc$, which we have just introduced. When $\bot$ is proven there, it will be possible to place $\bot$ in the parent subproof using the rule (Q$\sim\forall\bot$). The rest of the problem can be solved using strategies from propositional modal logic.

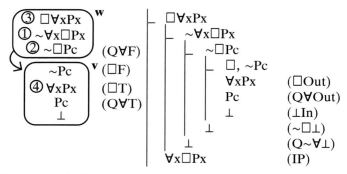

Unfortunately, the conversion method is not always so straightforward. There is a complication to be faced that can be illustrated by the following attempt to convert the qK-tree for (BF) into a proof:

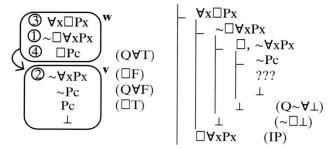

To the right, the first two steps of the tree have been converted into steps of a proof. The first step used (□F) to create a new world **v**, and the corresponding step of the proof was to create a boxed sub-proof headed by ~∀xPx. The next step was an application of (Q∀F), which created the subproof headed by ~Pc. We are faced with a puzzle since step 3 of the tree involves applying (∀Out) to ∀x□Px in the world **w** to produce □Pc, whereas in our proof, we have already constructed the subproof that represents the contents of the world **v**. We appear to need some way to return to the subproof for world **w** to apply (∀Out).

One solution that often works in such cases is to construct the steps of the proof in the order of their *appearance* in the tree, rather than the order in which the steps were *entered* into the tree. Since the use of (Q∀T) is the first step that appears in the tree, the corresponding step, the use of (∀Out), should be entered into the proof *before* the creation of the boxed subproof headed by □ and ∀xPx. The conversion process is now straightforward.

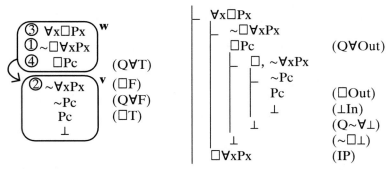

Note that placing □Pc in the third line of this proof did not cause a violation of the restriction on the (Q~∀⊥) rule because that step did not cause c to appear in any *hypothesis* for ~∀xPx.

EXERCISE 14.11   Convert all closed trees constructed in Exercise 14.8 into proofs. Double check that the restriction on (Q~∀⊥) is not violated in these proofs.

Although this strategy usually works, it does not provide a general solution to the problem of converting all trees into proofs. The reason is that the early use of a (∀Out) on a sentence with the form ∀x(AxvBx) may introduce the step AcvBc, which corresponds to a branch in the tree with Ac on one and Bc on the other branch. But in the corresponding proof, Ac and Bc will head subproofs within which (~Q∀⊥) must be applied, and this would violate the restriction on the (~Q∀⊥) rule. The problem is illustrated by the following partial proof, which attempts to convert the tree for the argument ∀x(□Pxv□Qx) / □∀x(QxvPx):

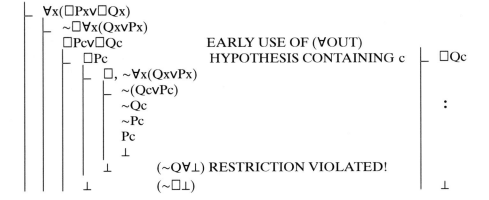

> **EXERCISE 14.12**   Construct the tree for the argument $\forall x(\Box Pxv\Box Qx)$ /
> $\Box\forall x(QxvPx)$.

We seem pulled two ways. It would seem best to postpone the use of ($\forall$Out) since this caused the introduction of hypotheses $\Box Pc$ containing c with the result that the restriction on ($\sim Q\forall\bot$) is violated. If the steps could be reordered so that the subproof headed by $\Box Pc$ could lie within the subproof headed by $\sim(QcvPc)$, the violation could be avoided. However, such a reordering does not seem possible since a boxed subproof lies between these two hypotheses, foiling any attempt at a reordering of the steps.

For a general solution to showing that arguments with closed fS-trees are always provable in fS, it is easier to employ the technique used for propositional logic presented in Section 7.10. It might be a good idea for the reader to review that section at this point. The strategy is to show that the branch sentence B* for any branch of a closed tree is inconsistent, that is, B* $\vdash \bot$. This follows immediately from the Tree Rule Lemma, which asserts that if the children of *B are inconsistent, then so is *B. All that is needed to extend the same argument to fS is to add cases for the rules ($\forall$T), ($\forall$F), ($\approx$In) and ($\approx$Out) to the Tree Rule Lemma. We give the reasoning for ($\forall$F) here and leave the others as an exercise.

($\forall$F). When rule ($\forall$F) is applied, *B is equivalent to a sentence with the form $C_1 \& \Diamond(C_2 \& \ .\ . \ \Diamond(C_n \& \sim\forall xAx) \ .\ .)$, and *B$'$ equivalent to $C_1 \& \Diamond(C_2 \& \ .\ . \ \Diamond(C_n \& \sim\forall xAx \& (Ec\&\sim Ac)) \ .\ .)$. The ($\forall$F) rule requires that c be new to the tree. Therefore c is not in *B, and so not in any of the C_i nor in $\forall xAx$. Since *B$'$ $\vdash \bot$, it follows by the * Lemma that C_1, $\Box$, C_2, .. $\Box$, C_n, $\sim\forall xAx$, $(Ec\&\sim Ac) \vdash \bot$. It follows that C_1, $\Box$, C_2, .. $\Box$, C_n, $\sim\forall xAx \vdash Ec\rightarrow Ac$ by (IP), (DN), and (Def&). Since c is not in any of these hypotheses nor in $\forall xAx$, ($\forall$In) may be used to obtain C_1, $\Box$, C_2, .. $\Box$, C_n, $\sim\forall xAx \vdash \forall xAx$. But C_1, $\Box$, C_2, .. $\Box$, C_n, $\sim\forall xAx \vdash \sim\forall xAx$ and so C_1, $\Box$, C_2, .. $\Box$, C_n, $\sim\forall xAx \vdash \bot$ by ($\bot$In). By the * Lemma it follows that *C_1 & $\Diamond(C_2$ & .. $\Diamond(C_n\&\sim\forall xAx)$ ..) $\vdash \bot$, and so *B $\vdash \bot$ as desired.

> **EXERCISE *14.13**   Complete the cases for ($\forall$T), ($\approx$In) and ($\approx$Out) in the
> Tree Rule Lemma of Section 7.10. (Hint: Use the Entailment Lemma of
> Section 7.10.)

EXERCISE 14.14   Use the method for converting trees into proofs to find proofs of the following facts:

a) The system fK+Ec→□Ec is equivalent to fK+(CBF).
b) (BF) is provable in fK+~Ec→□~Ec.
c) (BF) is provable in FB.

14.6. Trees for Systems that Include Domain Rules

In Section 13.9 a number of different ways were explored to strengthen fS, depending on the treatment of the quantifier domains.

(∃E)	∃xEx
(Q)	Et
(ED)	Ec→□Ec
(CD)	~Ec→□~Ec
(t∀)	∀xAx→(Et→At)
(RC)	(b≈c→□b≈c) & (~b≈c→□~b≈c)
(∃i)	L ⊢ ~t≈c / L ⊢ ⊥, no c in L, t

It is a simple matter to reflect these principles with trees. In the case of the first six axioms, simply use a tree rule that lets one add the appropriate axiom to any world of the tree. To guarantee that every possible step of a tree is carried out, it is assumed that the steps are ordered during tree construction to oscillate between applying an ordinary tree rule and adding instances of axioms. In the case of (∃E), the axiom need be added only once to each world. However, (Q) has infinitely many instances, one for each of the terms t in the language. It turns out that the large number of instances can easily be managed because the only instances that must be added to a tree are those for terms that have been introduced into the tree. So at each stage in tree construction, one will only need to add finitely many instances of (Q) to the tree. The same principle may be used to deal with introducing instances of (CD) and (ED). In the case of (t∀), there is even a larger variety in the possible instances since the number of possible instances of ∀xAx is also infinite. However, this axiom need only be added to a world on a branch of a tree when ∀xAx appears in that world and term t is in the tree. So again there are only finitely many instances of an axiom to add at each stage in tree construction. Tree construction for (ED), (CD), and (t∀) could have been simplified somewhat by introducing rules in place of these axioms as follows:

(ED)   Ec

―――――

$\Box$Ec

(CD)   ~Ec

―――――

$\Box$~Ec

(t$\forall$) $\forall$xAx

Et

―――――

At

However, we will presume that trees are created using the axioms in order to simplify the proof of the Tree Model Theorem in the next chapter.

It is necessary to find a way to reflect the rule ($\exists$i) with trees.

($\exists$i)   L $\vdash$ ~t$\approx$c

―――――――

L $\vdash$ $\bot$ provided c is not in L or t

The effect of this rule can be captured by a tree rule (tc) requiring that for each term t introduced to the tree, t$\approx$c is added to each world of a tree, where c is a constant chosen so that it is new to the tree.

t$\approx$c   (tc)

where c is new to the tree

Let fS be any system that results from adding to fK any selection of the rules or axioms we have just discussed and modal logic axioms (D), (M), (4), (B), (5), and (CD). Then a *fS-tree* is constructed by using the corresponding rules that have just been described.

EXERCISE 14.15   Complete trees to demonstrate the following:

a) $\vDash_{fK+(\exists E)}$ $\forall$xAx$\rightarrow$$\exists$xAx
b) $\vDash_{fK+(RC)}$ (b$\approx$c&$\Box$Pb)$\rightarrow$$\Box$Pc
c) $\vDash_{fK+(ED)}$ $\Box$$\forall$xAx$\rightarrow$$\forall$x$\Box$Ax
d) $\vDash_{fK+(CD)}$ $\forall$x$\Box$Ax$\rightarrow$$\Box$$\forall$xAx
e) $\vDash_{fK+(Q)}$ Ec$\rightarrow$$\Box$Ec
f) $\vDash_{fK+(Q)}$ ~Ec$\rightarrow$$\Box$~Ec
g) $\vDash_{fK+(\exists i)}$ Et$\leftrightarrow$$\exists$xx$\approx$t
h) $\vDash_{fK+(t\forall)}$ Et$\leftrightarrow$$\exists$xx$\approx$t

---

14.7. Converting Trees into Proofs in Stronger Systems

In this section, the method for converting fS-trees into proofs in fS will be extended to cover the case when rules discussed in the previous section are included in fS. What is needed is to show that when any of the rules or axioms are added to a fS-tree, the corresponding step can be carried out in a fS proof. The case of those tree rules that simply add axioms is easily dealt with since the corresponding system is able to prove these sentences in exactly the same way. (For a full-fledged proof, see the explanation at the end of Section 7.10.) So all that remains to show that fS-trees can always be converted into proofs is to consider the tree rule (∃i).

The corresponding tree rule for (∃i) in this case places t≈c in a world, where c is new to the tree. To show how to convert each tree into a proof, we will need to extend the Tree Rule Lemma of Section 7.10 to this new rule. Here is how the reasoning goes:

When tree rule (∃i) is applied, *B is equivalent to a sentence with the form $C_1 \& \Diamond(C_2 \& . . \Diamond(C_n \& A) . .)$, and *B′ equivalent to $C_1 \& \Diamond(C_2 \& . . \Diamond(C_n \& A \& t≈c) . .)$. The (∃i) rule requires that c be new to the tree. Therefore, c is not in *B, and so not in any of the C_i nor in t. Since *B′ ⊢ ⊥, it follows by the * Lemma that C_1, □, C_2, . . □, C_n, A, t≈c ⊢ ⊥. It follows that C_1, □, C_2, . . □, C_n, A ⊢ ~t≈c by (IP), and (DN). Since c is not in any of these hypotheses nor in t, the proof rule (∃i) may be used to obtain C_1, □, C_2, . . □, C_n, A ⊢ ⊥. By the * Lemma it follows that $*C_1 \& \Diamond(C_2 \& . . \Diamond(C_n \& A) . .) ⊢ ⊥$, and so *B ⊢ ⊥ as desired.

EXERCISE 14.16   Prove the following argument in oS4: ∀x(□Pxv□□Qx), ∃x□x≈t / □Ptv□□Qt by first constructing the tree and converting the tree into a proof.

EXERCISE 14.17   Show Et↔∃xx≈t is oS, with the help of the appropriate tree. Convert this tree into a proof in oS.

14.8. Summary of the Tree Rules

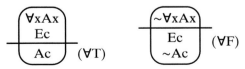

where c is new to the tree

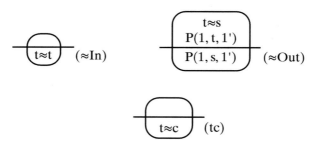

where c is new to the tree

where c is new to the tree

15

The Adequacy of Quantified Modal Logics

Many different systems of quantified modal logic have been presented in this book, each one based on the minimal system fK. In the next few chapters, we will show the adequacy of many of these logics by showing both their soundness and completeness. When S is one of the quantified modal logics discussed, and the corresponding notion of an S-model has been defined, soundness and completeness together amount to the claim that provability-in-S and S-validity match.

(Soundness)   If $H \vdash_S C$ then $H \vDash_S C$.
(Completeness)   If $H \vDash_S C$ then $H \vdash_S C$.

This chapter will be devoted to soundness and to some theorems that will be useful for the completeness proofs to come. Some of these results are interesting in their own right since they show how the various treatments of the quantifier are interrelated. Sections 15.4–15.8 will explain how notions of validity for the substitution, intensional, and objectual interpretations are shown equivalent to corresponding brands of validity on truth value models – the simplest kind of models. This will mean that the relatively easy completeness results for truth value models can be quickly transferred to substitution, intensional, and objectual forms of validity. Readers who wish to study only truth value models may omit those sections.

Two different strategies will be presented to demonstrate completeness for truth value models. Chapter 16 covers completeness using a variation on the tree method found in Chapter 8. The modifications needed to extend the completeness result to systems with quantifiers are fairly easy to supply. Chapter 17 presents completeness results using the canonical model technique of Chapter 9. This method is the standard technique found in the literature, but it requires fairly extensive modifications to the strategy used for propositional modal logic. Chapters 16 and 17 are designed to be read independently, so that one may be understood without the other.

The reader may be disappointed to discover that it is not always possible to extend completeness results for a propositional modal logic to the system that results from adding the quantifiers. We will not prove completeness results for quantified modal logics based on systems whose corresponding conditions include density or convergence, nor will we be able to obtain results for the general axiom (G) of Chapter 10. This is not our fault. We now know that at least some of these systems are in fact not complete (Cresswell, 1995). Exactly where the incompleteness holds, and how/whether it can be repaired by adding new rules, is an important open question in quantified modal logic.

To prove the soundness of systems of quantified modal logic, the soundness proof for the propositional systems must be supplemented with verification that the rules for the quantifiers preserve validity. We will show soundness for systems that use the intensional interpretation first (Sections 15.2 and 15.3), and then explain how the result may be extended to a proof for the substitution (15.9) and objectual (15.10) interpretations.

15.1. Preliminaries: Some Replacement Theorems

The adequacy proofs for the intensional interpretation depend on showing two basic properties of iS-models concerning replacement of terms for their values in hybrid sentences. The first result is called the Intensional Instance Theorem. It says that when the intension of t is i, then sentence At and the hybrid Ai have the same truth values in all worlds. (Remember, At is the result of replacing the term t for occurrences of a variable x bound by ∀x in ∀xAx, and Ai results from replacing i for x in the same way.)

Intensional Instance Theorem.
If $\mathbf{a}(t)=i$, then $\mathbf{a_w}(At)=\mathbf{a_w}(Ai)$ for all $w \in W$.

It is not difficult to see why this theorem should hold. When $\mathbf{a}(t)=i$, we have $\mathbf{a}(t)=\mathbf{a}(i)$, because the condition (f) ensures that $\mathbf{a}(f)$ is f in every iS-model. But if $\mathbf{a}(t)=\mathbf{a}(i)$, the result of replacing t for x in list l and the result of replacing i for x in list l will produce two lists, $[l]^t/x$ and $[l]^i/x$, with exactly the same values in all the possible worlds, that is, $\mathbf{a}([l]^t/x)=\mathbf{a}([l]^i/x)$. This will ensure that the values of atoms $Pltl'$ and $Plil'$ will be identical. Since the values of all complex sentences depend on the intensions of the atoms, it will follow that $\mathbf{a_w}(At)=\mathbf{a_w}(Ai)$ for any world $\mathbf{w}$. Although the intuition behind the proof of this theorem is simple, the details are tedious. So the proof of the Intensional Instance Theorem is given in an appendix at the end of this chapter.

The Intensional Instance Theorem provides a crucial fact needed to show soundness and completeness on the intensional interpretation. An analog of this theorem for *objects* d (members of the domain $\mathbf{D}$) rather than intensions would be the following:

(Bad Instance)   If $\mathbf{a_w}(t)=d$, then $\mathbf{a_w}(At)=\mathbf{a_w}(Ad)$ for all $\mathbf{w} \in \mathbf{W}$.

As the name suggests, this statement is incorrect, and its failure is the fundamental reason why formulating valid principles for the objectual interpretation is difficult. The reason (Bad Instance) does not hold is related to the problems concerning the objectual interpretation discussed in Section 13.6, problems that result from a failure of substitution. For example, when t is a nonrigid term such as 'the inventor of bifocals', and d is Benjamin Franklin, the truth of $\Box t{\approx}t$ ('it is necessary that the inventor of bifocals is the inventor of bifocals') does not entail the truth of the hybrid $\Box d{\approx}t$ ('it is necessary that d be the inventor of bifocals'). The point can be made more formally. In a model where $\mathbf{a_w}(t)=d$, $\mathbf{w}R\mathbf{v}$, and $\mathbf{a_v}(t){\neq}d$, $\mathbf{a_w}(\Box t{\approx}t)=T$ but $\mathbf{a_w}(\Box d{\approx}t)=F$.

EXERCISE 15.1   Verify that $\mathbf{a_w}(\Box d{\approx}t)=F$ when $\mathbf{a_v}(t){\neq}d$ and $\mathbf{w}R\mathbf{v}$.

However, (Bad Instance) does hold when t is *rigid*, that is, when $\mathbf{a_w}(t)=\mathbf{a_v}(t)$ for any $\mathbf{w}$ and $\mathbf{v}$ in $\mathbf{W}$. So the following will be proven for iS-models in the appendix of this chapter.

Rigid Instance Theorem.
If t is rigid and $\mathbf{a_w}(t)=d$, then $\mathbf{a_w}(At)=\mathbf{a_w}(Ad)$ for all $\mathbf{w} \in \mathbf{W}$.

We will also to appeal need to a third theorem about replacement of values that is familiar from predicate logic. It will also be given a proof in the appendix.

No t Theorem. If two iS-models are identical with the exception that their respective assignment functions $\mathbf{a}$ and $\mathbf{b}$ disagree only on the value of a single term t, and A is a wff (or hybrid) where t does not appear, then $\mathbf{a_w}(A)=\mathbf{b_w}(A)$. Furthermore, if t is not in L, then $\mathbf{a_w}(L)=\mathbf{b_w}(L)$.

The No t Theorem should be nearly obvious. It holds because the truth value of every sentence depends only on the values of the symbols it contains in the various possible worlds. If t does not occur in A, then changing the value of t cannot possibly affect the value of A. So if t is not in a list L, changing the value of t cannot change whether L is satisfied or not.

15.2. Soundness for the Intensional Interpretation

Assume S is a system that results from adding to fK axioms of a propositional modal logic that we already know is sound with respect to its corresponding semantics. We will show that the system S is also sound for the intensional interpretation of the quantifier by showing that the rules ($\approx$In), ($\approx$Out), ($\forall$Out), and ($\forall$In) preserve iS-validity.

To show that S is sound, one must prove that if $H \vdash_S C$ then $H \vDash_{iS} C$, for any argument H / C. Instead, something stronger will be proven, namely, that if $L \vdash_S C$, then $L \vDash_{iS} C$, when L is a *list* containing boxes as well as sentences. To do this, it helps to remind ourselves of the definition of '$L \vDash_{iS}$ C', which says that the modal argument L / C is iS-valid. The definition is found in Section 8.1, where the soundness proof for propositional modal logics is given. It depends on the following account of the notion of a list L being *satisfied* at $\mathbf{w}$ on an assignment $\mathbf{a}$ (in symbols $\mathbf{a_w}(L)=T$).

(L,$\Box$) $\mathbf{a_w}(L, \Box, H)=T$ iff $\exists \mathbf{v}\, \mathbf{a_v}(L)=T$ and $\mathbf{v}R\mathbf{w}$ and $\mathbf{a_w}(H)=T$.

The notation '$L \vDash_{iS} A$' is then defined as one would expect: $L \vDash_{iS} A$ iff for any iS-model $<\mathbf{W}, \mathbf{R}, \mathbb{D}, \mathbf{I}, \mathbf{a}>$ and any member $\mathbf{w}$ of $\mathbf{W}$, if $\mathbf{a_w}(L)=T$ then $\mathbf{a_w}(A)=T$.

We are now ready to show that the rules of S preserve iS-validity, that is, if the argument (or arguments) to which a rule is applied is (are) iS-valid, then so is the result of applying the rule. The demonstrations for all the rules of propositional modal logic are identical to those given in Section 8.1. All that remains is to show that the rules for $\forall$ and $\approx$ preserve validity, which is what follows. (The index 'iS' is dropped from '$\vDash$' in the remainder of this section to avoid eye strain.)

($\forall$Out) $L \vdash \forall xAx$

             $L \vdash Ec{\rightarrow}Ac$

Proof that (∀Out) preserves iS-validity. We must show that L ⊨ ∀xAx entails L ⊨ Ec→Ac. So assume both L ⊨ ∀xAx and L ⊭ Ec→Ac, and derive a contradiction. From L ⊭ Ec→Ac it follows that there is an iS-model <W, R, D, I, a> and a world w in W such that a_w(L)=T, and a_w(Ec→Ac)=F. But then by (→), a_w(Ec)=T and a_w(Ac)=F. By L ⊨ ∀xAx, a_w(∀xAx)=T. The situation can be pictured as follows:

$$\begin{array}{l} L \\ \sim(Ec{\to}Ac) \\ Ec \\ \sim Ac \\ \forall xAx \end{array} \quad \begin{array}{l} w \\ \\ (\to F) \\ L \vDash \forall xAx \end{array}$$

Now according to (cI), the intension **a**(c) of c must be some member i of **I**. So **a**(c)=i for this function i, hence a_w(c)=i(w). From a_w(Ec)=T and (Pl) it follows that a_w(c) ∈ a_w(E), that is: i(w) ∈ a_w(E). By the truth clause (i∀), it follows that a_w(Ai)=T. By the Intensional Instance Theorem, a_w(Ai)=T iff a_w(Ac)=T. Therefore a_w(Ac)=T. But this contradicts the previous result: a_w(Ac)=F, and so the demonstration is complete. The rest of the reasoning may be diagrammed as follows:

$$\begin{array}{l} L \\ \sim(Ec{\to}Ac) \\ Ec \\ \sim Ac \\ \forall xAx \\ Ei \\ Ai \\ Ac \\ \bot \end{array} \quad \begin{array}{l} w \\ \\ (\to F) \\ L \vDash \forall xAx \\ a(c)=i \\ (i\forall) \\ \text{Instance Theorem} \end{array}$$

Notice that placing the hybrid Ei in w expresses the fact that i(w) ∈a_w(E).

(∀In)   L ⊢ Ec→Ac

L ⊢ ∀xAx   provided c is not in L or ∀xAx

Proof that (∀In) preserves iS-validity. We are given L ⊨ Ec→Ac, where c is not in L or ∀xAx, and we must show that L ⊨ ∀xAx. Again the strategy will be to assume L ⊭ ∀xAx and derive a contradiction. From L ⊭ ∀xAx, it follows that there is an iS-model <W, R, D, I, a> and a world w in W such that a_w(L)=T and a_w(∀xAx)=F. By (i∀), it follows that for some function i in **I**, i(**w**) $\in$ **a$_w$**(E) and **a$_w$**(Ai)=F. We can diagram the situation as follows:

$$
\boxed{\begin{array}{c} L \\ \sim\forall xAx \\ Ei \\ \sim Ai \end{array}}^{\mathbf{w}} \quad (i\forall)
$$

At this point the proof takes an unusual turn because it will not be possible to derive a contradiction by considering only assignment **a**. Instead we will construct a new iS-model <**W, R, D, I, b**> with the same frame <**W, R**>, domain structure **D**, and set **I**, but with an assignment function **b** defined from **a** as follows: **b**(e)=**a**(e) when e is any predicate letter or term other than c, and **b**(c)=i. The values of the sentences given by **b** are fixed by the standard truth clauses: ($\approx$), (Pl), ($\perp$), ($\rightarrow$), ($\Box$), and (i$\forall$). Since **b** is identical to **a** except for what it assigns to c, and since c does not appear in L, we know by the No t Theorem that **b** agrees with **a** on these sentences and so **b$_w$**(L)=T. Since c is not in $\forall$xAx, it cannot be in the hybrid Ai either, so the No t Theorem also guarantees that **b$_w$**(Ai)=F. We may diagram this situation as follows:

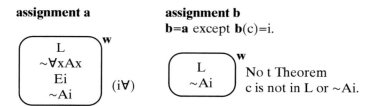

Note that since i(**w**) $\in$ **a$_w$**(E) and **a** and **b** agree on every expression other than c, i(**w**) $\in$ **b$_w$**(E). Since **b**(c)=i, and i(**w**) $\in$ **a$_w$**(E), it also follows that **b$_w$**(c) $\in$ **b$_w$**(E) and so **b$_w$**(Ec)=T by (Pl).

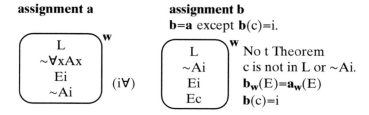

Furthermore, since L $\vDash$ Ec$\rightarrow$Ac, it follows from **b$_w$**(L)=T that **b$_w$**(Ec$\rightarrow$Ac)=T. It follows by the Intensional Instance Theorem and

$\mathbf{b_w}$(Ai)=F that $\mathbf{b_w}$(Ac)=F. But $\mathbf{b_w}$(Ec)=T and $\mathbf{b_w}$(Ac)=F yield $\mathbf{b_w}$(Ec→Ac)=F by (→). So there is a contradiction, and the demonstration is complete.

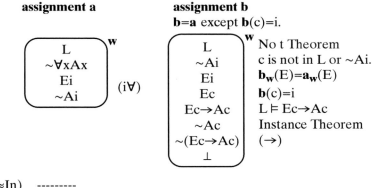

assignment a

assignment b

b=a except **b**(c)=i.

assignment a	assignment b	
L	L	No t Theorem
~∀xAx	~Ai	c is not in L or ~Ai.
Ei	Ei	$\mathbf{b_w}$(E)=$\mathbf{a_w}$(E)
~Ai	Ec	**b**(c)=i
(i∀)	Ec→Ac	L ⊨ Ec→Ac
	~Ac	Instance Theorem
	~(Ec→Ac)	(→)
	⊥	

(≈In)   ---------

L ⊢ t≈t

Proof that (≈In) preserves iS-validity. We must show that L ⊨ t≈t. So assume the opposite: L ⊭ t≈t. There then is an iS-model <**W**, **R**, **D**, **I**, **a**> and world **w** in **W**, such that $\mathbf{a_w}$(L)=T and $\mathbf{a_w}$(t≈t)=F. But by (≈) if $\mathbf{a_w}$(t≈t)=F, then $\mathbf{a_w}$(t)≠$\mathbf{a_w}$(t), which is clearly impossible. So L ⊨ t≈t.

(≈Out)   L ⊢ s≈t

L ⊢ Plsl′

L ⊢ Pltl′

Proof that (≈Out) preserves iS-validity. We are given that L ⊨ s≈t and L ⊨ Plsl′. We must show L ⊨ Pltl′. So we assume $\mathbf{a_w}$(L)=T and prove $\mathbf{a_w}$(Pltl′)=T. Since $\mathbf{a_w}$(L)=T, we have by L ⊨ s≈t that $\mathbf{a_w}$(s≈t)=T, and so by (≈), $\mathbf{a_w}$(s)=$\mathbf{a_w}$(t). It follows by (t_i) that $\mathbf{a_w}$(lsl′)=$\mathbf{a_w}$(ltl′), and so $\mathbf{a_w}$(lsl′) $\in\mathbf{a_w}$(P) iff $\mathbf{a_w}$(ltl′) $\in\mathbf{a_w}$(P).

(t_i) $\mathbf{a_w}((t_1,\ldots,t_n)) = (\mathbf{a_w}(t_1),\ldots,\mathbf{a_w}(t_n))$.

We know by L ⊨ Plsl′ that $\mathbf{a_w}$(Plsl′)=T, and so by (Pl) that $\mathbf{a_w}$(lsl′) $\in\mathbf{a_w}$(P). It follows that $\mathbf{a_w}$(ltl′) $\in\mathbf{a_w}$(P), hence $\mathbf{a_w}$(Pltl′)=T by (Pl).

15.3. Soundness for Systems with Domain Rules

In the last section, it was assumed that S was a system of logic that results from adding to fK axioms in a list of principles for propositional modal logic. However, in Section 13.9, new domain rules were introduced along with their corresponding conditions on the domains of iS-models. Let S be the result of adding as well one or more of those rules. To show that S is sound, it is necessary to show that each of its new rules is iS-valid when an iS-model meets their corresponding conditions.

Domain Rules		**Corresponding Domain Conditions**
(∃E)	∃xEx	For some i $\in$ **I**, i(**w**) $\in$ **Dw**.
(Q)	Et	**Dw=D**.
(ED)	Ec→□Ec	If **wRv** and $a_w(c) \in$ **Dw**, then $a_v(c) \in$ **Dv**.
(CD)	~Ec→□~Ec	If **wRv** and $a_v(c) \in$ **Dv**, then $a_w(c) \in$ **Dw**.
(RC)	(b≈c→□b≈c)& (~b≈c→□~b≈c)	$a_w(c) = a_v(c)$.
(∃i)	L ⊢ ~t≈c / L ⊢ ⊥, no c in L, t	For some i $\in$ **I**, i(**w**)=a_w(t).
(o)=(RC)+(∃i)		**I** is the set of all constant functions with values in **D**.
(o∃E)=(o)+(∃E)		(o) + **Dw** is not empty.
(oED)=(o)+(ED)		(o) + if **wRv**, then **Dw** $\subseteq$ **Dv**.
(oCD)=(o)+(CD)		(o) + if **wRv**, then **Dv** $\subseteq$ **Dw**.

Remember that an instance of an axiom may be placed within any sub-proof, so verifying an axiom A amounts to showing the validity of the argument L / A for any list L. To show that L / A is iS-valid, assume that <**W**, **R**, **D**, **I**, **a**> is an iS-model that meets the corresponding condition, let **w** be any member of **W** such that $a_w(L)$=T, and then show that $a_w(A)$=T. Here are the details for each axiom A.

(∃E)   ∃xEx   For some i $\in$ **I**, i(**w**) $\in$ **Dw**.

The condition guarantees that for some i $\in$ **I**, i(**w**) $\in$ **Dw**, therefore by (E), and (Pl), a_w(Ei)=T. So by (i∃), a_w(∃xEx)=T.

(Q)   Et   **Dw=D**.

The condition requires that **Dw=D**, so if a_w(t) $\in$ **D** then a_w(t) $\in$ **Dw**. But by the definition of an iS-model, the appropriate extension a_w(t) for a term t is a member of **D**. Therefore, a_w(t) $\in$ **Dw**. It follows by (E) that a_w(t) $\in a_w$(E) and so a_w(Et)=T by (Pl).

(ED)   Ec→□Ec   If **wRv** and $a_w(c) \in$ **Dw**, then $a_v(c) \in$ **Dv**.

EXERCISE *15.2   Show that $a_w(Ec \rightarrow \Box Ec)=T$ when the above condition holds. (Hint. Review the proof of the case for (CD) below.)

(CD) $\sim Ec \rightarrow \Box \sim Ec$ If wRv and $a_v(c) \in Dv$, then $a_w(c) \in Dw$.

To show $a_w(\sim Ec \rightarrow \Box \sim Ec)=T$ assume $a_w(\sim Ec)=T$ and prove $a_w(\Box \sim Ec)=T$, by assuming that v is any world such that wRv, and proving $a_v(\sim Ec)=T$. Since $a_w(\sim Ec)=T$, it follows by ($\sim$), (E), and (Pl) that $a_w(c) \notin Dw$. By the contracting domain condition (CD), if $a_v(c) \in Dv$ then $a_w(c) \in Dw$. Since $a_w(c) \notin Dw$, it follows that $a_v(c) \notin Dw$. So $a_v(\sim Ec)=T$ follows by ($\sim$), (E), and (Pl).

(RC) $(b \approx c \rightarrow \Box b \approx c) \& (\sim b \approx c \rightarrow \Box \sim b \approx c)$ $a_w(c)=a_v(c)$.

To show $a_w((b \approx c \rightarrow \Box b \approx c) \& (\sim b \approx c \rightarrow \Box \sim b \approx c))=T$, given the condition, it will be sufficient to show ($\approx \Box$) and ($\approx \sim \Box$), assuming that b and c are rigid.

($\approx \Box$) $a_w(b \approx c \rightarrow \Box b \approx c)=T$.
($\approx \sim \Box$) $a_w(\sim b \approx c \rightarrow \Box \sim b \approx c)=T$.

Proof of ($\approx \Box$). According to ($\rightarrow$), ($\approx \Box$) follows provided that if $a_w(b \approx c)=T$ then $a_w(\Box b \approx c)=T$. So assume $a_w(b \approx c)=T$, and show $a_w(\Box b \approx c)=T$, by assuming wRv and deducing $a_v(b \approx c)=T$ as follows. Since $a_w(b \approx c)=T$, we have $a_w(b)=a_w(c)$ by ($\approx$). Since b is rigid, b picks out the same object in all possible worlds. Since b and c pick out the same object in world w, and since c is also rigid, it follows that b and c pick out the same object in all possible worlds. So $a_v(b)=a_v(c)$, and hence by ($\approx$) $a_v(b \approx c)=T$, as desired.

EXERCISE *15.3   Prove ($\approx \sim \Box$).

($\exists$i) $L \vdash \sim t \approx c \,/\, L \vdash \bot$, no c in L, t   For some $i \in I$, $i(w)=d$.

It must be shown that ($\exists$i) preserves iS-validity. So suppose c is not in L or t, that $L \vDash \sim t \approx c$, and that $L \nvDash \bot$ for indirect proof. Then there is an iS-model $<W, R, \mathbb{D}, I, a>$ with world w in W where $a_w(L)=T$. The term t must have an extension $a_w(t)=d$ for some d in D. By the condition, there is a member i of I such that $i(w)=d$. Now construct the model $<W, R, \mathbb{D}, I, b>$ where b is like a except that the assignment function b is such that $b(c)=i$. Since c does not appear in L nor in t, it follows by the No t Lemma that $b_w(L)=a_w(L)=T$ and $b_w(t)=a_w(t)=d=i(w)=b_w(c)$. So by

($\approx$), $\mathbf{b_w}(t\approx c)$=T. But from L $\vDash$ ~$t\approx c$, it follows that $\mathbf{b_w}(t\approx c)$=F, which is a contradiction.

(o) = (RC)+($\exists$i)   I is the set of all constant functions with values in **D**.

When the condition holds, it follows by requirement (cI) on iS-models (namely, that $\mathbf{a}(c)$ is in **I**) that condition (RC) holds: namely, that $\mathbf{a}(c)$ is a constant function. It was already shown that axiom (RC) is iS-valid, given this condition, so (RC) will be iS-valid. Furthermore, when (o) holds, it follows that for each member d of **D**, there is a function i in **I** such that i($\mathbf{w}$)=d. By the fact that $\mathbf{a_w}(t)$ is always a member of **D**, condition ($\exists$i) follows, namely, that for each term t there is a member i of **I** such that i($\mathbf{w}$)=$\mathbf{a_w}(t)$. We already showed that the rule ($\exists$i) preserves validity under this condition, so it also preserves iS-validity when (o) holds.

EXERCISE 15.4   Show that when (o) and any of the following conditions holds in an iS-model, then the corresponding axiom is iS-valid.

*a) (o$\exists$E)=(o)+($\exists$E): $\exists$xEx   (o) + **Dw** is not empty.
*b) (oED)=(o)+(ED): Ec$\rightarrow\square$Ec   (o) + if **wRv**, then **Dw** $\subseteq$ **Dv**.
c) (oCD)=(o)+(CD): ~Ec$\rightarrow\square$~Ec   (o) + if **wRv**, then **Dv** $\subseteq$ **Dw**.

15.4. Expanding Truth Value (tS) to Substitution (sS) Models

In the discussion of the substitution interpretation in Sections 13.1 and 13.2, two different kinds of models were defined. The simpler ones were tS-models, which only assigned truth values to the sentences. The more sophisticated sS-models introduced a domain structure $\mathbb{D}$, and assigned values as well to the terms and predicate letters. In this section, it will be shown that it does not matter which of the two kinds of models is used because they provide equivalent accounts of validity.

ts Equivalence Theorem.   H $\vDash_{tS}$ C iff H $\vDash_{sS}$ C.

For the moment, sS-models are assumed to be sK-models that obey frame conditions for a given propositional modal logic S, but not for any of the quantifier domain rules. Since the rule ($\exists$i) is required for systems with nonrigid terms, we will assume here that the only terms in the language are the constants. In Sections 15.7 and following, we will consider the possibility that sS-models satisfy conditions on the quantifier domains as well so that we may accommodate nonrigid terms.

The ts Equivalence Theorem will have two different uses. It will help establish soundness for the substitution interpretation, and completeness of many different quantified modal logics. The result follows relatively easily once we explain how to construct for any given tS-model its ts-expansion, that is, a corresponding sS-model with the same frame that agrees with the tS-model on the values of all the sentences.

Given a tS-model $<\mathbf{W}, \mathbf{R}, \mathbf{a}^t>$, its *ts-expansion* $<\mathbf{W}, \mathbf{R}, \mathbb{D}, \mathbf{a}^s>$ is defined as follows. First, $\mathbf{a}^s$ agrees with $\mathbf{a}^t$ on the values of all the sentences.

$(\mathbf{a}^s A)$ $\mathbf{a}^s(A)=\mathbf{a}^t(A)$.

(Note that '$\mathbf{a}^s(A)=\mathbf{a}^t(A)$' means that the assignment functions $\mathbf{a}^s$ and $\mathbf{a}^t$ agree on the *intensions* of sentence A, from which it follows that $\mathbf{a}^s_\mathbf{w}(A)=\mathbf{a}^t_\mathbf{w}(A)$, for every world $\mathbf{w}$ in $\mathbf{W}$.) Terms t are assigned extensions that are *sets* of constants c such that $\mathbf{a}^s_\mathbf{w}(t\approx c)=T$.

$(\mathbf{a}^s t)$ $c \in \mathbf{a}^s_\mathbf{w}(t)$ iff c is a constant such that $\mathbf{a}^s_\mathbf{w}(t\approx c)=T$.

The structure $\mathbb{D}$ for the sS-model is defined by $(\mathbf{a}^s D)$ and $(\mathbf{a}^s Dw)$.

$(\mathbf{a}^s D)$ $d \in D$ iff for some term t and world w, $d=\mathbf{a}^s_\mathbf{w}(t)$.
$(\mathbf{a}^s Dw)$ $d \in Dw$ iff for some term t, $d=\mathbf{a}^s_\mathbf{w}(t)$ and $\mathbf{a}^s_\mathbf{w}(Et)=T$.

For predicate letters P, $\mathbf{a}^s_\mathbf{w}(P)$ is defined as follows:

$(\mathbf{a}^s P)$ $o \in \mathbf{a}^s_\mathbf{w}(P)$ iff for some list l', $\mathbf{a}^s_\mathbf{w}(l')=o$ and $\mathbf{a}^s_\mathbf{w}(Pl')=T$.

It is worth taking a moment to explain why we have chosen to define the extensions of the terms by $(\mathbf{a}^s t)$. The main difficulty to overcome in constructing $\mathbf{a}^s$ is to define extensions for the terms so that $(\approx)$ is satisfied. If, for example, each term is given an arbitrary extension $\mathbf{a}^s_\mathbf{w}(t)$, then there will be no guarantee that $\mathbf{a}^s_\mathbf{w}(s\approx t)=T$ entails $\mathbf{a}^s_\mathbf{w}(s)=\mathbf{a}^s_\mathbf{w}(t)$ as $(\approx)$ requires. A standard way of overcoming this problem is to let $\mathbf{a}^s_\mathbf{w}(t)$ be the set of all constants c such that $\mathbf{a}^s_\mathbf{w}(t\approx c)=T$. This way, when $\mathbf{a}^s_\mathbf{w}(s\approx t)=T$, it will follow (by $(\mathbf{a}^s A)$ and the truth condition $(t\approx)$) that $\mathbf{a}^s_\mathbf{w}(s\approx c)=\mathbf{a}^s_\mathbf{w}(t\approx c)=T$, for any constant c, with the result that the extensions of s and t will be the same as required.

There is a second, often-used method for overcoming the difficulty in satisfying $(\approx)$. Assume that the constants in the language are ordered in one (possibly infinite) list. Then $\mathbf{a}^s_\mathbf{w}(t)$ is defined as the earliest constant c on the list such that $\mathbf{a}^s_\mathbf{w}(t\approx c)=T$. This works because when $\mathbf{a}^s_\mathbf{w}(s\approx t)=T$, it is possible to show that $\mathbf{a}^s_\mathbf{w}(s)$ and $\mathbf{a}^s_\mathbf{w}(t)$ pick out exactly the same constant. It is an excellent check on the reader's understanding to trace through the coming theorems and lemmas to verify that the alternative method works as well.

Note that a^s automatically obeys (∃c) when the language at issue contains only the constants.

(∃c) For all t and w, there is a constant c such that $a^s{}_w(t≈c)=T$.

The reason is that when t is a constant b, there is a constant c such that $a^s{}_w(b≈c)=T$ because $a^s{}_w(b≈b)=T$ by (t≈In), so that the constant in question can be b itself. Note condition (∃c) could fail when new terms are introduced to the language, for when t is not a constant, it is not clear that $a^s{}_w(t≈c)=T$ for some constant c. This is why (∃c) is explicitly mentioned in the next theorem, for we will need to appeal to (∃c) in the course of its proof.

ts-Expansion Theorem. The ts-expansion $<W, R, D, a^s>$ of any tS-model $<W, R, a^t>$ that obeys (∃c) is an sS-model that obeys $a^t(A)=a^s(A)$.

Proof of the ts-Expansion Theorem. Let $<W, R, a^t>$ be any tS-model. Then the assignment function a^t assigns values to all sentences in every world and obeys (⊥), (→), (□), (∀), and (t≈). However, a^t does not assign anything to terms or predicate letters. It will be shown that the ts-expansion $<W, R, D, a^s>$ expands the assignment function a^t of the tS-model to a corresponding assignment a^s that agrees with a^t on the values of all the sentences, but also assigns values to terms, lists of terms, and predicate letters over a domain structure D in such a way that conditions (≈), (Pl), and (E) hold. Since a^s and a^t will agree on the values assigned the sentences, all other truth conditions for an sS-model will be obeyed. Since the frames of the two models are identical, $<W, R, D, a^s>$ inherits the frame conditions for S and so $<W, R, D, a^s>$ will qualify as an sS-model.

We begin by showing (≈). Note that a^s meets the condition (t≈) for ≈, since a^t does. For convenience we will refer to the two conjuncts of (t≈) as follows:

(t≈In) $a^s{}_w(t≈t)=T$.
(t≈Out) If $a^s{}_w(s≈t)=T$, then $a^s{}_w(Plsl')=a^s{}_w(Pltl')$.

These features of a^s will be the basis for proving some useful lemmas about ≈.

Substitution Lemma. If $a^s{}_w(s≈t)=T$ then $a^s{}_w(s≈c)=a^s{}_w(t≈c)$, and if $a^s{}_w(s≈c)=T$ and $a^s{}_w(t≈c)=T$, then $a^s{}_w(s≈t)=T$.

EXERCISE 15.5 Prove the Substitution Lemma. (Hint: Use $(t{\approx}In)$ and $(t{\approx}Out)$. It helps to review strategies for proving (Symmetry) and (Transitivity) for $\approx$ given in Section 12.3.)

$\approx$**Lemma.** $\mathbf{a^s_w}(s{\approx}t)=T$ iff for any constant c, $\mathbf{a^s_w}(s{\approx}c)=T$ iff $\mathbf{a^s_w}(t{\approx}c)=T$.

Proof of the $\approx$Lemma. By the Substitution Lemma, we have: if $\mathbf{a^s_w}(s{\approx}t)=T$ then $\mathbf{a^s_w}(s{\approx}c)=\mathbf{a^s_w}(t{\approx}c)$. So the lemma is proven from left to right. For the proof from right to left, suppose for any constant c, $\mathbf{a^s_w}(s{\approx}c)=T$ iff $\mathbf{a^s_w}(t{\approx}c)=T$, and prove $\mathbf{a^s_w}(s{\approx}t)=T$ as follows. By $(\exists c)$, there is a constant b such that $\mathbf{a^s_w}(t{\approx}b)=T$. Since $\mathbf{a^s_w}(s{\approx}c)=T$ iff $\mathbf{a^s_w}(t{\approx}c)=T$ holds for any constant c, it follows that $\mathbf{a^s_w}(s{\approx}b)=\mathbf{a^s}_w(t{\approx}b)=T$. By the Substitution Lemma, $\mathbf{a^s_w}(s{\approx}t)=T$ as desired.

With these lemmas in hand it is not difficult to show that the expanded assignment function $\mathbf{a^s}$ obeys $(\approx)$. Here is the proof:

$(\approx)$ $\mathbf{a^s_w}(s{\approx}t)=T$ iff $\mathbf{a^s_w}(s)=\mathbf{a^s_w}(t)$.

Proof.
$\mathbf{a^s_w}(s{\approx}t)=T$
iff for any c, $\mathbf{a^s_w}(s{\approx}c)=T$ iff $\mathbf{a^s_w}(t{\approx}c)=T$ $\approx$ Lemma
iff or any c, $c\in\mathbf{a^s_w}(s)$ iff $c\in\mathbf{a^s_w}(t)$ $(\mathbf{a^s}t)$ used twice
iff $\mathbf{a^s_w}(s)=\mathbf{a^s_w}(t)$ $\mathbf{a^s_w}(s)$ and $\mathbf{a^s_w}(t)$ have the same members

To prove that $\mathbf{a^s}$ obeys (Pl), it is useful to develop two lemmas concerning how assignment functions behave with respect to lists of terms. Let $l = t_1, .., t_i$ and $l' = t'_1, .., t'_i$ be two lists of terms of the same length i. Let $l'{\approx}l$ be the list of identity sentences $t'_1{\approx}t_1, .., t'_i{\approx}t_i$.

$l'{\approx}l$ **Lemma.** $\mathbf{a^s_w}(l')=\mathbf{a^s_w}(l)$ iff $\mathbf{a^s_w}(l'{\approx}l)=T$.

Proof. Remember $\mathbf{a^s_w}(l)$ is defined for lists $l = t_1, .., t_i$ as follows:

(t_i) $\mathbf{a_w}(t_1, .., t_i) = \mathbf{a_w}(t_1), .., \mathbf{a_w}(t_i)$

By (t_i), we have the following two facts:

$\mathbf{a^s_w}(l) = \mathbf{a^s_w}(t_1, .., t_i) = \mathbf{a^s_w}(t_1), .., \mathbf{a^s_w}(t_i)$
$\mathbf{a^s_w}(l') = \mathbf{a^s_w}(t'_1, .., t'_i) = \mathbf{a^s_w}(t'_1), .., \mathbf{a^s_w}(t'_i)$

So $\mathbf{a^s_w}(l') = \mathbf{a^s_w}(l)$
iff $\mathbf{a^s_w}(t'_1) = \mathbf{a^s_w}(t_1)$ and, .., and $\mathbf{a^s_w}(t'_i) = \mathbf{a^s_w}(t_i)$ previous two facts

iff $\mathbf{a^s_w}(t'_1 \approx t_1) = T$ and, .., and $\mathbf{a^s_w}(t'_i \approx t_i) = T$ ($\approx$) used i times
iff $\mathbf{a^s_w}(l' \approx l) = T$.   Definition of $l' \approx l$

Some l' Lemma.
$\mathbf{a^s_w}(Pl) = T$ iff for some l', $\mathbf{a^s_w}(l' \approx l) = T$ and $\mathbf{a^s_w}(Pl') = T$.

Proof of the Some l' Lemma. For the proof from left to right, suppose $\mathbf{a^s_w}(Pl) = T$. By ($t \approx In$) used many times, $\mathbf{a^s_w}(l \approx l) = T$. So for some l' (namely, l), $\mathbf{a^s_w}(l' \approx l) = T$ and $\mathbf{a^s_w}(Pl') = T$. For the proof from right to left, suppose for some l', $\mathbf{a^s_w}(l' \approx l) = T$ and $\mathbf{a^s_w}(Pl') = T$. Let $l = t_1, .., t_i$ and $l' = t'_1, .., t'_i$. Then $\mathbf{a^s_w}(t'_1 \approx t_1) = T$ and, .., and $\mathbf{a^s_w}(t'_i \approx t_i) = T$. By repeated use of ($t \approx Out$) replace each of the t'_j in Pl' with t_j to obtain Pl. So it follows from $\mathbf{a^s_w}(Pl') = T$ that $\mathbf{a^s_w}(Pl) = T$.

We are now ready to show (Pl) holds for $\mathbf{a^s}$.

(Pl) $\mathbf{a^s_w}(Pl) = T$ iff $\mathbf{a^s_w}(l) \in \mathbf{a^s_w}(P)$.

Proof of (Pl).
$\mathbf{a^s_w}(Pl) = T$
iff for some l', $\mathbf{a^s_w}(l' \approx l) = T$ and $\mathbf{a^s_w}(Pl') = T$ Some l' Lemma
iff for some l', $\mathbf{a^s_w}(l') = \mathbf{a^s_w}(l)$ and $\mathbf{a^s_w}(Pl') = T$ $l' \approx l$ Lemma
iff $\mathbf{a^s_w}(l) \in \mathbf{a^s_w}(P)$ ($\mathbf{a^s}P$)

Finally we must show that (E) holds for $\mathbf{a^s}$.

(E) $\mathbf{a^s_w}(E) = \mathbf{Dw}$.

Proof of (E). We show that for any d in $\mathbf{D}$, $d \in \mathbf{a^s_w}(E)$ iff $d \in \mathbf{Dw}$. Suppose that $d \in \mathbf{a^s_w}(E)$. Then by the definition ($\mathbf{a^s D}$) of $\mathbf{D}$ for the ts-expansion, for some term t, $d = \mathbf{a^s_w}(t)$. So $\mathbf{a^s_w}(t) \in \mathbf{a^s_w}(E)$ and by (Pl), $\mathbf{a^s_w}(Et) = T$, and so by ($\mathbf{a^s Dw}$), $d \in \mathbf{Dw}$. Now suppose $d \in \mathbf{Dw}$; then by ($\mathbf{a^s Dw}$), for some term t, $d = \mathbf{a^s_w}(t)$ and $\mathbf{a^s_w}(Et) = T$. By (Pl) $d = \mathbf{a^s_w}(t) \in \mathbf{a^s_w}(E)$.

This completes the proof of the ts-Expansion Theorem. It is not hard to prove the ts Equivalence Theorem now that the ts-Expansion Theorem is available.

ts Equivalence Theorem. $H \vDash_{tS} C$ iff $H \vDash_{sS} C$.

Proof of the ts Equivalence Theorem. It will suffice to show the following:

$H \nvDash_{sS} C$ iff $H \nvDash_{tS} C$.

To show this from left to right, assume $H \nvDash_{sS} C$, that is, that there is a sS-model $<\mathbf{W}, \mathbf{R}, \mathbb{D}, \mathbf{a^s}>$ that is a counterexample to H / C. To create a tS-model that is a counterexample to the same argument, let its frame be identical to the frame <**W, R**> for the sS-model and define its assignment function so that it agrees with the values $\mathbf{a^s}$ assigns to all the sentences. The result is a tS-counterexample to H / C.

> **EXERCISE 15.6** Explain why the model <**W, R, D, a^s**> defined above must be a tS-counterexample to H / C. In particular how do we know it is a tS-model?

For the direction from right to left, assume $H \nvDash_{tS} C$. So H / C has a tS-counterexample. Since we have assumed that constants are so far the only terms in the language, $(\exists c)$ holds, and so it follows by the ts-Expansion Theorem that a corresponding sS-model exists that leaves the values of all sentences the same in all worlds. So there is an sS-counterexample to H / C, that is, $H \nvDash_{sS} C$.

15.5. Expanding Substitution (sS) to Intensional (iS) Models

In this section, we learn how to expand each substitution interpretation model to create an intensional interpretation model that agrees with it on the values of all the sentences. This result is useful in several ways. It will allow us to exploit the proof that system S is sound for iS- (intensional interpretation) models to obtain the soundness of S for sS- (substitution interpretation) models. (See Section 15.9.) It will also help us transfer relatively easy completeness results for the substitution interpretation to the intensional interpretation. Finally, it will help establish the equivalence of the substitution and intensional interpretations.

These results all depend on an interesting fact. The substitution interpretation truth clause ($\forall$) holds in all iS-models that meet condition (s), which says that each member of **I** is the intension of some constant.

($\forall$) $\mathbf{a_w}(\forall x Ax)=T$ iff for every c, if $\mathbf{a_w}(Ec)=T$ then $\mathbf{a_w}(Ac)=T$.
(s) $i \in \mathbf{I}$ iff for some constant c, $i=\mathbf{a}(c)$.

si Lemma. Any iS-model that obeys (s) also obeys ($\forall$).

This lemma shows that the substitution interpretation can be exactly captured in iS-models that meet the extra condition (s). Since it will be shown later that (s) does not correspond to any additional axiom or rule, the equivalence of the concept of validity defined by the two interpretations follows.

Proof of the si Lemma. Suppose we have an iS-model with assignment function **a** that obeys (s). Since **a** obeys the intensional truth clause (i$\forall$), to show it also obeys the substitution truth clause ($\forall$), we need only demonstrate that the right-hand sides (r$\forall$) and (ri$\forall$) of the two conditions are equivalent.

(r$\forall$)   for all c $\in$ C, if $a_w(Ec)$=T then $a_w(Ac)$=T.
(ri$\forall$)   for all i $\in$ **I**, if i(**w**) $\in$ **Dw** then $a_w(Ai)$=T.

Proof from (r$\forall$) to (ri$\forall$). Suppose (r$\forall$). To show (ri$\forall$), assume that i is any member of **I** and i(**w**) is in **Dw** and show that $a_w(Ai)$=T as follows. By (s) there is some constant c such that i=a(c). Since i(**w**) $\in$ **Dw**, it follows that $a_w(c)$ $\in$ **Dw**, from which by (Pl) and (E) it follows that $a_w(Ec)$=T. By (r$\forall$), it follows that $a_w(Ac)$=T. But i=a(c), so the Intensional Instance Theorem (Section 15.1) yields the desired result: $a_w(Ai)$=T.

Proof from (ri$\forall$) to (r$\forall$). Suppose (ri$\forall$). To show (r$\forall$), assume that c is any constant such that $a_w(Ec)$=T and show $a_w(Ac)$=T as follows. From $a_w(Ec)$=T with (Pl) and (E) it follows that $a_w(c)$ $\in$ **Dw**. By (cI), a(c)=i for some function i in **I**. So we have that i(**w**) $\in$ **Dw** for this function i. By (ri$\forall$), it follows that $a_w(Ai)$=T. By the Intensional Instance Theorem, $a_w(Ac)$=T as desired.

Given the si Lemma, it is a straightforward matter to show how to construct the si expansion of any sS-model, which is a corresponding iS-model that leaves the values of all the sentences unaffected. For a given sS-model <**W**, **R**, $\mathbb{D}$, a^s>, the *si-expansion* <**W**, **R**, $\mathbb{D}$, **I**, a^i> is defined by the following:

(a^ie) $a^i(e)=a^s(e)$, when e is a term or predicate letter.
(a^i**I**)   i $\in$ **I** iff for some constant c, i=a^i(c).

The values $a^i_w(A)$ assigned by a^i to the sentences A are defined according to the truth conditions for an iS-model.

   si-Expansion Theorem.   The si-expansion <**W**, **R**, $\mathbb{D}$, **I**, a^i> of any sS-model <**W**, **R**, $\mathbb{D}$, a^s> is an iS-model that obeys $a^s(A)=a^i(A)$.

Proof of the si-Expansion Theorem. Note that (a^i**I**) guarantees (s) and (cI), the condition that a(c) $\in$ **I** for each constant c. Since the values of sentences are calculated using the truth conditions for an iS-model, the si-expansion <**W**, **R**, $\mathbb{D}$, **I**, a^i> clearly satisfies all the conditions for being an iS-model. To show $a^s(A)=a^i(A)$, note that a^s and a^i agree on all terms and predicate letters and differ only in the truth conditions for the quantifier. But by the si-Lemma, we know that a^i obeys ($\forall$), the substitution truth clause, so $\mathbf{a^s}$ and $\mathbf{a^i}$ agree on values assigned to all sentences including those involving quantifiers.

The final result of this section will be to explain how the equivalence of the intensional and substitution interpretations can be shown. The result depends on the si-Expansion Theorem, the soundness of S for the intensional interpretation proven in Sections 15.2 and 15.3, and the completeness of S on the substitution interpretation to be proven in following chapters. Since this result depends on the completeness of S for sS-validity to be proven later, it is important that the si-Equivalence Theorem not be appealed to in the course of that completeness proof.

si-Equivalence Theorem. $H \vDash_{sS} C$ iff $H \vDash_{iS} C$

Proof of the si-Equivalence Theorem. To show this from left to right assume that $H \vDash_{sS} C$ and note that the completeness of S for the substitution interpretation yields $H \vdash_S C$, from which $H \vDash_{iS} C$ follows by the soundness of S for the intensional interpretation. For the other direction, it will suffice to show if $H \nvDash_{sS} C$, then, $H \nvDash_{iS} C$. So suppose $H \nvDash_{sS} C$. So there is an sS-model that is a counterexample to H / C. By the si-Expansion Theorem, the si-expansion leaves the values of all sentences the same in all worlds. So there is an iS-counterexample to H / C, that is, $H \nvDash_{iS} C$.

15.6. An Intensional Treatment of the Objectual Interpretation

In this section, the groundwork is laid for proving soundness and completeness for the objectual interpretation. We will begin with a result that shows how the objectual interpretation can be captured within iS-models (models that use the intensional interpretation). The main idea is straightforward. In an oS (objectual interpretation) model, the domain **D** of quantification mentioned in (o∀) is a set of *objects*, whereas in an iS (intensional interpretation) model, the domain **I** mentioned in (i∀) contains individual concepts, that is, functions from **W** to **D**.

(o∀) $\mathbf{a_w}(\forall x A x) = T$ iff for $d \in \mathbf{D}$, if $d \in \mathbf{D}w$, then $\mathbf{a_w}(Ad) = T$.

(i∀) $\mathbf{a_w}(\forall x A x) = T$ iff for every $i \in \mathbf{I}$, if $i(\mathbf{w}) \in \mathbf{D}w$, then $\mathbf{a_w}(Ai) = T$.

When i is a *constant function*, one whose value i(**w**) is object d for each world **w**, i always produces the value d, regardless of which world it is applied to. So the function i will play exactly the role of its value d. Now consider the following condition (o) on iS-models:

(o)   **I** is the set of all constant functions with values in **D**.

This condition will guarantee that the domain **I** contains only and all constant functions that pick out members of **D**. However, these constant functions are for all practical purposes "stand ins" for their values. So one should expect that adding (o) as an additional condition on iS-models will produce a semantics that captures exactly the effect of the oS-models, models where the domain of quantification is **D**. That is what we intend to prove.

Let an ioS-model be any iS-model that obeys (o). Assume that for ioS-models, values of hybrids Ad are defined just as they were in objectual interpretation. We will show that any ioS-model automatically satisfies the objectual truth condition (o∀).

oi Lemma.   Every ioS-model satisfies (o∀).

Proof of the oi Lemma. Since ioS-models satisfy the intensional truth clause (i∀), we need only show that (ri∀) and (ro∀), the right-hand sides of the respective truth conditions, are equivalent.

(ri∀)   For all i $\in$ **I**, if i(**w**) $\in$ **Dw**, then a_w(Ai)=T.
(ro∀)   For all d $\in$ **Dw**, a_w(Ad)=T.

Proof from (ri∀) to (ro∀). Assume (ri∀) and d $\in$ **Dw** and show a_w(Ad)=T as follows. By (o), the constant function i with value d is in **I**. So i(**w**) $\in$ **Dw**, and by (ri∀) a_w(Ai)=T. By the Rigid Instance Theorem (of Section 15.1), a_w(Ad)=T as desired.

Proof from (ro∀) to (ri∀). Assume (ro∀), i $\in$ **I**, and i(**w**) $\in$ **Dw** and show a_w(Ai)=T as follows. The function i must be a constant function with some value d in **D**. So d $\in$ **Dw**, and by (ro∀), a_w(Ad)=T. By the Rigid Instance Theorem, a_w(Ai)=T as desired.

We noted in Section 13.9 that for the objectual interpretation, the following axioms correspond to conditions on oS-models as follows. So in this section, and the following one, let us assume that oS-models obey any of the corresponding *o-domain conditions* from this list and that ioS-models meet the same conditions.

(o∃E)	∃xEx	**Dw** is not empty.
(Q)	Et	**Dw**=**D**.
(oED)	Ec→□Ec	If **wRv**, then **Dw** $\subseteq$ **Dv**.
(oCD)	~Ec→□~Ec	If **wRv**, then **Dv** $\subseteq$ **Dw**.

We are now ready to prove the basis for the claim that oS- and ioS-models are equivalent. For each oS model <**W**, **R**, $\mathbb{D}$, a^o>, let its *oi-expansion* $<\mathbf{W}, \mathbf{R}, \mathbb{D}, \mathbf{I}, \mathbf{a^i}>$ be defined so that $\mathbf{I}$ is the set of all constant functions i with values in $\mathbf{D}$, and $\mathbf{a^i}(e)=\mathbf{a^o}(e)$, when e is a term or predicate letter, and $\mathbf{a^i}$ is defined over sentences by the truth clauses for an iS-model.

oi-Expansion Theorem. The oi-expansion $<\mathbf{W}, \mathbf{R}, \mathbb{D}, \mathbf{I}, \mathbf{a^i}>$ of any oS-model $<\mathbf{W}, \mathbf{R}, \mathbb{D}, \mathbf{a^o}>$ is an ioS-model that obeys $\mathbf{a^i}(A)=\mathbf{a^o}(A)$.

Proof of the oi-Expansion Theorem. Given any oS-model $<\mathbf{W}, \mathbf{R}, \mathbb{D}, \mathbf{a^o}>$, consider its oi-expansion $<\mathbf{W}, \mathbf{R}, \mathbb{D}, \mathbf{I}, \mathbf{a^i}>$. Since the only difference in truth conditions between ioS-models and oS-models is in the treatment of $\forall$, all that is required to show that $\mathbf{a^i}(A)=\mathbf{a^o}(A)$ holds is to explain why $\mathbf{a^i}$ obeys (o$\forall$). But that follows from the oi Lemma. In the light of the definition of $\mathbf{I}$, (o) holds, and the fact that (RC) holds in oS-models ensures (cI).

(cI) $\mathbf{a}(c) \in \mathbf{I}$.

Since $\mathbf{W}, \mathbf{R}$, and $\mathbb{D}$ in the two models are the same, $<\mathbf{W}, \mathbf{R}, \mathbb{D}, \mathbf{I}, \mathbf{a^i}>$ will inherit the o-domain conditions of the oS-model. Therefore, $<\mathbf{W}, \mathbf{R}, \mathbb{D}, \mathbf{I}, \mathbf{a^i}>$ meets all the conditions to qualify as an ioS-model.

In the light of the last theorem, the equivalence of oS and ioS semantics is easily secured. This equivalence theorem guarantees that we may obtain exactly the effect of the objectual interpretation by considering instead intensional models that meet condition (o).

oi Equivalence Theorem. $H \nvDash_{oS} C$ iff $H \nvDash_{ioS} C$.

Proof of the oi Equivalence Theorem. If $H \nvDash_{oS} C$, with the result that $<\mathbf{W}, \mathbf{R}, \mathbb{D}, \mathbf{a^o}>$ is an oS-counterexample to H / C, then by the oi-Expansion Theorem, its oi-expansion $<\mathbf{W}, \mathbf{R}, \mathbb{D}, \mathbf{I}, \mathbf{a^i}>$ is an ioS-counterexample to H / C. For the proof in the other direction, suppose $H \nvDash_{ioS} C$; then the model $<\mathbf{W}, \mathbf{R}, \mathbb{D}, \mathbf{a^o}>$ defined by $\mathbf{a^o}(e)=\mathbf{a^i}(e)$ for all expressions e is a counterexample to H / C. Since the ioS-model obeys (o$\forall$) by the io Lemma, it follows that $<\mathbf{W}, \mathbf{R}, \mathbb{D}, \mathbf{a^o}>$ obeys (o$\forall$), and so qualifies as an oS-counterexample to H / C. Since the two models differ only in that $\mathbf{I}$ is absent in $<\mathbf{W}, \mathbf{R}, \mathbb{D}, \mathbf{a^o}>$, and the o-domain conditions at issue do not mention $\mathbf{I}$, the latter model qualifies as an oS-counterexample to H / C, that is, $H \nvDash_{oS} C$.

15.7. Transfer Theorems for Intensional and Substitution Models

In this section, it will be shown how to transfer completeness results for truth value semantics to intensional semantics. The transfer theorems to be proven here state that once the completeness of system S for tS-validity has been shown, one can exploit that result to obtain a proof of the completeness of S for iS-validity and also for sS-validity. The proof of these transfer theorems will depend on an expansion theorem that links certain tS-models with corresponding iS-models. It is easy to tie together two previously shown expansion results to demonstrate that a tS-model can be expanded into a corresponding iS-model. The *ti-expansion* of a tS-model is simply the result of constructing its ts-expansion and then taking the si-expansion of the result. Putting the ts- and si-expansion theorems together, it follows that the ti-expansion $<$**W**, **R**, $\mathbb{D}$, **I**, **a**$>$ of any tS-model $<$**W**, **R**, $\mathbf{a^t}>$ that obeys ($\exists$c) is an iS-model that obeys $\mathbf{a^t}(A)=\mathbf{a}(A)$. However, this result dealt only with systems that are the result of adding propositional modal logic axioms to fK.

In Section 13.6, axioms and a rule were introduced that correspond to various conditions on the domains of quantification. A list of some of those *domain rules* along with their corresponding conditions follows:

Domain Rules		**Corresponding Domain Conditions**
($\exists$E)	$\exists$xEx	For some i $\in$ **I**, i(**w**) $\in$ **Dw**.
(Q)	Et	**Dw=D**.
(ED)	Ec$\rightarrow\Box$Ec	If **wRv** and $\mathbf{a_w}$(c) $\in$ **Dw**, then $\mathbf{a_v}$(c) $\in$ **Dv**.
(CD)	$\sim$Ec$\rightarrow\Box\sim$Ec	If **wRv** and $\mathbf{a_v}$(c) $\in$ **Dv**, then $\mathbf{a_w}$(c) $\in$ **Dw**.
(RC)	(b$\approx$c$\rightarrow\Box$b$\approx$c)& ($\sim$b$\approx$c$\rightarrow\Box\sim$b$\approx$c)	$\mathbf{a_w}$(c)=$\mathbf{a_v}$(c).
($\exists$i)	L $\vdash$ $\sim$t$\approx$c / L $\vdash$ $\bot$, no c in L, t	For some i $\in$ **I**, i(**w**)=$\mathbf{a_w}$(t).
(o)=(RC)+($\exists$i)		**I** is the set of all constant functions with values in **D**.
(o$\exists$E)=(o)+($\exists$E)		(o) + **Dw** is not empty.
(oED)=(o)+(ED)		(o) + if **wRv**, then **Dw** $\subseteq$ **Dv**.
(oCD)=(o)+(CD)		(o) + if **wRv**, then **Dv** $\subseteq$ **Dw**.

We intend to prove a ti-Expansion Theorem for systems that include domain rules. This will be helpful in providing completeness results for the stronger systems so constructed, which accommodate nonrigid terms. A difficulty to be faced in doing so is that it makes no sense to speak of tS-models meeting the domain conditions, because truth value models do not have any domains. However, there is a way around the problem. Let us say that an *axiom A is satisfied on a model* iff its assignment function assigns A the value T in all the possible worlds. Now let S be a system that results from adding to fK axioms for a propositional modal logic, and any selection of the above domain *axioms*: (∃E), (Q), (ED), (CD), and (RC). A *tS-model is now understood to be* any tK-model <**W**, **R**, **a**^{t}> that obeys (∃c), the frame conditions for the propositional modal logic axioms of S, satisfies its domain axioms, and also meets condition (r) if axiom (RC) is in S.

(∃c)   For teach term t, there is a constant c such that **a**^t_w(t≈c)=T.
(r)   If **a**^t_w(b≈c)=T then **a**^t_v(b≈c)=T.

Let us say that an axiom A *expresses its condition* iff whenever A is satisfied in any tS-model, its corresponding condition holds in that model's ti-expansion. In order to establish the expansion theorem, we will first prove that the domain axioms all express their corresponding conditions. (The reason we are forced to mention (r) in the definition of a tS-model is that without it (RC) does not express its corresponding condition.) We were forced to mention (∃c) because it is needed in order to use the ts-Expansion Theorem in the course of the proof of the ti-Expansion Theorem below.

Expression Theorem.   Each domain axiom of S expresses its corresponding condition.

Proof of the Expression Theorem. We need to show that the corresponding condition for each domain axiom of S holds in the ti-expansion of a tS-model that satisfies that axiom. Note that since a tS-model now obeys (∃c) by definition, it follows from the ts- and si- expansion theorems that the ti-expansion <**W**, **R**, $\mathbb{D}$, **I**, **a**> of a tS-model <**W**, **R**, **a**^{t}> agrees with it on the values for the sentences. Therefore, the ti-expansion will also satisfy any given domain axiom. Further useful facts about the assignment function **a** for the ti-expansion are stated here for ease of reference. They all follow directly from the definitions of ts- and si-expansions.

(**at**)   c ∈ **a**$_w$(t) iff c is a constant such that **a**$_w$(t≈c)=T.
(**aD**)   d ∈ **D** iff for some term t and some world **w**, d=**a**$_w$(t).
(**aDw**)   d ∈ **Dw** iff for some term t, d=**a**$_w$(t) and **a**$_w$(Et)=T.
(**aI**)   i ∈ **I** iff for some constant c, i=**a**(c).

Now we are ready to show that satisfaction of each axiom in the ti-expansion entails the corresponding condition on the domains.

(∃E)   ∃xEx   For some i ∈ **I**, i(**w**) ∈ **Dw**.

The axiom is satisfied by **a**, so we have $a_w(∃xEx)=T$. By (i∃), $a_w(Ei)=T$ for some i ∈ **I** such that i(**w**) ∈ **Dw**.

(Q)   Et   **Dw=D**.

In this case we have $a_w(Et)=T$. To prove **Dw=D**, it must be shown that d is in **Dw** exactly when d is in **D**. Since **Dw** is by definitions (**aD**) and (**aDw**) a subset of **D**, it follows that d is in **D** whenever d is in **Dw**. So all that remains is to show that assuming d is in **D**, it follows that d is in **Dw**. But if d is in **D**, it follows by (**aD**) that for some term t, $d=a_w(t)$. But $a_w(Et)=T$ together with (Pl) and (E) entails that $a_w(t)=d$ is in **Dw**.

(ED)   Ec→□Ec   If **wRv** and $a_w(c) ∈ D_w$, then $a_v(c) ∈ D_v$.

> **EXERCISE *15.7**   Complete the case for (ED). (Hint. Model your demonstration on the proof for (CD) given below.)

(CD)   ~Ec→□~Ec   If **wRv** and $a_v(c) ∈ Dv$, then $a_w(c) ∈ Dw$.

To prove the condition, assume **wRv** and $a_v(c) ∈ Dv$, and then prove $a_w(c) ∈ Dw$ as follows. Suppose for indirect proof that $a_w(c) ∉ Dw$. By (~), (Pl), and (E), $a_w(Ec)=F$, hence $a_w(~Ec)=T$. By $a_w(~Ec→□~Ec)=T$ and (→), $a_w(□~Ec)=T$ and so $a_v(~Ec)=T$ by **wRv** and (□). But by (~), (Pl), and (E), $a_v(c) ∉ Dw$, which contradicts $a_v(c) ∈ Dv$.

(RC)   (b≈c→□b≈c)&(~b≈c→□~b≈c) $a_w(c)=a_v(c)$.

Note that when (RC) is in the system, condition (r) holds. Two special cases of this condition yield (riff).

(r)   If $a_w(b≈c)=T$, then $a_v(b≈c)=T$.
(riff)   If $a_w(c≈b)=T$, then $a_v(c≈b)=T$, and if $a_v(c≈b)=T$ then $a_w(c≈b)=T$.

Therefore $a_w(c)=a_v(c)$ holds by the following reasoning:

$a_w(c≈b)=T$ iff $a_v(c≈b)=T$, for any b.	by (riff)
$b ∈ a_w(c)$ iff $b ∈ a_v(c)$, for any b.	two uses of (**at**)
$a_w(c)=a_v(c)$.	previous step, since $a_w(c)$ and $a_v(c)$ have the same members.

(∃i) $L \vdash \sim t \approx c / L \vdash \bot$, no c in L, t   For some $i \in I$, $i(\mathbf{w}) = \mathbf{a_w}(t)$.

To prove the condition, note that condition (∃c) holds by the definition of a tS-model. So there is a constant c such that $\mathbf{a_w}(t \approx c) = T$, and so by ($\approx$), $\mathbf{a_w}(t) = \mathbf{a_w}(c)$. It follows from (cI) that $\mathbf{a}(c) \in I$. So when i is $\mathbf{a}(c)$, there is an $i \in I$ such that $i(\mathbf{w}) = \mathbf{a_w}(t)$.

(o)=(RC)+(∃i)   **I** is the set of all constant functions with values in **D**.

To prove the condition, we will first show that every member of **I** is a constant function. Suppose $i \in I$. By (**aI**), $i = \mathbf{a}(c)$ for some constant c. But the reasoning for (RC) above guarantees that $\mathbf{a}(c)$ is a constant function. Next we will show that for each $d \in D$, there is a member $i \in I$ such that $i(\mathbf{w}) = d$. This follows because when $d \in D$, it follows by (**aD**) that for some term t, $d = \mathbf{a_w}(t)$. By the reasoning for (∃i) above, there is a member i of **I** such that $i(\mathbf{w}) = \mathbf{a_w}(t) = d$.

(o∃E)=(o)+(∃E)   (o) + **Dw** is not empty.

It was shown above that axiom (o) expresses condition (o). To prove **Dw** is not empty, note that we have already shown above that axiom (∃E) expresses the condition that for some $i \in I$, $i(\mathbf{w}) \in \mathbf{Dw}$.

(oED)=(o)+(ED)   (o) + if **wRv**, then $\mathbf{Dw} \subseteq \mathbf{Dv}$.

It was already shown that axiom (o) expresses condition (o). Now assume **wRv** and $d \in \mathbf{Dw}$ and prove that $d \in \mathbf{Dv}$ as follows. By (**aD**), we know that there is a term t and a world u such that $\mathbf{a_u}(t) = d$; but by (∃c) and ($\approx$), there is a constant c such that $\mathbf{a_u}(c) = \mathbf{a_u}(t) = d$. But (o) and (cI) guarantee that $\mathbf{a}(c)$ is a constant function. It follows that $\mathbf{a_w}(c) = \mathbf{a_v}(c) = \mathbf{a_u}(c) = d$, and so $\mathbf{a_w}(c) \in \mathbf{Dw}$. We already showed that (ED) expresses that if **wRv**, then if $\mathbf{a_w}(c) \in \mathbf{Dw}$ then $\mathbf{a_v}(c) \in \mathbf{Dv}$. So $\mathbf{a_v}(c) \in \mathbf{Dv}$. Since $\mathbf{a_v}(c) = d$, $d \in \mathbf{Dv}$ as desired.

EXERCISE *15.8   Complete the case for (oCD).

---

ti-Expansion Theorem.   The ti-expansion <**W**, **R**, $\mathbb{D}$, **I**, $\mathbf{a^i}$> of any tS-model <**W**, **R**, $\mathbf{a^t}$> is an iS-model that obeys $\mathbf{a^t}(A) = \mathbf{a^i}(A)$.

Proof of the ti-Expansion Theorem. Note that by definition, any tS-model <**W**, **R**, $\mathbf{a^t}$> obeys (∃c), so given <**W**, **R**, $\mathbf{a^t}$> use the ts-Expansion Theorem and the si-Expansion Theorem to show that the ti-expansion <**W**, **R**, $\mathbb{D}$, **I**, $\mathbf{a^i}$> of the tS-model obeys $\mathbf{a^t}(A) = \mathbf{a^i}(A)$. Since the two models have the same frames, the ti-expansion inherits the frame conditions for system S. Since the domain axioms of S are all satisfied in the tS-model, the fact that each axiom expresses its corresponding condition guarantees that the ti-expansion satisfies those corresponding conditions, and so it qualifies as an iS-model.

As stated, the ti-Expansion Theorem applies only to systems that result from adding the domain axioms on the above list to a quantified modal logic. However, in Chapters 18 and 19, we will consider new axioms, each of which expresses a corresponding condition. Since the proof of the ti-Expansion Theorem requires only that the axioms express their corresponding conditions, it will continue to hold when S includes these new axioms as well.

The ti-Expansion Theorem will be useful because it provides a method for transferring completeness proofs for truth value semantics to results for the intensional interpretation and the substitution interpretation, and to the objectual interpretation as well. Suppose we wish to show the completeness of some system S with respect to iS-models. Then all that will be necessary is to show the completeness with respect to the much simpler tS-models instead.

i Transfer Theorem. If system S is complete for tS-models, S is also complete with respect to iS-models.

Proof of the i Transfer Theorem. Assume S is complete for tS-models. To show that S is complete for iS-models, assume H $\nvdash_S$ C and prove H $\nvDash_{iS}$ C as follows. By the completeness of S with respect to tS-models it follows from H $\nvdash_S$ C that there is a tS-counterexample $<\mathbf{W}, \mathbf{R}, \mathbf{a}^t>$ to H / C. But by the ti-Expansion Theorem, the ti-expansion of $<\mathbf{W}, \mathbf{R}, \mathbf{a}^t>$ is an iS-counterexample to H / C, that is, H $\nvDash_{iS}$ C.

The close affinities between the intensional and substitution interpretations have already been noted. The next theorem shows that completeness results for tS-models transfer to the case of sS-models as well. Suppose that S is a system constructed from fK by adding propositional modal logic axioms and any of the domain axioms whose corresponding conditions fail to mention the domain **I**. Then the following theorem shows that completeness of S for sS-models follows from completeness for tS-models.

s Transfer Theorem. If system S is complete for tS-models, S is also complete with respect to sS-models.

Proof of the s Transfer Theorem. Assume S is complete for tS-models. To show that S is complete for sS-models, we prove the contrapositive. Assume H $\nvdash_S$ C and prove H $\nvDash_{sS}$ C as follows. By the completeness of

S with respect to tS-models it follows from H $\nvdash_S$ C that there is a tS-counterexample <**W**, **R**, **a**^{t}> to H / C. By the ti-Expansion Theorem, the ti-expansion <**W**, **R**, $\mathbb{D}$, **I**, **a**> of <**W**, **R**, **a**^{t}> is an iS-counterexample to H / C. Note that by (**aI**), this model obeys (s), so by the si Lemma of Section 15.5, it obeys ($\forall$), the substitution interpretation truth clause.

(s)   i $\in$ **I** iff for some constant c, i=**a**(c).
si Lemma.   Any iS-model that obeys (s) also obeys ($\forall$).

Now consider <**W**, **R**, $\mathbb{D}$, **a**>, the model that results from removing the domain **I** from the ti-expansion. The result is clearly an sS-counterexample to H / C, because the only difference between sS-models and iS-models is in the quantifier truth condition and the presence or absence of **I**. It follows that H $\nvdash_{sS}$ C as desired.

15.8. A Transfer Theorem for the Objectual Interpretation

A transfer theorem for the objectual interpretation can be shown with the help of a special case of the i Transfer Theorem. Let oS be a system that includes axiom (RC) and the rule ($\exists$i) in case there are nonrigid terms in the language. Note that by the definition of a tS-model, a *toS-model* for this system oS will satisfy both ($\exists$c) and (r).

($\exists$c)   For teach term t, there is a constant c such that **a**$_w$(t$\approx$c)=T.
(r)   If **a**$_w$(b$\approx$c)=T, then **a**$_v$(b$\approx$c)=T.

In the course of proving the i Transfer Theorem, it was shown that the ti-expansion of such a toS-model is an *ioS-model*, an iS-model that obeys the condition (o) stating that **I** contains exactly the constant functions with values in **D**. So the following result is immediate.

io Transfer Theorem.   If system oS is complete for toS-models, oS is also complete with respect to ioS-models.

The oi Equivalence Theorem of Section 15.6 established that ioS-validity and oS-validity are equivalent. So the transfer result for oS-models follows immediately.

o Transfer Theorem.   If oS is complete for toS-models, oS is also complete with respect to oS-models.

EXERCISE 15.9   Explain why the io Transfer Theorem is a special case of the i Transfer Theorem and then prove the o Transfer Theorem.

The o Transfer Theorem can be easily extended to systems that include new axioms to be introduced in later chapters. If nS is a system that results from adding *n*ew axioms to oS, each of which expresses its corresponding condition on oS-models, the reasoning of the ti-Expansion Theorem will extend to nS, and so the o Transfer Theorem will hold for nS as well. Presuming that a tnS-model is a toS-model that satisfies the new axioms, and a nS-model is an oS-model that satisfies the corresponding conditions for those axioms, we have the following:

> **Extended o Transfer Theorem.**   If nS results from adding axioms to oS, each of which expresses its corresponding condition, and if nS is complete for tnS-models, then nS is complete for nS-models.

EXERCISE 15.10   Prove the Extended o Transfer Theorem.

15.9. Soundness for the Substitution Interpretation

The proof of the ti-Expansion Theorem illustrates the close kinships between the substitution and intensional interpretations. This relationship can be exploited to show the soundness of S for truth value models, a result that is otherwise tedious to prove. The contrapositive of the ti-Expansion Theorem entails that if an argument is iS-valid, then it is also tS-valid. This result with the soundness of S for the intensional interpretation will provide everything we need. Remember that in tS-models, it makes no sense to enforce domain conditions since tS-models do not have any domains. When domain rules were included in system S, the definition of a tS-model was expanded in an *ad hoc* way to include the condition that any domain axioms were satisfied in the tS-model, that it obeyed ($\exists$c), and that it obeyed condition (r) if axiom (RC) is in S. Since there is no point in showing soundness of a system for these artificial conditions, let us assume for simplicity that system S does not contain any of the domain rules, so that the original conception of a tS-model is at issue in this section.

> **Soundness of S for Truth Value Models.**   If H $\vdash_S$ C then H $\vDash_{tS}$ C.

Proof. Suppose that H ⊢$_S$ C. By the soundness of S on the intensional interpretation (proven in Section 15.2) it follows that H ⊨$_{iS}$ C. Suppose that H ⊭$_{tS}$ C for Indirect Proof. Then H / C has a tS-counterexample <**W, R, a**>. By the ti-Expansion Theorem, the ti-expansion of <**W, R, a**> is an iS-counterexample to H / C, which contradicts H ⊨$_{iS}$ C.

Now that the proof of the soundness of S for truth value (tS) models is available, the proof of the soundness of S for sS-models is a direct result of the ts Equivalence Theorem of Section 15.4, which states that H ⊨$_{tS}$ C iff H ⊨$_{sS}$ C.

Soundness of S for Substitution Models.   If H ⊢$_S$ C then H ⊨$_{sS}$ C.

Although domain conditions make no sense in the context of tS-models, sS-models do include the domains **D** and **Dw**. It is a simple matter to expand the soundness result for systems that include domain axioms whose corresponding conditions mention these domains by showing that those axioms are sS-valid when the conditions are met.

EXERCISE 15.11   Show that axioms (Q), (ED), (CD), and (RC) are sS-valid when their corresponding conditions hold in sS-models. (Hint: Just "borrow" the proofs for the case of iS-models found in Section 15.3.)

15.10. Soundness for the Objectual Interpretation

The system oS was designed to manage the objectual interpretation, even when nonrigid terms are in the language. It results from adding to fS the axiom (RC) to make sure that the constants are rigid, and rule (∃i) to allow constants and nonrigid terms to interact in the right way when the latter are present. Assume that any of the domain axioms in the previous section might also be included in oS. The oS-soundness of oS may be shown by demonstrating that (∀Out), (∀In), (RC), and (∃i) and the domain axioms all preserve oS-validity. (The demonstrations for the ≈ rules are the same as those given for the soundness of iS.) However, in light of the oi Equivalence Theorem, there is a faster way to show the soundness of oS.

Soundness of oS.   If H ⊢$_{oS}$ C then H ⊨$_{oS}$ C.

Proof of the Soundness of oS. Suppose H ⊢$_{oS}$ C. Then H ⊨$_{ioS}$ C by the soundness proofs given in Section 15.3. By the oi Equivalence Theorem, H ⊨$_{oS}$ C.

Although this provides a quick result, it is an instructive exercise to prove the soundness of oS directly by verifying that all the rules of oS preserve oS-validity. That project is left to the next exercise.

EXERCISE 15.12   Verify that the rules of oS preserve oS-validity. (Hint: Review the cases for showing that the rules of S preserve iS-validity, making modifications as necessary. Note that the Rigid Instance Theorem was shown only for iS-models, so a new proof will be needed for oS-models.)

15.11. Systems with Nonrigid Terms

This section concerns what happens when (in addition to the constants) a set N of (possibly) nonrigid terms $n_1, n_2, .., n_i, ..$ is added to the language. In systems that that do not adopt (RC), there is no motivation for adding N, because the constants are nonrigid and may serve already for nonrigid expressions.

(RC) $(b{\approx}c{\rightarrow}\Box b{\approx}c)\&({\sim}b{\approx}c{\rightarrow}\Box{\sim}b{\approx}c)$

So assume that N is added to systems for the objectual interpretation that include (RC), where the constants are rigid. This will mean that terms in C (rigid) and those in N (nonrigid) have different logical behavior.

The first issue to resolve about the new terms is whether we should broaden ($\forall$Out) (the rule of universal instantiation) to (t$\forall$) so that instantiation is possible for all the terms including those in N.

(t$\forall$) $\forall xAx{\rightarrow}(Et{\rightarrow}At)$

It is possible to show that (t$\forall$) corresponds to the semantical condition that $\mathbf{a}(t) \in \mathbf{I}$. This means that the intension of every term t (including the nonrigid ones) is a substance, that is, an entity such as Benjamin Franklin, rather than a motley picked out by expressions such as "the inventor of bifocals." (See the discussion of substance in Section 13.6.) But in systems rS and oS, $\mathbf{I}$ is a set of constant functions. This suggests that for a new term n to satisfy $\mathbf{a}(n) \in \mathbf{I}$, its intension $\mathbf{a}(n)$ must be rigid, that is, it must pick out the same entity (Benjamin Franklin) in each possible world. But that conflicts with our decision that the new terms be nonrigid. It would seem that there is a fundamental conflict in any system that adopts (t$\forall$) with nonrigid terms, and this would appear supported by the fact that (t$\forall$) is invalid on the objectual interpretation.

However, (t∀) may make more sense given the intensional interpretation of the quantifier. This is easiest to appreciate in tense logic where the extension $a_w(n)$ of a term n is understood to be a time slice (at time **w**) of a temporally extended individual. (See the discussion in Section 13.8.) Then it would be possible for the intension of a term $a(n)$ to be nonrigid, while at the same time picking out a substance comprised of a unified collection of time slices. If it is presumed that such nonrigid terms always have intensions that count as substances, then (∀t) may be accepted. However, note that the adoption of (RC) seems incompatible with this choice, for the requirement (cI) that $a(c) \in I$ means that substances correspond to constant functions. The upshot is that the correct systems for a semantics of this kind would be ones that already reject (RC), in which case there is no need for any new nonrigid terms.

Since there is little motivation for systems that adopt (t∀), they will be treated only in the exercise below. Proofs of soundness are straightforward, and the ti-Transfer Theorem can be established for them by revising theorems in Section 15.4 and 15.4, replacing mention of C with the set T of terms throughout.

EXERCISE 15.13

a) Show that (t∀) is iS-valid when iS-models obey the condition $a(t) \in I$.

b) Prove the ti-Transfer Theorem for systems that include (t∀) and the condition $a(t) \in I$. (Hint: Note that tS-models that satisfy (t∀) automatically obey $a_w(∀xAx)=T$ iff for every *term t*, if $a_w(Et)=T$ then $a_w(At)=T$. The ti-expansion should now be defined so that $i \in I$ iff for some *term t*, $i=a(t)$. Note that (∃c) will be guaranteed under these circumstances since it claims that $a_w(t≈s)=T$ for some *term s*, which is trivial since the term s can be t.)

c) Explore what happens in the proof of the transfer theorem of b) for systems that adopt both (o) and $a(t) \in I$. What strengthening of (r) will be necessary to obtain the result that the ti-expansion obeys (o)? What variation on (RC) is going to be necessary to obtain completeness for such systems?

15.12. Appendix: Proof of the Replacement Theorems

Here we prove in detail the theorems about replacement used in this chapter. Accurate statement and proof of these theorem will require use of the official notation for substitution. So instead of writing: At, the full-dress notation will be employed: $[A]^t/x$. Let a g-term (for generalized term) be any term, any object in **D** or any individual concept, (i.e., a function from **W** into **D**). First, a formal definition of $[e]^g/x$ must be given, where e is any expression (including expressions formed from g-terms), g is any g-term, and x is any variable. We will use 'l' for any list of g-terms, 'P' for any predicate letter, including E or $\approx$, and 'A' and 'B' for any sentences including hybrids.

$[x]^g/x = g$.

$[e]^g/x = e$, when $e \neq x$.

$[\bot]^g/x = \bot$.

$[l, s]^g/x = [l]^g/x, [s]^g/x$, where s is any g-term.

$[Pl]^g/x = P[l]^g/x$.

$[A \rightarrow B]^g/x = [A]^g/x \rightarrow [B]^g/x$.

$[\Box A]^g/x = \Box[A]^g/x$.

$[\forall x A]^g/x = \forall x A$. (x is bound, so no substitution is carried out.)

$[\forall y A]^g/x = \forall y [A]^g/x$, when $x \neq y$.

Our next project will be to establish a simple lemma about multiple substitution, which will be useful for the theorems to come.

Order Lemma. If $x \neq y$, then $[[e]^i/x]^g/y = [[e]^g/y]^i/x$ where i is any individual concept.

Proof of the Order Lemma. The proof is by induction on the structure of e. When e is a term or a variable other than x or y, $[[e]^i/x]^g/y = e = [[e]^g/y]^i/x$. When e is x, $[[x]^i/x]^g/y = [i]^g/y = i = [x]^i/x = [[x]^g/y]^i/x$, and the proof is similar when e is y. Once the lemma is established for all terms or variables e, the result can easily be extended to lists and all sentences. The only case of any interest involves the quantifier. So suppose that $e = \forall z B$. We must show that $[[\forall z B]^i/x]^g/y = [[\forall z B]^g/y]^i/x$. Suppose that $x \neq z$ and $y \neq z$. Then $[[\forall z B]^i/x]^g/y = \forall z[[B]^i/x]^g/y$. By the inductive hypothesis, we have $[[B]^i/x]^g/y = [[B]^g/y]^i/x$. This with $[[\forall z B]^g/y]^i/x = \forall z[[B]^g/y]^i/x$ ensures that $[[\forall z B]^i/x]^g/y = [[\forall z B]^g/y]^i/x$ as desired. Now suppose that $x = z$, which by $x \neq y$ means that $y \neq z$. Then $[\forall z B]^i/x = [\forall x B]^i/x = \forall x B$. So $[[\forall z B]^i/x]^g/y = [\forall x B]^g/y = \forall x[B]^g/y$, since $y \neq x$. Furthermore, $[[\forall z B]^g/y]^i/x = [[\forall x B]^g/y]^i/x = [\forall x[B]^g/y]^i/x = \forall x[B]^g/y$ also. So we have $[[\forall z B]^i/x]^g/y = [[\forall z B]^g/y]^i/x$ in this case. The remaining case, where $y = z$, is similar. $\Box$

EXERCISE 15.14 Show that $[[\forall z B]^i/x]^g/y = [[\forall z B]^g/y]^i/x$ when $y = z$. Now give the proof of the Order Lemma in full detail.

We are now ready to state and prove the Intensional and Rigid Instance Theorems for iS-models. In order to save tedious repetition, it will be convenient to complete the demonstrations together by proving a more general claim. As we pointed out in Section 13.4, there is no need to include world subscripts when we write the extension of a rigid constant c. So '$a(t)$' may be used to indicate the *extension* of a rigid term t, since that extension does not depend on **w**. Under these circumstances, '$a(t)=d$' would indicate that t is a rigid term, whose extension is the object d. Using this notation, a general instance theorem may be stated as follows.

Instance Theorem.
If $a(t)=g$ then, $a_w([A]^t/x) = a_w([A]^g/x)$ for all $w \in W$.

When g ranges over **D**, so that '$a(t)=g$' indicates that t is a rigid constant, this result amounts to the Rigid Instance Theorem. When g ranges over individual concepts, the Intensional Instance Theorem is obtained. Note that when g is a member d of **D**, (d) guarantees $a_w(g)=g$. Since $a_w(g)=g=a_v(g)$, we may drop the subscript and write: $a(g)=g$. When g is an individual concept, (f) also guarantees $a(g)=g$.

(d) $a_w(d)=d$.
(f) $a_w(f)=f_w$.

Proof of the Instance Theorem. To show the Instance Theorem, assume $a(t)=g$, and then prove $a([A]^t/x) = a([A]^g/x)$ by induction on the length of A.

Case 1. A is an atom. Then A is $\bot$ or has the form Pl. (Since E and $\approx$ are considered to be predicate letters, atoms with shapes Et and $s \approx t$ are included in this case.)

When A is $\bot$, the proof is easy since $[\bot]^t/x=[\bot]^g/x$.

In case A has the form Pl, remember that $[x]^t/x = t$ and $[s]^t/x = s$ when s is not x. So it is easy to see that $a([s]^t/x) = a([s]^g/x)$ for any g-term s, for when s is not x, $[s]^t/x = s = [s]^g/x$, and when $s=x$, $a([s]^t/x) = a(t) = g = a(g) = a([s]^g/x)$. Since $a([s]^t/x) = a([s]^g/x)$ holds for all g-terms s, it follows that the corresponding property holds for lists of terms: $a([l]^t/x) = a([l]^g/x)$. Now let **w** be any member of **W**. It is not difficult to show

$\mathbf{a_w}([Pl]^t/x) = \mathbf{a_w}([Pl]^g/x)$ as follows:

$\mathbf{a_w}([Pl]^t/x)=T$
iff $\mathbf{a_w}(P[l]^t/x)=T$ $[Pl]^t/x=P[l]^t/x$
iff $\mathbf{a_w}([l]^t/x) \in \mathbf{a_w}(P)$ (Pl)
iff $\mathbf{a_w}([l]^g/x) \in \mathbf{a_w}(P)$ $\mathbf{a}([l]^t/x)=\mathbf{a}([l]^g/x)$
iff $\mathbf{a_w}(P[l]^g/x)=T$ (Pl)
iff $\mathbf{a_w}([Pl]^g/x)=t.$ $[Pl]^g/x=P[l]^g/x$

Case 2. A has the form B→C. We must show $\mathbf{a_w}([B{\to}C]^t/x)=T$ iff $\mathbf{a_w}([B{\to}C]^g/x)=T$ for all **w** in **W**. This is done as follows:

$\mathbf{a_w}([B{\to}C]^t/x)=T$
iff $\mathbf{a_w}([B]^t/x{\to}[C]^t/x)=T$ $[B{\to}C]^t/x=[B]^t/x{\to}[C]^t/x$
iff $\mathbf{a_w}([B]^t/x)=F$ or $\mathbf{a_w}([C]^t/x)=T$ (→)
iff $\mathbf{a_w}([B]^g/x)=F$ or $\mathbf{a_w}([C]^g/x)=T$ Inductive Hypothesis
iff $\mathbf{a_w}([B]^g/x{\to}[C]^g/x)=T$ (→)
iff $\mathbf{a_w}([B{\to}C]^g/x)=T.$ $[B{\to}C]^g/x=[B]^g/x{\to}[C]^g/x$

Case 3. A has the form □B. We show $\mathbf{a_w}([\Box B]^t/x)=T$ iff $\mathbf{a_w}([\Box B]^g/x)=T$ for all **w** in **W** as follows:

$\mathbf{a_w}([\Box B]^t/x)=T$
iff $\mathbf{a_w}(\Box[B]^t/x)=T$ $[\Box B]^t/x=\Box[B]^t/x$
iff if **wRv**, then $\mathbf{a_v}([B]^t/x)=T$ (□)
iff if **wRv**, then $\mathbf{a_v}([B]^g/x)=T$ Inductive Hypothesis
iff $\mathbf{a_w}(\Box[B]^g/x)=T$ (□)
iff $\mathbf{a_w}([\Box B]^g/x)=T.$ $[\Box B]^g/x=\Box[B]^g/x$

Case 4. A has the form ∀yB. We show $\mathbf{a_w}([\forall yB]^t/x)=T$ iff $\mathbf{a_w}([\forall yB]^g/x)=T$ for all **w** in **W** as follows. Assume first that x=y. Then $[\forall yB]^t/x = \forall yB = [\forall yB]^g/x$, so clearly $\mathbf{a_w}([\forall yB]^t/x)=T$ iff $\mathbf{a_w}([\forall yB]^g/x)=T$ in this case. Now assume x≠y. We show $\mathbf{a_w}([\forall yB]^t/x)=T$ iff $\mathbf{a_w}([\forall yB]^g/x)=T$ as follows:

$\mathbf{a_w}([\forall yB]^t/x)=T$
iff $\mathbf{a_w}(\forall y[B]^t/x)=T$ $[\forall yB]^t/x=\forall y[B]^t/x$ for x≠y
iff if $i \in \mathbf{I}$ and $i(\mathbf{w}) \in \mathbf{D}w$, then $\mathbf{a_w}(([B]^t/x]^i/y)=T$ (i∀)

iff if i $\in$ **I** and i(**w**) $\in$ **Dw**, then $\mathbf{a_w}([[B]^i/y]^t/x)=T$ Order Lemma
iff if i $\in$ **I** and i(**w**) $\in$ **Dw**, then $\mathbf{a_w}([[B]^i/y]^g/x)=T$ Inductive Hypothesis
iff if i $\in$ **I** and i(**w**) $\in$ **Dw**, then $\mathbf{a_w}([[B]^g/x]^i/y)=T$ Order Lemma
iff $\mathbf{a_w}(\forall y[B]^g/x)=T$ (i$\forall$)
iff $\mathbf{a_w}([\forall yB]^g/x)=T$ $[\forall yB]^g/x=\forall y[B]^g/x$
      for x$\neq$y

This completes the proof of the Instance Theorem, and so the Intensional and Rigid Instance Theorems have been proven. We turn now to the proof of the No t Theorem.

No t Theorem. If two iS-models are identical with the exception that their respective assignment functions **a** and **b** disagree only on the value of a single term t, and A is a wff (or hybrid) where t does not appear, then $\mathbf{a_w}(A)=\mathbf{b_w}(A)$. Furthermore, if t is not in L, then $\mathbf{a_w}(L)=\mathbf{b_w}(L)$.

Proof of No t Theorem. The proof is by induction on the length of A. When A is atomic, the proof is easy, for when A has the form Pl and no t is in l, then $\mathbf{a_w}(l)=\mathbf{b_w}(l)$, which by (Pl) ensures that $\mathbf{a_w}(Pl)=\mathbf{b_w}(Pl)$. The inductive cases and the case for $\perp$ are all straightforward.

EXERCISE 15.15   Prove the inductive cases for the No t Theorem.

16

Completeness of Quantified Modal Logics Using Trees

The completeness of quantified modal logics can be shown with the tree method by modifying the strategy used in propositional modal logic. Section 8.4 explains how to use trees to demonstrate the completeness of propositional modal logics S that result from adding one or more of the following axioms to K: (D), (M), (4), (B), (5), (CD). In this chapter, the tree method will be extended to quantified modal logics based on the same propositional modal logics. The reader may want to review Sections 8.3 and 8.4 now, since details there will be central to this discussion. The fundamental idea is to show that every S-valid argument is provable in S in two stages. Assuming that H / C is S-valid, use the Tree Model Theorem (of Section 8.3) to prove that the S-tree for H / C closes. Then use the method for converting closed S-trees into proofs to construct a proof in S of H / C from the closed S-tree. This will show that any S-valid argument has a proof in S, which is, of course, what the completeness of S amounts to.

16.1. The Quantified Tree Model Theorem

In order to demonstrate completeness for quantified modal logics, a quantified version of the Tree Model Theorem will be developed here. This will also be useful in showing the correctness of trees for the quantified systems. Proofs of the appropriate tree model theorems are complicated by the fact that there are so many different systems to be considered in quantified modal logic. Several different interpretations of the quantifiers have been developed. However, the transfer theorems proven in Sections 15.7 and 15.8 show how results for all these systems can be obtained from a proof of completeness for truth value models (tS-models). So a demonstration of the Tree Model Theorem will be given for tS-validity. Let us assume that S is a system that results from adding any collection of the modal logic axioms (D), (M), (4), (B), (5), and (CD) to fK and any of the principles in the below list:

(∃E)   ∃xEx
(Q)   Et
(ED) $Ec \rightarrow \Box Ec$
(CD) $\sim Ec \rightarrow \Box \sim Ec$
(t∀) $\forall x Ax \rightarrow (Et \rightarrow At)$
(RC) $(b \approx c \rightarrow \Box b \approx c)$ & $(\sim b \approx c \rightarrow \Box \sim b \approx c)$
(∃i) $L \vdash \sim t \approx c / L \vdash \bot$, provided c is not in L or t

Assume the S-tree is constructed according to the instructions in Section 14.6. Finally, *it is a requirement on S that if the language contains terms other than the constants, then the rule (∃i) must be included in S.*

For each of these systems S, the corresponding tS-model is defined so that a *tS-model* <**W**, **R**, **a**> is any tK-model that obeys (∃c), obeys the frame conditions for the rules of S, satisfies each domain axiom of S, and (r) if (RC) is in S.

(∃c)   For teach term t, there is a constant c such that $\mathbf{a_w}(t \approx c) = T$.
(r)   If $\mathbf{a_w}(b \approx c) = T$ then $\mathbf{a_v}(b \approx c) = T$.

For simplicity in the proof, the tree model theorem formulated here asserts the contrapositive of the claim that every tS-valid argument had a closed S-tree.

Quantified Tree Model Theorem.
If the S-tree for H / C is open, then $H \nvDash_{tS} C$.

Proof of the Quantified Tree Model Theorem. Assume the S-tree for H / C has an open branch. The basic strategy of the proof is to construct the tree model for that branch that is a S-counterexample to H / C. The *tree model* (for an open branch) <**W**, **R**, **a**> is defined as follows. **W** is the set of all worlds on the open branch. **R** is defined so that **wRv** iff there is an arrow in the tree from **w** to **v**. The assignment function **a** is defined for a language that contains exactly those terms and predicate letters that appear in the open branch. It assigns values to *atomic sentences* A (sentences with the forms ⊥, and Pl) so that $\mathbf{a_w}(A) = T$ iff A is in world **w**.

(**a**A)   If A is an atom, then $\mathbf{a_w}(A) = T$ iff A appears in **w**.

The truth values of the complex sentences are determined by $(\rightarrow)$, $(\Box)$, and $(\forall)$.

If we can show that the tree model is a tS-counterexample to H / C, the proof of the Quantified Tree Model Theorem will be complete. It should be clear that the principles for adding arrows to the S-tree ensure that the frame $<W, R>$ obeys the conditions for S. It satisfies the relevant truth conditions by definition. If we can establish that the domain rules are satisfied, that $(t\approx)$ and $(\exists c)$ hold, and that (r) holds if (RC) is in S, then the tree model will qualify as a tS-model.

To help establish that the tree model is a tS-counterexample to H / C, we will prove the Open Branch Lemma for a language that contains the quantifier. Remember that a sentence A is said to be *verified* iff whenever A appears in any world w in the tree, a assigns it true at w, (i.e., $a_w(A)=T$).

Open Branch Lemma.
Every sentence is verified on the tree model.

Once the Open Branch Lemma is in place, it is easy to see that $<W, R, a>$ qualifies as a tS-counterexample to H / C, for H and $\sim$C are found at the head of the opening world o of the tree, and so $a_o(H)=T$ and $a_o(C)=F$.

Proof of the Open Branch Lemma. The proof of this lemma proceeds almost exactly as it did in the case of propositional modal logic (Section 8.3). The proof is by mathematical induction on the size of a formula A, where size is defined by the number of symbols other than $\perp$ in A. The base case is proven as in the case for propositional logic. The only modification needed for the inductive case (IC) is to demonstrate cases where A has one of the forms $\forall xBx$ and $\sim\forall xBx$.

(IC)   If all sentences smaller in size than A are verified, so is A.

The proof of (IC) requires assuming (IH) and showing that it follows that A is verified.

(IH)   All sentences smaller in size than A are verified.

To say A is verified means that if A is in world w, then $a_w(A)=T$. So to prove that A is verified, assume (1) and prove $a_w(A)=T$.

(1)   A is in world w.

Cases 1–7 where A has one of the shapes Pl, ~Pl, ~~B, ~(B→C), ~□B, B→C, or □B are proven exactly as they were in propositional modal logic. (See Section 8.3.) Only two more cases remain.

Case 8. A has the form ~∀xBx. By (1), ~∀xBx is in **w**. (∀F) was applied to ~∀xBx to place Ec and ~Bc in **w** for some constant c new to the tree. The terms of the language are the terms present in the tree, so c is one of those terms. By (IH), both Ec and ~Bc are verified, and so $\mathbf{a_w}(Ec)=T$ and $\mathbf{a_w}(\sim Bc)=T$, hence $\mathbf{a_w}(Bc)=F$. So it is false that for every constant c, if $\mathbf{a_w}(Ec)=T$, then $\mathbf{a_w}(Bc)=T$. By (∀), $\mathbf{a_w}(\forall xBx)=F$. As a result, $\mathbf{a_w}(\sim\forall xBx)=T$, and hence A is verified.

Case 9. A has the form ∀xBx. By (1), we know that ∀xBx is in **w**. To show that ∀xBx is verified, we need to prove that $\mathbf{a_w}(\forall xBx)=T$ on the tree model. By (∀), $\mathbf{a_w}(\forall xBx)=T$ provided that for any constant c, if $\mathbf{a_w}(Ec)=T$ then $\mathbf{a_w}(Bc)=T$. So suppose that $\mathbf{a_w}(Ec)=T$ for one of those constants c. This case will be completed when we show $\mathbf{a_w}(Bc)=T$. Now Ec must be in **w**, because if Ec were not, then by the definition (**aA**), $\mathbf{a_w}(Ec)$ would be F, which it is not. Since Ec is in **w**, it follows by (∀T) that Bc must be in **w**, and since Bc is shorter than A, it is verified by (IH). It follows that $\mathbf{a_w}(Bc)=T$. We have completed the proof that if $\mathbf{a_w}(Ec)=T$ then $\mathbf{a_w}(Bc)=T$ for every constant c in the language, and so it follows by (∀) that $\mathbf{a_w}(\forall xBx)=T$ and A is verified in this case.

The Open Branch Lemma has now been proven. So we know the tree model is a counterexample to H / C. But to show the Quantified Tree Model Theorem, we need to know that the tree model is a tS-model, in order to establish that H / C has a <u>tS</u>-counterexample. So to complete the proof of this theorem, we must show the tree model satisfies the domain rules, obeys (t≈) and (∃c), and obeys (r) if (RC) is in S.

Proof that the tree model satisfies the domain axioms. Note that by the rules for tree construction, every instance of an axiom written in the language of the tree model must appear on every open branch. Since the Open Branch Lemma assures us that these axioms are verified, they must be true at every world on the tree model.

(t≈) $\mathbf{a_w}(t\approx t)=T$ and if $\mathbf{a_w}(s\approx t)=T$ and $\mathbf{a_w}(Plsl')=T$ then $\mathbf{a_w}(Pltl')=T$.

Proof that the tree model obeys (t≈). The proof is straightforward in the light of (**aA**) since the tree rules (≈In) and (≈Out) guarantee the following property for any world **w** in the tree.

t≈t is in **w** and if s≈t and Plsl′ are in **w** then so is Pltl′.

Next, we must verify that the tree model obeys (∃c) and that (r) is obeyed given (RC) is in S. That (∃c) is obeyed when nonrigid terms are in the language can be shown using facts about the S-tree rules that must have been applied to the open branch.

(∃c)   For teach term t, there is a constant c such that $a_w(t \approx c) = T$.

Proof that the tree model obeys (∃c). In case the constants are the only terms in the language, (∃c) holds immediately, for when t is a constant, there is always a constant c (namely, t) such that $a_w(t \approx c) = T$ by (t≈). In case there are terms other than the constants in the language, it was required that rule (∃i) be in S. But when (∃i) is a rule of S, the corresponding tree rule (tc) for S says explicitly to add t≈c to each world, where c is a constant new to the tree. So the condition follows by (aA).

(r)   If $a_w(b \approx c) = T$ then $a_v(b \approx c) = T$.

Proof that the tree model obeys (r) when (RC) is in S. By the fact that (RC) is satisfied in the tree model, it follows from (→) and (~) that if $a_w(b \approx c) = T$, then $a_w(\Box b \approx c) = T$, and if $a_w(b \approx c) = F$, then $a_w(\Box b \approx c) = F$. So when **wRv**, and $a_w(b \approx c) = T$, it follows by (□T) that $a_v(b \approx c) = T$. Similarly when **wRv**, and $a_w(b \approx c) = F$, it follows that $a_v(b \approx c) = F$. We can express this with the following pair of diagram rules, called (R≈):

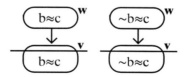

Note that each tree begins with an opening world **o**, and any world subsequently introduced into the S-tree is an ancestor of **o**, in the sense that for each world **w** of the tree model (including **o** itself), there is a chain of (zero or more) arrows extending from **o** to **w**. So for each **w** in **W**, there is a number n such that $oR^n w$. Furthermore, whenever $oR^n w$, the value of b≈c in **w** is identical to its value in **o**, for if $a_o(b \approx c) = T$, then $a_w(b \approx c) = T$, by many applications of (R≈), and if $a_o(b \approx c) = F$, then $a_w(b \approx c) = F$ for the same reason. It follows that every member **w** of **W** agrees with **o** on the value of b≈c, hence any two members **w**, **v** of **W** must agree with each other on the value of b≈c, and so (r) must hold.

16.2. Completeness for Truth Value Models

When it comes to the truth value models, both halves of what is needed for proving completeness are now in place. When S is any quantified modal logic discussed in Chapter 14, the method for converting a closed S-tree into an S-proof was given in Sections 14.5 and 14.7. Furthermore, the Quantified Tree Model Theorem has just been proven. So the completeness of S for tS-models follows immediately.

Completeness of S for tS-Models. If $H \vDash_{tS} C$ then $H \vdash_S C$.

Proof. Suppose $H \vDash_{tS} C$. Then by the contrapositive of the Quantified Tree Model Theorem, the S tree for H / C is closed. This closed tree can be converted into a proof by the methods of Sections 14.5 and 14.7. So $H \vdash_S C$.

16.3. Completeness for Intensional and Substitution Models

In this section, we will show the completeness of systems for the intensional and substitution interpretations. Let S be any system that results from adding to fK any selection of modal logic axioms (D), (M), (4), (B), (5), (CD) and domain axioms from the list below.

Domain Rules		**Corresponding Domain Conditions**
(∃E)	∃xEx	For some $i \in \mathbf{I}$, $i(\mathbf{w}) \in \mathbf{Dw}$.
(Q)	Et	$\mathbf{Dw}=\mathbf{D}$.
(ED)	Ec→□Ec	If $\mathbf{wRv}$ and $\mathbf{a_w}(c) \in \mathbf{Dw}$, then $\mathbf{a_v}(c) \in \mathbf{Dv}$.
(CD)	~Ec→□~Ec	If $\mathbf{wRv}$ and $\mathbf{a_v}(c) \in \mathbf{Dv}$, then $\mathbf{a_w}(c) \in \mathbf{Dw}$.
(RC)	(b≈c→□b≈c)&(~b≈c→□~b≈c)	$\mathbf{a_w}(c)=\mathbf{a_v}(c)$.
(∃i)	L ⊢ ~t≈c / L ⊢ ⊥, no c in L, t	For some $i \in \mathbf{I}$, $i(\mathbf{w})=\mathbf{a_w}(t)$.
(o)=(RC)+(∃i)		**I** is the set of all constant functions with values in **D**.
(o∃E)=(o)+(∃E)		(o) + **Dw** is not empty.
(oED)=(o)+(ED)		(o) + if $\mathbf{wRv}$, then $\mathbf{Dw} \subseteq \mathbf{Dv}$.
(oCD)=(o)+(CD)		(o) + if $\mathbf{wRv}$, then $\mathbf{Dv} \subseteq \mathbf{Dw}$.

The i Transfer Theorem of Section 15.7 shows that completeness of S for iS-models that meet the corresponding conditions follows from a proof of the completeness of S with respect to truth value (tS) models. But that was shown in the previous section. So the result is immediate.

i Transfer Theorem.   If system S is complete for tS-models, S is also complete with respect to iS-models.

Completeness of S for iS-Models.   If $H \vDash_{iS} C$ then $H \vdash_S C$.

Now let S be any system that results from adding to fK any selection of modal logic axioms (D), (M), (4), (B), (5), (CD) and domain axioms (Q), (ED), (CD), and (RC). Completeness of S for sS-models follows immediately from the s Transfer Theorem of Section 15.7.

s Transfer Theorem.　　If system S is complete for tS-models, S is also complete with respect to sS-models.

Completeness of S for sS-Models.　　If $H \vDash_{sS} C$ then $H \vdash_S C$.

16.4. Completeness for Objectual Models

Completeness for systems that use the objectual interpretation can be demonstrated in a similar way. Let us presume for a moment that there are nonrigid terms in the language. Let S be any system that results from adding to fK, any selection of modal logic axioms (D), (M), (4), (B), (5), (CD), and o-domain axioms from the list below.

(∃E)	∃xEx	**Dw** is not empty.
(Q)	Et	**Dw=D**.
(ED)	Ec→□Ec	If **wRv**, then **Dw ⊆ Dv**.
(CD)	~Ec→□~Ec	If **wRv**, then **Dv ⊆ Dw**.

Let oS be the result of adding (RC) and (∃i) to S. It was shown in Section 12.8 (Exercises 12.16 and 12.20) that Ec→□Ec equivalent to (CBF) or ∀x□Ex, and ~Ec→□~Ec is equivalent to (BF) in oK, so the completeness results will continue to hold when these alternative axioms are used in oS.

(CBF)	□∀xAx→∀x□Ax
(BF)	∀x□Ax→□∀xAx

The completeness of oS follows from the o Transfer Theorem of Section 15.8, provided that we can show that oS is complete for toS-models, where toS-models are tS-models that satisfy (r).

(r)　　If $\mathbf{a_w}(b \approx c)=T$ then $\mathbf{a_v}(b \approx c)=T$.

o Transfer Theorem.　　If oS is complete for toS-models, oS is also complete with respect to oS-models.

So all that remains is to show that oS is complete for toS-models. To make headway on this, it is worth reviewing a special case of the Quantified Tree

Model Theorem, where the system S at issue is oS, that is, a system that includes (RC) and (∃I).

o Tree Model Theorem.
If the oS-tree for H / C is open, then H $\vdash_{\text{toS}}$ C.

The proof of this special case of the Quantified Tree Model Theorem has already been given in Section 16.2. When the system at issue is oS, we know that the corresponding oS-tree is constructed using (RC). In the proof of the Quantified Tree Model Theorem given in Section 16.2, it was shown that when H / C has an open tree of this kind, the tree model is a tS-model that satisfies (r). But a toS-model is, by definition, a tS-model that meets this condition. So the tree model is a toS-counterexample to H / C, hence H $\vdash_{\text{toS}}$ C.

The completeness of oS for toS-models is now just around the corner.

Completeness of oS for toS-Models. If H $\vDash_{\text{toS}}$ C then H $\vdash_{\text{oS}}$ C.

Proof. Suppose H $\vDash_{\text{toS}}$ C. Then by the contrapositive of the o Tree Model Theorem, the oS tree for H / C is closed. This closed tree can be converted into a proof by the methods of Sections 14.5 and 14.7. So H $\vdash_{\text{oS}}$ C.

This last result with the o Transfer Theorem guarantees completeness of oS for oS-validity.

Completeness of oS for oS-Models. If H $\vDash_{\text{oS}}$ C then H $\vdash_{\text{oS}}$ C.

Note that it has been assumed for this proof that nonrigid terms are in the language. When they are absent, it is possible to show the completeness for oS-models of the weaker system rS=S+(RC), which lacks (∃i).

EXERCISE *16.1   Show the completeness of rS with respect to oS-models when the only terms are the constants.

EXERCISE 16.2   Show that system oS5, which is the result of adding (RC), (∃i), and the axioms of S5 to fK is complete with respect to oS models that have universal frames, where a frame is universal when **wRv** for all **w** and **v** in **W**. (Hint: Show the tree model for any system that includes the S5 axioms is universal. See Exercise 8.7b for help on this.)

EXERCISE 16.3 (Project)   Use the tree method to prove completeness of a system where the strong interpretation (≡) of ≈ is used. Use the intensional interpretation of the quantifier.

(≡) $\mathbf{a_w}(s{\approx}t)=T$ iff $\mathbf{a}(s)=\mathbf{a}(t)$.

(Hint: What changes in the principles for ≈ will be needed? How will these changes affect the proof of the theorems that play a role in the completeness proof?)

16.5. The Adequacy of Trees

In Section 8.7, it was shown that the tree method for propositional modal logic is correct in the sense that closed S-trees identify exactly the S-valid arguments. The proof depended on soundness and completeness results using the method of trees. Exactly the same strategy can be used in the case of quantified modal logics discussed in this book. Let S be any system for which we have defined S-trees. The demonstration that S-trees are *adequate* shows that the S-tree for H / C is closed iff H / C is S-valid. The structure of the reasoning is illustrated in the following diagram:

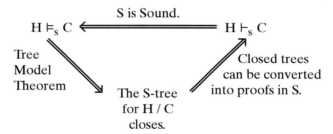

EXERCISE 16.4   Using the diagram above, explain in more detail why S-trees are adequate. (Hint. If necessary, review the explanation in Section 8.7.)

17

Completeness Using Canonical Models

Here we give completeness proofs for many quantified modal logics, using a variant of the method of maximally consistent sets. Although the previous chapter already established completeness for many quantified modal logics using the tree method, there are good reasons for covering the method of maximally consistent sets as well. First, this is the standard approach to obtaining completeness results, so most students of modal logic will want some understanding of the method. Second, the tree method applied only to those systems for which it was shown how to convert a tree into a proof. The method of maximally consistent sets applies to more systems, though it has limitations described below in Section 17.2.

17.1. How Quantifiers Complicate Completeness Proofs

One might expect that proving completeness of quantified modal logic could be accomplished by simply "pasting together" standard results for quantifiers with those for propositional modal logic. Unfortunately, it is not so easy. In order to appreciate the problems that arise, and how they may be overcome, let us first review the strategies used to show completeness for propositional modal logic with maximally consistent sets. Then it will be possible to outline the difficulties that arise when quantifiers are added.

The basic idea behind completeness proofs that use maximally consistent sets is to show that any argument H / C that is not provable has a counterexample. This is done by showing that given H ⊬ C, the set H, ~C is consistent, and so can be extended to a maximally consistent set **h** by the Lindenbaum Lemma. The canonical model is then constructed, and **h** is used to show there is a counterexample to H / C.

When the quantifier ∀ is in the language, it is no longer possible to base this tactic on maximally consistent sets. To see why, let us consider first the simpler case where classical rules (Q∀In) and (Q∀Out) for the quantifier are used, along with the substitution interpretation truth clause (Q∀).

(Q∀) $\mathbf{a_w}(\forall xAx)=T$ iff for every constant c, $\mathbf{a_w}(Ac)=T$.

It will be important to be able to show (Q∀) holds in the canonical model. Since the canonical model is defined so that $\mathbf{a_w}(A)=T$ iff $\mathbf{w} \vdash A$ for maximally consistent sets **w**, guaranteeing (Q∀) amounts to showing the following:

$\mathbf{w} \vdash \forall xAx$ iff for every constant c, $\mathbf{w} \vdash Ac$.

There is no problem showing this from left to right because that is guaranteed by features of maximally consistent sets and the (Q∀Out) rule.

EXERCISE 17.1   Show that if $\mathbf{w} \vdash \forall xAx$, then for every constant c, $\mathbf{w} \vdash Ac$ when the system at issue is qK.

However, the other direction is a problem. In fact, there are maximally consistent sets **w** that prove instances Ac for each constant c, even though ∀xAx is not provable from **w**. To see why, note that the set consisting of ~∀xAx and Ac for each constant c is consistent, so it can be extended to a maximally consistent set that cannot contain ∀xAx.

The solution to this difficulty is to base the completeness proof on what are called saturated sets, where *saturated sets* **w** are maximally consistent sets that meet a further condition (oc), sometimes called *omega completeness*.

(oc)   If $\mathbf{w} \not\vdash \forall xAx$, then for some constant c, $\mathbf{w} \not\vdash Ac$.

The contrapositive of this condition guarantees that whenever $\mathbf{w} \vdash Ac$ for every constant c, $\mathbf{w} \vdash \forall xAx$. This means that for saturated sets **w**, the truth condition (Q∀) will hold in the canonical model as is required.

So it appears that if the canonical model is defined so that **W** contains all and only the saturated sets, the problem will be resolved. Note, however, that it is now necessary to formulate and prove a new version of the

Lindenbaum Lemma. Instead of showing that every consistent set can be extended to a maximally consistent set, it is necessary now to show that every consistent set can be extended to a *saturated* one.

This requires modifying the construction given in the Lindenbaum Lemma used to create a maximally consistent set. In the original construction, one begins with the consistent set M, orders the sentences A_1, A_2, .., A_i, .., and adds sentences to M in sequence, forming a series of sets: M_1, M_2, .. M_i, .. so that either A_i or $\sim A_i$ is added to M_i depending on which choice leaves the result M_{i+1} consistent. Unfortunately, this procedure does not guarantee (oc). To overcome the problem, the standard thing to do is to adopt the following procedure. When a sentence A_i with the form $\sim\forall xBx$ is to be added to M_i to form M_{i+1}, one also adds an instance $\sim Bc$ where c is a constant that has not appeared in M_i. It is important that the constant chosen is new to M_i because otherwise, it is not possible to establish that the result remains consistent. It is a straightforward matter to show that this procedure works, and so establishes the *Saturated Set Lemma*, that is, the claim that consistent sets can be extended to saturated sets.

The requirement that the constant c be new when Ac is added during the saturated set construction raises new issues. Consider what happens when one hopes to construct a saturated set from a consistent set M whose sentences already contain all the constants of the language. Since no new constants are available, the saturated set cannot be constructed in that language. This is not a problem in the proof of the completeness of *nonmodal* quantificational logic. Given H $\nvdash$ C, so that the set H, $\sim$C is consistent, one simply considers a language larger than the one in which the argument H / C is written, and uses the Saturated Set Lemma to obtain the desired saturated set **h** written in that new language. When the canonical model is constructed for the new language, it is easy to see that it serves as a counterexample to the original argument.

The same strategy would work to show completeness of a classical *quantified* modal logic qS were it not for one thing. In this case it is necessary to show that the canonical model simultaneously meets truth conditions (Q∀) and (□), so it will be necessary to demonstrate both of the following:

$\vdash \forall xAx$ iff for every constant c, $\mathbf{w} \vdash Ac$.
$\vdash \Box A$ iff for all $\mathbf{v} \in \mathbf{W}$, if $\mathbf{wRv}$, then $\mathbf{v} \vdash A$.

Notice that in the completeness proof for propositional modal logic, demonstration of the second fact requires a proof of ($\nvdash\Box$), and the proof of this makes an essential appeal to the Lindenbaum Lemma.

($\nvdash\Box$)   If $\mathbf{w}\nvdash\Box A$, then for some $\mathbf{v}\in\mathbf{W}$, $\mathbf{wRv}$, and $\mathbf{v}\nvdash A$.

(Assuming $\mathbf{w}\nvdash\Box A$, one shows that V, $\sim A$ is consistent, where $B\in V$ iff $\Box B\in\mathbf{w}$. But then one needs the Lindenbaum Lemma to create from V, $\sim A$ a maximally consistent set $\mathbf{v}$ such that $\mathbf{wRv}$, and $\mathbf{v}\nvdash A$.) So in the case of quantified modal logic, it will be necessary to appeal to the Saturated Set Lemma a second time to prove that there is a saturated set $\mathbf{v}$ such that $\mathbf{wRv}$, and $\mathbf{v}\nvdash A$ in order to establish that the canonical model obeys the $\Box$ truth condition. The problem is that there is no guarantee that there are enough constants missing from the set V, $\sim A$ to use in the saturated set construction. As a matter of fact since $\Box(Pc\rightarrow Pc)$ is a theorem, it follows that $Pc\rightarrow Pc$ is a member of V, $\sim A$ for every constant c in the language, so there are no new constants at all. If we attempt to remedy the problem by constructing the world $\mathbf{v}$ in a larger language L', then one is trapped in a vicious circle. Now one must prove the canonical model obeys the quantifier truth condition ($Q\forall$) for language L' instead of the original language. This will force us to define $\mathbf{W}$ in the canonical model as the set of all saturated sets written in L'. But when this is done, and one returns to the proof of ($\nvdash\Box$), one needs to find new constants foreign to a set V, $\sim A$ *written in L'.* Of course, there is no guarantee that there are such constants, and we are right back where we started. Note that exactly the same problem will arise whether we adopt classical or free logic approaches to the quantifier.

There are many different methods that one may use to overcome this fundamental problem (Garson 2001, Section 2.2). However, each works only for a subset of the quantified modal logics. A method that encompasses a fairly wide selection of quantified modal logics will be presented here. (A more general result is found in Garson (2005).) The basic idea behind the method is to generalize the definition of omega completeness so that it is possible to show that any set V, $\sim A$ from which we hope to construct saturated set $\mathbf{v}$ is already omega complete, so that no new constants are needed to create the desired saturated set.

17.2. Limitations on the Completeness Results

It is important to make clear the limitations on the completeness results to be given in this chapter. For the moment, let system S be the result of adding to fK propositional modal logic axioms, and domain axioms discussed in Section 15, but *not* (RC) and *not* the rule (∃i). In Sections 17.5 and 17.6 we will explain how to extend the results to systems that include these principles. An important restriction concerning these stronger systems is that *when (RC) is present and terms other than the constants are in the language, it is necessary also to include the rule (∃i).*

There is also a restriction on the propositional modal logic on which S is based. In the case of propositional modal logics with conditions on models such as density and convergence, the completeness proof involves a *third* appeal to the Saturated Set Lemma. For this reason, the method given here will not work to show completeness of quantifier versions of those systems. In fact, it is known that it is impossible to prove completeness for some of these systems because they are in fact *not* complete (Cresswell, 1995). The proofs given here will show the completeness of modal logics S only when the canonical model obeys frame conditions that are preserved by subframes, which means that the condition holds in the frame of the canonical model, and continues to hold when members of its set of worlds **W** are deleted.

The official definition of preservation by subframes goes like this. A condition on frames for propositional modal logic S is *preserved by subframes* iff it holds in the canonical model for propositional logic S, and whenever the condition holds for frame <**W′**, **R′**>, it also holds for any *subframe* <**W**, **R**>, that is, any frame <**W**, **R**> such that **W** ⊆ **W′** and **R** ⊆ **R′**, where **R** ⊆ **R′** means that for all **w**, **v** in **W**, **wRv** iff **wR′v**. All conditions on **R** involving universal quantification over worlds are preserved by subframes. For example, reflexivity, shift reflexivity, transitivity, symmetry, the euclidean condition, and linearity are conditions that qualify. The reason is that when a universal claim holds for a domain **W**, then it holds for each member of **W**; and so it holds for members in any subset of **W**. Seriality, density, and convergence do not qualify because these conditions involve *existential* quantification over **W**. A true claim that there exists a member in **W** with a certain property might fail in a subset of **W** that omits some of its members. Despite the fact that seriality is not preserved by subframes, there is a way to modify the method presented here to obtain completeness proofs for that condition. Unfortunately, the method does not work for density, and in fact, we know that completeness must fail for convergence (Cresswell, 1995). It also does not work for universality, the condition that **wRv** for all **w** and **v** in **W**, since the canonical model for S5 is not universal; but completeness can be proven nonetheless by modifying the method given here. (See Exercise 17.13.)

The completeness proof follows the same pattern used for propositional logic in Chapter 9. After the basic ideas are presented in the next section, it will be shown how to obtain completeness results for tS-models – truth value models with the substitution interpretation. This together with the various Transfer Theorems developed in Chapter 15 will allow us to extend the completeness results to the more sophisticated treatments of the quantifier. This will serve as a framework for proofs for most of the quantified modal logics mentioned in this book, everything from systems with constant domains that accept the Barcan Formulas, to systems that use the objectual interpretation with nonrigid terms.

17.3. The Saturated Set Lemma

The completeness proof for S will follow the discussion in Section 9.1. When we write 'M ⊢ A' in the case of a set M, we mean that H ⊢$_S$ A for some (finite) list H whose members are all in M. In order to manage cases involving the quantifier, the notion of an ∀-set will be introduced. The basic idea is that when such a set entails Ec→Ac for all constants c in the language, then it should also contain ∀xAx. The reason that we are interested in such sets is that they obey the analog of (∀), the substitution truth clause for the quantifier. In quantified model logic, however, we need a more general version of this idea.

To explain it, some new notation is needed. When L / C is an argument, the *corresponding sentence* L–3C is the result of applying (□In) and (→In) repeatedly to the argument L / C. For example, when L / C is the argument A, □, B, □ / C, then the corresponding sentence L–3C may be constructed in stages as follows:

A, □, B, □ / C
A, □, B / □C   (□In)
A, □ / B→□C   (→In)
A / □(B→□C)   (□In)
A→□(B→□C)   (→In)

> **EXERCISE 17.2**   Construct L–3C in cases where L / C has L is empty, where L / C = □, A, □, B / C and where L / C = □, □, □ / C.

The following Lemma should be nearly obvious.

   –3 **Lemma.**   When L′ is finite L, L′ ⊢ C iff L ⊢ L′–3C.

Proof of the ⊃ *Lemma.* Suppose L, L′ ⊢ C. Then L ⊢ L′⊃C by repeated uses of (□In) and (→In). Suppose L ⊢ L′⊃C. Then L, L′ ⊢ C by repeated uses of (□Out) and (→Out).

M *is a* ∀*-set* (for a given language) if and only if it obeys the following property, for any list L:

(∀-set)   If M ⊢ L⊃(Ec→Ac) for all constants c of the language, then M ⊢ L⊃∀xAx.

We will say that M is *saturated* for a language if and only if M is a maximal, consistent ∀-set for that language.

As already explained, the reason we are interested in ∀-sets is so that we will be able to construct a model that satisfies (∀), the truth clause for the substitution interpretation of the quantifier. You may wonder why a simpler condition is not used, namely, the result of deleting 'L⊃' from the definition.

If M ⊢ Ec→Ac for all constants c of the language, then M ⊢ ∀xAx.

However, this condition will not accomplish everything we need for the completeness proof. The gist of the problem is that the more general property is necessary to simultaneously guarantee (∀) and (□) together in the canonical model. At the appropriate point in the proof, the need for the more complex definition of a ∀-set will be noted.

The main reasoning of the completeness proof will be to establish an analog of the Lindenbaum Lemma, that is, to show that every consistent set can be extended to a saturated set. First, the way will be prepared with some lemmas concerning what we call ready sets. A set M *is ready* iff either M is a ∀-set or there are infinitely many constants of the language that fail to appear in M.

Ready Addition Lemma. If M′ is finite and M is ready, then M∪M′ (the union of M with M′) is ready.

Proof of the Ready Addition Lemma. Suppose M′ is finite and M is ready. If the reason M is ready is that there are infinitely many constants of the language not in M, then since M′ is finite, there will still be infinitely many constants not in M∪M′ and so M∪M′ is ready. If the reason M is ready is that it is a ∀-set, then M∪M′ is also a ∀-set and so ready as well by the following reasoning. Suppose that M∪M′ ⊢ L⊃(Ec→Ac) for every constant c of the language. It follows (by (CP) and (&In)) that M ⊢ H→(L⊃(Ec→Ac)) for every constant c of the language, where H is the conjunction of the members of M′. But by the definition of L⊸3, H→(L⊸3(Ec→Ac)) is just H, L⊸3(Ec→Ac). Since M is a ∀-set it follows then that M⊢ H, L⊸3∀xAx, from which it follows by (MP) and (&Out) that M∪M′ ⊢ ∀xAx. Therefore M∪M′ is a ∀-set, and so ready in this case as well.

Ready Lemma. If M is ready and consistent for a given language, and contains ∼(L⊸3∀xAx), then M, ∼(L⊸3(Ec→Ac)) ⊬ ⊥, for some constant c of the language.

Proof of the Ready Lemma. Suppose M is ready, consistent, and contains ∼(L⊸3∀xAx). To show that M, ∼(L⊸3(Ec→Ac)) ⊬ ⊥, for some constant c of the language, suppose the opposite and derive a contradiction. So suppose that M, ∼(L⊸3(Ec→Ac))⊢ ⊥ for every constant c. A contradiction can be obtained as follows. By (IP) it follows that M ⊢ L⊸3(Ec→Ac), for every constant c. If the reason that M is ready is that M is a ∀-set, then it follows immediately that M ⊢ L⊸3∀xAx. If M is ready because there are infinitely many constants of the language not in M, then M ⊢ L⊸3∀xAx also holds for the following reason. L is finite, so there are infinitely many constants not in M, L, or ∀xAx. Let b be one of these constants. Since M ⊢ L⊸3(Ec→Ac), for any c, we have M ⊢ L⊸3(Eb→Ab), and so H ⊢ L⊸3(Eb→Ab) for some list H of members of M. So by the ⊸3 Lemma, H, L ⊢ Eb→Ab. Since b is not in H, L, or ∀xAx, (∀In) may be applied to H, L⊢ Eb→Ab to obtain H, L⊢ ∀xAx. By the ⊸3 Lemma, it follows that H ⊢ L⊸3∀xAx, and hence M ⊢ L⊸3∀xAx. So for whichever reason M is ready, it follows that M ⊢ L⊸3∀xAx. But we also have that ∼(L⊸3∀xAx) is in M, and this conflicts with the consistency of M. Therefore it follows that M, ∼(L⊸3(Ec→Ac)) ⊬ ⊥ for some constant c.

We are now in a position to prove a quantified modal logic version of the Lindenbaum Lemma.

Saturated Set Lemma.
If M is consistent and ready, then M has a saturated extension.

Proof of the Saturated Set Lemma. Suppose M is consistent and ready. We will explain how to construct a saturated set m that is an extension of M, using a variant of the proof strategy for the Lindenbaum Lemma. We order all the sentences of the language in an infinite list: $A_1, A_2, .. A_i, ..$ and create a series of lists: $M_1, M_2, .. M_i, ..$ following the main outlines of the recipe used for propositional logics, starting with $M_1 = M$.

$$M_{i+1} = M_i, A_i \quad \text{if } M_i, A_i \nvdash \bot.$$
$$M_{i+1} = M_i, \sim A_i \quad \text{if } M_i, A_i \vdash \bot.$$

However, there will be one change in the definition of M_{i+1}. Suppose that a sentence of the form $\sim(L\text{--}3\forall xAx)$ is A_i, the candidate for addition to M_{i+1}. If the addition of this sentence would be consistent (i.e., if M_i, $\sim(L\text{--}3\forall xAx) \nvdash \bot$), then add **both** $\sim(L\text{--}3\forall xAx)$ and $\sim(L\text{--}3(Eb\rightarrow Ab))$ to M_i to form M_{i+1}, where b is a constant chosen so that M_{i+1} is consistent. There is such a constant by the following reasoning. M is ready, and only finitely many sentences were added to M to form M_i, $\sim(L\text{--}3\forall xAx)$, so by the Ready Addition Lemma, M_i, $\sim(L\text{--}3\forall xAx)$ is ready. Since M_i, $\sim(L\text{--}3\forall xAx) \nvdash \bot$, and $\sim(L\text{--}3\forall xAx)$ is in M_i, $\sim(L\text{--}3\forall xAx)$, it follows by the Ready Lemma that M_i, $\sim(L\text{--}3\forall xAx)$, $\sim(L\text{--}3(Ec\rightarrow Ac)) \nvdash \bot$ for some constant c.

Let m be the union of M with the set of all sentences added in forming any of the M_i. Clearly m is maximal, and each set M_i in this construction is clearly consistent by the same reasoning given in the Lindenbaum Lemma. By the M Lemma of Section 9.1, m is consistent. Below it is shown that m is a $\forall$-set, and so m is the desired saturated extension of M, and the proof of the Saturated List Lemma is complete.

Proof that m is a $\forall$-set. Suppose that $m \vdash L\text{--}3(Ec\rightarrow Ac)$ for every constant c. We will show that $m \vdash L\text{--}3\forall xAx$, by showing that $m \nvdash L\text{--}3\forall xAx$ leads to a contradiction. Suppose $m \nvdash L\text{--}3\forall xAx$. Then by (IP), m, $\sim(L\text{--}3\forall xAx) \nvdash \bot$. But $\sim(L\text{--}3\forall xAx)$ must be A_i, the ith member of the list of all sentences for some value of i. If m, $\sim(L\text{--}3\forall xAx) \nvdash \bot$, then M_i, $\sim(L\text{--}3\forall xAx) \nvdash \bot$ (since M_i is a subset of m). But then $\sim(L\text{--}3(Eb\rightarrow Ab))$ was added to form M_{i+1} for some constant b. Hence $m \vdash \sim(L\text{--}3(Eb\rightarrow Ab))$. However, we already supposed $m \vdash L\text{--}3(Ec\rightarrow Ac)$ for every constant c, so in particular, $m \vdash L\text{--}3(Eb\rightarrow Ab)$. This conflicts with the consistency of m. Therefore, we must conclude that $m \vdash L\text{--}3\forall xAx$, and so m is a $\forall$-set.

17.4. Completeness for Truth Value Models

Now that the Saturated Set Lemma has been proven, we turn to the details of the completeness proof for S with respect to truth value models (tS-validity). Remember that this result is limited because so far, the system S contains neither (RC) nor the rule ($\exists$i). We wish to show that if H / C is tS-valid, then H / C can be proven in S.

Completeness for tS-Models (for systems without (RC) or ($\exists$i)).
If $H \vDash_{tS} C$, then $H \vdash_S C$.

Proof of the Completeness of S. We will actually show the contrapositive: if H $\nvdash_S$ C, then H / C has a tS-counterexample. So assume H $\nvdash_S$ C. Then by (IP), H, $\sim$C $\nvdash_S$ $\bot$. Consider the quantified modal language that contains all the symbols appearing in H, $\sim$C. Create a new language from this one by adding infinitely many constants that do not appear in H, $\sim$C. For this new language H, $\sim$C is ready, so it is a member of the set of all consistent and ready sets. Therefore by the Saturated Set Lemma, there is a saturated extension **h** of H, $\sim$C in this new language.

Now let us define the canonical model for S that will serve as a counterexample to H / C. The definition closely resembles the one used for propositional modal logics except that saturated sets now play the role of maximally consistent sets.

The *canonical model* <**W**, **R**, **a**> for S is defined over the new language as follows:

(Def **W**)   **W** is the set of all saturated sets.
(Def **R**)   **w****R****v** iff for all sentences B, if **w** $\vdash$ $\Box$B then **v** $\vdash$ B.
(Def **a**) $\mathbf{a_w}(A)$=T iff **w** $\vdash$ A.

If it can be shown that the canonical model just defined is a tS-model, we will have constructed a tS-counterexample to H / C. To see why, note that the saturated set **h** constructed from H, $\sim$C entails $\sim$C and all members of H, so by (Def **a**), $\mathbf{a_h}$(H, $\sim$C) = T, and so $\mathbf{a_h}$(H)=T and $\mathbf{a_h}$(C)=F.

All that remains for the completeness proof is to show that the canonical model for S is a tS-model. To do so, we must verify that **W** is nonempty, that **R** is binary relation on **W**, and that **a** obeys the following conditions: ($\bot$), ($\rightarrow$), ($\Box$), ($\forall$), (t$\approx$), and ($\exists$c). We must show also that its frame <**W**, **R**> obeys the corresponding conditions for system S. In case there are any domain axioms in S, we must show also that the canonical model satisfies those axioms. The proofs that **W** is nonempty, that **R** is binary relation on **W**, and that **a** obeys ($\bot$) and ($\rightarrow$) are identical to the corresponding cases in propositional logic. (See Section 9.2.) Let us now cover the remaining issues.

($\Box$) $\mathbf{b_w}(\Box A)$=T iff for all **v** $\in$ **W**, if **w****R****v**, then $\mathbf{a_v}(A)$=T.

Proof that **a** *obeys* ($\Box$). In the light of (Def **a**), ($\Box$) follows if we can show ($\vdash\Box$) and ($\nvdash\Box$).

($\vdash\Box$)   If **w** $\vdash$ $\Box$A, then for all **v** $\in$ **W**, if **w****R****v**, then **v** $\vdash$ A.
($\nvdash\Box$)   If **w** $\nvdash$ $\Box$A, then for some **v** $\in$ **W**, **w****R****v**, and **v** $\nvdash$ A.

Proof of (⊢□). Suppose **w** ⊢ □A, and let **v** be any member of **W** such that **wRv**. By (Def**R**), for any sentence B, if **w** ⊢ □B, then **v** ⊢ B. So **v** ⊢ A.

The following lemmas, which were already proven in Section 9.2, will be used in the proof of (⊬□). Remember that V is defined by (V∈).

(V∈) B ∈ V iff □B ∈ **w**.

Extension Lemma.
If M′ is an extension of M, then if M ⊢ A then M′ ⊢ A.

V-Lemma. **w** is an extension of □V.

Consistency Lemma. If **w** ⊬ □A, then V, ~A is consistent.

R Lemma. If **v** is an extension of V, ~A then **wRv**.

EXERCISE 17.3 Review the proofs of the previous four lemmas to verify that the presence of quantifiers does not affect the reasoning given in Section 9.2.

One more lemma is needed to show that V, ~A can be extended to a saturated set. To do this using the Saturated Set Lemma, we will need to know not only that V, ~A is consistent but also that it is a ∀-set so that it will follow that V, ~A is ready.

EXERCISE 17.4 To practice steps taken in the reasoning of the next lemma, show the following, by working out examples when L is the list C, □, D, □.

a) □(L−∋A) = □, L −∋ A
b) B→(L−∋A) = B, L −∋ A

∀-Set Lemma. V, ~A is a ∀-set.

Proof. To show V, ~A is a ∀-set, assume V, ~A ⊢ L −∋ (Ec→Bc) for all c, and show that V, ~A ⊢ L −∋ ∀xBx as follows. From the assumption, it follows by (CP) that V ⊢ ~A, L −∋ (Ec→Bc) for all c. By (GN), □V ⊢ □,~A, L −∋ (Ec→Bc) for all c. Since **w** is an extension of □V, it follows by the Extension Lemma that **w** ⊢ □, ~A, L −∋ (Ec→Bc) for all c. But **w** is a ∀-set and so for any list L′, if **w** ⊢ L′ −∋ (Ec→Bc) for all c, then **w** ⊢ L′ −∋ ∀xAx. So when L′ is the list □,~A, L, it follows that **w** ⊢ □, ~A, L −∋ ∀xAx. (This is the point in the proof that illustrates why the more general definition of a ∀-set was needed. If 'L−∋' had been missing in that definition, it would not have been possible to argue from the fact that **w** is a ∀-set to the result that V, ~A is a ∀-set.) Since **w** is maximal, either □, ~A, L ⫣ ∀xBx or its negation is in **w**. But the negation cannot be in **w** since that would make **w** inconsistent. Therefore □, ~A, L ⫣ ∀xBx is in **w** with the result that ~A, L ⫣ ∀xBx is in V. So V ⊢ ~A, L ⫣ ∀xBx, and V, ~A ⊢ L ⫣ ∀xBx by (MP).

Proof of (⊬□). Suppose **w** ⊬ □A. The Consistency Lemma guarantees that V, ~A is S-consistent. The ∀-Set Lemma guarantees that V, ~A is a ∀-set. So by the Saturated Set Lemma, we can extend V, ~A to a saturated set **v** in **W**. By the fact that **v** is an extension of V, ~A it follows by the R-Lemma that **w**R**v**. Since **v** is an extension of V, ~A, it also follows that ~A ∈ **v**, and hence by the consistency of **v** that **v** ⊬ A. We have found a saturated set **v** in **W** with the feature that **w**R**v** and **v** ⊬ A, which finishes the proof of (□⊬).

(∀)   **a**_{**w**}(∀xAx)=T iff for every constant c, if **a**_{**w**}(Ec)=T then **a**_{**w**}(Ac)=T.

Proof of (∀). By (Defa) it will be sufficient for establishing (∀) to show (⊢∀) and (⊬∀).

(⊢∀)   If **w** ⊢ ∀xAx, then for every constant c, if **w** ⊢ Ec, then **w** ⊢ Ac.
(⊬∀)   If **w** ⊬ ∀xAx, then for some constant c, **w** ⊢ Ec and **w** ⊬ Ac.

Proof of (⊢∀). Assume **w** ⊢ ∀xAx and that c is any constant such that **w** ⊢ Ec. By (∀Out), **w** ⊢ Ec → Ac, hence by (MP), **w** ⊢ Ac.

Proof of (⊬∀). Assume **w** ⊬ ∀xAx. Since **w** is saturated, **w** is a ∀-set. So in the special case where L is empty, we have that if **w** ⊢ Ec→Ac for every constant c, then **w** ⊢ ∀xAx. But by our assumption **w** ⊬ ∀xAx, so it follows that it cannot be true that **w** ⊢ Ec→Ac for every constant c. Therefore, for some constant c, **w** ⊬ Ec→Ac, which means Ec→Ac is not in **w**. By the fact that **w** is maximal, ~(Ec→Ac) is in **w**, and by the derived rule (→F), we have both **w** ⊢ Ec and **w** ⊢ ~Ac. Since **w** is consistent, **w** ⊬ Ac. So for this constant c, **w** ⊢ Ec and **w** ⊬ Ac.

(t≈)   **a**_{**w**}(t≈t)=T and if **a**_{**w**}(s≈t)=T and **a**_{**w**}(Plsl′)=T, then **a**_{**w**}(Pltl′)=T.

Proof of (t≈). By (Defa), (t≈) follows if we can show (1) and (2).

(1)   **w** ⊢ t≈t.
(2)   If **w** ⊢ t≈s and **w** ⊢ Pltl′ then **w** ⊢ Plsl′.

But (1) and (2) follow from the presence of (≈In) and (≈Out) in fS.

(∃c)   For all t and **w**, there is a constant c such that $a_w(t \approx c) = T$.

Proof of (∃c). Since the only terms so far in the language are the constants, all we must show is that for each constant b, there is a constant c such that $a_w(b \approx c) = T$. But this follows from (t≈), which guarantees $a_w(b \approx b) = T$, so that the constant c in question can be b itself. (Note that condition (∃c) could fail when new terms are introduced to the language.)

Our final project is to show that the frame <**W**, **R**> of the canonical model obeys the frame conditions corresponding to the propositional modal logic axioms of S. We have assumed that the conditions on **R** at issue are preserved by subframes. In the course of the completeness proofs for the propositional modal logics, we proved that for any system containing the axioms of S, the frame <**W′**, **R′**> for the canonical model obeys the corresponding properties for those axioms. The very same reasoning applies to show those same frame conditions would hold for the canonical model for S if only <**W′**, **R′**> were its frame. Remember **W′** contained the maximally consistent sets. In the canonical model for S, however, its frame <**W**, **R**> is defined so that **W** contains *saturated* sets, that is, maximally consistent sets that are also ∀-sets. Therefore, <**W**, **R**> is a subframe of <**W′**, **R′**>. Since the conditions on **R** for system S are preserved by subframes, we know that <**W**, **R**> obeys them as well.

It is possible to show also that seriality holds for the canonical model if the axiom (D) is in S. Let **w** be any member of **W**. Since **w** is maximal, it must contain any theorem of S including $\sim\Box\bot$ that derivable from (D). So $w \vdash \sim\Box\bot$ and by (Def**a**), the canonical model is such that $a_w(\sim\Box\bot) = T$ and so $a_w(\Box\bot) = F$. But we proved that the canonical model obeys (□), and so there must be a world **v** in **W** such that **wRv** and $a_v(\bot) = F$. So for each world **w** in **W** there is a word **v** in **W** such that **wRv**. Therefore the canonical model's frame is serial when (D) is in S, which means that the completeness proof will be forthcoming in this case, even though seriality is not preserved by subframes.

17.5. Completeness for Systems with Rigid Constants

Here we will explore the completeness question for systems that include the axiom (RC), whose corresponding condition asserts that the constants are rigid.

(RC) $(b \approx c \rightarrow \Box b \approx c)$ & $(\sim b \approx c \rightarrow \Box \sim b \approx c)$ $a_w(c) = a_v(c)$

Now let rS be a system that is the result of adding (RC) to one of the systems S already described at the end of Section 17.2. *Note that it is a requirement on the language of rS that the constants are the only terms in the language.* The completeness proof for rS follows the outlines of the strategy used in the previous section but unfortunately the presence of (RC) does not guarantee that the canonical model has rigid constants. So it is necessary to complicate the construction of the canonical model and adjust the proof to fit. Remember that in case (RC) is present, it was stipulated that a tS-model must satisfy the condition (r).

(r)   If $\mathbf{a_w}(b{\approx}c)=T$ then $\mathbf{a_v}(b{\approx}c)=T$.

So we will show the completeness of system rS with respect to *trS*-models, that is, tS-models that obey (r). Note that (∃i) *is not present in rS*. In the following section, it will be explained how to manage systems that include (∃i).

Completeness of rS for trS-Models (for systems without (∃i)).
If $H \vDash_{tS} C$ then $H \vdash_{rS} C$.

Proof. Assume that $H \nvdash_{rS} C$. Then H, ~C $\nvdash_{rS} \perp$, and so the Saturated Set Theorem guarantees that H, ~C can be extended to a saturated set **o**. The canonical model for rS is then defined from **o** so that its set of possible worlds **W** is restricted to reflect the fact that the constants are rigid. Let us call a saturated set *r-normal* when the sentences it entails of the form b≈c are exactly the sentences of that form entailed by **o**. So **w** is *r-normal* exactly when **o** ⊢ b≈c iff **w** ⊢ b≈c, for any two constants b and c. The canonical model <**W**, **R**, **a**> for rS is identical to canonical model for S defined in the previous section, except that the set of possible worlds **W** is restricted to the r-normal saturated sets.

(DefrW)   **W** = the set of **r-normal** saturated sets.

All that remains is to show that the canonical model so defined is a trS-model. It should be obvious from (DefrW) that (r) is satisfied, for in the light of (Defa) and the fact that **w** is r-normal, $\mathbf{a_o}(b{\approx}c)=\mathbf{a_w}(b{\approx}c)$ for all **w** in **W**. Finally, we can show that <**W**, **R**> obeys the appropriate frame conditions by noting that those conditions are all preserved by subframes and that **W** in the present model is a subset of **W** in the canonical model for S defined in the previous section. The rest of the demonstration is identical to the proof given there, with the exception that a modification of the proof for ($\Box\nvdash$) is needed.

($\nvdash\Box$)   If $\mathbf{w} \nvdash \Box A$, then for some $\mathbf{v} \in \mathbf{W}$, $\mathbf{w}R\mathbf{v}$, and $\mathbf{v} \nvdash A$.

Proof of ($\Box\nvdash$). We must show that if $\mathbf{w} \nvdash \Box A$, then there is a saturated set $\mathbf{v}$ *in* W, such that $\mathbf{w}R\mathbf{v}$ and $\mathbf{v} \nvdash A$. The reasoning given for that case in Section 17.4 still shows that there is a saturated set $\mathbf{v}$ such that $\mathbf{w}R\mathbf{v}$ and $\mathbf{v} \nvdash A$, but it does not guarantee that $\mathbf{v}$ is a member of $\mathbf{W}$ unless we can also show that $\mathbf{v}$ is r-normal. To prove that, it must be shown that $\mathbf{o} \vdash b{\approx}c$ iff $\mathbf{v} \vdash b{\approx}c$. We know that $\mathbf{w}$ is r-normal because it is in $\mathbf{W}$, so all that remains is to show $\mathbf{w} \vdash b{\approx}c$ iff $\mathbf{v} \vdash b{\approx}c$, which breaks into two cases as follows:

(r$\approx\vdash$)   If $\mathbf{w} \vdash b{\approx}c$ then $\mathbf{v} \vdash b{\approx}c$.
(r$\approx\nvdash$)   If $\mathbf{w} \nvdash b{\approx}c$ then $\mathbf{v} \nvdash b{\approx}c$.

For the *proof of* (r$\approx\vdash$) assume $\mathbf{w} \vdash b{\approx}c$. Then by the axiom (RC), $\mathbf{w} \vdash \Box b{\approx}c$, and so by the fact that $\mathbf{w}R\mathbf{v}$ and (Def$R$), it follows that $\mathbf{v} \vdash b{\approx}c$.

For the *proof of* (r$\approx\nvdash$) assume $\mathbf{w} \nvdash b{\approx}c$. Then $b{\approx}c$ is not in $\mathbf{w}$. By the maximality of $\mathbf{w}$, $\sim b{\approx}c$ is in $\mathbf{w}$, and hence $\mathbf{w} \vdash \sim b{\approx}c$, from which $\mathbf{w} \vdash \Box{\sim}b{\approx}c$ follows by (RC). By the fact that $\mathbf{w}R\mathbf{v}$ and (Def$R$), it follows that $\mathbf{v} \vdash \sim b{\approx}c$, and so since $\mathbf{v}$ is consistent, $\mathbf{v} \nvdash b{\approx}c$.

17.6. Completeness for Systems with Nonrigid Terms

So far, completeness has been shown only when ($\exists$i) is absent from S. Since ($\exists$i) is required to handle nonrigid terms, it follows that the language of S does not contain nonrigid terms. But this is a heavy price to pay since nonrigid terms are commonplace in ordinary language. Let us consider what can be done to prove completeness for systems with nonrigid terms that include ($\exists$i).

($\exists$i) $L \vdash \sim t{\approx}c \,/\, L \vdash \bot$ where c is not in L nor in t

Let system oS be the result of adding ($\exists$i) to rS, and assume now that the language includes terms other than the constants. The completeness proof for oS will require a major overhaul. Let us say that set M is a $\approx$-set when the following property holds:

($\approx$-set)   If $M \vdash L{-}\exists{\sim}t{\approx}c$ for every constant c, then $M \vdash L{-}\exists{\sim}t{\approx}t$.

Notice how the condition ($\approx$-set) mimics the content of the ($\exists$i) rule while at the same time deploying the strategy used in the definition of a ∀-set. (The sentence ~t≈t serves as the contradiction ⊥ in the rule.) A ≈*saturated* set is a ≈-set that is also saturated. We need to show an analogue of the Saturated List Lemma, this time for ≈saturated sets. Let us say that a set M is ≈*ready* when it is both a ∀-set and a ≈-set, or there are infinitely many constants of the language not in M. It is helpful to first show the following analogues of the Ready Addition Lemma, the Ready Lemma, and the Saturated Set Lemma:

≈Ready Addition Lemma.
If M′ is finite, and M is ≈ready, then M∪M′ is ≈ready.

EXERCISE *17.5   Using the proof of the Ready Addition Lemma as a guide, prove the ≈Ready Addition Lemma.

≈Ready Lemma. If M is ≈ready, consistent, and contains ~(L−3~t≈t), then M, ~(L−3~t≈c) ⊬ ⊥, for some constant c of the language.

EXERCISE *17.6   Using the reasoning of the Ready Lemma as a guide, show the ≈Ready Lemma.

≈Saturated Set Lemma.
If M is consistent and ≈ready, then M has a ≈saturated extension.

EXERCISE *17.7   Using the reasoning of the Saturated Set Lemma as a guide, prove the ≈Saturated Set Lemma. (Hint: Modify the definition of M_{i+1} so that when A_i is ~(L−3~t≈t), and M_i, ~(L−3~t≈t) ⊬ ⊥, add both ~(L−3~t≈t), and ~(L−3~t≈c) to form M_{i+1}, where c is chosen so that M_{i+1} is consistent. You will need to show that m on your construction is a ≈-set, which you may do following the strategy of the proof that m is a ∀-set given at the end of Section 17.3.)

With these new lemmas in hand, completeness of oS for truth value semantics is proven using the same strategy we have established in previous sections. Let a toS-model be any tS-model that obeys (r).

Completeness of oS for toS-Models.   If H ⊨$_{toS}$ C then H ⊢$_{oS}$ C.

Proof. From H ⊬$_{oS}$ C, we obtain a consistent set H, ~C that is extended to a ≈saturated set **o** written in a language with infinitely many new constants.

We then define the canonical model and show it is a toS-model. Since **o** will belong to the **W** of that model, we will have a toS-counterexample to H / C. The canonical model <**W**, **R**, **a**> is defined as in the previous section, with the exception the **W** is restricted to the ≈saturated sets.

(Def≈**W**)   **W** is the set of all ≈saturated sets.

We then show that the canonical model for S is a toS-model, just as we did in Section 17.5, using ≈saturated rather than saturated sets throughout. Only two adjustments to the proof are necessary. First a change is needed in the proof that the canonical model obeys (□). The proof of (□⊬) now requires a demonstration that V, ~A is a ≈-set, so as to show that V, ~A is ≈ready and so can be extended to a ≈saturated set **v**. So it is necessary to establish the following lemma:

≈**-Set Lemma.**   V, ~A is a ≈-set.

EXERCISE *17.8   Show the ≈-Set Lemma.

EXERCISE 17.9   Prove that the canonical model defined in this section obeys (□).

The second adjustment required in the proof that the canonical model is a toS-model is in the proof that it obeys (∃c).

(∃c)   For all t and **w**, there is a constant c such that $a_w(t≈c)$=T.

Now that there are terms other than the constants, showing the canonical model obeys (∃c) requires a special argument. However, the use of ≈saturated sets in the canonical model provides what is needed.

Proof of (∃c). This follows immediately from (Def**a**), if (cReady) can be shown.

(cReady)   For every term t, there is a constant c such that **w** ⊢ t≈c.

Proof of (*cReady*). Let t be any term. Since **w** is ≈saturated, we have the following:

If **w** ⊢ L−∃~t≈c for every constant c, then **w** ⊢ L−∃~t≈t.

In the special case where L is empty, this comes to the following:

If **w** ⊢ ~t≈c for every constant c, then **w** ⊢ ~t≈t.

But since **w** is consistent, **w** ⊬ ~t≈t, for **w** ⊢ t≈t by (≈In). So it follows that **w** ⊬ ~t≈c for some constant c. We know that **w** is maximal, so either **w** ⊢ ~t≈c or **w** ⊢ t≈c. Since the former is not the case, **w** ⊢ t≈c for this c.

EXERCISE 17.10 (Project)   Give a proof of the completeness of oS for toS-validity in all its details.

This finishes the proof of the completeness of oS. So we now know that S, rS, and oS are all complete for tS-validity. However, there is one system we have yet to cover, namely, the system that results from adding only (∃i) to S. Completeness for this system can be shown using almost exactly the strategy of the completeness proof for oS. Simply delete mention of (RC) and (r) in that proof.

EXERCISE 17.11   Prove the completeness of S+(∃i) for tS-models.

17.7. Completeness for Intensional and Substitution Models

When we began the completeness project, we excluded systems that used (RC) and (∃i). In the previous two sections, we have explained how to overcome those limitations at the expense of corresponding complications. It follows that we now have a general completeness result for all systems S formed by adding to fK axioms whose frame conditions are preserved by subframes, and any of the domain rules including (RC) and (∃i). Let 'S' refer now to any of these systems. We can summarize the previous results as follows:

Completeness for tS-models (Unrestricted).
If H ⊨$_{tS}$ C then H ⊢$_S$ C.

Given the transfer theorems developed in Chapter 15, this result may be deployed to show completeness for the intensional and substitution interpretations. The results are immediate given the appropriate transfer theorems. Suppose first that S is formed by adding to fK, axioms whose frame conditions are preserved by subframes, and any of the domain rules. Then completeness of S for iS-validity follows from the i Transfer Theorem.

i Transfer Theorem.   If system S is complete for tS-models, S is also complete with respect to iS-models.

Completeness for iS-Models. If H ⊨$_{iS}$ C then H ⊢$_S$ C.

Now suppose that S is formed by adding to fK, axioms whose frame conditions are preserved by subframes, and any of the domain rules whose conditions do not mention **I**. Completeness of S for sS-validity follows immediately from the s Transfer Theorem.

s Transfer Theorem. If system S is complete for tS-models, S is also complete with respect to sS-models.

Completeness for sS-Models. If H ⊨$_{sS}$ C then H ⊢$_S$ C.

17.8. Completeness for the Objectual Interpretation

Let oS be a system that results from adding to fK, (∃i), (RC) any selection of propositional modal logic axioms whose frame conditions are preserved by subframes, and o-domain axioms from the below list:

(∃E)	∃xEx	**Dw** is not empty.
(Q)	Et	**Dw=D**.
(ED)	Ec→□Ec	If **wRv**, then **Dw** ⊆ **Dv**.
(CD)	~Ec→□~Ec	If **wRv**, then **Dv** ⊆ **Dw**.

It was shown in Section 12.8 (Exercises 12.17 and 12.20) that Ec→□Ec is equivalent to (CBF) or ∀x□Ex, and ~Ec→□~Ec is equivalent to (BF) in oK, so the completeness results will continue to hold when these alternative axioms are used in oS.

(CBF)	□∀xAx→∀x□Ax
(BF)	∀x□Ax→□∀xAx

The completeness of oS follows from the o Transfer Theorem of Section 15.8, provided that we can show that oS is complete for toS-models. But that was shown in Section 17.6.

o Transfer Theorem. If system S is complete for toS-models, S is also complete with respect to oS-models.

Completeness oS for toS-Models. If H ⊨$_{toS}$ C then H ⊢$_{oS}$ C.

Completeness of oS for oS-Models. If H ⊨$_{oS}$ C then H ⊢$_{oS}$ C.

EXERCISE 17.12   Universality, the condition that **wRv** for all **w** and **v** in **W**, is not preserved by subframes because it does not hold in the canonical model for its corresponding propositional modal logic S5. All that the axioms for S5 require of the canonical model for S5 is that the frame be reflexive, transitive, and symmetric, and there are such frames that are not universal. Prove that system oS5 is complete with respect to oS-models that have universal frames. (Hint: Review the hint for Exercise 9.5. Adapt a similar strategy to defining the canonical model for the quantified modal logic.)

18

Descriptions

18.1. Russell's Theory of Descriptions

English phrases that begin with 'the', such as 'the man' and 'the present king of France', are called definite descriptions (or descriptions for short). So far, we have no adequate logical notation for descriptions. It is possible to translate 'the man is bald' by choosing a constant c for 'the man', a predicate letter P for 'is bald', and writing: Pc. However, treating the description as if it were a constant will cause us to classify some valid arguments as invalid.

For example, it should be clear that (1) entails (2).

(1) Aristotle is the philosopher who taught Alexander the Great.
(2) Aristotle taught Alexander the Great.

If we choose the constants: a for Aristotle, and g for Alexander the Great, we might notate (2) as (2′).

(2′) Tag

If we treat "the philosopher who taught Alexander the Great" as a constant g, then (1) is notated by (1′).

(1′) a≈g

However, there is no logical relationship between the atomic sentences (1′) and (2′) that would cause us to recognize that the argument from (1′) to (2′) is valid. Clearly we need a way to notate the internal structure of 'the philosopher who taught Alexander the Great' if we are ever to show that (1) entails (2) in logic.

In order to do that, let us introduce the symbol ! for 'the'. We can use ! with variables much as we do with quantifiers, and notate (3) by (3').

(3) the philosopher who taught Alexander the Great
(3') !x(Px&Txg)

Here (3') reads 'the x such that x is a philosopher and x taught Alexander the Great'. To notate (1), we can now write (1!).

(1) Aristotle is the philosopher who taught Alexander the Great.
(1!) a≈!x(Px&Txg)

Similarly to notate (4) we write (4!).

(4) The present king of France is bald.
(4!) B!xPx

We have introduced the new symbol ! to help explain the validity of the inference from (1) to (2). But to show that the argument is valid, we will need some logical principles to govern the use of !. Russell, in his famous paper "On Denoting" (1905), presents a method for handling arguments involving descriptions. It is to translate each sentence containing a description into a corresponding formula of predicate logic. Once the descriptions have been eliminated by this method, the result can be shown valid using the principles of QL.

The translation that Russell proposed is (Russell's Def !).

(Russell's Def !)   B!xPx =$_{df}$ ∃x(Px & ∀y(Py→y≈x) & Bx)

This says that the sentence:

B!xPx

(read 'the present king of France is bald'), can be rewritten in quantification theory as:

∃x(Px & ∀y(Py→y≈x) & Bx)

which says that there is something that is a present king of France, nothing else is a present king of France, and it is bald. The second conjunct ensures that there is no more than one present king of France. It reflects the idea that when we use 'the' we mean to pick out a unique individual.

It will simplify matters to introduce the following abbreviation:

(Def1)   1Ac =$_{df}$ Ac & ∀y(Ay→y≈c)

We can read 1Pc as 'c and only c is a present king of France'. Using this abbreviation, Russell's definition comes to (Def!).

(Def!) $B!xAx =_{df} \exists x(1Ax \& Bx)$

So the translation for 'The present king of France is bald' comes to: 'something is such that it and only it is a present king of France and it is bald'. Once we translate (1) and (2) into QL with the help of Russell's method, it is not too difficult to show that (2) follows from (1).

EXERCISE 18.1   Show that (1) entails (2) using Russell's method of descriptions. (Hint: $a\approx!x(Px\&Txg)$ comes to (1″) and (2) is notated by (2′).

(1″) $\exists x(1(Px\&Txg) \& a\approx x)$ or $\exists x((Px\&Txg) \& \forall y((Py\&Tyg)\rightarrow y\approx x) \& a\approx x)$
(2′) aTg

Construct a new subproof headed by $1(Pc\&Tcg)\&a\approx c$ to set up for a later use of ($\exists$Out). From this $Pc\&Tcg$ follows by (Def1). Then apply $\approx$Out to Tcg and $a\approx c$ to obtain Tag. The result does not contain c, so ($\exists$Out) allows the derivation of Tag outside the subproof and the proof is complete.)

EXERCISE 18.2   Translate the following sentences into formulas of logic using the ! notation for descriptions. Invent your own predicate letters and explain their meaning.

(a) The round square is round.
(b) The tallest man loves the tallest woman.
(c) The cat is on the mat by the fireplace.

EXERCISE 18.3   The following sentence is ambiguous. (So is (c) above, but the ambiguity is not so striking.)

(d) I visited the fat lady at the circus.

In one sense, I was at the circus during the visit to a fat lady, and in the other, 'fat lady at the circus' identifies which lady I visited. Give two translations of (d) using the ! notation, then say which goes with which sense of (d).

EXERCISE 18.4   Take all formulas produced in the previous two exercises and translate them according to Russell's theory of descriptions, first using the abbreviation 1P, and then without it.

18.2. Applying Russell's Method to Philosophical Puzzles

Russell's method for handling descriptions is useful because it shows us how to replace descriptions with the standard notation of classical predicate logic. As a result, we do not need to formulate any new logical rules to govern the behavior of descriptions. The rules of QL will be sufficient to handle any argument once the descriptions have been eliminated.

Russell's method has philosophical as well as logical interest. He used it to help solve some interesting problems concerning the philosophy of language. We will present here some of the problems that Russell mentions in his famous article "On Denoting", along with their solutions using the method of descriptions.

Problem 1. How can 'There is no present king of France'
be contingently true as we believe?

It seems that the description 'the present king of France' must refer to something if the following sentence ($\sim\exists$PKF) is to make any sense.

($\sim\exists$PKF)   The present king of France does not exist.

But if it does refer, then it presumably refers to something that exists. By this reasoning, ($\sim\exists$PKF) could never be true, and yet it is true. This puzzle puts a strong pressure on us to find something else to which the description does refer, such as a thought or idea; a pressure to which many philosophers succumbed. The same problem turns up in quantificational logic, because according to it, the formula $\exists xx\approx t$ is a theorem. If 'the present King of France' is to be treated as a constant t, then ($\sim\exists$PKF) has the shape $\sim\exists xx\approx t$. In QL, this is a logical contradiction, and so, not contingently true.

Solution: This puzzle is resolved on Russell's Theory by denying that descriptions are referring terms. According to Russell, ($\sim\exists$PKF) has the form: $\sim\exists yy\approx!xPx$, which amounts to $\sim\exists y\exists z(1Pz\&y\approx z)$. This in turn is equivalent to $\sim\exists y1Py$, which claims that no one thing is a present king of France. This is what ($\sim\exists$PKF) seems to say. Notice that $\exists y1Py$ is not a theorem of logic, and so we have no problem explaining the fact that ($\sim\exists$PKF) is contingent. The problem arose, says Russell, because we failed to recognize that 'the present King of France' is not to be treated as a term. On Russell's analysis, there is no term that corresponds to this phrase, and so no need to find a referent for the phrase.

EXERCISE 18.5   Use a tree to create a qK-counterexample to ∃y1Py.

Problem 2. What did King George want to know?

Suppose King George wants to know whether Scott is the author of Waverley, and suppose that Scott is in fact the author of Waverley. By substituting 'Scott' for 'the author of Waverley' in 'King George wants to know whether Scott is the author of Waverley', we conclude that King George wanted to know whether Scott was Scott. However, no one wonders whether Scott is identical to himself. The puzzle is that we have an argument that appears to have true premises and a false conclusion, which also seems valid.

Scott is the author of Waverley.
<u>King George wanted to know whether Scott is the author of Waverley.</u>
King George wanted to know whether Scott is Scott.

The argument appears valid because the first premise seems to have the shape of an identity: $s \approx !xWx$. By the rule of substitution of equalities, we should be able to replace one of the two terms for the other in the second premise, and so arrive at the conclusion. On the other hand, this could not be a valid argument since it has true premises (King George did in fact want to know whether Scott was the author of Waverley) and a false conclusion.

Solution: The solution of this problem, according to Russell's analysis, depends on our distinguishing between the primary and secondary occurrence interpretations of the second premise. If we use the shorthand 'K' for the expression 'King George wanted to know whether', then we may represent these two interpretations in a language with a modal operator **K** as follows.

(Primary Occurrence) $\exists x(1Wx \ \& \ Ks \approx x)$
(Secondary Occurrence) $\mathbf{K}\exists x(1Wx \ \& \ s \approx x)$

The primary occurrence reading makes the claim that there is something that is in fact the only author of Waverley (namely, Scott) and King George wanted to know whether that person was Scott. In this case, what King George wonders about is the person Scott. This is sometimes called the *de re* interpretation (Latin for 'concerning the thing'). Here, the second premise attributes to King George an interest in whether Scott (the person who in fact was the only author of Waverley) was Scott. This premise is false, and so the puzzle concerning our argument disappears.

The secondary occurrence interpretation says that King George wonders about whether there is exactly one author of Waverley who is Scott. This is sometimes called the *de dicto* reading (Latin for 'concerning the sentence'). Under this interpretation, the premise is true, but the argument is no longer valid. Russell explains the invalidity of the argument form by pointing out that although the first premise appears to have the form of an identity: s≈!xWx, its translation according to his theory does not: ∃x(1Wx & s≈x). When the descriptions in the argument are translated away, the argument does not have the form of a substitution of identical terms.

Problem 3. Is the round square both round and square?
Clearly the round square is round, and clearly the round square is square. But something cannot be both round and square.

Solution: On Russell's theory, 'The round square is round' translates to ∃x(1(Rx&Sx)&Rx). This is clearly false since it claims that there is a round square. Both 'the round square is round' and 'the round square is square' are false, given their translations according to Russell's theory of descriptions, and they are false simply because no such thing exists.

18.3. Scope in Russell's Theory of Descriptions

When Russell's theory of description is used, one must take care in applying (Def!) to complex sentences involving ~ and □. Consider (~PKF).

(~PKF)   The present king of France is not bald.

Since the description notation for 'the present king of France is bald' is B!xPx, ~B!xPx would be the notation for (~PKF). On Russell's theory, B!xPx translates to ∃y(By & 1Py), and so we expect ~B!xPx to translate to the negation of that, namely, (~∃).

(~∃)   ~∃x(1Px&Bx)

However, (~∃) reads 'Nothing is both the only present king of France and bald', and this is not what we ordinarily mean by (~PKF) when we say that the present king of France is not bald. Given that there is no present king of France, there is no such king that is bald, and so (~∃) is true. However, (~PKF), 'The present king of France is not bald', is false, or perhaps meaningless.

A correct translation of what we ordinarily mean by (~PKF) is (~B), which claims that there is an only king of France, which is not bald.

(~B) $\exists x(1Px\&\sim Bx)$

Here the scope of the negation is Bx, and not to the whole sentence $\exists x(1Px\&Bx)$.

This shows that there two different ways to apply (Def!) to (~PKF) depending on how the scope of ~ is treated. One needs to distinguish, as it were, the primary from secondary occurrences of negation in (~PKF). It follows that the notation ~B!xPx is ambiguous as it stands since one might unpack it as either (~$\exists$) or (~B). Russell solved the problem by introducing special notation to make clear how the scope of ~ is to be settled in the final result. Here !xPx is treated like a quantifier rather than a term, so that one may distinguish between (~$\exists$) and (~B) as follows:

~[!xPx]B!xPx for (~$\exists$): ~$\exists x(1Px\&Bx)$
[!xPx]~B!xPx for (~B): $\exists x(1Px\&\sim Bx)$

The importance of attending to scope in Russell's theory becomes even clearer for the modal operator $\square$. Consider the following sentence where b is a constant standing for Benjamin Franklin, and B reads 'is the inventor of bifocals'.

1Bb & $\square b\approx b$

This sentence is presumably true, for it says that Benjamin Franklin was the only inventor of bifocals, and he was necessarily identical to himself. From the principles of classical quantificational logic QL, the following sentence ($\exists\square$) can be derived by (Q$\exists$In):

($\exists\square$) $\exists x(1Bx \& \square b\approx x)$

A naive application of Russell's definition (Def!) would yield the following:

$\square b\approx !xBx$

This appears to claim that Benjamin Franklin is necessarily the inventor of bifocals. We have objected to this claim in Section 13.6, and for good reason. Being the inventor of bifocals is not a necessary property of Benjamin Franklin because somebody else might easily have qualified had history been slightly different. However, it appears that we have obtained this unpalatable result from 1Bb & $\square b\approx b$ in classical logic alone.

Arthur Smullyan (1948) explains why this reasoning is fallacious. The notation □b≈!xBx is ambiguous between (∃□) and (□∃).

(∃□)   ∃x(1Bx & □b≈x)
(□∃)   □∃x(1Bx & b≈x)

But it is (□∃) and not (∃□) that asserts that Benjamin Franklin is necessarily the inventor of bifocals. (∃□) asserts only that there is exactly one inventor of bifocals who is necessarily identical with himself. The unpalatable version of □b≈!xBx is (□∃), and this cannot be obtained from 1Bb & □b≈b in classical logic.

The need to indicate scope complicates the notation for descriptions and underscores a point that has been made in Sections 12.3 and 12.4, namely, that the Russell's strategy is not compatible with treating definite descriptions as genuine terms. If !xPx were a genuine term, then ~B!xPx would have the shape ~Bt, where ambiguity of scope can not arise.

The fact that the Russellian analysis does not treat !xPx as a term can be appreciated in another way. When !xPx≈!xPx (for 'the present king of France is identical to the present king of France') is translated according to the theory, we obtain a sentence that asserts the existence of exactly one present king of France. Since there is no present king of France, !xPx≈!xPx must be false, and not a logical truth. If !xPx counts as a term, however, !xPx≈!xPx would amount to an instance of (≈In), and so qualify as a theorem.

EXERCISE 18.6   Translate !xPx≈!xPx into predicate logic using Russell's theory, and show that the result is equivalent to ∃x1Px.

18.4. Motives for an Alternative Treatment of Descriptions

One of the best known complaints against Russell's theory concerns the fact that sentences involving descriptions entail the existence and uniqueness of what is described. However, there are many sentences of English where this does not seem to be the case. Consider the following examples:

(1) The accident was averted.
(2) The omega minus particle was never found, so physicists now believe that it does not exist.

If Russell's theory is right, (1) entails that there is exactly one accident, and (2) entails that there is exactly one omega minus particle. Clearly these sentences do not mean to assert the existence and uniqueness of such things. Even 'the cat is on the mat', which was a favorite example used by Russell in other contexts, is not correctly treated by his theory. We simply don't count 'the cat is on the mat' false on the grounds that there happens to be more than one cat in the world.

EXERCISE 18.7   Prove $\exists x \exists y(Cx \& Cy \& {\sim} x \approx y) \to {\sim} \exists x(1Cx \& \exists y(1My \& Oxy))$, and explain what this has to do with the previous discussion.

Russell may reply that his theory doesn't apply to such uses of 'the accident', 'the omega minus particle', 'the cat', and 'the mat'. However, the vast majority of phrases with the shape 'the P' in English do not behave as Russell predicts. More often, the context of use of a description helps us decide what it refers to. In most of its uses (for example), 'the cat' behaves more like 'the cat in a domain of things I am now discussing'.

Strawson (1950) is famous for making a related objection. On Russell's theory, 'the present king of France is bald' is false, for it entails the existence of a present king of France, and of course, there is none. However, Strawson urges that 'the present king of France is bald' is not false, when the term 'the present king of France' lacks a referent. Instead of *entailing* the existence of a unique present king of France, the sentence *presupposes* that there is one. If the presupposition fails, the sentence is not false, it simply fails to make a statement, and so lacks a truth value.

The problem that sentences like (1)–(2) do not appear to entail existence and uniqueness of what is described becomes more pressing in quantified modal logic. Russell's theory is normally deployed using a standard or classical theory of quantification. In Section 12.9 it was shown that classical rules require a single possibilist domain of quantification where $\exists x Ax$ reads: 'there is a possible object x such that A'. So on this account, (1) entails the existence and uniqueness of a *possible* accident. Although it is an improvement that (1) no longer entails the existence of an *actual* accident, the implication that there is only *one* possible accident is ludicrous in the extreme. On a theory that there are many more possible objects than actual ones, the prospects for satisfying the uniqueness condition for a description would seem even more remote.

These objections do not close the door on Russell's theory of descriptions. It could be rescued with a theory of how the context of utterance narrows down the domain of quantification to the few objects that are the topic of discussion in a given context. With such a theory in hand, the uniqueness problem might be resolved. It is interesting to reflect on the fact that the actualist interpretation of the quantifier, where the domain depends on the possible world at issue, promises to provide the right tools for fleshing out such a theory. If possible worlds are understood to include information about the context of utterance, then a domain that varies from one possible world to another could be sensitive to context in the right way. So it appears that there are better prospects for solving the uniqueness problem with an actualist treatment of the quantifiers, one that requires free logic rather than classical rules.

Although the application of Russell's theory of descriptions to modal logic could be developed in such a way, this book will explore an alternative system !S, which does not rely on Russell's method. Since not all philosophers are able to accept Russell's theory, such an alternative will be worth exploring. In !S, descriptions are treated as genuine terms – terms that are typically nonrigid. !S handles definite descriptions directly, without the need for complex translation methods. The description !xPx will qualify as a term in this logic, and there will be no need for the complex notation that was required in Russell's theory to indicate scope in sentences such as ~B!xPx, and □b≈!xBx. Problems involving scope simply do not arise in !S. Furthermore, it will be shown in Section 18.10 that !S can resolve (in its own way) the philosophical puzzles presented in Section 18.2 that helped motivate Russell's method.

18.5. Syntax for Modal Description Theory

System !S for modal description theory will be developed as an extension of the system oS for the objectual interpretation. It will treat descriptions as complex nonrigid terms. In order to provide a firm foundation for the theorems in the next few sections, we need to define a language for modal description theory. Since !S is built from oS, we may presume, if we like, that E is defined by (DefE), rather than being a primitive symbol of the language. The language for !S will contain the same basic symbols as were in oS except the description operator ! is included as well. So the symbols of !S include the universal quantifier ∀, the description symbol !, an unlimited supply of *variables* x, y, z, x′, . . , a set of *constants* b, c, b′, c′, . . , a set of *predicate letters* P, Q, R, P′, . . , the propositional logic symbols ⊥, →, □, the identity sign ≈, and finally the parentheses, and the comma.

The definition of the atomic sentences of the language is complicated by the presence of descriptions. One problem that must be faced is that strings of symbols such as P!xGxt are ambiguous. P!xGxt may be read as the result of filling the two-place predicate letter P with two terms !xGx and t. On the other hand, it might be interpreted as the result of filling the one-place predicate P with the description !xGxt, where G is a two-place predicate. The official notation for atomic sentences uses parentheses and commas to clear up such ambiguities. An atomic sentence (for example R(t, s)) is formed by appending a parenthesized *list* of the terms (for example (t, s)) to a predicate letter (R). On this approach, the two possible readings of the ambiguous formula P!xQxt are distinguished as follows: P(!xG(x), t) and P(!xG(x, t)). Although the official notation requires that terms in an atomic sentences appear in a list, writing the extra parentheses and commas can become tiresome, so the parentheses and commas will be omitted when no ambiguities arise.

Now we are ready to define the sets of sentences and terms together in a single definition.

The Definition of Terms and Sentences of !S.

1. Constants are terms.
2. If At is a sentence, and x is a variable, then !xAx is a term.
3. If l is a list of terms and P is a predicate letter, then Pl is a sentence.
4. If A, B, and At are sentences, x is a variable, and both s and t terms, then ⊥, s≈t, (A→B), □A, and ∀xAx are sentences.
   No sequences of symbols count as terms or sentences unless they qualify by clauses 1–4.

It is crucial to this definition that both terms and sentences are defined together, for atomic sentences such as P(!xAx) may contain complex descriptions !xAx, where At is a very complex sentence that may itself contain predicate letters and other terms including (complex) descriptions.

Note that although !x in the formula !xAx has the appearance of a quantifier, it plays a very different role in the syntax of !S. Quantifiers like ∃x form sentences ∃xAx from an instance Ac. On the other hand, !xAx forms a *term*, not a sentence. Although a sentence is the sort of expression that can be true or false, a term cannot have a truth value, and instead picks out an individual. The syntactical role of terms is to join with the predicates to form sentences, so for example, the term 'the present king of France' can be joined with 'is bald' to form the sentence 'the present king of France is bald'. It follows that although !xAx may have the superficial form of a sentence, it is actually a term, which must be combined with a predicate to obtain a sentence.

18.6. Rules for Modal Description Theory: The System !S

If descriptions are added to quantified modal logic, new rules are needed to govern the ! notation. The following axiom, when added to oS, defines the system !S of modal free description theory. Furthermore !S-trees may be defined by simply including (!) among the tree rules for oS.

!S = oS + (!)

(!) $\forall y(1Ay \leftrightarrow y \approx !xAx)$

Given (!) is available in !S, ($\forall$Out) may be applied to derive the following:

$Ec \rightarrow (1Ac \leftrightarrow c \approx !xAx)$.

This reports that if c exists, then c is the only A iff c is identical to the A. In the light of the derivability of this formula, it is easy to see that the following more convenient rules of inference are derivable in !S:

(!Out)	$c \approx !xAx$	(!In)	$1Ac$
	Ec		Ec
	--------		--------
	$1Ac$		$c \approx !xAx$

It is also not hard to prove (!) from the above two rules. So it really does not matter whether we define !S with the axiom or this pair of rules.

Some formulations of free description theory use the rule (E!Out) instead of (!Out) (Thomason 1970, p. 63, A9$'$).

(E!Out) $E\ !xAx$

$\exists x 1 Ax$

But again it will not matter which of those two rules is used since the resulting systems prove exactly the same arguments.

To illustrate proof strategies in !S, here is a demonstration that (E!Out) is derivable given (!Out) and other rules of oS.

E !xAx

∃yy≈!xAx	(see Exercise 12.22)
└─ Ec & c≈!xAx	
Ec	(&Out)
c≈!xAx	(&Out)
1Ac	(!Out)
∃y1Ay	(∃In)
∃y1Ay	(∃Out)

This proof illustrates a useful strategy for exploiting an available sentence of the form Et. It is to unpack Et by (DefE) and then immediately set up a new subproof headed by Ec & c≈t for the purposes of eventually using (∃Out).

> **EXERCISE. 18.8**   Show E!xAx↔∃y1Ay in !S. (Hint. For the proof from left to right use (E!Out). For the proof from right to left set up a subproof for (∃Out) and apply (!In).)

The following proof that (!Out) may be derived from oS+(!In)+(E!Out) raises an interesting issue concerning substitution of ≈. Here is an outline of the demonstration:

c≈ !xAx
Ec

∃yy≈ !xAx	(∃In)
E!xAx	(DefE)
∃y1Ay	(E !Out)
└─ Eb &1Ab	
Eb	(&Out)
1Ab	(&Out)
b≈ !xAx	(!In)
!xAx≈c	(c≈!xAx and the symmetry of ≈)
b≈c	(≈Out)
1Ac	**(R≈Out)**
1Ac	(∃Out)

In the next to last line, 1Ac has been obtained from 1Ab and b≈c, using (R≈Out), the rule that allows the full substitution of identities in the case of rigid terms. (See Section 12.11.) Note that this substitution would not be legal for terms in general, for the substitution of identities does not follow for non-rigid terms when the substitution is carried out within the scope of □.

In !S, the rule of universal instantiation (!∀Out) appropriate for descriptions is derivable in the special case where the description follows a predicate letter Q.

(!∀Out) ∀xQx / ∃x1Px→Q!xPx

EXERCISE 18.9 Prove (!∀Out) is derivable in !S, where Q is any predicate letter.

In Exercise 18.8, you proved that E!xPx (which says that !xPx exists) and ∃x1Px (which says there is exactly one P) are equivalent in !S. So (!∀Out) may be written in an equivalent form, which resembles the free logic principle of universal instantiation for descriptions.

∀xQx / E!xPx→Q!xPx

Note, however, that this principle does not work in general, for the proof of ∀xAx / E!xPx→A!xPx is blocked in case Ax is an intensional expression.

EXERCISE 18.10 Attempt a proof of ∀x□Qx / E!xPx→□Q!xPx and explain why the proof is blocked.

One of the reasons the proof is blocked is that (∀Out) allows instantiation only to constants c. In !S, we do not allow (nor do we want) the rule (t∀) of universal instantiation for all terms, for as we pointed out in Section 13.6, this rule is invalid for nonrigid terms, and descriptions are typically nonrigid.

(t∀) ∀xAx / Et→At

Another interesting feature of !S is that P!xPx cannot be proven there. (See Exercise 18.17a below.) So we are not forced to claim, for example, that the round square is round and square. The closest we can come in !S to P!xPx is E!xPx→P!xPx, which says in the case of our example that the round square is round and square *if it exists.*

EXERCISE 18.11   Prove E!xPx / P!xPx in !S. (Hint. Apply (E!Out) to E!xPx and set up a subproof headed by Ec&1Pc for (∃Out). Apply (!In) and watch for an opportunity to make a substitution.) Would the proof be possible where P replaced by □P throughout?

Given the fact that nothing can be both round and square, we conclude in !S that the round square does not exist.

EXERCISE 18.12   Suppose ∀x(Rx↔~Sx). Prove ~E!x(Rx&Sx) in !S. (Hint. Suppose E!x(Rx&Sx) for (IP). By (E!Out) you may obtain ∃x1(Rx&Sx). Set up a subproof for (∃Out) headed by Ec&1(Rc&Sc). By (Def1) this amounts to (Rc&Sc) & ∀y((Ry&Sy)→y≈c). Then derive a contradiction using ∀x(Rx↔~Sx)).

EXERCISE 18.13   Prove the following in !S:

a) E!xPx / !xPx≈!yPy (Hint: Assume E!xPx and apply (E!Out). Set up a subproof for (∃Out) headed by Ec & 1Pc, and then use (!In) twice, once for the variable x and the other for the variable y.)

b) ~E!x~x≈x (Hint: Assume E!x~x≈x for (IP) and apply (E!Out). Set up a subproof for (∃Out) headed by Ec & 1~c≈c, and use (Def1) to obtain a contradiction.)

c) ∃x∃y(~x≈y & Px & Py) / ~E!xPx (Hint: Assume E!xPx and apply (E!Out). Set up a subproof headed by Ec & 1Pc for (∃Out). Then set up (∃Out) subproofs twice more using ∃x∃y(~x≈y & Px & Py). Watch for an opportunity to exploit (Def1) to obtain a contradiction.)

d) E!xPx, ∀x(Px↔Qx) / !xPx≈!xQx (Hint: Use the initial strategy for the previous problem, constructing a subproof headed by Ec & 1Pc. Obtain c≈!xPx by (!In). Use ∀x(Px↔Qx) and (Def1) to obtain a proof of 1Qc, and then apply (!In) again to obtain c≈!xQx.)

e) E!xx≈t / t ≈ !xt≈x (Hint: Use the initial strategy for the previous two problems to set up a subproof headed by Ec & 1c≈t. Unpack 1c≈t by (Def1), and create a proof of 1t≈c. Now apply (!In) to obtain c ≈ !xt≈x, from which t ≈ !xt≈x follows directly from c≈t. This exercise is difficult because the notation !xt≈x (and !xx≈t) is hard to "read" especially during applications of the ! rules. It helps to practice applying (!Out) to Ec and !xt≈x before you attempt this exercise just to get used to the process.)

The axiom (!) may be added to stronger logics as well. However, one must be careful about the strength of the underlying logic. For example, in the case of constant quantifier domains, (!) may be added to the system oS+(Q) for classical quantification forming system !qS.

!qS = oS + (Q) + (!).

Trees and proofs for this system may be simplified using the following description rules:

(!QOut)   c≈!xAx   (!QIn)   1Ac
          ------   ------
          1Ac   c≈!xAx

EXERCISE *18.14   Translate sentences (1) and (2) below. Then attempt a proof of the resulting argument form in !S. What blocks the proof? Now prove the argument in !qS.

(1) Aristotle is the philosopher who taught Alexander the Great.
(2) Aristotle taught Alexander the Great.

Although this seems an attractive simplification of !S, the resulting system is not sound. To see why, note that the axiom (Q) yields E!x~x≈x, which is incompatible with the results of Exercise 18.13b.

18.7. Semantics for !S

Our next project will be to give a semantics for modal description theory, based on the objectual interpretation. The idea is to supplement the definition of a oS-model with a semantical condition that explains how the extension of a description is calculated. We have already remarked in Section 18.4 (where objections to Russell's theory were discussed) that one who uses the sentence 'the cat is on the mat' does not think that there is exactly one cat in the universe. Instead the speaker has in mind a special domain defined by the context of utterance – one that contains exactly one cat. The varying domain approach to quantified modal logic is especially well suited to capturing this idea. Presume now that domain **Dw** contains the things that a speaker had in mind in a "world" **w** that includes the context supplied by him or her. The fundamental idea behind the semantics for ! is that !xAx should refer to the unique object in the speaker's domain such that Ad is T, provided that there is such an individual. Let us introduce formal notation to help express this idea. The notation '$1a_w(Ad)$' indicates that d is the unique object existing in **Dw** such that $a_w(Ad)=T$.

$1a_w(Ad)$ iff d is the only member of **Dw** such that $a_w(Ad)=T$.

If there is such an object d, it will be the referent of !xAx. On the other hand, there may be no such object. Under those circumstances, it is not clear how we should assign a referent to !xAx, or even that !xAx should receive any referent at all. The idea that !xAx may have no referent will be explored further in Exercise 18.20 below. For the moment, however, let us assume that !xAx is to be given a referent. Then at least one thing is clear; the referent given to !xAx should not be an object in **Dw** because if any referent of !xAx is in **Dw**, it ought to be the unique existing thing d for which $a_w(Ad)=T$, and there is no such d.

Putting these two ideas together, the following is the condition that explains how !xAx is assigned a referent:

(!)   If for some object d, $1a_w(Ad)$, then $a_w(!xAx)=d$,
        otherwise $a_w(!xAx) \notin$ **Dw**.

A *!S-model* will be any oS-model that also satisfies (!). !S-validity is defined from the notion of a !S-model in the usual way.

In order to satisfy condition (!), there will have to be a member outside of **Dw** to which !xAx can be assigned whenever there is no unique member d such that $a_w(Ad)=T$. Since all terms refer to objects in **D**, this object will have to be in **D** but outside **Dw**. It will always be necessary to find such an object because of descriptions such as !x~x≈x, where $1a_w(\sim d \approx d)$ cannot hold for any d. Intuitively, the requirement that there be a member of **D** outside **Dw** is not especially burdensome, since one expects there to be at least one possible object that fails to exist in **Dw**, especially given the understanding that **Dw** is a narrow domain especially defined by the speaker's concerns. Note, however, that the constant domain condition (Q) is not compatible with requirement (!) since $a_w(!xAx) \notin$ **Dw** can never hold when **D=Dw**.

(Q)   **D=Dw**.

It follows that a viable description theory that employs (!) can not be based on classical logic. This incompatibility is a reflection of the unsoundness of !qS noted in the previous section.

18.8. Trees for !S

Trees for !S are constructed by adding to the tree rules for oS the rule that any instance of axiom (!) may be added to any world during construction of the tree. In case the tree does not close, it will be necessary to add each of the infinitely many instances of (!). Therefore, it will be necessary to adopt the strategy of Section 14.6 to oscillate between applying tree rules and adding instances of axioms during tree construction. Using the axiom leads to complex trees because (∀T) may be applied to it in many ways, and furthermore the use of ↔ rules or (Def↔) complicates any tree. Using the derived rules (!Out), (!In), and (E!Out) in trees can simplify tree construction. However, although a closed tree that results from the use of these rules will clearly demonstrate that the argument for which it is constructed has a proof, there are valid arguments that may not have closed trees if these rules were adopted in place of the axiom. So officially, the axiomatic formulation of trees is assumed. Nevertheless it is convenient to allow the use of the derived rules in trees since they can simplify trees considerably.

EXERCISE 18.15   Construct trees for the arguments proven in exercise 18.13.

Since trees do not serve as a decision procedure for predicate logic, it follows that !S-trees could not serve as a decision procedure for validity in a language that includes descriptions. However, !S-trees do serve as a quasi-decision procedure in the following sense. From the adequacy proof to be given in the next section, it follows that when an argument is !S-valid, the !S-tree will eventually close after finitely many steps. On the other hand, when an argument is !S-invalid, !S-trees will be infinite since there are infinitely many instances of the axiom (!) to add to each world. Despite this problem, it is often possible to use !S-trees to construct a partial tree for a !S-invalid argument that will yield a !S-counterexample to it. Consider, for example, the following argument:

$$\exists x(1Bx \ \& \ \Box b{\approx}x) \ / \ \Box b{\approx}!xBx$$

An informal explanation for why a reading of this principle is unacceptable was given in Section 18.3. Even when classical quantifier principles are used, it does not follow from the fact that there is someone (namely, Benjamin Franklin) who is the first inventor of bifocals and necessarily identical to Benjamin Franklin, that it is necessary that Franklin is the first inventor of bifocals. Here is a partial tree for this argument that quickly yields a diagram for a !qK-counterexample. Note that for efficiency, (!QIn) is used in the tree rather than the axiom (!).

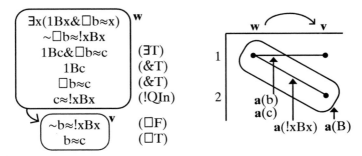

18.9. Adequacy of !S

In this section, the adequacy of !S will be proven, where !S is the result of adding axiom (!) to any system oS that we have so far shown to be adequate. The result will depend on the following helpful lemmas. The first says that the hybrid sentence $\forall y(Ay{\rightarrow}y{\approx}d)$ is true at a world **w** iff any object e in **Dw** such that $a_w(Ae)=T$ must be d.

=d Lemma.
   $a_w(\forall y(Ay{\rightarrow}y{\approx}d))=T$ iff   if $e \in \mathbf{Dw}$ and $a_w(Ae)=T$, then e=d.

Proof.
$a_w(\forall y(Ay{\rightarrow}y{\approx}d))=T$ iff
for any $e \in \mathbf{Dw}, a_w(Ae{\rightarrow}e{\approx}d)=T$ iff   (o$\forall$)

for any $e \in \mathbf{Dw}$, if $\mathbf{a_w}(Ae)=T$ then $\mathbf{a_w}(e{\approx}d)=T$ iff $(\rightarrow)$
for any $e \in \mathbf{Dw}$, if $\mathbf{a_w}(Ae)=T$ then $e=d$. $(\approx)$ and (d)

The next lemma says that $1\mathbf{a_w}(Ad)$ holds exactly when d exists at $\mathbf{w}$ and the hybrid sentence 1Ad is true there as well.

1 Lemma. $1\mathbf{a_w}(Ad)$ iff $d \in \mathbf{Dw}$ and $\mathbf{a_w}(1Ad)=T$.

Proof. For the proof from left to right, assume $1\mathbf{a_w}(Ad)$, that is, that d is the only member of $\mathbf{Dw}$ such that $\mathbf{a_w}(Ad)=T$. So for any member e of $\mathbf{Dw}$ such that $\mathbf{a_w}(Ae)=T$, $e=d$. By the $=d$ Lemma, $\mathbf{a_w}(\forall y(Ay{\rightarrow}y{\approx}d))=T$. This with $\mathbf{a_w}(Ad)=T$, (&) and (Def1) yields $\mathbf{a_w}(1Ad)=T$. For the proof in the other direction, note that from the assumption that $\mathbf{a_w}(1Ad)=T$, it follows that $\mathbf{a_w}(Ad)=T$ and $\mathbf{a_w}(\forall y(Ay{\rightarrow}y{\approx}d))=T$. By the $=d$ Lemma, if $e \in \mathbf{Dw}$ and $\mathbf{a_w}(Ae)=T$, then $e=d$. So it follows that d is the only member of $\mathbf{Dw}$ such that $\mathbf{a_w}(Ad)=T$, which is what $1\mathbf{a_w}(Ad)$ claims.

A third lemma states the semantical condition that corresponds to the (!) axiom being true.

(!) Axiom Lemma. $\mathbf{a_w}(\forall y(1Ay{\leftrightarrow}!xAx{\approx}y))=T$ iff
    for any $d \in \mathbf{Dw}$, $\mathbf{a_w}(1Ad)=T$ iff $\mathbf{a_w}(!xAx)=d$.

Proof.
$(\forall y(1Ay{\leftrightarrow} !xAx{\approx}y))=T$ iff
for any $d \in \mathbf{Dw}$, $\mathbf{a_w}(1Ad{\leftrightarrow} !xAx{\approx}d)=T$ iff $(o\forall)$
for any $d \in \mathbf{Dw}$, $\mathbf{a_w}(1Ad)=T$ iff $\mathbf{a_w}(!xAx{\approx}d)=T$ iff $(\leftrightarrow)$
for any $d \in \mathbf{Dw}$, $\mathbf{a_w}(1Ad)=T$ iff $\mathbf{a_w}(!xAx)=d$ (d) and $(\approx)$

We are now ready to proof the soundness and completeness of !S.

Soundness of !S.   If $L \vdash_{!S} C$ then $L \vDash_{!S} C$.

Proof. We know that oS is oS-sound, so to show soundness of !S, it is necessary to show only that the (!) axiom is !S-valid. But in the light of the (!) Axiom Lemma we need demonstrate only the following:

    For any $d \in \mathbf{Dw}$, $\mathbf{a_w}(1Ad)=T$ iff $\mathbf{a_w}(!xAx)=d$.

To prove this, let d be any member of $\mathbf{Dw}$. To show $\mathbf{a_w}(1Ad)=T$ iff $\mathbf{a_w}(!xAx)=d$, first assume $\mathbf{a_w}(1Ad)=T$. By the 1 Lemma, $1\mathbf{a_w}(Ad)$, so by (!), $\mathbf{a_w}(!xAx)=d$. Now suppose $\mathbf{a_w}(!xAx)=d$. Since $d \in \mathbf{Dw}$, we have $\mathbf{a_w}(!xAx) \in \mathbf{Dw}$. But by (!), $\mathbf{a_w}(!xAx) \notin \mathbf{Dw}$ if there is no object e such that $1a_w(Ae)$. So there must be such an object e. However, if $1a_w(Ae)$, it follows by (!) again that $a_w(!xAx)=e$, and so d=e. Hence $1a_w(Ad)$, from which $a_w(1Ad)=T$ follows by the 1 Lemma.

Completeness of !S. If H $\vDash_{!S}$ C then H $\vdash_{!S}$ C.

Proof. We prove the contrapositive: if H $\nvdash_{!S}$ C, then H $\nvDash_{!S}$ C. So assume H $\nvdash_{!S}$ C. Use the completeness method of either Section 16.4 (using trees) or 17.8 (using the canonical model) to establish H $\nvDash_{t!S}$ C, where a t!S-model is a toS-model that satisfies the axiom (!). This establishes the completeness of iS with respect to t!S-models. At this point the Extended o Transfer Theorem of Section 15.8 will guarantee that !S is complete for !S-models, provided that we can show that axiom (!) expresses the semantical condition (!) on oS-models.

Extended o Transfer Theorem. If nS results from adding axioms to oS, each of which expresses its corresponding condition, and if nS is complete for tnS-models, then nS is complete for nS-models.

So to show completeness it is sufficient to show that axiom (!) expresses the condition (!).

(!) If for some object d, $1a_w(Ad)$, then $a_w(!xAx)=d$,
     otherwise $a_w(!xAx) \notin \mathbf{D}w$.

To show axiom (!) expresses the condition (!), we need to show that the ti-expansion of any t!S-model obeys (!). Since the t!S-model satisfies (!), we have $a_w(\forall y(1Ay \leftrightarrow !xAx \approx y))=T$. To prove (!), we need only prove the two conditionals that form it.

Suppose $1a_w(Ad)$. We must show that $a_w(!xAx)=d$. The fact that $1a_w(Ad)$ yields $d \in \mathbf{D}w$ and $a_w(1Ad)=T$ by the 1 Lemma. By $a_w(\forall y(1Ay \leftrightarrow !xAx \approx y))=T$ and the (!) Axiom Lemma, we have that $a_w(1Ad)=T$ iff $a_w(!xAx)=d$, so $a_w(!xAx)=d$.

Suppose there is no d such that $1a_w(Ad)$. We must show that $a_w(!xAx) \notin \mathbf{D}w$. We know $a_w(!xAx)$ is assigned to some member e of $\mathbf{D}$. We will show that this e is not a member of $\mathbf{D}w$ by Indirect Proof. Assuming $e \in \mathbf{D}w$, and the (!) Axiom Lemma, we have $a_w(1Ae)=T$ iff $a_w(!xAx)=e$. But $a_w(!xAx)=e$, so $a_w(1Ae)=T$. This with $e \in \mathbf{D}w$ and the 1 Lemma yields $1a_w(Ae)$, which conflicts with the first supposition. So $d \notin \mathbf{D}w$, that is, $a_w(!xAx) \notin \mathbf{D}w$.

EXERCISE 18.18   Review the discussion of the Good Samaritan Paradox in Section 2.4. Now that notation for descriptions is available, a more sophisticated solution to the problem may be attempted. Use the following vocabulary to translate the paradoxical argument into the language of free description theory.

Bxy   x binds y
Wx   x is a wound of the traveler
g   Good Samaritan

Use trees to show that in free logic Bg!xWx $\nvdash$ ∃yWy, establishing that there is no danger in free logic of obtaining OBg!xWx $\vdash$ O∃yWy using (GN) with the deontic operator O. On the other hand, show that E!xWx, Bg!xWx $\vdash$ ∃yWy, but explain why the result of applying (GN) to it: OE!xWx, OBg!xWx $\vdash$ O∃yWy does not result in an intuitively valid argument with true premises.

EXERCISE 18.19   The semantics given in this chapter is weak in some respects. Devise !K-models to show that (instances of) the following two principles are !K-invalid:

(1) t ≈ !xx≈t
(2) ∀x(Ax↔Bx) / !xAx≈!xBx.

Do you think (1) and (2) are intuitively correct? In Exercise 18.13e you showed E!xx≈t $\vdash_{!S}$ t ≈ !xx≈t. Show also that ∀x(Ax↔Bx), E!xAx $\vdash_{!K}$!xAx≈!xBx. Given that these somewhat weaker principles are available in !S, are your intuitions pacified? Assuming they are not, explain how to add conditions to !S-models to validate (1) and (2). Then show completeness of the strengthened logics.

EXERCISE 18.20   (Project). Strawson (1950) takes the position that the sentence 'the present king of France is bald' is not false as Russell claims. It is instead undefined since the description 'the present king of France' has no referent. Provide a Strawsonian semantics for description theory by revising the semantics for free description theory given in this section. Assume that an assignment function may be partial, that is, it may leave values for some expressions undefined. Your aim should be to define the semantics so that the resulting concept of validity is equivalent to the one given in Section 18.6. You should also prove that equivalence. Here are hints about how the semantics should go. First, sentences that contain undefined terms will also be undefined, but otherwise the standard truth conditions hold. Let '?a_w(e)' indicate that expression e is undefined by **a** at world **w**. Here are sample conditions for the "Strawsonian" semantics:

If t occurs in sequence l and ?a_w(t), then ?a_w(l).
If ?a_w(l), then ?a_w(Pl), but otherwise a_w(Pl)=T iff a_w(l) ∈ a_w(P).

If ?$\mathbf{a_w}$(A) or ?$\mathbf{a_w}$(B) then ?$\mathbf{a_w}$(A→B),
  but otherwise $\mathbf{a_w}$(A→B)=T iff $\mathbf{a_w}$(A)=F or $\mathbf{a_w}$(B)=T.
If ?$\mathbf{a_v}$(A) for any $\mathbf{v}$ such that $\mathbf{wRv}$, then ?$\mathbf{a_w}$(□A),
  but otherwise $\mathbf{a_w}$(□A)=T iff if $\mathbf{wRv}$, then $\mathbf{a_v}$(A)=T.
If ?$\mathbf{a_w}$(Ad) for any d ∈ $\mathbf{Dw}$, then ?$\mathbf{a_w}$(∀xA),
  but otherwise $\mathbf{a_w}$(∀xA)=T iff for all d ∈ $\mathbf{Dw}$, $\mathbf{a_w}$(Ad)=T.

What clause would be appropriate for !xAx? There are problems to be faced in providing a definition of validity when partial assignments are used. How does one guarantee that standard truths such as Pc→Pc come out valid? When c is not defined on a model, Pc→Pc will be undefined as well, with the result that Pc→Pc is not always T in every model, and so presumably not valid. One way to deal with this is to modify a basic idea from the semantics for propositional logic. Consider the propositional variable p. As a variable, p has no particular meaning in English, so we may think of its value as undefined. But p→p may be validated nonetheless. Let us fill in the value of p in an arbitrary way. Regardless of how we do that, we can never refute p→p. Whether p is T or F, p→p is T. This is why p→p is considered valid even though p is undefined. You may adopt a similar idea to define validity for a Strawsonian semantics. Let assignment **c** be a *completion* of (partial) assignment **a** if **c** agrees with **a** on the values of all expressions defined by **a**, but also fills in values for all expressions not defined by **a** in some way that satisfies (!). A (partial) assignment function *a* *satisfies a set H of sentences in world w* (in short: $\mathbf{a_w}$(H)=T), provided that every member of H is T at **w** on some arbitrary completion of **a**. Now that notation: '$\mathbf{a_w}$(H)=T' is defined, the notions of a counterexample and valid argument are defined in the usual way. You may also be interested in the partial model semantics found in (van Fraassen 1966) and (van Fraassen and Lambert, 1967), where a somewhat stronger logic is developed.

18.10. How !S Resolves the Philosophical Puzzles

Russell's theory was designed to handle philosophical problems connected with descriptions. Let's see how the modal description theory !S handles the same issues.

Problem 1. How can 'The present king of France doesn't exist' be contingently true?

Solution: The translation for 'the present king of France does not exist' in the notation of !S is ~E!xPx. Since E!xPx is not a theorem of !S, we are not left with the puzzle that a sentence that is contingently true is treated as a contradiction. It would seem that we are left with a puzzle. If the sentence ~E!xPx is to make sense and so be true, then !xPx would have to have a referent; yet the sentence itself says that !xPx does not refer to anything real. The solution to the problem is simply to deny that a term of a sentence must refer to an existent object in order for the sentence to have a meaning, and hence to take on a truth value. We can challenge our opponent's basic premise by asking him to explain how sentences like 'Pegasus is a winged horse' and 'Pegasus is not a hippopotamus' (which are clearly both true) can be treated on a theory that denies truth values to all sentences whose terms refer to things that do not exist. In the semantics for !S, terms may refer to possible objects, and sentences that contain such terms have truth values.

Problem 2. Did King George really want to know whether Scott was Scott?

Solution: The argument has the form of a substitution of identical terms.

$$s \approx !xAx$$
$$\underline{Ks \approx !xAx}$$
$$Ks \approx s$$

But we deny the correctness of substituting identities in the scope of the intensional operator **K** (which reads 'King George wanted to know whether . .').

Problem 3. Is the round square both round and square?

Solution: The round square is not round, and it is not square. In fact, it is not. It does not exist. We can prove neither R!x(Rx&Sx) nor S!x(Rx&Sx) in free logic unless we also have E!x(Rx&Sx). (The round square exists.) But we showed in Exercise 18.12 that given the premise that being round and being square are incompatible, it follows that ~E!x(Rx&Sx). (The round square does not exist.)

19

Lambda Abstraction

19.1. *De Re* and *De Dicto*

We have already encountered the *de re – de dicto* distinction at a number of points in this book. In this section, we will investigate the distinction more carefully, explain methods used to notate it, and develop quantified modal logics that are adequate for arguments involving the new notation.

Some of the best illustrations of the *de re – de dicto* distinction can be found among sentences of tense logic. For example, consider (S).

(S)   The president was a crook.

This sentence is ambiguous. It might be taken to claim of the present president that he (Bush at the time this was written) used to be a crook. On the other hand, it might be read 'At some time in the past the president (at that time) was a crook'. On this last reading, we are saying that the whole *sentence* (or *dictum* in Latin) 'the president is a crook' was true at some past time. This is the *de dicto* reading of (S). Here both 'the president' and 'is a crook' are read in the past tense. We can represent this interpretation of (S) by applying the past tense operator P to the sentence 'the president is a crook', so that both 'the president' and 'is a crook' lie in its scope.

P(the president is a crook)   *de dicto* reading of (S)

On the first reading of (S), we are saying a certain *thing* (in Latin *res*) has a past tense property: of having been a crook. This is the *de re* reading of (S). Here we read 'the president' in the present tense, and 'is a crook' in the past tense. We can represent this reading by restricting the scope of the past tense operator P to the predicate 'is a crook'.

the president P(is a crook)   *de re* reading of (S)

The distinction between these two readings of (S) is a crucial one, for given that Bush never was a crook, and that Nixon was, the *de dicto* version of (S) is true, while the *de re* version is false.

EXERCISE 19.1   Distinguish between *de re* and *de dicto* applications of the intensional operators in the following sentences:

a) The number of planets is necessarily greater than 7.
b) King George wanted to know whether Scott was the author of Waverley.

Given standard assumptions about what is (mathematically) necessary and about what people might want to know, which of the readings of these sentences are true and which false?

Though notational and semantical machinery exists for handling *de dicto* applications of intensional operators, we have no way to treat the *de re* applications since intensional operators, so far, do not bind predicates. This section will discuss two standard approaches to notating the *de re* – *de dicto* distinction. One method involves the use of Russell's theory of descriptions.

When descriptions are translated into quantificational logic according to Russell's theory, more than one result may be obtained depending on how the scope of the operators is treated. (See Section 18.2.) For example, 'King George wanted to know whether Scott was the author of Waverley' has two readings, which may be represented using a modal operator **K** (for 'King George wanted to know whether') as follows:

Secondary Occurrence   **K**∃x(1Wx&s≈x)
Primary Occurrence   ∃x(1Wx&**K**s≈x)

This difference in scope may be exploited to give an account of the *de re* – *de dicto* distinction. For example, consider (S).

(S)   The president was a crook.

This can be represented in description notation by (S′) (where R reads 'is the president').

(S′)   **PC!xRx**

When !xRx is translated, two different results may be obtained depending on whether the past tense operator **P** binds the whole sentence ∃x(Cx&1Rx) or the open sentence Cx in the result.

P∃x(1Rx&Cx)   *de dicto*
∃x(1Rx&**P**Cx)   *de re*

Notice that the first of these says that in the past there was exactly one president who was a crook, and this is the *de dicto* reading of (S), whereas the second claims that there is (now) exactly one president, and he was a crook, which is the *de re* reading.

> **EXERCISE 19.2**   Represent the sentences of Exercise 19.1 in description notation. Then translate away the description in each in two ways, and label them according to whether they represent *de dicto* or *de re* readings.

Although this method for representing the *de re – de dicto* distinction is perfectly acceptable, it has some limitations. The main problem is that there are sentences that have both *de re* and *de dicto* readings but fail to contain any description to which Russell's translation method can be applied. For example, consider (K).

(K)   Philip believes that Ortcutt is a spy,

This sentence has a *de re* and a *de dicto* reading. The *de dicto* reading makes the claim that the person whom Philip believes to be Ortcutt is a spy. (Here the intensional operator **B** is introduced for 'Philip believes that'.)

B(ortcutt is a spy)   *de dicto*

On the other hand, the *de re* reading says that whoever is in *fact* Ortcutt is believed by Philip to be a spy.

Ortcutt **B**(is a spy)   *de re*

It is not too difficult to imagine a situation where these two readings of (K) have different truth values. Just suppose that a reliable friend has told Philip that Ortcutt is the doorman at the Russian Embassy, and that his friend happens to be wrong about this. Suppose Philip has good evidence that the doorman at the Russian embassy is a spy, and suppose that the person who is in fact Ortcutt is someone whom Phillip does not know. Under these circumstances the *de dicto* reading of (K) will be true, for Philip does believe that the person he believes to be Ortcutt (namely, the doorman) is a spy. However, the *de re* reading is false, because although Philip does believe of the doorman that he is a spy, the man Ortcutt does not have the property of being believed by Philip of being a spy since Philip does not know Ortcutt, and so has no beliefs about him one way or the other. The upshot is that there are sentences where we need to make the *de re – de dicto* distinction that do not explicitly contain descriptions.

EXERCISE 19.3   Give another example of a sentence that fails to contain descriptions where we need to make the *de re – de dicto* distinction. Give an example that does not involve the intensional operator 'believes that'.

If we are to formulate the two senses of sentences like (K) using Russell's theory, we will be forced to claim that 'Ortcutt' in (K) is a covert description (say 'the Ortcuttizer'). We have criticized this treatment of proper names in Section 12.4, when Russell's theory was proposed as a method for preserving classical logic in face of the problem of nonreferring terms. If we wish to avoid the problems mentioned there, we must find some other method for notating the *de re – de dicto* distinction in sentences that fail to contain descriptions.

A second alternative is to notate *de re* sentences using the method of abstraction. A new operator λ called the *abstraction operator* is introduced into the notation (Stalnaker and Thomason, 1968). This operator converts a sentence Ac into *predicate*: λxAx. So, for example, when Gc reads 'c is green', then λxGx reads 'is green'. The main function of the λ operator is to create complex predicates from complex sentences. Complex predicates such as 'is believed by Philip to be a spy' and 'is necessarily greater than 7' and 'is black or blue but not necessarily black or blue' can be notated by forming first the appropriate complex sentences, and then applying λx to convert them into the corresponding predicates. For example, to represent 'is believed by Philip to be a spy', form first the representation of the sentence 'c is believed by Philip to be a spy', namely, **B**Sc, to which we apply λx to obtain λx**B**Sx. Then one can notate the *de re* version of (K) by combining the predicate λx**B**Sx with the term o to obtain λx**B**Sx(o),

(K)   Philip believes that Ortcutt is a spy.
λx**B**Sx(o)   *de re*

whereas the *de dicto* version is notated as follows:

BS(o)   *de dicto*

Note that λxSx(o) says that Ortcutt has the property: λx x is a spy, that is, the property expressed by 'is a spy', so λxSx(o) and So are equivalent to each other. This means that the *de dicto* reading of (K) can also be notated this way:

BλxSx(o)   *de dicto*

This helps us appreciate that the difference between the *de re* and *de dicto* interpretations of (K) is a matter of scope. It depends on the order in which **B** and λx appear in the two formulas.

λx**B**Sx(o)   *de re*
BλxSx(o)   *de dicto*

EXERCISE 19.4   Notate the *de re* interpretations of the following sentences using λ.

a) The number of planets is necessarily greater than 7.
b) John is black and blue but not necessarily black and blue.
c) The president is necessarily a citizen, but not necessarily an honest man.

Note that parentheses are included around 'o' in 'λx**B**Sx(o)' and '**B**λxSx(o)'. This follows the official the syntax defined in Chapter 12, which says that predicate letters are followed by *lists* of terms, and that lists are enclosed in parentheses. According to this policy, the notation for a sentence formed from a predicate letter P and a term t is 'P(t)'. In this book, the parentheses have usually been dropped: Pt. However, in the case of complex predicates, the parentheses are needed to help resolve ambiguity, and they actually make formulas easier to read, especially when there are complex terms such as descriptions as well. So the parentheses around terms will be included in sentences involving λ.

19.2. Identity and the *De Re – De Dicto* Distinction

Keeping track of the difference between *de re* and *de dicto* applications of an intensional operator is crucial when it comes to evaluating arguments involving identity. Remember the failure of substitutivity of identical terms in the scope of an operator was a pervasive feature for intensional operators. For example, the truth of the premises and falsity of the conclusion of the following argument can be used to show that substitution fails in the scope of 'necessarily'.

9 is the number of planets.
<u>9 is necessarily greater than 7.</u>
The number of planets is necessarily greater than 7.

The application of this test, however, is ticklish. There are two ways to read the conclusion, and it is only on the *de dicto* reading that the conclusion is false. On the *de re* reading, the sentence says that the number of planets (which is 9) has a certain property, namely, being necessarily greater than 7. Since 9 *is* necessarily greater than 7, it follows from the identity of 9 with the number of planets that 'the number of planets is necessarily greater than 7' is true on the *de re* reading. In general, when a sentence is given the *de re* reading, the substitution of terms that refer to the same thing goes through in contexts where it would not be allowed given the *de dicto* reading. '9' *can* be substituted for 'the number of planets' in 'the number of planets is necessarily greater than 7' when this sentence is given the *de re* reading, but it cannot on the *de dicto* reading. This difference in behavior can be explained by the fact that on the *de re* reading 'the number of planets' does not lie in the scope of 'necessarily', whereas on the *de dicto* reading it does. We can appreciate the situation by giving notation for the argument on both the *de re* and *de dicto* readings.

DE DICTO		DE RE	
9≈!xNx	*invalid* because	9≈!xNx	*valid* because
□(9>7)	!xNx is replaced	λx□(x>7)(9)	!xNx is replaced for
□(!xNx>7)	for 9 in the scope	λx□(x>7)(!xNx)	9 outside the scope
	of □		of □

On the left (in the *de dicto* case), the '9' in the second premise lies inside the scope of □, whereas it lies outside that scope on the right.

A good notation for the *de re* – *de dicto* distinction will allow us to quickly determine which term positions lie inside (and which outside) the scope of an operator. Otherwise we will have trouble assessing the validity of arguments that involve the substitution of terms that appear in true identity statements. Although the λ notation does make the distinction clear, the notation is complex enough that the scope is not all that easy to assess. To help overcome the problem, let us introduce the abbreviation that allows the deletion of the cumbersome λ notation.

(□(P))   □(P) =$_{df}$ λx□Px

Then the second premise of the *de re* version of the argument comes to $\Box(>7)(9)$. Allowing the subject term '9' at the head of the sentence (as is done in English) results in a considerably more legible notation: $9\Box(>7)$. Then the *de re* and *de dicto* versions of the 'number of planets' argument can be expressed in a way that clearly indicates that the *de re* version is valid since substitution of !xNx for 9 lies outside the scope of $\Box$.

DE DICTO		DE RE	
$9\approx$!xNx	*invalid* because	$9\approx$!xNx	*valid* because
$\underline{\Box 9>7}$	!xNx is replaced	$\underline{9\Box(>7)}$	!xNx is replaced for
$\Box$!xNx>7	for 9 beneath $\Box$	!xNx$\Box(>7)$	9 outside $\Box$

One might introduce the notation $\Box(P)$ directly by defining the syntax so that the modal operator $\Box$ binds predicate letters as well as sentences (Garson, 1981). However, that device will not allow one to construct the full range of complex predicates that the λ notation and variables allow. So in the quantified modal logic to be defined here, λ is a primitive symbol, and we introduce abbreviations that help overcome visual clutter related to the use of λ.

We have already remarked in the previous section that the Russellian method for handling the *de re – de dicto* distinction does not work in cases where there are no descriptions to translate. This and other problems with Russell's theory were discussed in Sections 12.3 and 12.4. So for safety, an alternative system for abstraction will be developed here – one that does not depend on Russell's method.

19.3. Principles for Abstraction: The System λS

When abstraction notation is used, the correct principles for substitution of identities are easily formulated. Remember that the rule ($\approx$Out) was restricted so that it applied only to atomic sentences.

($\approx$Out)   s$\approx$t, P(l, s, l') / P(l, t, l')
where P is a predicate letter (including $\approx$)

It is an easy matter to modify the statement of ($\approx$Out) in the appropriate way, when λ is in the language. Simply understand 'P' to range over predicate letters *as well as all abstractions of the form λxAx*, where Ac is a well-formed sentence. It will follow that the result of notating the *de re* version of the 'planets' argument in λ notation will qualify as an instance of ($\approx$Out) and so reflect the validity of the argument as desired.

9≈!xNx
λx(□x>7)(9)
λx(□x>7)(!xNx)

Here the term positions (9) in the second premise and (!xNx) in the conclusion follow the predicate λx(□x>7). Since λx(□x>7)(9) and λx(□x>7)(!xNx) have the forms PIsl′ and PItl′, the (≈Out) rule warrants the substitution and all is well. This makes sense because neither 9 nor !xNx lies in the scope of the intensional operator □.

Unfortunately, new problems arise if the standard axiom for abstraction is adopted.

(The Principle of Abstraction)   λxAx(t) ↔ At

At first, it would seem that this principle is uncontroversial. Since λxAx(t) merely says that t has the property of being A, it would seem that λxAx(t) and At should be equivalent. However, there is a problem if an intensional operator appears in At. For example, when Ax is □x>7 and t is !xNx, the principle of abstraction asserts that the *de re* and *de dicto* translations of the conclusion of the 'planets' argument are equivalent.

λx□x>7(!xNx) ↔ □!xNx>7

But this would be fatal to any attempt to distinguish the deductive behavior of *de re* and *de dicto* sentences. If we are to use the method of abstraction to handle *de re* applications of intensional operators, we must carefully restrict the principle of abstraction so as to avoid the identification of *de re* with *de dicto*.

The solution to the problem adopted in this book will be to adopt rigid constants and formulate abstraction for constants only. So a corrected version of the axiom is (λ).

(λ)   λxAx(c) ↔ Ac

In Section 19.5 below, the adequacy of a system that uses this principle will be demonstrated.

19.4. Syntax and Semantics for λS

Let us begin with a formal account of a language for a system λS that includes the λ operator. The definition will simultaneously define 'sentence', 'term', and 'predicate'.

The Definition of Sentences, Terms and Predicates of λS.

1. Constants are terms.
2. If At is a sentence, and x is a variable, then !xAx is a term and λxAx is a predicate.
3. If l is a list of terms and P is a predicate, then Pl is a sentence.
4. If A, B, and At are sentences, x is a variable, and both s and t terms, then $\perp$, s$\approx$t, (A$\rightarrow$B), $\square$A, and $\forall$xAx are sentences.

No sequences of symbols count as sentences, terms, or predicates unless they qualify by clauses 1–4.

We already have the semantical machinery needed to handle cases of *de dicto* applications of the intensional operators. To handle *de re* applications, we need to define models that obey the appropriate semantical condition for λ. What is needed is a condition that indicates what the extension $a_w(\lambda xAx)$ of the predicate λxAx should be. But λxAx is a predicate that indicates some property, so $a_w(\lambda xAx)$ should pick out the set of objects that have this property. Since the members of predicate letters were *lists* of objects, even in the case of one-place predicates, let us presume that the extension $a_w(\lambda xAx)$ of λxAx is the set containing exactly those (one-item) lists (d) of objects d that bear the relevant property. But what is the relevant property? It is that (d) is a member of $a_w(\lambda xAx)$ exactly when d satisfies Ax, that is, when $a_w(Ad)=T$. It follows that (λ) is the desired condition for fixing the extension of λxAx.

(λ)   (d) $\in a_w(\lambda xAx)$ iff $a_w(Ad)=T$.

Once (λ) is in place, the truth clause (Pl) can be used to fix the truth values of atomic sentences that include λ. To see why, note that (λPl) is a special case of (Pl).

(λPl) $a_w(\lambda xAx(t))=T$ iff $a_w((t)) \in a_w(\lambda xAx)$.
(Pl) $a_w(Pl)=T$ iff $a_w(l) \in a_w(P)$.

Since (t) is a special case of (t_i), when n = 1, the overall result is (λPl).

(t) $a_w((t)) = (a_w(t))$.
(t_i) $a_w((t_1, \ldots, t_n)) = (a_w(t_1), \ldots, a_w(t_n))$.
(λt) $a_w(\lambda xAx(t))=T$ iff $(a_w(t)) \in a_w(\lambda xAx)$.

It is visually annoying to include the outside parentheses in the lists: (d) and $(a_w(t))$, so these will be dropped when no ambiguity would arise. Using this convention, (λt) and (λ) may be simplified as follows:

(λt) $a_w(\lambda xAx(t))=T$ iff $a_w(t) \in a_w(\lambda xAx)$.
(λ)   d $\in a_w(\lambda xAx)$ iff $a_w(Ad)=T$.

Now let a *λS-model* be any !S-model for a language for λS that obeys (λ). It is interesting to work out the truth conditions in λS-models for sentences involving the *de re* and *de dicto* readings. Consider the truth behavior of a *de re* sentence of the shape $\Box(P)t$, where P is a one-place predicate, and t is a name. Since $\Box(P)t$ is shorthand for $\lambda x\Box(Px)(t)$, we can use (λ) to work out the semantical behavior of $\Box(P)t$. $\Box(P)t$ says that what t refers to has a certain property, namely, of being necessarily P. This means that the referent of t ought to fall into the extension of P in all worlds accessible from our own. So the semantical clause for the *de re* sentence $\Box(P)t$ would be expected to read as follows:

(DR) $\mathbf{a_w}(\Box(P)t)=T$ iff if $\mathbf{wRv}$, then $\mathbf{a_w}(t) \in \mathbf{a_v}(P)$

It is interesting to note that (DR) is easy to derive from (λ) as follows. We know that $\mathbf{a_w}(t)$ must refer to some object d in D. So we have the following:

$(\Box(P)t)=T$
iff $\mathbf{a_w}(\lambda x\Box(Px)(t))=T$ $(\Box(P))$
iff $\mathbf{a_w}(t) \in \mathbf{a_w}(\lambda x\Box Px)$ (λt)
iff $d \in \mathbf{a_w}(\lambda x\Box Px)$ $\mathbf{a_w}(t) = d$
iff $\mathbf{a_w}(\Box Pd) = T$ (λ)
iff if $\mathbf{wRv}$ then, $\mathbf{a_v}(Pd) = T$ $(\Box)$
iff if $\mathbf{wRv}$ then, $\mathbf{a_v}(d) \in \mathbf{a_v}(P)$ (Pl)
iff if $\mathbf{wRv}$ then, $d \in \mathbf{a_v}(P)$ (d): $\mathbf{a_v}(d) = d$
iff if $\mathbf{wRv}$ then, $\mathbf{a_w}(t) \in \mathbf{a_v}(P)$ $\mathbf{a_w}(t) = d$

It is instructive to compare this clause with the truth conditions that we obtain using the standard semantics for the *de dicto* sentence $\Box Pt$.

(DD) $\mathbf{a_w}(\Box Pt)=T$ iff   if $\mathbf{wRv}$, then $\mathbf{a_v}(t) \in \mathbf{a_v}(P)$.

EXERCISE 19.5   Show that (DD) is the case using the standard truth clauses governing atomic sentences and $\Box$.

The two conditions (DR) and (DD) are identical except for one thing, namely, that where we have $\mathbf{a_w}(t)$ in (DR), we have $\mathbf{a_v}(t)$ in (DD). In the *de re* case we check the referent $\mathbf{a_w}(t)$ of t in the *original* world **w** to see whether it falls in the extension of P in all worlds accessible from **w**, whereas in the *de dicto* case we check each accessible world **v** to see whether the referent of t *in that world* **v** is in the extension of P for that world. The difference between the two cases can be appreciated by thinking of the *de re* case as identical to the *de dicto*, save that in the *de re* case we always test the referent of t for *the original world* of the evaluation.

The diagrams that we used for representing models are quite helpful in making clear what the distinction between *de re* and *de dicto* amounts to. We already know how to calculate the truth value of a *de dicto* sentence $\Box$Pt on a diagram, for example, the following one:

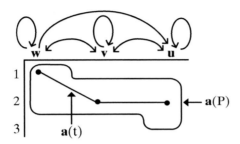

Here we see that $\Box$Pt is T at **w** because the extension of t remains inside the extension of P in all worlds accessible from **w**. What about the value of the *de re* sentence on the same model? Here we must check to see whether $\mathbf{a_w}(t)$ is in the extension of P in all worlds accessible from **w**, and so we must check to see whether the object 1 in our diagram is inside the boundary for P at **w**, **v**, and **u**. We see that it is not, and in fact $\mathbf{a_w}(t)$ lies outside the extension of P in both **v** and **u**. To help us see this fact about the diagram, let us draw a horizontal dotted line to represent the value of $\mathbf{a_w}(t)$. By sighting along this line, we can see that $\mathbf{a_w}(t)$ falls out of P's bounds in worlds **v** and **u**.

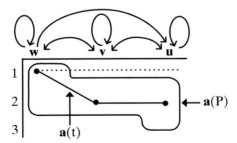

Notice that although $\Box$(P)t is F at **w**, $\Box$(P)t turns out to be T at **v**. We can see this by drawing a horizontal dotted line through the point $\mathbf{a_v}(t)$ and seeing that it stays inside the extension of P in all the worlds accessible from **v**.

EXERCISE 19.6   Calculate the following extensions on the following diagrams.

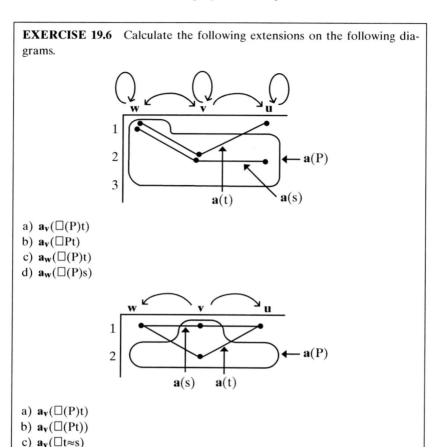

a) $a_v(\Box(P)t)$
b) $a_v(\Box Pt)$
c) $a_w(\Box(P)t)$
d) $a_w(\Box(P)s)$

a) $a_v(\Box(P)t)$
b) $a_v(\Box(Pt))$
c) $a_v(\Box t\approx s)$
d) $a_v(t\Box(\approx s))$ that is $a_v(\lambda x\Box(x\approx s)(t))$

Diagrams help us appreciate the conditions under which *de re* and *de dicto* sentences are equivalent. When t is a rigid term, that is, when t refers to the same object in all worlds, then the line for its intension is horizontal, and so coincides with the dotted line we would draw in calculating the values of *de re* sentences involving it. This means that when t is rigid, the sentences $\Box(Ft)$ and $\Box(F)t$ must have the same truth values. It follows that if we adopt a semantics where we assume that all the terms are rigid, then the *de re – de dicto* distinction collapses. Second, even if t is nonrigid, we can find a *de dicto* sentence that is equivalent to $\Box(F)t$, as long as we can be sure that a rigid constant of the right kind is available. To illustrate this, suppose that we have a model where c is a rigid constant that refers to the same object that t does in world **w**. Then the intension for c will be a horizontal line that points to $a_w(t)$, and this line will exactly coincide with the dotted line we would draw to assess the value at **w** of *de re* sentences.

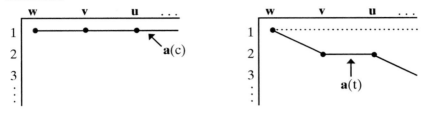

So any diagram that made □(P)t at **w** would make □Pc T at **w** and vice versa.

This feature of rigid terms and *de re* sentences suggests another way to indicate the *de re – de dicto* distinction. Since any *de re* sentence is equivalent to a *de dicto* sentence involving a rigid constant that refers to the right object, we can simply use such *de dicto* sentences to express the contents of the *de re* sentences. One difficulty with this tactic should be pointed out. For a given term t, the choice we make for c depends on the possible world. In the above pair of diagrams, □(P)t and □Pc do not have the same truth values at **v**, or **u**. The dotted line we would draw for world **v** in the right-hand diagram points to object 2, and so we would need to find a new constant b to express the contents of □(P)t in world **v**. As a result, the sentence we choose for expressing the *de re* application of modality is not fixed by any one definition, but changes as the world at issue changes.

So far, our discussion of *de re* sentences has not taken account of the possibility that objects may fail to exist in certain situations. As a matter of fact, it seems reasonable to suppose that for any object, there is a world where it fails to exist. If this is true, then our present semantical definition for *de re* modality seems too harsh. For example, the *de re* sentence 'the president is necessarily a man' will be false in our world if there is a world where the extant president (Bush at the time of this writing) does not fall into the extension of 'is a man'. Given that there is a world accessible from ours where Bush doesn't exist at all, it would seem that Bush couldn't be in the extension of any predicate in that world, and so we would have to rule the sentence false.

However, this reasoning rests on a debatable assumption, one that is initially attractive, but probably false. The assumption is that if an object fails to exist in a world, then it cannot fall in the extension of any predicate in that world. This assumption can be challenged by pointing to such true sentences as 'Pegasus is a horse'. Though Pegasus does not exist, we still want to say that this sentence is true, and so we must allow the object Pegasus to be a member of the extension of 'is a horse'. Similarly, we could preserve the truth of 'the president is necessarily a man' by making sure that Bush is in the extension of 'is a man' in all accessible worlds.

On the other hand, the insistence that Bush *must* be in the extension of 'is a man' even in worlds where he does not exist seems to be a technical trick that does not sit well with our intuitions. For this reason it seems worthwhile to work out the semantics for a version of *de re* modality where we only inspect worlds where the object at issue exists. Let us use the notation [E] for this conception of *de re* modality. The semantical clause for the sentence [E](P)t says that it is true at **w** just in case the extension d of t (at **w**) falls in the extension of P in all worlds **w** where d exists.

(EDR) $a_w([E](P)t)=T$ iff if **wRv** and $a_w(t) \in Dv$, then $a_w(t) \in a_v(P)$.

EXERCISE 19.7   Construct a model where $\Box(P)t$ is F and [E](P)t is T at some world.

EXERCISE *19.8   Show how to define [E](P)t using λ. Demonstrate (EDR) given your definition.

19.5. The Adequacy of λS

In this section the adequacy of λS will be shown. Remember that λS is !S plus the axiom (λ), and λS-models are !S-models that satisfy the condition (λ). Here it is shown that λS is both sound and complete.

Soundness of λS.   If $L \vdash_{\lambda S} C$ then $L \vDash_{\lambda S} C$.

Proof. We know that !S is !S-sound, so to show soundness of λS, it is necessary to show only that the (λ) axiom is λS-valid, that is, that (λ) is valid in any !S-model that meets the semantical condition (λ). To show $a_w(\lambda x A x(c) \leftrightarrow Ac)=T$ for any λS-model $<$**W, R, $\mathbb{D}$, a**$>$, note first that an assignment function for a λS-model must assign an appropriate extension to each term, so $a_w(c)$ must be identical to some object d in **D**. According to the truth condition ($\leftrightarrow$) for $\leftrightarrow$, it will be sufficient for proving

$\mathbf{a_w}(\lambda xAx(c)\leftrightarrow Ac)=T$ to show that $\mathbf{a_w}(\lambda xAx(c))=T$ iff $\mathbf{a_w}(Ac)=T$. This is done as follows:

$(\lambda xAx(c))=T$
iff $\mathbf{a_w}(c)\in\mathbf{a_w}(\lambda xAx)$ (λt)
iff $d\in\mathbf{a_w}(\lambda xAx)$ $\mathbf{a_w}(c)$ is d
iff $\mathbf{a_w}(Ad)=T$ (λ)
iff $\mathbf{a_w}(Ac)=T$ Rigid Instance Theorem

(Remember that λS-models have rigid constants, which is why the Rigid Instance Theorem applies.)

Completeness of λS. If $H \vDash_{\lambda S} C$ then $H \vdash_{\lambda S} C$.

Proof. We prove the contrapositive: if $H \nvdash_{\lambda S} C$, then $H \nvDash_{\lambda S} C$. So assume $H \nvdash_{\lambda S} C$. Use the completeness method of either Section 16.4 (using trees) or Section 17.8 (using the canonical model) to establish $H \nvDash_{t\lambda S} C$, where a tλS-model is a t!S-model that satisfies the axiom (λ). This establishes the completeness of λS with respect to tλS-models. At this point the Extended o Transfer Theorem of Section 15.8 will guarantee that λS is complete for λS-models, provided that we can show that axiom (λ) expresses the semantical condition (λ).

Extended o Transfer Theorem. If nS results from adding axioms to oS, each of which expresses its corresponding condition, and if nS is complete for tnS-models, then nS is complete for nS-models.

Note that λS is oS plus both (!) and (λ) and it was already shown in Section 18.8 that axiom (!) expresses the condition (!). To show that axiom (λ) expresses its condition (λ), we need to show that the ti-expansion of any tλS-model obeys (λ). Since the tλS-model satisfies (λ), the truth condition $(\leftrightarrow)$ for $\leftrightarrow$ yields the following:

(λc) $\mathbf{a_w}(\lambda xAx(c))=T$ iff $\mathbf{a_w}(Ac)=T$.

By construction, the ti-expansion of the tλS-model obeys the following. (See Section 15.7.)

(aD) $d\in\mathbf{D}$ iff for some term t and some world $\mathbf{w}$, $d=\mathbf{a_w}(t)$.

But we also know that any tλS-model obeys ($\exists$c). (See Section 15.8.)

($\exists$c)   For teach term t, there is a constant c such that $\mathbf{a_w}(t\approx c)=T$.

Putting (aD) and ($\exists$c) together, it follows that (aoD).

(aoD) $d\in\mathbf{D}$ iff for some constant c and some world $\mathbf{w}$, $d=\mathbf{a_w}(c)$.

We are ready to show that (λ) holds in the ti-expansion.

(λ) $d \in a_w(\lambda x A x)$ iff $a_w(Ad)=T$.

Proof of (λ). Let d be any member of $\mathbf{D}$, and let $\mathbf{w}$ be any member of $\mathbf{W}$. By (aoD), there is a constant c, and a world $\mathbf{u}$ such that $d=a_u(c)$. Since the axiom (RC) is in λS, the Expression Theorem of Section 15.7 entails that the constants are all rigid. It follows that $d=a_w(c)$. Note also that the reasoning of the ti-Expansion Theorem of Section 15.7 guarantees that the ti-expansion is an iS-model. So (Pl), and hence (λt) holds. Given all this, the proof is straightforward.

$d \in a_w(\lambda x A x)$
iff $a_w(c) \in a_w(\lambda x A x)$ $d=a_w(c)$
iff $a_w(\lambda x A x(c))=T$ (λt)
iff $a_w(Ac)=T$ (λc)
iff $a_w(Ad)=T$ Rigid Instance Theorem

19.6. Quantifying In

Quantifying into intensional contexts (or 'quantifying in' for short) occurs when a quantifier binds a variable that lies in the scope of an intensional operator and the intensional operator lies in the scope of that quantifier. For example, formulas with the shape $\exists x \Box P x$ exhibit quantifying in since the scope of $\Box$ includes a variable x that is bound by $\exists x$, a quantifier whose scope includes $\Box$. The formula $\Box \exists x P x$ is not an example of quantifying in because here $\Box$ does not lie in the scope of $\exists x$. Quine has argued in several places (most famously in "Reference and Modality" [1961]) that quantifying in is incoherent. Quine calls term positions where substitution of identities fails *opaque contexts*. His view is that quantification into opaque contexts is illicit. If he is right, then either we must never write formulas like $\exists x \Box P x$, or we must provide a translation procedure to eliminate them in favor of formulas where quantification into opaque contexts does not occur. The only reasonable hope of doing so would be to adopt the Barcan Formulas, so that $\exists x \Diamond P x$ can be converted to $\Diamond \exists x P x$, and $\forall x \Box P x$ to $\Box \forall x P x$. But even that would not provide a way to trade $\exists x \Box P x$ for $\Box \exists x P x$. Furthermore, one is still faced with formulas like $\exists x (Gx \& \Diamond Fx)$, where an attempt to 'hoist' the $\Diamond$ outside of the quantifier $\exists x$ is blocked by the fact that $\Diamond(Gc\&Fc)$ is not equivalent to $(Gc\&\Diamond Fc)$.

> **EXERCISE 19.9** Give an English counterexample that shows that (Gc&◇Fc) and ◇(Gc&Fc) are not equivalent. (Hint: Use a tree to created a fK-counterexample to help you see what is needed. Try an assignment that makes (Gc&◇Fc) true and ◇(Gc&Fc) false.)

This book has so far proceeded using opaque contexts without comment, and it argues for systems of quantified modal logic that reject the Barcan Formulas. It is important, then, to provide a defense against Quine's arguments. Quine contends that quantification into opaque contexts is incoherent because failure of substitution at a term position undermines the normal referring function of terms and variables that occur there. This in turn undermines coherency of quantification into those contexts. Consider the argument below, which is a famous example of the failure of substitution:

9≈n   9 is the number of planets.
□9>7   Necessarily 9 is greater than 7.
□n>7   Necessarily the number of planets is greater than 7.

(To simplify the discussion, the argument has been symbolized to the left, using 'n' as an abbreviation for 'the number of planets'.) The premises of this argument are presumably true, but at least on one reading, the conclusion is false. This shows that the term position where '9' occurs in the second premise □9>7 is an opaque context. Quine argues that terms in opaque contexts do not play their normal referring roles. Both '9' and 'the number of planets' refer to nine, so something other than these term's referents must explain why the truth values of □9>7 and □n>7 differ. What *does* account for the difference has to do with differences in the *ways of describing* or the *manner* of referring to nine. '9' refers to nine directly, as it were, whereas 'the number of planets' gets at nine indirectly.

Now consider (∃□) where we quantify in.

(∃□)   ∃x(necessarily, x is greater than 7).

The objectual truth condition claims that (∃□) is true iff the hybrid sentence □d>7 holds for some object d in the domain.

□d>7   Necessarily d is greater than 7.

Note that □d>7 results from replacing d either for '9' in □9>7 or for 'n', that is, 'the number of planets' in □n>7. However, the truth values of

□9>7 and □n>7 were sensitive to the manner in which nine is described. Since d is some *object*, it does not describe anything at all, and so crucial information needed to make sense of the truth value of □d>7 has been lost.

Presumably we think (∃□) is true because nine is necessarily greater than 7, and so something is necessarily greater than 7. But Quine asks, 'What number is the object d that supports the purported truth of □d>7?' Presumably it is nine. But nine just is the number of planets, and the number of planets is *not* an object d that makes □d>7 true since □n>7 is false. Quine's objection, then, rests on the idea that opaque contexts deprive terms of their normal directly referring roles since the *manner* of reference is implicated as well. But the standard truth conditions for quantifiers depend on their variable positions having normal referring roles, where the manner of referring is irrelevant.

This reasoning may seem persuasive. However, note that at least on one reading, Quine's reasoning employs the substitution of identities in intensional contexts, which we have urged is questionable. When he argues that there is something incoherent about the truth conditions for □d>7 when d is nine, he presumes that the fact that nine is the number of planets entails that we must be pulled two ways when evaluating □d>7. □9>7 prompts us to rule it true, whereas □n>7 prompts us to rule it false. However, the fact that □n>7 is false would exert pressure on us to think that □d>7 is false only if substitution of 'the number of planets' for d in □d>7 were legitimate. But this amounts to substitution into intensional contexts, which is invalid. By recognizing the failure of substitution and the phenomenon of nonrigid designation, one may provide a clear standard for evaluating □d>7 when d is nine. Because '9' is presumably a rigid term referring to nine, it follows by a legitimate replacement of nine for '9' that the truth of □9>7 entails the truth of □d>7. The fact that □n>7 is false is no problem because 'the number of planets' is a nonrigid term. It refers to different numbers in possible worlds with different numbers of planets. Since substitution fails for nonrigid terms, there is all the room we need to hold that □n>7 is false whereas □d>7 is true. The upshot is that we are not pulled in two ways as Quine contends, and so we need not accept the view that quantification is impossible in term positions that lack a directly referring role.

There is a second way of diagnosing Quine's objection, which will require a separate reply. Quine may believe that substitution of 'the number of planets' for d in $\Box$d>7 is legitimate because he gives this sentence the *de re* reading (d$\Box$>7).

(d$\Box$>7) d$\Box$(>7)=λx$\Box$x>7(d)

Using the *de re* analysis throughout, the original argument has the following form:

9≈n
9$\Box$(>7)
n$\Box$(>7)

On this interpretation, both '9' and 'n' (i.e., 'the number of planets') lie outside the scope of $\Box$ and so the substitution of these terms is correct given 9≈n. On this analysis of the situation, Quine would be right to use substitution of 'the number of planets' for d in d$\Box$>7 to conclude that n$\Box$(>7).

Does this mean that Quine's reasoning against quantifying in goes through on the *de re* reading? The answer is that it does not. Even if one could demonstrate that there is something incoherent about the truth value for d$\Box$>7, this could pose a problem only for understanding the truth conditions of quantified sentences such as $\exists$xx$\Box$(>7). But here quantifying in does not occur since the variable bound by $\exists$x lies *outside* the scope of $\Box$.

Furthermore, the argument would go through only if there were a tension in evaluating d$\Box$(>7) when d is nine. But there is no such tension. In the *de re* case, the argument form is valid since the substitution occurs outside the scope of $\Box$. The premises are true, and therefore so is the conclusion n$\Box$(>7). This matches the intuition that 'the number of planets is necessarily greater than 7' is true on the *de re* reading, because the *object* referred to by 'the number of planets' (namely, 9) *is* necessarily greater than 7. It follows that there is no difference in the truth values of 9$\Box$(>7) and n$\Box$(>7) that could be used to argue an instability in the truth value for d$\Box$(>7).

Quine's argument is seductive because of the difficulties we all have in detecting differences in scope of modal operators. At the crucial juncture where he reasons that $\Box$d>7 should be false since $\Box$n>7 is false, we are liable to credit his reasoning by adopting the *de re* reading. The fact that he needs the *de dicto* reading to obtain a result about quantifying in may easily pass us by.

EXERCISE 19.10   Suppose we give (1) the *de re* and (2) the *de dicto* reading.

(1) Necessarily 9 is greater than 7.

(2) Necessarily the number of planets is greater than 7.

What objections to Quine's reasoning against quantifying in would be appropriate now?

Quine's argument against quantifying in has produced a giant literature, and there is no room in this book to do it justice. Garson (2006) provides a useful entry point to the topic in case you would like to study the issue more deeply. However, two important contributions are worth reviewing here. One of the telling responses to Quine was the work of Arthur Smullyan (1948). In Section 12.3 it was pointed out that if terms are replaced by descriptions whenever an apparent failure of substitution occurs, and Russell's theory of descriptions is applied, one may develop a logical system without any restrictions on a rule of substitution. On this analysis, there are no opaque contexts, and so Quine's argument does not even get off the ground.

A second influential response to Quine was given by Kaplan in "Quantifying In" (1969). It involves selecting a privileged class of terms (the so-called vivid names). Although the truth values of $\Box 9>7$ and $\Box n>7$ are sensitive to the two ways nine is described ('9' vs. 'n'), Kaplan argues that there is no corresponding indeterminacy in $\Box d>7$ because one of these ways is privileged. Since '9' is a more direct way to get at nine, $\Box 9>7$ and not $\Box n>7$ is used to resolve the truth status of $\Box d>7$.

Given the force of these and other responses, Quine has conceded that his argument does not show quantifying in is (strictly) incoherent. However, he has continued to object to quantifying in on other grounds. He contends that appeals to privileged ways of describing things, to rigid terms, or to any other way of making the truth value of $\Box d>7$ cogent boils down to having to make sense of the idea that some objects bear necessary properties that other objects do not. Quine complains that this amounts to an unacceptable form of essentialism. What sense can it make to assert of an object itself (apart from any way of describing it) that it has necessary properties?

In a well-known passage from *Word and Object* (1960, p. 199), Quine supports the view that essentialism is unacceptable. Consider sentences (1)–(5).

(1) Mathematicians are necessarily rational.
(2) Mathematicians are not necessarily two-legged.
(3) Cyclists are necessarily two-legged.
(4) Cyclists are not necessarily rational.
(5) John is a cyclist and John is a mathematician.

Assuming that these are all true, he asks us whether John is necessarily rational. Now John is both a cyclist and a mathematician (by (5)), but from (1) we conclude that he is rational, and from (4) we conclude he is not. It seems that under the description 'cyclist', John isn't necessarily rational, but under the description 'mathematician', he is. This prompts Quine to propose that it is only for an object-under-a-description that one can make a distinction between necessarily and contingent properties. However, he admits that one *might* develop a philosophical theory about *objects* (like John) quite apart from their descriptions, which claims that certain properties are essential for being a given object. For example, we might claim that rationality (say) is part of the essence of John, whereas two-leggedness is not, as Aristotle might have done. But then what do we do with the fact that we may want to claim (3) (cyclists are necessarily two-legged) and that John is a cyclist? It seems that for an essentialist theory, the only way out, given that John is not necessarily two-legged, is to deny (3). Medieval Neo-Aristotelians struggled with a similar issue. One wants to say that *qua* cyclist, John is essentially two-legged, and that *qua* mathematician, he is essentially rational, and *qua* man, something else perhaps. But then what is John, *qua* the object John? Is there an essence of an object taken simply as an object? Is there no way to find an object's essence apart from how it is categorized, or does the object come with its essential categories built-in somehow?

These are important issues for an essentialist to clarify, but regardless of how they are resolved, it can be shown that something is wrong with Quine's challenge. It is possible at least for the essentialist to hold (1)–(5) without a contradiction. The essentialist can say that since (3) and (1) hold, and John is both a cyclist and a mathematician, it follows that John is necessarily two-legged *and* necessarily rational; this is a simple consequence of the following formalization of (1), (3), and (5).

(F1) $\forall x(Mx \rightarrow \Box Rx)$
(F3) $\forall x(Cx \rightarrow \Box 2x)$
(F5)   Cj & Mj

EXERCISE 19.11   Show that □Rj & □2j follows from (F1), (F3), (F5) using standard quantification theory. What must we add to get the deduction in free logic?

But what of (2) and (4)? Don't these show that John is neither necessarily rational nor necessarily two-legged? They would if they had the forms (F~2) and (F~4).

(F~2)   ∀x(Mx→~□2x)
(F~4)   ∀x(Cx→~□Rx)

In that case, we could use reasoning similar to that of the preceding exercise to arrive at a contradiction. But (F~2) and (F~4) are not proper formalizations of (2) and (4). If (2) is a plausible claim at all, it cannot be represented with a formula that claims that *every* mathematician is not necessarily two-legged, for suppose the mathematician is our cyclist friend John. The correct formalization of (2) must be (~F2) or perhaps (~□F2).

(~F2)   ~∀x(Mx→□2x)
(~□F2)   ~□∀x(Mx→2x)

(~F2) denies merely that all mathematicians are necessarily two-legged, whereas (~□F2) denies the necessity of all mathematicians being two-legged. In either case the translation does not allow the deduction of the claim ~□Rj or ~□2j ('John is not necessarily rational' or 'John is not necessarily two-legged'). I believe that (~□F2) is probably the best way to translate the intent of (2), for it is equivalent to ◇∃x(Mx&~2x), which says it is possible for there to be a mathematician without two legs. (~F2) does not capture (2) very well because (~F2) is equivalent to ∃x(Mx&~□2x), which says that some mathematician exists who is not necessarily two-legged. That doesn't seem to me to capture the spirit of (2), since (2) does not entail the existence of anything.

Although this response shows that essentialism need not be contradictory, Quine or others might still find other philosophical reasons to object to essentialism. The most effective reply to this move has been to point out that even if sentences that quantify in make assertions that are philosophically objectionable, this is hardly a reason to ban quantifying in from logic. Quantified modal logic should provide an impartial framework for the analysis and evaluation of all philosophical positions, whether we like them or not. If quantifying in can be used to express even unpalatable versions of essentialism, then this is a point in its *favor*. In any case, if Quine is right that quantifying in is by its nature essentialist, then this amounts to a retraction of his first contention that quantifying in is (literally) incoherent. If it were incoherent, it could not express essentialism, since it would express nothing at all.

The semantics for quantified modal logic that has been developed in this book serves as further evidence that there is nothing wrong with quantifying in. It has been shown here that by formalizing straightforward intuitions about the quantifiers, there are quantified modal logics that are consistent and complete where bound variables lie in opaque contexts. We have not merely stipulated that a sentence like $\exists x \Box Fx$ is intelligible, we have given a semantics that tells us exactly what its truth conditions are. If the intuitions behind this semantics make any sense at all, so must quantifying into intensional contexts.

Quine will surely object to this defense, for he challenges possible worlds semantics with complaints concerning the philosophical credentials of the concepts of a possible world and a possible object. However, the notions of a possible world and possible object are such a crucial foundation for the semantics for modal logic that these complaints speak more against the entire project of developing modal logic than against quantification into opaque contexts in particular. It would take another book to adequately present Quine's challenges and to discuss the answers to be given to them. This book is long enough.

Answers to Selected Exercises

Exercise 4.8g

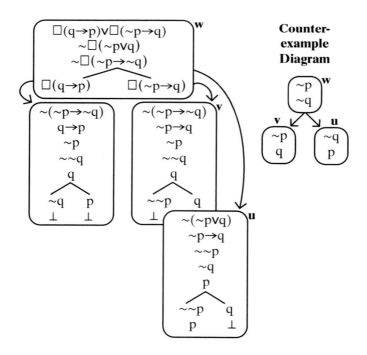

Exercise 5.3

$\mathbf{a_w}(DA)=T$ iff for each $\mathbf{v}$ in $\mathbf{W}$, if $\mathbf{wR_Dv}$ then $\mathbf{a_v}(A)=T$.

Exercise 5.6

(One possible solution) Let us say that world **v** is the neighbor of world **w** when it contains all the things that exist in **w**, and has almost exactly the same physical laws as **w**. Suppose that □A is T in **w** iff A is T in all neighbors of **w**. The neighborhood relation **R** is not symmetric because **v** can be the neighbor of **w**, when **v** contains objects that do not occur in **w**, in which case **wRv** could hold, whereas while **vRw** does not. Transitivity fails because it is possible for the laws of **w** and **v** to be almost exactly the same and the laws of **v** and **u** to be almost exactly the same without the laws of **w** and **u** being sufficiently similar to make **v** a neighbor of **w**.

Exercise 6.1c

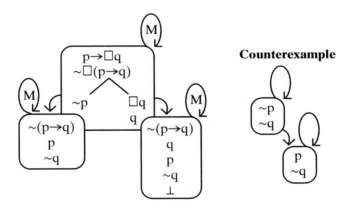

Counterexample

Exercise 6.1d

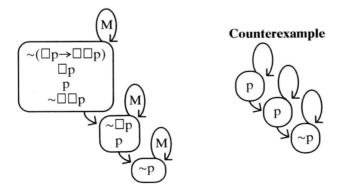

Counterexample

Exercise 6.1e

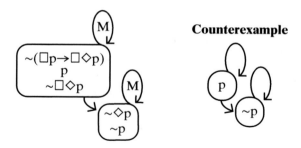

Counterexample

Exercise 6.1f

The tree rule for K + (□M) would say that if you have an arrow from world **w** to world **v**, then you must add a "loop" arrow from **v** back to **v**. This will guarantee that **R** is shift reflective.

Exercise 6.5

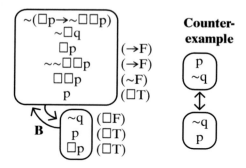

Counter-example

Exercise 7.24

Solution for (◇⊥)

A ⊢ ⊥	Given
⊢ ~A	(CP), (Def~)
⊢ □~A	(Nec)
⊢ ~~□~A	(DN)
⊢ ~◇A	(Def◇)
◇A ⊢ ⊥	(Def~), (MP)

Exercise 7.25

$C_1 \& \Diamond(C_2 \& .. \Diamond(C_n \& A)..) \vdash \perp$ iff
$\vdash C_1 \& \Diamond(C_2 \& .. \Diamond(C_n \& A)..) \to \perp$ iff   by (CP) and (MP)
$\vdash \sim[C_1 \& \Diamond(C_2 \& .. \Diamond(C_n \& A)..)]$ iff   by (Def$\sim$)
$\vdash C_1 \to \Box(C_2 \to .. \Box(C_n \to \sim A)..)$ iff   shown in the text
$C_1, \Box, C_2, .. \Box, C_n \vdash \sim A$ iff   by (CP), (MP), ($\Box$In) and ($\Box$Out)
$C_1, \Box, C_2, .. \Box, C_n, A \vdash \perp.$ by (CP), (MP) and (Def$\sim$)

Exercise 7.27

($\sim$F). In this case, *B is equivalent to *($\sim\sim$A) and *B$'$ equivalent to *($\sim\sim$A&A). But $\sim\sim$A $\vdash \sim\sim$A&A. So given that *B $\vdash \perp$, *B$' \vdash \perp$ by the Entailment Lemma.

($\perp$In). In this case, *B is equivalent to *(A&$\sim$A) and *B$'$ equivalent to *(A&$\sim$A&$\perp$). But A&$\sim$A $\vdash$ A&$\sim$A&$\perp$ by ($\perp$In). So given that *B$' \vdash \perp$, *B $\vdash \perp$ by the Entailment Lemma.

($\Box$F). In this case, *B is equivalent to *($\sim\Box$A) and *B$'$ equivalent to *($\sim\Box$A&$\Diamond\sim$A). But $\sim\Box$A $\vdash \sim\Box$A&$\Diamond\sim$A by ($\sim\Box$). So given that *B$' \vdash \perp$, *B $\vdash \perp$ by the Entailment Lemma.

Exercise 8.3

We assume that $L \vDash_K \Box A$, and show $L, \Box \vDash_K A$ as follows. Suppose that $L, \Box \nvDash_K A$ for indirect proof. Then there is a model with a world **w** where $\mathbf{a_w}(L, \Box)$=T and $\mathbf{a_w}(A)$=F.

$$L, \Box \nvDash_K A$$
$$\boxed{L, \Box}^{\mathbf{w}} \quad \mathbf{a_w}(L, \Box) = T$$
$$\boxed{\sim A} \qquad \mathbf{a_w}(A) = F$$

By definition (L,$\Box$), there must be a world **v** such that $\mathbf{a_v}(L)$=T and **vRw**.

$$\boxed{L}^{\mathbf{v}} \quad (L, \Box)$$
$$\mathbf{vRw} \downarrow \quad L, \Box \nvDash_K A$$
$$\boxed{L, \Box}^{\mathbf{w}} \, \mathbf{a_w}(L, \Box) = T$$
$$\boxed{\sim A} \quad \mathbf{a_w}(A) = F$$

We know that $L \vDash_K \Box A$, so $\mathbf{a_v}(\Box A)$=T.

$$\boxed{\begin{array}{c} L \\ \Box A \end{array}}^{\mathbf{v}} \begin{array}{l} (L, \Box) \\ L \vDash_K \Box A \end{array}$$
$$\mathbf{vRw} \downarrow \quad L, \Box \nvDash_K A$$
$$\boxed{\begin{array}{c} L, \Box \end{array}}^{\mathbf{w}} \mathbf{a_w}(L, \Box) = T$$
$$\boxed{\sim A} \quad \mathbf{a_w}(A) = F$$

By (□T) it follows that $a_w(A)=T$, which is impossible.

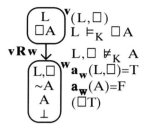

Exercise 8.5

By (1), ~(B→C) appears in world **w**. When (→F) is applied to ~(B→C), B and ~C are placed in **w**. By (IH), both B and ~C are verified because both B and ~C are smaller in size than A. Since these sentences are both in **w**, $a_w(B)=T$ and $a_w(\sim C)=T$. So $a_w(C)=F$ by (~). By the truth condition (→), $a_w(B\rightarrow C)=F$ and so $a_w(\sim(B\rightarrow C))=T$ by (~). So $a_w(A)=T$ in this case.

Exercise 9.1

Suppose that not **wRv**. Then by (DefR), it is not the case that for all sentences A, if **w** ⊢ □A then **v** ⊢ A. This means that for some sentence A, **w** ⊢ □A and **v** ⊬ A. By (Defa), it follows that $a_w(\square A)=T$ and $a_v(A)=F$.

Exercise 9.3

Suppose **wRv** and $a_v(A)=T$. We must show that $a_w(\lozenge A)=T$. By (Def◇) and (~), this amounts to showing that $w(\square\sim A)=F$. That is shown by indirect proof. Assume that $a_w(\square\sim A)=T$; then by (□T), $a_v(\sim A)=T$. But this conflicts with $a_v(A)=T$, and so the proof is complete.

Exercise 9.4c

To show that **R** is connected when (L) is provable, assume the opposite and demonstrate a contradiction as follows. Assuming **R** is not connected, we have that **wRv** and **wRu** but **v** is not **u** and not **vRu** and not **uRv**. We will show that this leads to a contradiction. Since **u** and **v** differ, there must be a sentence C such that C is in **v** but not in **u**. Since not **vRu**, it follows by (~R) that for some sentence B, □B is in **v** and ~B is in **u**. Similarly from not **uRv**, it follows there is a sentence A such that □A is in **u** and ~A is in **v**. By (Defa) we have the following values: $a_u(C)=F$, $a_u(B)=F$, $a_u(\square A)=T$, $a_v(C)=T$, $a_v(\square B)=T$ and $a_v(A)=F$. By (v) and (~), $a_u(B\lor C)=F$, so by

(→), **a**_u(□A→(BvC))=F. Hence by (□), **a**_w(□(□A→(BvC)))=F. But every instance of (L) is provable from **w**, including the following one: □(□A→(BvC)) v □(((BvC)&□(BvC))→A). By (Def**a**), **a** assigns this sentence T in world **w**. Since its left disjunct is F in **w**, it follows by (v) that the right disjunct is T in **w**, and so by (□T), and **wRv** ((BvC)&□(BvC))→A is T in **v**. Since **a**_v(C)=T, it follows by (v) that **a**_v(BvC)=T. Since **a**_v(□B)=T, and □B ⊢_K □(BvC), it follows by the Closed Lemma that **a**_v(□(BvC))=T. So by (&), **a**_v((BvC)&□(BvC))=T, which means that **a**_v(A)=T. But we had **a**_v(A)=F, which yields the desired contradiction.

Exercise 11.2

The following diagram shows (B) is provable in M5.

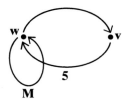

S5 = M5   by definition
  = MB5   by this exercise, (B) is provable in M5
  = M4B5   (4) is provable in MB5 (by Exercise 11.1b).
  = M45   (B) is provable in M45 (since provable in M5)
  = M4B   (5) is provable in M4B (by Exercise 11.1a)
  = D4B   (M) is provable in D4B (shown in the text)
  = D4B5   (5) is provable in D4B (shown in the text).
  = DB5   (4) is provable in DB5 (by Exercise 11.1b)

Exercise 12.14

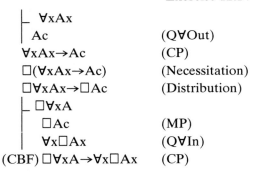

⌐ ∀xAx	
│ Ac	(Q∀Out)
∀xAx→Ac	(CP)
□(∀xAx→Ac)	(Necessitation)
□∀xAx→□Ac	(Distribution)
⌐ □∀xA	
│ □Ac	(MP)
│ ∀x□Ax	(Q∀In)
(CBF) □∀xA→∀x□Ax	(CP)

Exercise 12.16b

Proof of (ED) in fK+(CBF)

```
⌐ □
│ ⌐ Ec
│   Ec→Ec      (CP)*
│   ∀xEx       (∀In)
│ □∀xEx        (□In)
│ ∀x□Ex        (CBF), (MP)
│ Ec→□Ec       (∀Out)
```

* (By our lights, the one-line subproof ⊢ Ec entails Ec→Ec by (CP) since the top and bottom sentences of that subproof are both Ec. Of course the top and bottom sentences are the very same one, but there is nothing wrong with appealing to the same line twice in a proof.)

Proof of (CBF) in fK+(ED)

```
⌐ □∀xAx
│ ⌐ Ec
│ │ Ec→□Ec      (ED)
│ │ □Ec         (MP)
│ │ ⌐ □
│ │ │ Ec        (□Out)
│ │ │ ∀xAx      (□Out)
│ │ │ Ec→Ac     (∀Out)
│ │ │ Ac        (MP)
│ │ □Ac         (□In)
│ │ Ec→□Ac      (CP)
│ ∀x□Ax         (∀In)
```

Exercise 12.22

Et, ~∃xx≈t, c≈t ⊢ ∀x~x≈t	Definition of ∃ and ~~A ⊢ A
Et, ~∃xx≈t, c≈t ⊢ Ec→~c≈t	(∀Out)
Et, ~∃xx≈t, c≈t ⊢ Ec	(≈Out)
Et, ~∃xx≈t, c≈t ⊢ ~c≈t	(MP)
Et, ~∃xx≈t ⊢ ~c≈t	(CP) and A→~A ⊢ ~A
Et, ~∃xx≈t ⊢ ⊥	(∃i)
Et ⊢ ∃xx≈t	(IP)

Exercise 13.3

We show $a_w(Et)=T$ iff $a_w(\exists xx\approx t)=T$. For the proof from left to right assume $a_w(Et)=T$. Then by (Et), $a_w(t) \in Dw$. Since terms are all constants, t is c for some choice of c, so we have $a_w(Ec)=T$ and $a_w(c)=a_w(t)$. So by $(\approx)$, $a_w(c\approx t)=T$, hence $a_w(\exists xx\approx t)$ by $(\exists)$. For the proof from right to left assume $a_w(\exists xx\approx t)$. Then by $(\exists)$ and $(\approx)$, $a_w(Ec)=T$ and $a_w(c)=a_w(t)$, for some constant c. By (Et), $a_w(c) \in Dw$, so $a_w(t) \in Dw$. Note the proof depends on being able to identify term t with some constant and this may not hold when new terms are introduced to the language.

Exercise 14.8i

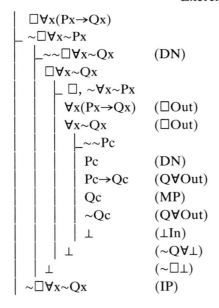

Exercise 14.13

$(\forall T)$. In this case, *B is equivalent to *$(\forall xAx)$ and *B′ amounts to *$(\forall xAx\&(Ec\rightarrow Ac))$. But $\forall xAx \vdash \forall xAx\&(Ec\rightarrow Ac)$. So given that *B′ $\vdash \bot$, *B $\vdash \bot$ by the Entailment Lemma.

Exercise 15.2

To show $a_w(Ec\rightarrow\Box Ec)=T$, assume $a_w(Ec)=T$ and prove $a_w(\Box Ec)=T$ by assuming that **v** is any world such that **wRv**, and proving $a_v(Ec)=T$. Since

$\mathbf{a_w}$(Ec)=T, it follows by (E) and (Pl) that $\mathbf{a_w}$(c) $\in \mathbf{Dw}$. By the expanding domain condition (ED), it follows that $\mathbf{a_v}$(c) $\in \mathbf{D_v}$. So $\mathbf{a_v}$(Ec)=T follows by (E) and (Pl).

Exercise 15.3

Proof of ($\approx\sim\Box$). According to ($\rightarrow$), ($\approx\sim\Box$) follows provided that if $\mathbf{a_w}$($\sim$b$\approx$c)=T, then $\mathbf{a_w}$($\Box\sim$b$\approx$c)=T. So assume $\mathbf{a_w}$($\sim$b$\approx$c)=T, and show $\mathbf{a_w}$($\Box\sim$b$\approx$c)=T, by assuming $\mathbf{wRv}$ and deducing $\mathbf{a_v}$($\sim$b$\approx$c)=T as follows. Since $\mathbf{a_w}$($\sim$b$\approx$c)=T, $\mathbf{a_w}$(b$\approx$c)=F by ($\sim$). By ($\approx$) we have $\mathbf{a_w}$(b)$\neq\mathbf{a_w}$(c). Since b and c are rigid, it follows that $\mathbf{a_v}$(b)$\neq\mathbf{a_v}$(c), and hence by ($\approx$), $\mathbf{a_v}$(b$\approx$c)=F. By ($\sim$), $\mathbf{a_v}$($\sim$b$\approx$c)=T as desired.

Exercise 15.4a

(o∃E)=(o)+(∃E): ∃xEx   (o) + $\mathbf{Dw}$ is not empty.

We showed already that (∃E) is valid when condition (∃E) holds, namely, that for some i $\in \mathbf{I}$, i($\mathbf{w}$) $\in \mathbf{Dw}$. But when $\mathbf{Dw}$ is not empty, there must be some member d in $\mathbf{Dw}$, and by (o) it follows that there is a constant function i in $\mathbf{I}$ with d as a value. So condition (∃E) holds, which guarantees that axiom (∃E) is valid on models that obey (o∃E).

Exercise 15.4b

(oED)=(o)+(ED): Ec→$\Box$Ec   (o) + If $\mathbf{wRv}$, then $\mathbf{Dw} \subseteq \mathbf{Dv}$.

We already showed that (ED) is valid when condition (ED) holds, namely, that if $\mathbf{wRv}$ and $\mathbf{a_w}$(c) $\in \mathbf{Dw}$ then $\mathbf{a_v}$(c) $\in \mathbf{Dv}$. But the condition (oED) entails this condition by the following reasoning. Suppose $\mathbf{wRv}$ and $\mathbf{a_w}$(c) $\in \mathbf{Dw}$. It is possible to show $\mathbf{a_v}$(c) $\in \mathbf{Dv}$ as follows. By (oED), $\mathbf{Dw} \subseteq \mathbf{Dv}$, and $\mathbf{a_w}$(c) $\in \mathbf{Dv}$. But (o) guarantees that $\mathbf{a}$(c) is a constant function because $\mathbf{a}$(c) is in $\mathbf{I}$ by (cI). So $\mathbf{a_w}$(c)=$\mathbf{a_v}$(c), and so $\mathbf{a_v}$(c) $\in \mathbf{Dv}$, which is the desired result.

Exercise 15.7

(ED)   Ec→$\Box$Ec   If $\mathbf{wRv}$ and $\mathbf{a_w}$(c) $\in \mathbf{Dw}$, then $\mathbf{a_v}$(c) $\in \mathbf{Dv}$.

To prove the condition, assume $\mathbf{wRv}$ and $\mathbf{a_w}$(c) $\in \mathbf{Dw}$, and then prove $\mathbf{a_v}$(c) $\in \mathbf{Dv}$ as follows. By (Pl) and (E), $\mathbf{a_w}$(Ec)=T. By $\mathbf{a_w}$(Ec→$\Box$Ec)=T, it follows by ($\rightarrow$) that $\mathbf{a_w}$($\Box$Ec)=T and so $\mathbf{a_v}$(Ec)=T by $\mathbf{wRv}$ and ($\Box$). But by (Pl) and (E), $\mathbf{a_v}$(c) $\in \mathbf{Dv}$.

Exercise 15.8

(oCD)=(o)+(CD)   (o) + If **wRv**, then **Dv** $\subseteq$ **Dw**.

It was already shown that axiom (o) expresses condition (o). Now assume **wRv** and d $\in$ **Dv**, and then prove d $\in$ **Dw** as follows. By (**aD**), we know that there is a term t and a world **u** such that $a_u(t)$=d, but by ($\exists$c) and ($\approx$), there is a constant c such that a_u(c)=a_u(t)=d. But (o) and (cI) guarantee that **a**(c) is a constant function. It follows that a_w(c)=a_v(c)=a_u(c)=d. So a_v(c) $\in$ **Dw**. We already showed that (CD) expresses that if **wRv** and a_v(c) $\in$ **Dv** then a_w(c) $\in$ **Dw**. So a_w(c) $\in$ **Dw**. Since a_w(c)=d, d $\in$ **Dw** as desired.

Exercise 16.1

According to the i Transfer Theorem of Section 15.7, we need show only that rS is complete for *trS-models*, that is, tS-models that obey (r). This can be proven as follows. As a special case of the Quantified Tree Model Theorem, the tree model for any open rS-tree for argument H / C obeys (r), and so qualifies as a trS-model that serves as a trS-counterexample to H / C. Note that we do not need the presence of the rule ($\exists$i) in S to establish that the tree model obeys ($\exists$c). So assuming H $\vDash_{trS}$ C, it follows by the contrapositive of the Quantified Tree Model Theorem that the rS-tree for H / C is closed. It follows that H $\vdash_{rS}$ C since we know how to convert such tree into a proof using the methods of Section 14.5 and 14.7.

Exercise 17.5

Proof of the $\approx$Ready Addition Lemma. Suppose M$'$ is finite and M is $\approx$ready. If the reason M is $\approx$ready is that there are infinitely many constants of the language not in M, then since M$'$ is finite there will still be infinitely many constants not in M$\cup$M$'$ and so M$\cup$M$'$ is $\approx$ready. If the reason M is $\approx$ready is that it is both a $\forall$-set and a $\approx$-set, then M$\cup$M$'$ is a $\forall$-set by the argument given in the Ready Addition Lemma (Section 17.3). That M$\cup$M$'$ is also a $\approx$-set can be shown as follows. Let M$'$ be any finite set, and suppose that M$\cup$M$'$ $\vdash$ L $\rightarrow$ ~t$\approx$c for every constant c of the language. It follows by (CP) that M$\vdash$ H, L $\rightarrow$ ~t$\approx$c for every constant c of the language, where H is the list of members of M$'$. Since M is a $\approx$-set it follows then that $M \vdash H, L \, \text{\textbf{--}3} \sim t \approx t$, from which it follows that $M \cup M' \vdash \sim t \approx t$, by (MP). Therefore, $M \cup M'$ is $\approx$ready in this case as well.

Exercise 17.6

Proof of the $\approx$Ready Lemma. Suppose M is $\approx$ready, consistent, and contains $\sim(L\text{--}3\sim t \approx t)$. There must be a constant c of the language such that $M \nvdash L\text{--}3\sim t \approx c$, because otherwise $M \vdash L\text{--}3\sim t \approx c$ for every constant c, which leads to a contradiction as follows. If the reason that M is $\approx$ready is that M is a $\approx$-set, then we would have $M \vdash L\text{--}3\sim t \approx t$ immediately. If M is $\approx$ready is because there are infinitely many constants not in M, then $M \vdash L\text{--}3\sim t \approx t$ also holds for the following reason. L is finite, so there are infinitely many constants not in M, L or $\sim t \approx t$. Let b be one of those constants. By $M \vdash L\text{--}3\sim t \approx c$, for every constant c, it follows that $M, L \vdash \sim t \approx b$, and so $H, L \vdash \sim t \approx b$, for some list H of members of M. So by the $\text{--}3$ Lemma $H, L \vdash \sim t \approx b$. Constant b is not in H, L, or t, so we can apply ($\exists$i) to obtain $H, L \vdash \perp$. From this it follows by the rule (Contra) (from $\perp$ anything follows) that $H, L \vdash \sim t \approx t$, and so by the $\text{--}3$ Lemma, and the fact that H contains members of M, $M \vdash L\text{--}3\sim t \approx t$. So regardless of the reason M was $\approx$ready, $M \vdash L\text{--}3\sim t \approx t$. But we also have that $\sim(L\text{--}3\sim t \approx t)$ is in M, which conflicts with the consistency of M. So we must conclude that $M \nvdash \sim(L\text{--}3\sim t \approx c)$, for some constant c.

Exercise 17.7

Proof of the $\approx$Saturated Set Lemma. Order the sentences $A_1 .., A_i, ..$ and create a series of sets: $M_1, M_2, .. M_i, ..$ in the manner mentioned in the proof of the Saturated List Lemma, except that when A_i is $\sim(L\text{--}3\sim t \approx t)$, and $M_i, \sim(L\text{--}3\sim t \approx t) \nvdash \perp$, then add both $\sim(L\text{--}3\sim t \approx t)$ and $\sim(L\text{--}3\sim t \approx c)$ to form M_{i+1}, where c is chosen so that M_{i+1} is consistent. That there is such a constant c is guaranteed by the $\approx$Ready Lemma. The reason is that $M_i, \sim(L\text{--}3\sim t \approx t)$ is consistent, and it is $\approx$ready by the $\approx$Ready Addition Lemma because M is $\approx$ready and only finitely many sentences were added to form $M_i, \sim(L\text{--}3\sim t \approx t)$. Finally, $\sim(L\text{--}3\sim t \approx t)$ is in $M_i, \sim(L\text{--}3\sim t \approx t)$, so by the $\approx$Ready Lemma, $M_i, \sim(L\text{--}3\sim t \approx t), \sim(L\text{--}3\sim t \approx c) \nvdash \perp$ for some constant c.

Now let m be the set of all sentences in M plus those added during the construction of any of the M_i. Clearly m is maximal, and each set M_i in this construction is clearly consistent by the same reasoning given in the

Lindenbaum Lemma. By the M Lemma of Section 9.1, m is consistent. It is also a saturated set by the reasoning of the Saturated Set Lemma. So to show that m is the desired ≈saturated extension of M, all that is needed is a proof that m is a ≈-set.

To do that, suppose m ⊢ L−3~t≈c for every constant c. We will show that M ⊢ L−3~t≈t by showing that m ⊬ L−3~t≈t leads to a contradiction. Suppose m ⊬ L−3~t≈t. Then by (IP), m, ~(L−3~t≈t) ⊬⊥. But ~(L−3~t≈t) must be A_i, the ith member of the list of all sentences for some value of i. If m, ~(L−3~t≈t) ⊬⊥, then M_i, ~(L−3~t≈t) ⊬⊥ (since M_i is a subset of m). But then ~(L−3~t≈b) was added to form M_{i+1} for some constant b. Hence m ⊢ ~(L−3~t≈b). However, we already supposed m ⊢ L−3~t≈c for every constant c, so in particular m ⊢ L−3~t≈b. This conflicts with the consistency of m. Therefore, we must conclude that m ⊢ L−3~t≈t, and so m is a ≈-set.

Exercise 17.8

Proof of the ≈-Set Lemma. To show V, ~A is a ≈-set, assume V, ~A ⊢ L −3 t≈c for all c, and show that V, ~A ⊢ L−3~t≈t as follows. From the assumption it follows that V ⊢ ~A, L −3 ~t≈c for all c. By (GN) □V ⊢ □,~A, L −3 ~t≈c for all c. Since **w** is an extension of □V, it follows that **w** ⊢ □,~A, L −3 ~t≈c for all c. But **w** is a ≈-set, so **w** ⊢ □, ~A, L −3 ~t≈t. Since **w** is maximal, either □, ~A, L −3 ~t≈t or its negation is in **w**. But the negation cannot be in **w** since that would make **w** inconsistent. Therefore □, ~A, L −3 ~t≈t is in **w** with the result that ~A, L −3 ~t≈t is in V. So V ⊢ ~A, L −3 ~t≈t, and V, ~A ⊢ L −3 ~t≈t by (MP).

Exercise 18.14

(1′) a≈!x(Px&xTg)
(2′) aTg

What blocks the proof is that Ea is needed but not available. In !qS, Ea is proven from (Q). This with (!Out) (and symmetry of ≈) yields 1aTg, from which aTg follows by (Def1).

Exercise 19.8

The definition would be: [E](P)t = λx□(Ex→Px)(t). The demonstration that (EDR) holds goes like this.

We know $\mathbf{a_w}(t)=d$ for some d in **D**.

$\mathbf{a_w}([E](P)t)=T$

iff $\mathbf{a_w}(\lambda x\square(Ex\rightarrow Px)(t))=T$	Definition of $[E](P)t$
iff $\mathbf{a_w}(t)\in\mathbf{a_w}(\lambda x\square(Ex\rightarrow Px))$	(λt)
iff $d\in\mathbf{a_w}(\lambda x\square(Ex\rightarrow Px))$	$\mathbf{a_w}(t)=d$
iff $\mathbf{a_w}(\square(Ed\rightarrow Pd))=T$	(λ)
iff if $\mathbf{wRv}$ then $\mathbf{a_v}(Ed\rightarrow Pd)=T$	$(\square)$
iff if $\mathbf{wRv}$ and $\mathbf{a_v}(Ed)=T$ then $\mathbf{a_v}(Pd)=T$	$(\rightarrow)$
iff if $\mathbf{wRv}$ and $\mathbf{a_v}(d)\in\mathbf{Dv}$ then $\mathbf{a_v}(d)\in\mathbf{a_v}(P)$	(Pl) twice
iff if $\mathbf{wRv}$ and $d\in\mathbf{Dv}$ then $d\in\mathbf{a_v}(P)$	(d): $\mathbf{a_v}(d)=d$
iff if $\mathbf{wRv}$ and $\mathbf{a_w}(t)\in\mathbf{Dv}$, then $\mathbf{a_w}(t)\in\mathbf{a_v}(P)$	$\mathbf{a_w}(t)=d$

Bibliography of Works Cited

Aqvist, L. (1984) "Deontic Logic," Chapter 11 of Gabbay and Guenthner (1984), 605–714.

Aqvist, L. (1967) "Good Samaritans Contrary-to-Duty Imperatives, and Epistemic Obligations," *Nous*, 1, 361–379.

Anderson, A. (1967) "Some Nasty Problems in the Formal Logic of Ethics," *Nous*, 1, 345–360.

Barcan, R. (1946) "A Functional Calculus of First Order Based on Strict Implication," *Journal of Symbolic Logic*, 2, 1–16.

Bencivenga, E. (1986) "Free Logics," Chapter 6 of Gabbay and Guenthner (1986), 373–426.

Boolos, G. (1993) *The Logic of Provability*, Cambridge University Press, Cambridge.

Boolos, G., Burgess, J., and Jeffrey, R. (2002) *Computability and Logic*, Cambridge University Press, Cambridge.

Bowen, K. (1979) *Model Theory for Modal Logic*, Reidel, Dordrecht.

Bressan, A. (1973) *A General Interpreted Modal Calculus*, Yale University Press, New Haven.

Bull, R., and Segerberg, K. (1984) "Basic Modal Logic," Chapter 1 of Gabbay and Guenthner (1984), 1–88.

Burgess, J. (1984) "Basic Tense Logic," Chapter 2 of Gabbay and Guenthner (1984), 89–134.

Carnap, R. (1947) *Meaning and Necessity*, University of Chicago Press, Chicago.

Chellas, B. (1980) *Modal Logic: An Introduction*, Cambridge University Press, Cambridge.

Copi, I., and Gould, J. (1967) *Contemporary Readings in Logical Theory*, Macmillan, New York.

Corsi, G. (2002) "A Unified Completeness Theorem for Quantified Modal Logics," *Journal of Symbolic Logic*, 67, 1483–1510.

Cresswell, M. J. (1991) "In Defence of the Barcan Formula," *Logique et Analyse*, 135–6, 271–282.

Cresswell, M. J. (1995) "Incompleteness and the Barcan Formulas," *Journal of Philosophical Logic*, 24, 379–403.

Cresswell, M. J. (1985) *Structured Meanings*, MIT Press, Cambridge, MA.

Davidson, D., and Harman, G. (eds.) (1972) *Semantics of Natural Language*, Reidel, Dordrecht.

Dunn, M. (1986) "Relevance Logic and Entailment," Chapter 3 of Gabbay and Guenthner (1986), 117–224.

Fitting, M., and Mendelsohn, R. (1998) *First Order Modal Logic*, Kluwer, Dordrecht.

Fitting, M. (2004) "First Order Intensional Logic," *Annals of Pure and Applied Logic*, 127, 171–193.

Gabbay, D. (1976) *Investigations in Modal and Tense Logics with Applications to Problems in Philosophy and Linguistics*, Reidel, Dordrecht.

Gabbay, D., and Guenthner, F. (eds.) (1984) *Handbook of Philosophical Logic*, vol. 2., Reidel, Dordrecht.

Gabbay, D., and Guenthner, F. (eds.) (1986) *Handbook of Philosophical Logic*, vol. 3., Reidel, Dordrecht.

Gabbay, D., and Guenthner, F. (eds.) (2001) *Handbook of Philosophical Logic*, second edition, vol. 3, Kluwer, Dordrecht.

Gallin, D. (1975) *Intensional and Higher-Order Modal Logic*, North Holland, Amsterdam.

Garson, J. (1978) "Completeness of Some Quantified Modal Logics," *Logique et Analyse*, 21, 153–164.

Garson, J. (1981) "Prepositional Logic," *Logique et Analyse*, 24, 4–33.

Garson, J. (1984) "Quantification in Modal Logic," Chapter 5 of Gabbay and Guenthner (1984), 249–307.

Garson, J. (1987) "Metaphors and Modality," *Logique et Analyse*, 30, 123–145.

Garson, J. (2001) "Quantification in Modal Logic," in Gabbay and Guenthner (2001), 267–323 (revised and updated version of Garson (1984)).

Garson, J. (2005) "Unifying Quantified Modal Logic," *Journal of Philosophical Logic*, 34, 621–649.

Garson, J. (2006) "Quantifiers and Modality," entry in the *Encyclopedia of Philosophy*, Second edition, Macmillan, New York.

Grandy, R. (1976) "Anadic Logic," *Synthese*, 82, 395–402.

Hilpenin, R. (1971) *Deontic Logic: Introductory and Systematic Readings*, Humanities Press, New York.

Hintikka, J. (1970) "Existential and Uniqueness Presuppositions," in Lambert (1970), 20–55.

Hughes, G., and Cresswell, M. (1968) *An Introduction to Modal Logic*, Methuen, London.

Hughes, G., and Cresswell, M. (1984) *A Companion to Modal Logic*, Methuen, London.

Hughes, G., and Cresswell, M. (1996) *A New Introduction to Modal Logic*, Routledge, London.

Kaplan, D. (1969) "Quantifying In." In D. Davidson and J. Hintikka, (eds.), *Words and Objections*, Reidel, Dordrecht.

Kripke, S. (1963) "Semantical Considerations in Modal Logic," *Acta Philosophica Fennica*, 16, 83–94.

Kripke, S. (1972) "Naming and Necessity," in Davidson and Harman (1972), 253–355.

Lambert, K. (ed.) (1969) *The Logical Way of Doing Things*, Yale University Press, New Haven.

Lambert, K. (ed.) (1970) *Philosophical Problems in Logic*, Reidel, Dordrecht.

Lambert, K. and van Fraassen, B. (1972) *Derivation and Counterexample*, Dickenson Publishing Company, New York.

Leblanc, H. (1976) *Truth-Value Semantics*, North-Holland, Amsterdam.

Lemmon, E., and Scott, D. (1977) *The 'Lemmon Notes': An Introduction to Modal Logic*, Basil Blackwell, Oxford.

Lewis, D. (1968) "Counterpart Theory and Quantified Modal Logic," *Journal of Philosophy*, 65, 113–126.

Lewis, D. (1973) *Counterfactuals*, Harvard University Press, Cambridge, MA.

Linsky, B., and Zalta, E. (1994) "In Defense of the Simplest Quantified Modal Logic," *Philosophical Perspectives*, 8, (Logic and Language), 431–458.

Mares, E. (2004) *Relevant Logic*, Cambridge University Press, Cambridge.

Montague, R. (1974) *Formal Philosophy*, Yale University Press, New Haven.

Nute, D. (1984) "Conditional Logic," Chapter 8 of Gabbay and Guenthner (1984), 387–439.

Parks, Z. (1976) "Investigations into Quantified Modal Logic," *Studia Logica*, 35, 109–125.

Prior, A. (1967) *Past, Present and Future*, Clarendon Press, Oxford.

Quine, W. (1960) *Word and Object*, MIT Press, Cambridge, MA.

Quine, W. (1961) "Reference and Modality," Chapter 8 of *From a Logical Point of View*, Harper & Row, New York.

Quine, W. (1963) "On What There Is," Chapter 1 of *From a Logical Point of View*, Harper Torch Books, Harper Row, New York, pp. 1–19.

Rescher, N., and Urquhart, A. (1971) *Temporal Logic*, Springer Verlag, New York.

Russell, B. (1905) "On Denoting," *Mind*, 14, 479–493.

Sahlqvist, H. (1975) "Completeness and Correspondence in First and Second-Order Semantics for Modal Logic," in Kanger, S. (ed.), *Proceedings of the Third Scandanavian Logic Symposium*, North Holland, Amsterdam, 110–143.

Smullyan, A. (1948) "Modality and Description," *Journal of Symbolic Logic*, 13, 31–37.

Smullyan, R. (1968) *First Order Logic*, Springer Verlag, New York.

Strawson, P. (1950) "On Referring," *Mind*, 59, 320–344.

Stalnaker, R., and Thomason, R. (1968) "Abstraction in First Order Modal Logic," *Theoria*, 34, 203–207.

Thomason, R. (1969) "Modal Logic and Metaphysics," in Lambert (1969), 119–146.

Thomason, R. (1970) "Some Completeness Results for Modal Predicate Calculi," in Lambert (1970), 56–76.

Williamson, T. (1998) "Bare Possibilia," *Erkenntnis*, 48, 257–273.

van Fraassen, B. (1966) "Singular Terms, Truth Value Gaps, and Free Logic," *Journal of Philosophy*, 63, 481–495.

van Fraassen, B., and Lambert, K. (1967) "On Free Description Theory," *Zeitschrift für Mathematik, Logik und Grundlagen der Mathematik*, 13, 225–240.

Index

449

CPSIA information can be obtained at www.ICGtesting.com
Printed in the USA
BVOW010322300112

281531BV00006B/5/P